SCHOOL OF
ORIENTAL AND AFRICAN STUDIES
UNIVERSITY OF LONDON

London Oriental Series
Volume 5

THE HON. MOUNTSTUART ELPHINSTONE

LONDON ORIENTAL SERIES · VOLUME 5

SOCIAL POLICY AND SOCIAL CHANGE IN WESTERN INDIA
1817–1830

BY

KENNETH BALLHATCHET
Lecturer in Modern Indian History
School of Oriental and African Studies

LONDON
OXFORD UNIVERSITY PRESS
NEW YORK   TORONTO

Oxford University Press, Amen House, London E.C.4

GLASGOW   NEW YORK   TORONTO   MELBOURNE   WELLINGTON
BOMBAY   CALCUTTA   MADRAS   KARACHI   KUALA LUMPUR
CAPE TOWN   IBADAN   NAIROBI   ACCRA

First edition 1957
Reprinted 1961

REPRINTED LITHOGRAPHICALLY IN GREAT BRITAIN
AT THE UNIVERSITY PRESS, OXFORD
BY VIVIAN RIDLER
PRINTER TO THE UNIVERSITY

PREFACE

SOCIAL history has been called history with the politics left out, but a change of government may involve great social changes. When it happens, groups associated with the old government may lose wealth, power, influence, and prestige, while those associated with the new may gain correspondingly. I have tried to analyse, first, the extent to which this type of social change took place when the British conquered the Peshwa's territories in Western India.

Besides the immediate changes which thus resulted from the overthrow of the Maratha Government and the establishment of the British in its place, the different administrative methods of the British affected the social structure and social institutions of the whole country, lowering the status of the village headmen, enfeebling the vigour of the village committees, and producing many other slow, insidious, and inordinate mutations.

Moreover, the British at this time were in a reforming mood. Stimulated by the Evangelical and Utilitarian movements, they were attempting social reforms in all their Indian possessions—encouraging education and discouraging customs like the suicide of widows. I have tried to examine the effects of such reforming zeal in Western India.

I have traced these developments in the light of the career of the Hon. Mountstuart Elphinstone. Before the outbreak of war he held the post of Resident at the Peshwa's Court. After it he was appointed Commissioner to settle the Deccan territories conquered from the Peshwa. The first part of this book deals with the time when he was setting up a provisional system of government there. When he became Governor of Bombay the Deccan was annexed to the Bombay Presidency, and in the second part of this book the prospect widens to include the whole of the territories under that government. By way of epilogue the third part is a brief survey of the ways in which the policies and tendencies which began under Elphinstone continued under his friend Sir John Malcolm who succeeded him as Governor of Bombay. I am making a fuller study of Malcolm in a separate book.

Elphinstone often disclaimed any intention of making big changes. He sometimes said that all he wanted to do was to remedy any serious abuses that might appear in the existing system. During

the months of war he could indeed do little more than meet the
needs of the moment. After the war, however, he had more time for
reflection, and we can then begin to find some general principles
running through his different policies.

He disliked the system of government which had been established by Lord Cornwallis in Bengal, with its detailed and inflexible
Regulations administered by English Judges who seemed to respect
neither the privileges of the aristocracy nor the customs of the
people. He had more liking for the methods being developed in
Madras under the influence of his friend Sir Thomas Munro. There
at least less power was given to English Judges and some attempt
was made to take account of Indian customs. Munro, however,
lacked Elphinstone's desire to preserve the position of the aristocracy and give them a positive function in society. At the same time,
Elphinstone was attracted by the doctrines of the Utilitarians. Yet
fundamentally his desire to protect the aristocracy and to follow
Maratha methods of government was at variance with the spirit of
Utilitarianism. I have tried to throw light upon the tension which
resulted.

I am deeply grateful to the late Lord Elphinstone for allowing me
to study the Mountstuart Elphinstone papers. I have also used
the official records of the East India Company in the India Office
Library, together with some unofficial material preserved there—
in particular, some of Sir John Malcolm's private correspondence.
For this my thanks are due to the Librarian and Keeper of the
Records. I must also thank the Librarian of the Church Missionary
Society for allowing me to consult the Western India Mission
records in the Society's archives, and the Librarian of the University of Nottingham for allowing me to study the private papers of
Lord William Bentinck in the Portland Collection. I have also
made incidental use of the W. H. Mill papers in the Bodleian
Library at Oxford, and for permission to do this my thanks are due
to the Keeper of Western Manuscripts there.

This book has emerged from a thesis for which I was granted the
degree of Doctor of Philosophy by the University of London. The
thesis was written under the supervision of Professor C. H. Philips,
and I have gained much from his incisive comments, from his
sympathetic encouragement, and from the freedom which he gave
me to pursue my own ideas. For helpful advice and criticism I am
also indebted to Dr. Vera Anstey, Dr. C. C. Davies, Dr. T. G. P.

Spear, and Dr. E. T. Stokes. Mrs. June Ewing typed most of the manuscript and also made some helpful suggestions as she did so.

The Central Research Funds Committee of the University generously helped to pay some of the expenses which I incurred in the course of my researches. The Publications Committee of the School of Oriental and African Studies have honoured me by paying for the publication of this book in the London Oriental Series. In this connexion I must add a final word of thanks to Mr. J. R. Bracken, the Secretary of that Committee, for his deft and tactful guidance through the difficulties of publication.

My wife's help has been invaluable throughout, and especially in the preparation of the Index.

K. A. B.

CONTENTS

LIST OF ILLUSTRATIONS

PART ONE

1

INTRODUCTION

A t the beginning of the nineteenth century the Peshwa Baji Rao
still administered from Poona the large and prosperous territories
of the Maratha state. Nominally the ministers of the Rajas of Satara,
the Peshwas had in fact for some fifty years exercised supreme
power and left the Rajas with little more than the name of sovereign.
They had also succeeded in maintaining the independence of their
state against the advancing British power.

But in 1801 Baji Rao rashly provoked the irascible Jaswant Rao
Holkar by having his brother trampled to death beneath an elephant.
In search of revenge Holkar soon invaded the Peshwa's territories
and captured Poona, Baji Rao having fled to Bassein in search of
help from the British. The British were eager to oblige him, but
first they made him conclude a subsidiary alliance—the form of
union which they had specially devised for Indian princes in distress. By the Treaty of Bassein (1802) he accordingly ceded some
land to meet the cost of a British force to be stationed within his
territories and promised to consult the British before he entered
into relations with any other state.

With such friends he was soon restored to power, but not to
independence. He had in effect surrendered the right to have a
foreign policy. Henceforth the figure of the British Resident was to
cast a lengthening shadow over his court. Indeed, in the person of
Mountstuart Elphinstone the Resident was soon standing not only
between the Peshwa and foreign princes but also between him and
his own overmighty subjects.

The Hon. Mountstuart Elphinstone was the last and greatest of
the British Residents at Poona. He had come out to India in the
service of the East India Company in 1795 at the age of fifteen. A
picture of him at that time shows a handsome youth—with a strong
nose, full lips, and sombre, brooding eyes.

He had at first gone to Benares as an Assistant to the Register, Edward Strachey, and under the Judge and Magistrate, Samuel Davis, but he was soon transferred to 'the diplomatic line', and in 1801 was sent to Poona as an Assistant to the Resident.[1]

It was then that he first met the Peshwa. His first impressions were favourable: he called him 'a very handsome, dignified, unaffected person', although he added that there was 'something vulgar in his mouth'.[2]

In the Maratha War of 1803 he served as a sort of political assistant under General Wellesley, the future Duke of Wellington, who was so impressed by his abilities that he told him that he should have been a soldier.[3]

Thereafter he held various diplomatic posts—Resident with the Raja of Berar, Resident with Sindhia, envoy to Kabul—until in 1811 he was appointed Resident at Poona. He was a man capable of taking full advantage of the strategic position which the Treaty of Bassein had given to the Resident.

He had learnt much of India. His work had given him occasion to travel widely, and early in his career he resolved to 'employ my time in learning something of the country through which I pass instead of indulging in mere unprofitable thought'.[4]

This note of self-reproach often recurs in his journals, and there is much self-searching inquiry in them. He would often resolve to make better use of his time. He gave up taking snuff because of 'the utility of accustoming oneself to breaking habits and to other exertions of self-denial'.[5] He had perhaps caught the spirit of Evangelicalism. Not, however, its doctrines: his attitude to religion was very like that of an eighteenth-century deist.

His application to intellectual effort also has something of the earnestness of the Evangelicals without their narrowness. He read widely, deeply, and strenuously—Greek, Latin, Persian, English, French, Italian. Here is just one example from a journal which he kept at Nagpur in 1808 when he had a friend with him:

We rise at four and read Sophocles, generally about 200 lines, till it is time to ride. We sometimes read on our return, which takes place about seven. After breakfast business generally prevents our beginning Xeno-

---

[1] *Personal Records*, vii. 519.

[2] Elphinstone, Journal, 11.2.1802 (hereafter, for the sake of brevity, I will refer to him in these footnotes by his initials, M.E.), Colebrooke, *Life*, i. 46.

[3] Anecdote in Colebrooke, op. cit. 111.

[4] Journal, ibid. 29.   [5] Journal, 15.7.1812, ibid. 272.

phon, which is our forenoon's lesson, till eleven; we then read twenty or thirty pages, eat a sandwich, and read separately—I Tacitus and the books on the French Revolution—till two; then we read Grotius till evening.[1]

His literary tastes were catholic. Among contemporary writers he was very fond of Byron, and he himself had that intense interest in his emotions that was characteristic of the Romantic movement. When he was campaigning in 1803, for example, he went alone one 'dark, cloudy evening' to the battlefield of Assaye shortly after the fighting and examined the grim scene attentively, until 'at last I began to feel a good deal of horror—awful, but not unpleasant. . .'.[2] One day a few years later he described how he had been overcome at 'writing Europe letters and thinking of home', and added, 'A common observer would not have thought me feeling great pleasure, for I was shut up in my bedroom, and crying all the time, but I enjoyed it more than I can describe.'[3] A book like Southey's life of Nelson could also move him to tears.[4]

Again, his interest in history suggests a kinship with the Romantic movement. He was always responsive to the melancholy of past grandeur. He once described with feeling a visit to an ancient temple: 'Captain Sydenham went into the temple to play on the flageolet, and I to walk in the colonnade. The instrument, though but indistinctly heard where I was, had a mild and pleasing sound, and the whole scene was solemn and sublime. . . .'[5]

With his intensely emotional nature he enjoyed the company of women. As a young Assistant at the Poona Residency he noted with appreciation the 'sly and graceful' ways of the dancing-girls, and recorded in his journal that he liked 'nautching' better than ever before.[6] Then there was a visit to Calcutta in 1807—'such lots of women, and laughing, and philandering, that I was in heaven'.[7]

But he never married. He resolved to stay in India until he had saved enough to give him £1,500 when he retired—although by then, he mused gloomily in 1816, he would be forty-two—'too old to set up a wife and family, and likewise too old to mix in society so as to be able to do without them'.[8]

[1] Journal, Apr. 1808, ibid. 166.
[2] M.E. to Strachey, 3.10.1803, ibid. 74 f.
[3] M.E. to Strachey, 4.4.1806, ibid. 142.
[4] Journal, 14.7.1817, ibid. 363.
[5] Journal, 24.7.[1815], ibid. 286.   [6] Journal, 8.2.1802, ibid. 45.
[7] M.E. to Strachey, 13.8.1807, ibid. 161.
[8] M.E. to Strachey, 29.11.1816, ibid. 344.

Such feelings of depression did not last, however, for he was a man of moods—as he himself realized. 'Sometimes dejected without a cause', he would record in his journal that he had wasted time in daydreams, and he would deplore the habit of 'spending nearly as much time in an ideal world of my own creation as in actual life'.[1] At other times there would be outbursts of energy: 'two days' hard and pleasant hunting, though only four hogs killed' is a remark typical of one of these periods of intense activity.[2]

He led a strenuous life all the time he was in India. Pigsticking and hard riding were his great recreations. An officer who knew him well records that 'he was a reckless horseman, sat loosely, and giving his horse his head, he generally galloped from eight to ten miles every morning; a horse seldom lasted him more than a year or two'.[3]

He would not let himself be outdone. It is related that on one occasion when he went to see a massive waterfall someone mentioned that a certain officer had walked across a 'narrow, slippery, and dangerous ledge' above it. Elphinstone, the story runs, 'immediately turned round to the speaker, and said, "Are you sure?" and on the fact being confirmed ... said, "Well, then, let you and I try if we cannot do so also"; and he instantly led the way, all the Staff being necessarily obliged to follow his example.'[4]

His determination not to be surpassed may well have been strengthened by his pride of birth. In 1818 he thanked his uncle, Lord Keith, for having declined a baronetcy on his behalf: 'It would have annoyed and embarrassed me to have been obliged to accept a baronetcy, and thus to admit the superiority of an honour which I should have shared with half the aldermen in London, over that which I derive from my birth, and which can never be held but by a gentleman.'[5]

But his pride of birth never betrayed him into complacency. He was restless and ambitious, but his ambitions were as soundly based upon his abilities and accomplishments as upon his birth. As Bishop Heber wrote several years later, he was 'in every respect an extraordinary man'.[6]

[1] Journal, 31.1.1817, Colebrooke, *Life*, i. 352.
[2] Journal, 20.8.1817, ibid. 366.
[3] Briggs, quoted by Colebrooke, *Memoir*, 70.   [4] Ibid. 72.
[5] M.E. to Lord Keith, 3.10.1818, Colebrooke, *Life*, ii. 47.
[6] Heber, *Narrative of a Journey*, ii. 219.

As Resident, Elphinstone soon found cause to intervene both in the domestic and in the foreign affairs of the Peshwa's Government. On the one hand, he curbed Baji Rao's passionate determination to crush his great territorial magnates with the help of the subsidiary force, and arranged instead a settlement at Pandharpur in 1812 by which they promised to serve the Peshwa according to custom provided that the Peshwa in his turn respected their customary rights. On the other hand, he tried to promote a settlement of the Peshwa's disputes with Baroda, and guaranteed the safety of an envoy sent to Poona for that purpose.

He soon came to distrust Baji Rao and to realize how much he resented British influence. He saw him as a crafty and vindictive ruler, restrained by cowardice and indecision. He despised both his religious and his sensual excesses, observing with distaste that 'the greater part of his time that is not occupied by religion is devoted to vicious indulgences'.[1]

He saw with misgiving that Baji Rao was falling increasingly under the influence of an ignorant, unprincipled, and dissolute favourite, Trimbakji Dengle. When Gangadhar Shastri, the envoy from Baroda, was assassinated, Elphinstone felt convinced that Trimbakji was behind it, and forced Baji Rao to surrender him into British custody. Trimbakji's subsequent escape and Baji Rao's failure to recapture him, accompanied by some vacillating and in-conclusive military preparations, persuaded Elphinstone to exact a more stringent treaty in June 1817. Among other humiliating pro-visions, Baji Rao had to acknowledge his entire dependence upon the British Government in all external relations.

After this tension there was a lull. Elphinstone was soon recording in his journal how he was longing for 'change, bustle, interest, distinction'.[2] In October 1817 he resolved, 'I must keep up my relish for society, for hog hunting, and for all kinds of enterprise and activity, and avoid the strange, torpid, solitary, shy habits I had fallen into last year.'[3]

But his fears of monotony and boredom were unjustified. Con-trary to his own judgement, a large proportion of the subsidiary force had been temporarily withdrawn to the north to join a wide-spread campaign against the marauding bands of Pindaris that had been ravaging vast areas of country. On 5 November 1817 Baji

---

[1] M.E. to Governor-General (1815) quoted in Colebrooke, *Life*, i. 289.
[2] Journal, 27.6.1817, ibid. 362.   [3] Journal, 8.10.1817, ibid. 378.

Rao took advantage of the situation and attacked the remnant, but without success.

After two more British victories,[1] the war degenerated into a pursuit of Baji Rao. Wearied by the hardships of the march, depressed by the growing numbers of deserters, tormented by suspicions of his remaining adherents, he managed to continue his flight until 3 June, when he at last surrendered.[2]

His fate had already been decided. In December 1817 the Governor-General in Council told Elphinstone that Baji Rao was to be deposed and that his territories were to be annexed by the East India Company.[3]

Elphinstone, unrivalled in his knowledge of the Marathas and of their country, was appointed 'Sole Commissioner for the settlement of the territory conquered from the Peishwah'; he was told to provide as he thought fit for the temporary administration of the country and to employ any officers whom he thought suitable for the work.[4]

The shape of the new system of government was in fact left to his discretion. He had no clear-cut plans. All that he could do for the time being was to choose his men and provide for the needs of war.

[1] At Koregaon on 1 Jan. 1818 and at Ashti on 19 Feb.
[2] He surrendered to Sir John Malcolm. For Baji Rao's suspicions of his adherents see, for example, Malcolm to Supreme Government, 31.5.1818, P.R.C. xiii. 367 f.; Malcolm to Supreme Government, 4.6.1818, ibid. 374 ff.
[3] Supreme Government to M.E., 15.12.1817, ibid. 270 ff.
[4] Ibid. His salary was later fixed at Rs.50,000 a year plus expenses, with effect from 15 Dec. 1817 (Supreme Government to M.E., 14.7.1818, Bom. S.C. 30.9.1818, 946 ff.).

2

THE NEW RULERS TAKE CHARGE

THE work of administration had begun before Elphinstone received his instructions in December 1817. The city of Poona was taken less than a fortnight after the outbreak of war. The Maratha forces left it unprotected, and when the British under General Lionel Smith advanced upon it, a substantial citizen came out to ask for 'protection for the bankers and merchants'. He was in fact the banker who had generally handled the Company's business there. With his help guards were posted at strategic points, and—as Elphinstone reported with satisfaction—although 'some trifling excesses were committed in the suburbs before there was time to take precautions', nevertheless 'the city suffered no injury and the loss of property was quite insignificant considering all circumstances'.[1]

Elphinstone advised General Smith to appoint Lieutenant H. D. Robertson, the General's Persian Interpreter, to be the officer commanding in the city.[2] He considered that the selection of a capable man for this post was 'an object of much importance as the care of the police and in fact the government of the city were necessarily vested in him'. Robertson seemed to have excellent qualities: he 'understands the language, knows the natives, is accustomed to business, and is of a conciliating temper'.[3]

Poona itself was no mean city. In 1819 Elphinstone estimated its population to be about 110,000.[4] This he thought was between one-tenth and one-fifth less than when the Peshwa lived there with his court, his soldiers, and his dependants. Then it had been the centre of the Maratha Empire, with all the pomp and luxury of a capital. There is a contemporary picture by a European artist of a scene in the Ganesh Mahal of the Shaniwar Palace in 1790: Sir Charles Malet is handing a treaty to the Peshwa Sawai Madhav

---

[1] M.E. to Governor-General, 23.11.1817, P.R.C. xiii. 254 ff.
[2] Henry Dundas Robertson, Bombay Army; Ensign 1807, Lieutenant 1810.
[3] M.E. to Governor-General, 23.11.1817. He soon came to regard Robertson as 'the best qualified for civil business of all the gentlemen employed in the Paishwa's country' (M.E. to J. Elphinston, 29.10.1818, *Elphinstone*).
[4] M.E., *Report on the Territories Conquered from the Peshwa*, 5.

Rao; the young ruler, richly clothed, rests against sumptuous cushions; the painted walls are hung with deeply folded drapery; he is surrounded by the chivalry of Maharashtra, and the atmosphere is heavy with subdued magnificence.

With the British conquest, however, what Bagehot would have called the dignified part of the state was swept away. The contrast was immediately apparent. When Lieutenant Macleod,[1] a sensitive and observant young officer, went to see the Shaniwar Palace soon after the British had taken Poona, he was 'a good deal' disappointed by what he saw: in his journal he recorded how

Robertson occupied the common Durbar & a small room off it, where there was a picture of Marquis Wellesley & a miniature of Sir Barry Close stuck with a little wax against the wall—the Durbar room is quite plain excepting a row of carved wooden pillars . . . down each side. The Gunnesh Mahl is a handsome lofty room . . . The famous image of Gunnesh had been removed. The room appeared to much disadvantage, being hung with white cloths to keep off dust, & quite empty.[2]

However, the new rulers had no intention of abolishing forms and ceremonies that might reassure public opinion. Robertson, for example, doubted the utility of the 120 nightwatchmen who went the rounds in bodies of twelve preceded by a trumpeter: 'I fancy they seldom caught any vagrants or did much good in any way.' But he continued the custom in order that 'the notion of security attached to the sounding of the hour might be maintained among the inhabitants'. He also continued the system of firing a night and morning gun and of apprehending any person found in the streets during the night, with the same object in view—that of 'deadening as much as possible the feelings of alarm attendant upon a translation from an old to a new state of things'.[3]

On the other hand, while the new rulers retained the existing division of the city into a number of districts, each with one or more officials having a general responsibility for law and order, they made a significant change in the position of those officials. Under the Maratha Government they had enjoyed powers which were in effect judicial and in extent indefinite: it had been their

[1] John Macleod, an engineer officer on the Bombay establishment; Marathi interpreter to M.E., formerly aide-de-camp to Sir Evan Nepean, subsequently Assistant to Chaplin, finally Agent at Bushire, where he died (*Eur. MSS. Catalogue, s.v.* 295).

[2] Macleod, Journal, 21.11.1817, *Eur. MS.* 295, 95.

[3] H. D. Robertson to M.E., 30.11.[1817], Bg. S.C. 31.7.1818, 305.

duty to settle any disputes that arose between the inhabitants of their districts. Now they were strictly forbidden to do more than try to reconcile the parties. As Robertson explained at the time: 'I conceived it to be an object of the first importance to allow my servants no latitude or power and by taking on myself the trouble of keeping every particle of authority in my own hands to establish . . . in the commencement of our rule in the Marhatta capital a favourable impression of the sovereignty of the British Government'.[1]

Robertson himself certainly had authority enough. Under the Maratha Government there had been no rigid separation of powers. Of necessity there was none under the new Government: Robertson was Judge and Magistrate, besides having charge of the police. He had a Shastri—a learned Brahman—to advise him on points of Hindu law, and a Registrar and several assistants to take down the depositions of parties and witnesses in open court. He himself heard these depositions, cross-examined, and after consulting the Shastri either gave judgement himself or referred the case to arbitration.[2]

He was also the Collector. Soon after he had installed himself in Poona he was told by Elphinstone to settle the country within a march of the city[3]—this being the area which could be protected by the dispatch of troops. On Elphinstone's instructions he granted to the ryots—or peasants—large remissions of the revenue due from them to the Government. In this way, so he reported optimistically, he had demonstrated to them that 'Government[s] were made for the sake of the people and not the people (as the Marhattas believed) for the sake of the Government'.[4]

Soon Elphinstone was able to sketch out the lines of future policy. On 26 February 1818 he formally appointed Robertson Provisional Collector and Magistrate of Poona and laid down some general principles for him to observe.[5] In due course he sent similar instructions to his other Collectors.[6]

Robertson was now to bring under British authority as much territory as he could. To help in this, Elphinstone authorized him

---

[1] Ibid. [2] Ibid.

[3] One march or eight kos—a kos being equal to about two miles (H. D. Robertson to M.E., 19.2.1818, Bg. S.C. 31.7.1818, 307).

[4] H. D. Robertson to M.E., 1.1.1818, ibid. 306.

[5] M.E. to H. D. Robertson, 26.2.1818, Choksey, *Last Phase*, 212 ff.

[6] M.E. to Briggs, 11.3.1818, Bg. S.C. 31.7.1818, 89; M.E. to Pottinger, 2.4.1818, ibid. 105; M.E. to Grant, 8.4.1818, ibid. 131.

to engage 1,000 sibandis (irregular soldiers). Elphinstone's shrewd advice concerning the best type of recruit is typical of his general approach to social problems. He told Robertson to employ only 'men of military habits', and to discourage cultivators from leaving the land. Security should be obtained for good behaviour, and sibandis of doubtful loyalty should be employed at a distance from their homes so that 'their defection would leave their families exposed to the supposed effects of your resentment'. Sibandis might well be made more efficient than they usually were, but Robertson was reminded that 'it does not suit our policy to preserve a permanent military spirit among them', and that it would be desirable 'to allow them in time to sink into Judges' and Collectors' peons'.[1]

With the instruments at his disposal, Robertson accordingly extended the area of his Collectorate as the circumstances of war permitted. Eventually it comprised the land between the Nira and the Bhima, bounded on the west by the Ghats. He later estimated its population to be about 500,000.[2]

Elphinstone ordered the abolition of revenue farming. Instead, the revenue was to be collected from the Patels, or village headmen, and the amount assessed by reference not to past years of prosperity but to the actual state of cultivation at the present. Oppressive or unpopular taxes were to be abolished. Lands held free of revenue were not to be interfered with.[3] In short, everything possible was to be done to reassure people concerning the new government.

Elphinstone also gave Robertson some general instructions about the administration of justice. Any village helping the Peshwa was to be punished for rebellion by martial law. Other crimes were to be dealt with 'according to the forms of justice usual in the country modified as you may think expedient, and in all cases you will endeavour to enforce the existing laws and customs, unless where they are clearly repugnant to reason and natural equity'. The custom of the country was to be so closely followed that Brahmans were to remain exempt from the death penalty except for treason or plundering the country as bandits. Civil suits were also to be judged according to the existing law and custom of the country and by means of arbitration whenever possible.[4]

The new government would continue to pay the cost of 'all

[1] M.E. to H. D. Robertson, 26.2.1818, Choksey, *Last Phase*, 212 ff.
[2] H. D. Robertson to Chaplin, n.d., Bom. R.C. 19.3.1823, 1457.
[3] M.E. to H. D. Robertson, 26.2.1818, Choksey, *Last Phase*, 212 ff.
[4] Ibid.

established religious institutions'. But Elphinstone qualified this general principle by excluding what he called 'magical ceremonies' and also Baji Rao's personal charities. What was religious and what was magical might well have been a matter of opinion in a Utilitarian era: Elphinstone, however, specifically ordered Robertson to keep up the annual ceremony for rain, together with similar rites 'of ancient institution', as also such of Baji Rao's charities as seemed 'required by humanity'. Robertson thus had plenty of scope for discretion.[1]

For his part, Robertson was convinced of the administrative value of respectability: 'considering immorality as the source from which heinous offences and crimes are derived', he explained, 'I became solicitous (however arduous the task is in appearance) to endeavour to reform the depraved habits which prevailed'. He forbade liquor-sellers to live within half a mile of the city: this 'removed the temptation which these houses presented to debauchery'. There were many gambling-dens: these he prohibited. In his zeal he went even further. 'The greatest evil', he thought, was 'infidelity to the marriage bed.' He hoped that reform in this sphere would be of political value: 'a check to this practice sanctioned by a Brahmin Prince if quickly put in force by the British Government, would occasion a comparison highly favourable to the British name'. He took speedy and effective advantage of his opportunity when he discovered that the police had arrested a Brahman for having committed adultery with a widow of the same caste, had optimistically demanded from 20 to 15 rupees from him, and had eventually freed him when he paid them 6 rupees. Robertson was careful that the initiative should seem to come not from himself but from the Shastri of his Court, so that he himself would not appear as one anxious to change the shape of things. The new and the old were deftly combined in his handling of the situation. The Brahman and his mistress were sent around the town with the public crier proclaiming their disgrace: the lady's face was blackened and her garments were tied to those of her lover. This was a traditional punishment. But Robertson's proclamation which described the crime and announced the punishment was so framed as to exhibit

---

[1] Robertson at first determined to reduce the cost of religious establishments in his area from Rs.27,000 to Rs.20,000. But when he examined in detail what this would actually mean he decided that the risk of arousing a desire for Baji Rao's return would be too great. He therefore maintained them upon the old footing (H. D. Robertson to M.E., 8.4.1818, Choksey, *Last Phase*, 219 ff.).

the even-handedness of British justice in that it also related how the offending Brahman had been awarded 20 rupees as compensation for his ill-treatment at the hands of the police.[1]

Elphinstone returned from his campaigning to stay at Poona for a couple of days in March 1818. In his own words, 'all the principal people' who were still in the city came to see him. He also invited 'all the Brahmins who were eminent for their learning or reputation': over 200 of them came, and among them he distributed presents. 'The expense of these presents', he told the Governor-General, 'was great, but in my opinion fully recompensed by the impression that will be created among the Hindoos by this proof [that] the persons whom they respect are not intended to be neglected under the new Govt.' However, not many of the aristocracy of Poona were there: 'the houses of the great', he noted, 'are almost all empty'. Many of the great had in fact fled to Wai. Nevertheless, 'the other orders' seemed to him 'as numerous as ever', and had 'every appearance of security and content'.[2]

While he was at Poona he lived in one of the Peshwa's palaces. 'The Peshwa's great hall', he wrote in his journal, 'is now my reception room.' But his nature was of too fine a grain for him to glory in the transfer of power: 'Poona, when approached, is unchanged in appearance; but the destruction of all our houses destroys every feeling of quiet and home, and the absence of the Hindoo Government occasions a void that alters the effect of everything. Our respect for the place is gone, and the change is melancholy. How must the natives feel this, when even we feel it!'[3]

He was ever anxious to conciliate public opinion and to soften the impact of the changes which he knew must come. Towards the end of the month he visited Wai. He understood and appreciated why it was always so much frequented by Hindus—'the beauty of its situation, its sanctity as being near the source of the Krishna, and its numerous temples, ghauts and gardens'. At that time he found it 'crowded by the greatest part of the respectable inhabitants of Poona who retired there previously to our occupation of that capital'. During the few hours that he could spend at Wai he was visited by 'most people of note about the place and received assurances from all of them of their submission to our Government'. As

[1] Proclamation by H. D. Robertson, Choksey, *Last Phase*, 223 f.
[2] M.E. to Governor-General, 20.3.1818, Bg. S.C. 1.5.1818, 103.
[3] M.E., Journal, 17.3.[1818], Colebrooke, ii. 30.

he had done at Poona he received the Brahmans and gave them presents: 'the number that came', he told the Governor-General, 'was from 5 to 600, and upwards of 40 were the most eminent for their learning and sanctity in the Paishwa's late dominions'. And he concluded, 'this class has not yet shown any disposition at all hostile to the British Government'.[1]

Robertson took a similarly optimistic view of the state of public feeling in Poona itself. When the city was first occupied he thought that the attitude of the people in general had been 'strong against us'. This later developed into a cautious neutrality. But as soon as they realized that their city would never again come under the rule of Baji Rao, the inhabitants seemed less anxious to hide their willingness to collaborate with the new government: 'some of the most respectable and sensible members of the community visited me in the day time instead of as formerly during the night'. Robertson firmly believed in 'the policy of pleasing the people of Poona', for 'this city has for many years given the tone to the feeling of the Maratha Empire'. Indeed, it seemed that many of 'the lower classes' believed that because he was in charge of Poona he had succeeded to supreme power: 'men come to me from the Concan, from Candeish, from other quarters, with complaints, and it is quite impossible to convince them that I cannot decide on their affairs and they go away satisfied that I am unwilling to listen to their grievances'.[2]

There was already apparent a great change in the manner of administration: as Robertson noted in April, 'the parade and bustle of the former Government have subsided into a comparative calm'.[3] But in other ways normal conditions seemed to have returned to Poona: in the same month Lieutenant Macleod recorded in his journal that the city 'seemed quite crowded, and everyone looked busy and confident, the shops well supplied and frequented, and everything appeared to have recovered its former condition'.[4]

To the south, Elphinstone had an able colleague in the renowned

[1] M.E. to Governor-General, 31.3.1818, Bom. S.C. 15.4.1818, 628 ff. P.R.C. xiii. 324 ff.
[2] H. D. Robertson to M.E., 8.4.1818, Choksey, *Last Phase*, 219 ff.
[3] Ibid.
[4] Macleod, 20.4.1818, *Eur. MS.* 295, 218 f.

Colonel Thomas Munro of the Madras Army. Munro had already proved himself to be an outstanding administrator, and he had done much to persuade the home authorities of the wisdom of governing India by Indian rather than English methods. Shortly before the war he had been appointed to take charge of the cessions which were to be made by the Peshwa in the Southern Maratha country under the Treaty of Poona in June 1817.

The majority of the population in the territories between the Krishna and the Varada which now became his responsibility was in fact of Kanarese and not of Maratha stock. It was later estimated that the Marathas were at most only one-eighth or one-tenth of the whole; according to Elphinstone, 'what there is of them seems to consist of soldiers and Bramins with a full share of the vice of those classes'.[1]

Munro was quick to realize the political significance of the social divisions which he found there. He was soon reporting to the Governor-General that the Maratha jagirdars—or chieftains[2]—and their principal servants were 'considered, in some measure, as strangers and conquerors'; although 'the best of the horse' were 'in general Mahrattas, and no doubt attached to their chiefs', nevertheless 'the infantry in the forts and villages' were 'mostly Canarese, and ready to join any power that will pay them'. The civil population, too, seemed to have reason for welcoming the British: 'all the trading classes', he wrote, 'are anxious for the expulsion of the Mahrattas, because they interrupt their trade by arbitrary exactions, and often plunder them of their whole property'; the village headmen, he thought, were also 'very generally desirous of being relieved from the Mahratta dominion'.[3]

He had few troops. He might well have used them to garrison his headquarters at Dharwar. Instead, he encouraged the inhabitants to withhold the payment of revenue from the Maratha officers, urged them to rise against the Marathas, and sent small detachments to support those villages which did. There were many small forts in the Southern Maratha country, their garrisons ranging from about thirty to about four hundred men. He organized what

[1] M.E., *Report*, 8; Munro to Governor-General, 28.11.1817, Gleig, ii. 14.

[2] Jagir: the assignment of the revenues of an area of land. Jagirdar: the holder of such an assignment. The great jagirdars in this area also exercised extensive political, or at least administrative and judicial powers, and were often referred to as chieftains.

[3] Munro to Governor-General, 28.11.1817, Gleig, ii. 15.

today might be called a fifth column. He had what he called 'partisans' in many of these forts, who with the help of the inhabitants would gradually expel those of the garrisons who came from beyond the Krishna.[1] His progress was triumphal. A contemporary, Captain James Grant, described it in the following terms: 'he sent his irregulars to the right and left of his column of march, who occupied the villages, fought with spirit on several occasions, stormed fortified places, and took possession in name of "Thomas Munro Buhadur" '.[2] As he went forward he left Amildars—local officials—behind him to pacify and govern the conquered areas.

The villagers seemed well disposed. As early as 18 December 1817 he was claiming that at least nine-tenths of the inhabitants were in favour of the British.[3] Their support was sometimes active: for example, after an engagement near Sholapur in which the Marathas had been routed, 'of those who remained many were plundered and even put to death by the villagers'.[4]

A large proportion of the population were directly subject to the great jagirdars, or chieftains. A few years after the war it was estimated that there were 778,000 souls in the jagirdars' estates, compared with 684,000 in those areas of the Southern Maratha country which came under direct British rule.[5]

One of his most important tasks was to arrange, in consultation with Elphinstone, terms of submission for these jagirdars. But he did not relish this work: 'I am tired of sitting for hours every day with the Vakeels of a set of high-titled chiefs, who have long since been beaten into submission, and who follow the standard of Bajee Row, without any intention of fighting against us.'[6] When the fighting was done, he retired from his post in June 1818. Two years later he became Governor of Madras.

To succeed him at Dharwar he recommended William Chaplin of the Madras civil service, at that time Collector of Bellari: 'he possesses great temper—an excellent judgement and has had much experience'.[7] Indeed, Munro thought him 'the fittest person in the Madras Civil Service';[8] 'he has more talent and more extensive

[1] Munro to M.E., 20.12.1817, Gleig, iii. 224.
[2] Grant (later Grant-Duff), *History*, ii. 520.
[3] Munro to M.E., 18.12.1817, Gleig, iii. 222.
[4] M.E. to Governor-General 24.5.1818, Bg. S.C. 3.7.1818, 234.
[5] The actual figures were 778,183 and 684,193 (Chaplin, *Report*, 4).
[6] Munro to Alexander Munro (his brother), 6.4.1818, Gleig, iii. 241 f.
[7] Munro to M.E., 5.5.1818, ibid. 251.
[8] Munro to M.E., 26.4.1818, ibid. 250.

general views than any of the Civil Servants under Madras'.[1] But besides his intellectual ability, it transpired that Chaplin had a lively sense of humour and—as often happens when these two qualities are combined—a tendency to sarcasm which aroused resentment among his subordinates when he eventually succeeded the suave and catholic-spirited Elphinstone as Commissioner in the Deccan.

However great may have been the military importance of the Southern Maratha country, with its powerful jagirdars, the traditions of the Maratha Empire pointed northwards—to Satara.

Among the fundamental principles which were to guide Elphinstone in the new 'arrangement', he was told to make some 'provision in land' for the Raja of Satara, the descendant of Shivaji and nominal head of the Maratha Empire. In this he was given a wide discretion:

The provision for the Raja of Sattara may be made either by an assignment of land in jagheer or by establishing him in a small and compact sovereignty under such stipulations as shall secure the supremacy of the British Government. You will decide between these two arrangements, or on the adoption of any other calculated to secure the same object, namely, the conciliation of the tribe of Mahrattas to the new order of things, and the establishment of a counterpoise to the remaining influence of the former Brahmin Government.[2]

When he saw this letter, Munro wrote to Elphinstone to impress upon him the desirability of erecting 'some local government which should give employment to the military classes of the people', and so reduce the likelihood of unrest in the new British territories. He cited Mysore as a case in point.[3]

In short, Elphinstone had the alternative of bestowing an estate or a kingdom upon the heir of Shivaji: he gave him a kingdom. He distinguished four main functions which the new state was to perform: it would furnish 'an honourable maintenance to the representatives of the ancient princes of this country'; secondly, it would be 'a counterpoise to the remaining influence of the former Brahmin Government', as was proposed in his instructions from the Governor-General; thirdly, as Munro had pointed out, it would provide for some of the soldiers thrown out of employment when

[1] Munro to M.E., 12.5.1818, Gleig, iii. 252.
[2] Supreme Government to M.E., 15.12.1817, P.R.C. xiii. 270 ff.
[3] Munro to M.E., 19.1.1818, Bg. S.C. 31.7.1818, 75.

the war ended; fourthly, the Raja, as a Hindu prince, would maintain 'some of the civil and religious orders whom it might be difficult to dispose of under our own direct Government'.[1]

Shortly before the war, Baji Rao, realizing the importance of keeping within his control the head of the Maratha Empire, had imprisoned the Raja of Satara and his family at Wasota. Soon after the war began he had them brought to his camp. For the time being, therefore, the British had to content themselves with possession of the town of Satara, which they captured in the evening of 10 February. 'The line and garrison joked with each other as the latter was marching out', and the British troops occupied the town quietly. At noon on the following day, in order to make the situation clear, the British flag was hoisted for a moment and then pulled down; it was at once replaced by the Raja's.[2] Elphinstone 'assembled the Rajah's officers and principal inhabitants and laid open our views which', he thought, 'were received with much satisfaction by the auditors'.[3] To add weight to the counterpoise against Baji Rao's influence, Elphinstone drew up a proclamation stating the case against him, outlining the British plans for the future, and calling upon all in the Peshwa's service to withdraw from it within two months on pain of forfeiting their lands.[4] This proclamation was not, however, generally circulated in the Deccan until a force had arrived to besiege the great Fort of Singarh on 20 February.[5] This was because Elphinstone did not think it prudent to declare the British intention to assume the government of the country 'until we were prepared effectually to support our declaration', and until the likelihood of final victory by the British was more apparent 'in the native country of Marhattas, where I believe a national feeling still exists sufficient to prevent the people from assisting a foreign conqueror'. But he saw no need for such caution south of the Krishna, and at the end of January he authorized Munro to tell the people in his territories 'that they shall hereafter be British subjects'.[6]

[1] M.E. to Grant, 8.4.1818, ibid. 131.
[2] M.E., Journal, 11.2.1818, Colebrooke, ii. 27.
[3] M.E. to Governor-General, 7.3.1818, P.R.C. xiii. 313 ff.
[4] Proclamation of 11.2.1818, ibid. 299 ff.
[5] M.E. to Governor-General, 7.3.1818, ibid. 313 ff. The Deccan army had in fact been divided into two divisions, one under General Smith with the task of pursuing Baji Rao, the other under General Pritzler with the task of capturing forts. Pritzler at length took Singarh on 2 Mar.
[6] M.E. to Munro, 31.1.1818, Bg. S.C. 31.7.1818, 76.

General Smith's victory at Ashti delivered into his custody the persons of the Raja of Satara and his family. Smith at once asked Elphinstone to take them off his hands: 'The Raja's family is rather a nuisance to me; they insist on my not leaving them, and I cannot keep up any useful pursuit with them.'[1]

When Elphinstone met the Raja he thought that his gratitude to General Smith for rescuing him from Baji Rao's control was 'very engaging'. The Raja seemed 'about twenty; not handsome, but good-humoured and frank', and 'not destitute of intelligence'. Elphinstone thought that his brothers had 'nearly the same character, with rather better looks'. His mother seemed 'a woman of some talent and address', 'a fine old lady, who has been handsome, and has still very fine eyes'. Elphinstone's reception was formal: 'they observe all the Eastern sovereignty, neither rising on the entrance of strangers, nor returning salutes'.[2]

Elphinstone accompanied Raja Pratapsingh to Satara, and on 29 March saw him enter his capital 'in procession with the pomp of a prince and the delight of a schoolboy'.[3]

The character of the first British Resident to be appointed to the Court of Satara was of some importance, for he would have to lead the Raja's feet into the ways of British administrative practice. Elphinstone chose Lieutenant James Grant, an army officer on his own staff. He has been called 'a raw British soldier',[4] but this description hardly fits him. He studied deeply in Maratha history, as his published work was to show. He was keenly interested in the people around him. He presumably had a strong constitution, for he was accustomed to boast that he was the only man in his regiment who could ever walk to bed, and he used to drink a bottle of port every night.[5] When in 1821 he was attacked by cholera morbus the 'spasms were trifling and never got above my legs', and he soon

---

[1] Smith to M.E., 20.2.1818, Colebrooke, ii. 28.

[2] M.E., Journal, 4.3.1818, ibid. 29; M.E. to Governor-General, 5.3.1818, Bg. S.C. 24.4.1818, 23. Pratapsingh was born in 1793 (G. S. Sardesai, *New History of the Marathas*, iii. 504).

[3] M.E., Journal, 29.3.1818, Colebrooke, ii. 31.

[4] G. S. Sardesai, *New History of the Marathas*, iii. 510.

[5] M. E. Grant Duff, *A Victorian Vintage*, Introduction, vi. James Grant added the name Duff on succeeding in 1825 on his mother's death to the estates of the Duffs of Eden, Banffshire. He added the name Cuninghame when his wife came into some property in 1850.

recovered in spite of the remedies which he used: '8 grains camphor
and 2 of opium every hour with *brandy and eau de Cologne* (for
both which last I called lustily) at last subdued the disease'. 'I
drank three bottles of brandy in as many days', he reported triumph-
antly to Elphinstone, 'so you see thin people sometimes can stand
more than stouter folks.'[1] Perhaps it is hardly surprising that he
suffered increasingly from headaches, and had to retire for this
reason in 1823.

The Raja was formally enthroned on 10 April. He and his
brothers, mounted upon elephants, went in procession through
the town. When he dismounted at the palace 'three or four sheep
were killed . . . and a quantity of holy water poured out'. A pavi-
lion or mandap had been erected in the court of the palace; there
stood Shivaji's throne, 'a little old-fashioned couch', which had
been 'covered with rich cloths'. Lieutenant Macleod was again
disappointed: 'the mandap was but shabby, there were no dancing
girls nor illuminations'. The Raja seated himself upon the throne.
There was a short pause. Then rosewater and flowers were distributed, and Elphinstone and his party took their leave. On the
following day the Raja paid him a visit. Elphinstone gave presents
of jewels and cloths to the Raja, his brothers, and his retinue, and
rosewater and flowers were again distributed.[2]

At Elphinstone's suggestion the boundaries of the new state
were fixed at the Ghats on the west, the Nira on the north, the
Nizam's frontier on the east, and the Krishna and Warna on the
south.[3] It was estimated in 1821 that the Raja's net annual revenues
would be little short of 15 lakhs of rupees.[4] In fact, for the twenty
years of Pratapsingh's reign they averaged Rs.1,456,603.[5]

At Satara Grant found himself in a situation that required all
his tact and diplomacy. In April 1818 Elphinstone had told him
that 'the Raja's flag may be hoisted in the villages' and that 'it may
also be explained to the inhabitants that they are the Raja's subjects'.
On the other hand, Elphinstone added that 'it will be proper to
impress on them as well as on the Raja that it is not intended to

[1] Grant to M.E., 15.12.1821, *Elphinstone*.
[2] Macleod, Journal, 10.4.1818, *Eur. MS.* 295, 215 f.
[3] M.E. to Grant, 8.4.1818, Bg. S.C. 31.7.1818, 131; M.E. to Supreme
Government, 18.6.1818; Supreme Government to M.E., 14.7.1818, P.R.C. xiii.
394 ff., 418 ff.
[4] Political letter from Bombay, 7.3.1821, para. 46, Bom. P.L.R. viii. 110 ff.
[5] T. C. Ogilvy, Report, S.B.R., n.s. xli. 167.

revive even in name the Empire of Seevajee'. Grant had to secure
the Raja's goodwill, but he had also to make it quite clear that the
authority of the British Government was in reality supreme. Otherwise, 'the machine we are setting up will be liable to be turned
against us'. For the present, Grant was authorized to take full
charge of the Government—'a natural arrangement, while everything is to be done with our troops and our money'. As the Raja
gained experience of administration and as his state developed
enough revenue to maintain itself, Grant was gradually to hand
over power. Meanwhile, Elphinstone paved the way for Grant by
telling the Raja that 'the final settlement of his government will in
a great measure be regulated by the disposition he evinces during
this period of probation.'[1] He also entrusted the management of the
southern jagirdars to the Collector of Dharwar rather than to the
Political Agent at Satara, partly because 'it is an object not to make
them look to Satara as their Head Quarters or keep their Vakeels
assembled at that Court'.[2]

Grant set to work to win the Raja's confidence. He did this
partly by direct argument—'persuading him that his interests and
mine were the same, that our fortunes were linked together, that
my rise depended on his future greatness', and so on.[3] Grant also
developed an ingenious strategy;

above all things [he explained to Elphinstone] he must think that every
act of mine and his is *controlled*, and that an infringement of your orders
if reported would bring instant ruin upon him. I must be his friend
and adviser, bound by my public duty to insist on his acting with
economy, justice & moderation, but privately disposed to report as few
faults as can possibly be avoided consistent with my situation, at the
same time that I should be displaced immediately if you discovered that
I had allowed anything improper to pass unnoticed or without reporting
it to you.[4]

And he emphasized to the Raja how dangerous it would be to
offend Elphinstone. On one occasion he told 'the poor little Raja',
as he wrote afterwards to Elphinstone, 'that though you were
great in your friendship *you were terrible in your wrath*'.[5]

Grant soon came to feel a certain affection for the Raja. In May

[1] M.E. to Grant, 8.4.1818, Bg. S.C. 31.7.1818, 131.
[2] M.E. to Governor-General, 18.6.1818, P.R.C. xiii. 394 ff.
[3] Grant to M.E., 23.3.1819, R. D. Choksey, *Aftermath*, 260 ff.
[4] Grant to M.E., n.d. [Feb. 1819?], *Elphinstone*.
[5] Grant to M.E., 23.4.1818, *Elphinstone*.

1818 he was writing of him as 'a very good fellow. I really like him very much though the young scamp ought not to meddle with other people's wives'.[1] By November 1818 he had developed a healthy respect for the Raja's diplomatic abilities: 'he is as sly the little fellow as you can conceive, and I see how he tries to cheat me in the way he tells me (as a great secret) how he cheats others'.[2] This, however, did not lessen his affection for the Raja: 'I like the sinner with all his faults, he does not tell me lies.'[3]

One of Grant's earliest and most difficult tasks was to limit the Raja's personal expenditure. Elphinstone told Grant that for the present it should be 'about three lacks of rupees per annum'.[4] The Raja first demanded 'nearly half a crore', but Grant 'had no difficulty in making him acknowledge the absurdity of this, and he freely admitted that he had taken the advice of other people . . . who had told him that it was proper to give in a large estimate as in fact half a lack and half a crore were all the same to the Company's Government when inclined to bestow favour'. He then said that 'we can manage on twenty lacks for the ensuing year'. Grant finally told him how much Elphinstone was willing to allow, to which he replied that 'it was impossible'. Grant then remarked that he himself thought 3 lakhs of rupees 'most handsome', and the interview seems to have ended in an unsatisfactory way: 'we parted less cordially than we had ever done before'.[5]

He decided not to continue the argument personally, but to act through his confidential agent: 'I sent Ballajee Punt because I should have found difficulty in avoiding personal altercation.' Balaji Pant proved 'of the greatest use', and the Raja finally agreed to Rs.25,000. He asked for Rs.2,000 extra to use in charity: Grant decided to give him Rs.1,000 and allow for further purchases up to an additional Rs.1,000. This figure of Rs.26,000 a month came to Rs.12,000 a year more than Elphinstone had originally proposed.[6]

[1] Grant to M.E., 4.5.1818, ibid.   [2] Grant to M.E., 8.11.1818, ibid.
[3] Grant to M.E., 24.2.1819, ibid.
[4] M.E. to Grant, 8.4.1818, Bg. S.C. 31.7.1818, 131.
[5] Grant to M.E., 23.3.1819, Choksey, *Aftermath*, 260 ff.
[6] It was distributed in the following proportions:

Raja	.	.	.	.	.	Rs.15,075
Rani	.	.	.	.	.	Rs. 1,152
Raja's brothers	.	.	.	.	Rs. 7,500
Raja's mother	.	.	.	.	Rs. 2,273
						Rs.26,000

Ibid. Also Grant to M.E., 26.4.1818, *Elphinstone*.

Shortly after this achievement, Grant was dismayed to hear that Sir Thomas Hislop might soon visit Satara. 'I have got the Raja to lock up all his finery and to restore the old fashion of plain clothes, and another display *like the Coronation* will upset all his fine plans and destroy the effects of all Ballajee Punt's persuasions.'[1] His fears seem to have come to nothing, for there is no record of any such extravagance, and the Raja's habits of economy continued.

Elsewhere, British rule was established with less ceremony and in much the same way as at Poona, against the shifting background of a war which was almost daily changing in direction and impetus as the Peshwa turned indecisively from one course to another. The general pattern of administration was the same. All civil matters, even the collection of revenue, were necessarily subordinated to war. When General Smith occupied the town of Ahmadnagar in November 1817 he entrusted its government to the Fort Adjutant, Captain Gibbon. At Elphinstone's suggestion he told him to settle as much country as possible within reach of the garrison.[2] This concentration of authority in the hands of one man was in accordance both with the military situation and with previous Maratha practice.[3] But it meant that Elphinstone had to take particular care to find a man of ability for so responsible a post.

Captain Gibbon seemed to lack some of the qualities required by his situation. One of the first tasks of a new administrator was to take charge of the records of the former government—this was generally regarded as a matter of course. But it turned out that Captain Gibbon had sold 'enormous heaps of them' as waste paper to the banias of Ahmadnagar.[4] Loud complaints were soon heard

---

[1] Grant to M.E., 27.[4.1818], *Elphinstone*.

[2] M.E. to Governor-General, 23.11.1817, P.R.C. xiii. 254 ff. Ahmadnagar had been the depot of the subsidiary force since its conquest from Sindhia in 1803. Thereafter the British remained there on sufferance until the Treaty of Poona, which provided for the transfer to the Company in perpetual sovereignty of the Fort of Ahmadnagar (Governor-General to Court of Directors, 4.9.1817, P.P. 1818, xi. 369, 45–49). The cession included the adjoining country within 2,000 yards of the foot of the glacis. But when Smith arrived at Ahmadnagar on 8 November the town had still not been given up to the British. He took possession of it 'at once' (Smith to Lt.-Gen. Sir T. Hislop, 20.11.1817, Bg. S.C. 16.1.1818, 55).

[3] Under Baji Rao's rule, the administration of all civil and criminal justice had been in the hands of the person who farmed the revenue of the town of Ahmadnagar and the surrounding country (Waman Rao Apte) (Pottinger to M.E., 1.5.1818, Bg. S.C. 31.7.1818, 300).

[4] Pottinger to M.E., 12.5.1819, *Elphinstone*.

all over his district against his drastic way of collecting the revenue:
'it would appear that every bushel of grain (particularly gram
and wheat) in the country has been *seized* by Captain Gibbon's
people . . . he has actually left nothing for seed for next year'.[1]
Worse still, he did not seem to know what to do with the grain once
he had got hold of it. 'His *private* dwelling house here is full of it.'[2]
Moreover, the ryots complained that they had neither been paid
in cash nor had been awarded any deduction in the amount of
revenue to be demanded from them.[3]

Elphinstone selected Lieutenant Henry Pottinger for the permanent appointment of Collector of Ahmadnagar. He had already
won fame as a daring explorer. After going to Sind in the Hankey
Smith mission of 1809, he had volunteered with a friend to
explore the country between India and Persia. The local inhabitants had not been deceived by the elaborate disguise adopted by
the two friends, but Pottinger returned safely to Bombay and in
1816 his report on his travels was published. After his return to
Bombay he was appointed to the staff of the Governor, Sir Evan
Nepean, who brought him to Elphinstone's notice. Before appointing him to Ahmadnagar, Elphinstone had in fact had personal
experience of his abilities in the post of assistant to the Resident at
Poona. He was quite a competent Collector, though his career at
Ahmadnagar was not entirely without fault. It was diplomatic work
which seemed most to stimulate his ability and energy. He soon
began to feel the pressure of the routine work of administration:
often receiving from twenty to thirty letters a day from his Kamavisdars, he claimed that he was kept in his office every day from
six in the morning to 'near seven' in the evening.[4] When he heard
that Grant was leaving Satara he asked Elphinstone if he could go
there: political work would be more congenial. 'It would be a relief
to me from duties which I find so laborious and unceasing, that I
have never an *instant* to look into a book or I may say *think* of anything beyond the routine of my office, for I assure you it is only
[by] fagging incessantly [that] I keep my business from falling into
arrears.'[5] He renewed his request when he heard rumours that
Grant's successor might be retiring.[6] At last, in 1825, Elphinstone
appointed him Resident in Cutch. Whilst in that post he renewed

[1] Pottinger to M.E., 1.4.1818, ibid.
[2] Pottinger to M.E., 12.4.[1818], ibid.
[3] Pottinger to M.E., 1.4.1818, ibid.   [4] Pottinger to M.E., 8.8.1819, ibid.
[5] Pottinger to M.E., n.d., ibid.   [6] Pottinger to M.E., 1.9.1824, ibid.

his acquaintance with Sind to such effect that in 1836 he became Political Agent there. For his services in Sind he was made a baronet in 1840. After further diplomatic achievements he became Governor of Hong Kong in 1843, Privy Councillor in 1844, Governor of the Cape in 1846, Governor of Madras in 1847. In the words of the *Dictionary of National Biography*, while Governor of Madras he was 'somewhat inert and dilatory in the disposal of public business. . . . He was better fitted to deal firmly with a crisis than to conduct ordinary administrative duties.' High office, in fact, had not changed him. There is an undated portrait of him in middle life— the features fleshy, almost Italianate, but strong.[1]

His Collectorate soon extended from the river Bhima to the Chandor hills, with a population estimated in 1821 to be some 453,000.[2] Its resources were considerable: Macleod remarked that the valley of Ahmadnagar was 'probably one of the richest in this part of the Deccan'[3] But the country had suffered severely during recent years. Pottinger once declared that there was not a single village under his authority which had not at one time or another within the past two decades been deserted, plundered, or burned: the people had endured not only the terrible famine of 1803–4 but also the devastation caused by the armies of Sindhia and Holkar.[4]

The present war was a further disaster. Pottinger tried to save the interests of the new government and its subjects from the zeal of its friends: 'I am certain', he told Elphinstone in April 1818, 'that the dreadful oppression of the Nizam's officers is driving 1,000's of people to be rebels.'[5] He wrote to the Resident at Hyderabad in the hope that he would exercise a restraining influence and

suggested that the Nizam's officers should be instructed to *threaten* any of Bajee Row's people who may be refractory, but not to go further than threats, as it is better that some places should remain in the enemy's hands till a regular force can be ordered down there, than [that] the ryots should be terrified, and possibly plundered, by a rabble like the Nizam's irregular troops who would fancy they were serving us by sparing nothing.[6]

---

[1] *Dublin University Magazine*, vol. xxviii, no. clxvi (Oct. 1846), facing p. 426.

[2] Within the Collectorate there were also many villages belonging to Sindhia, Holkar, and the Nizam, with a population of some 172,000 (Bom. R.C. 1.9.1823, 2714).

[3] Macleod, Journal, 11.10.1817 and 13.10.1817, *Eur. MS.* 295, 73 ff.

[4] Pottinger, Memorandum, n.d., Bom. R.C. 19.3.1823, 2729.

[5] Pottinger to M.E., 22.4.[1818], *Elphinstone*.

[6] Pottinger to M.E., 12.4.[1818], ibid.

He also tried to repair the damage which had been done by Captain Gibbon's enthusiasm in seizing all the grain: he decided to pay the headmen at the bazaar price for all the grain which had been taken from their villages.[1] He thought that his own behaviour towards them also had a beneficial effect:

> I have had whole *flocks* of Patails to visit me, and make Salaam, since I arrived here, and can discover nothing but happiness amongst them at their change of masters. I have done everything in my power to add to this feeling, and have explained to them individually and collectively the principles on which we mean to govern the country, at which they expressed great satisfaction[2].

To the north of the Deccan tableland lies Khandesh. Elphinstone described it as 'low and hot'.[3] It is shut in by mountains—on the north by the Satpura, on the south-west by the Sahyadri, and on the south-east by the Ajanta and Satmala ranges. To the east lay the territories of Sindhia and the Nizam. Some parts were still well cultivated. But as a whole the province had suffered greatly from the famine of 1803–4, from devastation in war, and from mis-government in peace. 'The greater part of Candeish', Elphinstone wrote in 1819, 'is covered with thick jungle, full of tigers and other wild beasts, but scattered with the ruins of former villages.'[4]

The British victory at Mahidpur in December 1817 won them Holkar's territories in that area. Malcolm, who made peace with Holkar in January 1818, selected Captain John Briggs of the Madras infantry establishment to take charge of these cessions.[5]

Briggs was a distant relative of Malcolm's, and had served on the staff of his mission to Persia. Later, in 1816, Briggs had joined Elphinstone at Poona as Third Assistant at the Residency, his main duty being to translate the intelligence reports sent in by Elphinstone's agents at the different Indian courts.[6] He was ambitious. Soon after his appointment by Malcolm he was asking Elphinstone if he could remain in Khandesh as Collector: 'You see I already calculate on being your agent in Candeish', he wrote to Elphinstone on one occasion in February 1818, 'but in fact I am prepared

[1] Pottinger to M.E., 12.4.[1818], ibid.
[2] Ibid.   [3] M.E., *Report*, 5.   [4] M.E., *Report*, 3.
[5] The cessions were made by the Treaty of Mandasor, 6 Jan. 1818 (Aitchison, iv. 29 ff.).
[6] He was actually appointed to Poona in 1815 (Bell, 48).

to be anything under you.'[1] Elphinstone did allow him to stay there
as Collector and Political Agent. He remained there until 1823,
when he succeeded Grant at Satara.

Once appointed, he proved extremely tenacious of his rights. He
was continually pressing Elphinstone to define his authority as
against that of the military commander in Khandesh—first General
Doveton, later Colonel MacDowell. Elphinstone's response was
typically statesmanlike: 'be assured that there is no such thing as
clearly defined and absolute authority which can be increased without managing and consulting and sometimes giving way to other
people, Bonaparte had nothing of the kind'.[2] By his continual complaints and demands for a definition of his authority Briggs finally
brought down upon himself one of the few serious rebukes which
Elphinstone ever found it necessary to administer to any of his
subordinates.[3] This brought him to his senses; as soon as he had
made apology, Elphinstone restored the former friendly relation-
ship between them.[4] Certainly, some of his complaints give the
impression that he was overwrought: he once wrote to Elphinstone
that he suspected that General Doveton and Colonel Macdowell
'plot together under the rose'.[5] Certainly, he suffered from bad
health. He had severe headaches: 'these attacks are produced
generally at the change of the moon'. 'Four days continued operation of large doses of calomel and repeated opening medicines of
various sorts' could not completely cure one of his headaches.[6]
Certainly, he was greatly overworked: 'For fifteen months I was
never in the same place twenty days, and during that period I can
hardly be said to have enjoyed one night of undisturbed repose or
been permitted to sit down at an appointed hour to my meals, while
frequently I have been unable to close my packet of twenty or
twenty-five public despatches for the day, before midnight.'[7]

But he was the sort of man who throve on difficulties and dispu-
tations and found them wherever he went. A portrait of him at the
age of 78 shows him still with a keen, aggressive expression: the
lips thin and firmly compressed together.[8] While waiting on board
the *Upton Castle* in Bombay Harbour to return to England, in
January 1827, he occupied his time by writing on the Company's

[1] Briggs to M.E., 15.2.1818, *Elphinstone*.   [2] M.E. to Briggs, 6.6.1818, ibid.
[3] M.E. to Briggs, 23.6.1818, ibid.   [4] M.E. to Briggs, 1.7.1818, ibid.
[5] Briggs to M.E., 14.5.1818, ibid.   [6] Briggs to M.E., 19.7.1818, ibid.
[7] Briggs to Chaplin, para. 45, 16.4.1825, B.C. 1022, 371.
[8] Bell, *Briggs*, frontispiece.

thick foolscap a detailed account of his controversy with Simson, his successor, about the sale of his bungalow at Satara to the latter.[1] When he returned to India and was appointed Senior Commissioner in Mysore in 1831 he was soon involved in bitter controversy with the Governor of Madras.[2] As Bentinck pointed out, his main fault seems to have been that he lacked sufficient 'temper, prudence and discretion'.[3] He finally returned to England in 1836, and rose to the rank of major-general in 1838. As an unemployed major-general his allowances amounted to £1,750 a year and enabled him to devote himself in comfort to liberal causes.[4] He joined the Anti-Corn Law League. He invariably voted with the minority in the many Satara debates in the Court of Proprietors. He was in fact a born radical. Like Mr. Honeythunder, he harnessed his pugnacious instincts to the promotion of philanthropic principles.[5]

The problems of Khandesh in 1818 certainly demanded all his energy and enthusiasm. Some of the forts there were held by Arab garrisons, and there was bitter fighting. The fall of Trimbak on 25 April, which left the British in possession of the whole of the Godaveri valley, was accompanied by savagery unusual in this war.[6] Briggs was sincerely distressed:

The enormities committed by the Europeans & natives in this town, on the day of their arrival here, exceed anything, The property, the very food & clothing, and the household gods were carried off, the temples polluted, & some go so far as to say the women suffered the same abomination, but certain it is, they were stript and lying naked in the streets. Col. MacDowell did all he could to restore the property to the inhabitants, and some men were taken up and are to be punished if found guilty, but the fact is that the detachment at the end of the campaign is perfectly wild and there is no discipline at all in it, among the Europeans particularly, and I am sorry to say that many of the officers are as notorious for their depredations as the men, and none seem[s] to think it essential to maintain discipline by checking it. The Col. always refers me to his orders, but they are not obeyed. . . . It is in vain for us to administer the government wisely, to endeavour to gain the hearts of the inhabitants by conciliatory measures, if our army is to be the bane, instead of the support of our operations. I shall request Colonel MacDowell to

[1] Briggs, Memorandum, 15.1.1827, *Elphinstone*.
[2] Bell, *Briggs*, chap. x–xii.
[3] Bentinck to Briggs, 13.11.1832, ibid. 207–8.   [4] Ibid. 234.
[5] See *Edwin Drood*, chap. xvii.
[6] MacDowell to M.E., 25.4.1818, Bom. P.C. 20.5.1818, 2928; M.E. to Governor-General, 9.5.1818, Bom. S.C. 20.5.1818, 661 ff.

have the plunderers, the Europeans in particular, punished in the *streets of the town* of Trimbuc, and I shall recall the Bramins from Nassuck and other places where they have gone and give a sum of money from 500 to 1,000 Rupees on account of Govnt. to enable them to make any ceremony they may choose, so as to do away by all means in my power the unfortunate impression which is likely to go abroad of our character.[1]

Elphinstone thoroughly approved of Briggs's attitude: 'never scruple to give large sums when Temples of note are really polluted. It shows our anxiety to respect the religion of the country.'[2]

Like the other Collectors, Briggs extended the area of his authority as the military situation permitted. His province was large, but not well populated: the total population under him was estimated in 1821 to be about 418,000.[3] He found that there was a widespread anxiety among villages which had suffered from the Arabs or the Bhils that the British Government should protect them. The Arabs he was soon able to deal with. The Bhils he never properly subdued.

Apart from these two local problems, his general instructions from Elphinstone were similar to those received by the other Collectors. In framing these instructions Elphinstone followed the content and in many respects the form of his first general declaration of administrative policy, which he had made to Robertson the Collector of Poona in February 1818. The prosecution of the war and the extension of British authority were the first essentials. Innovations were as far as possible to be avoided: the Collectors were to continue the existing system of revenue and judicial administration—apart from abolishing great abuses like the farming of the revenue.[4]

Elphinstone, Munro, Chaplin, Robertson, Grant, Pottinger, and Briggs—these were the first builders of the new order in the territories conquered from the Peshwa. They would have laboured in vain, however, had they not been given the willing service of talented Indians eager to collaborate with the new government. The majority of local officials seem to have stayed at their posts, prepared to serve the British as faithfully as they had served the

[1] Briggs to M.E., 25.4.1818, *Elphinstone*.
[2] M.E. to Briggs, 4.5.1818, ibid.
[3] Briggs, *Answers to questions*, n.d., Bom. R.C. 19.3.1823, 2077.
[4] M.E. to Briggs, 11.3.1818, Bg. S.C. 31.7.1818, 89; M.E. to Pottinger, 2.4.1818, ibid. 105; M.E. to Grant, 8.4.1818, ibid. 131.

Peshwa. During the war Elphinstone made no change in this situation. He allowed his Collectors to make fresh appointments whenever the need arose, but he was anxious to employ the officials of the former government wherever possible in order to minimize the social changes involved in the transfer of power. Later, in order to train up the local men in British administrative methods, he decided to import some Indian officials who had served the Company in Madras. This problem he left until after the war.[1]

For the time being it was his policy to avoid all unnecessary changes in either the men or the measures of the former government.

[1] M.E. to Collectors, 10.7.1818, Bg. S.C. 29.8.1818, 9.

3

THE IDEAS BEHIND THE NEW SYSTEM

DURING the war it was a matter of convenience, even of necessity, to avoid all unnecessary changes in the existing system of government. A custom like the farming of the revenue had to be abolished because it conflicted too violently with Western ideas. But in general Elphinstone tried to avoid innovations.

This might be a necessity in war. Elphinstone made of it a virtue in the peace that followed. 'My employment is very humble', he wrote to a friend in August 1818. 'It is to learn which system is in force, and to preserve it unimpaired. This, I think, ought to be the great duty of a provisional Government; and I shall think I have done a great service to this country if I can prevent people making laws for it until they see whether it wants them.'[1] He therefore strongly opposed the introduction of the detailed Regulations of the Bengal or Bombay governments into the Deccan. 'Even if they could be quietly imposed', he wrote to the Governor-General, 'it is a question whether our regulations would be beneficial to the people in their present state, and it is very doubtful how they would be received. Many novelties must accompany every revolution, and if to these we voluntarily add an entire change in the laws, it is easy to conceive the odium and prejudices we shall raise up against us.' The impact of the new order of things must be cushioned. 'There seems', he added with perhaps a touch of irony, 'there seems no ground for fearing that we shall be remiss in introducing our own system, and it is better that it should gradually encroach on the institutions of the country, than that it should overwhelm them at once, and leave the inhabitants without any known objects by which they could direct their course.'[2]

There were also more positive reasons for opposing the introduction of Regulations. He had a good opinion of the Maratha system; he wanted to preserve as much of it as he could because he thought that it had served the Marathas well.

The present system is probably not bad in itself as the country has

[1] M.E. to Erskine, 4.8.1818, Colebrooke, ii. 46.
[2] M.E. to Governor-General, 18.6.1818, Bg. S.C. 26.9.1818, 3.

prospered under it, notwithstanding the feebleness and corruptions with which it was administered. At all events it is generally known and understood. It suits the people whom indeed it has helped to form, and it probably is capable of being made tolerably perfect by gradual improvements introduced as they appear to be called for.[1]

He had had good opportunity to observe the results of the Maratha system during his years as Resident at Poona. There were aspects of it which he disliked, but he considered that it had on the whole great merits. As he confided to Pottinger early in 1819, 'it cannot be denied that the Paishwa's Govt. was weak & corrupt & as little can it be denied that the freedom from great crimes & from accumulation of civil causes is such as would be an object of envy to our oldest provinces in Bengal'.[2]

Indeed, there had been growing for some years a vigorous opposition to the system of government established by Lord Cornwallis in Bengal, with its separation of powers, its complicated, detailed and extensive Regulations, and its general reliance upon English ideas and methods. Elphinstone was not alone in wanting to develop a system more in harmony with Indian ways. Nor did he derive his opinions solely from his observation of the results of the Maratha system.

His first appointment in India had been under Samuel Davis, the Judge and Magistrate of Benares, a man of learning and of ideas. Davis had formed a good opinion of Indian methods of government. When he went back to England he found a strategic position from which to attack the Cornwallis system. He was invited by a Select Committee of the House of Commons to make an analysis of the internal government of Bengal and Madras. At his own suggestion his investigations were confined to Bengal, and the internal government of Madras was analysed by James Cumming, the clerk in charge of the Revenue and Judicial Department of the Board of Control. The work of each in his own field formed the basis of the Fifth Report issued by the Select Committee of the House of Commons in 1812, which criticized the Cornwallis system in Bengal and praised its rival, the system worked out by Munro in Madras with the aim of using Indian methods as far as possible.[3]

[1] Ibid.   [2] M.E. to Pottinger, 7.1.1819, *Elphinstone.*
[3] Samuel Davis returned to England in 1806 and became a Director of the East India Company in 1809 (C. R. Markham (ed.), *Narrative of the Mission of George Begle*, lxxi, n.; *Brief Notice of the Services of Mr. Cumming*, 63 ff. n.).

Elphinstone acknowledged how much Davis had influenced him. Explaining to Davis his determination to maintain the traditional system of government in the Deccan, he wrote in 1819 that

> It was from your opinions at Benares that I was led to think well of the plan. It is certain that under good Kings the native system was sufficient to keep the country in a very high state of prosperity; a few weak monarchs were enough to throw it into complete disorder; but as our Govt. might possess the consistency which is unattainable in a despotic monarchy, it follows that the native system under us ought to produce permanent happiness to our subjects.[1]

Munro, the leading figure in the opposition to the Cornwallis system of Bengal, himself did much to shape Elphinstone's views. Elphinstone not only sought his advice in day-to-day problems of administration, but also studied his published writings with attention.[2] He once wrote in his journal, after a cordial visit from Munro, that he 'felt as much respect for him as for a father, and as much freedom as with a brother'.[3]

He liked Munro's efforts to make use of Indian institutions and methods in the administration of justice. On the other hand, he had less sympathy with Munro's policy of making revenue settlements with the individual peasant cultivator instead of with more substantial landholders. As he explained to his friend Strachey in 1822: 'I am not democratic enough to insist on a ryotwar system: I think that the aristocracy of the country whether it consists of heads of villages or heads of zemindarees should be kept up but I also think its rights and the opposite rights of the ryots should be clearly defined and the latter especially effectually defended.'[4]

This was the Strachey of his Benares days—the same Edward Strachey whom Carlyle knew and liked, who once took Carlyle and his 'dear Kitty' to Paris, and whom Carlyle later remembered with affection as 'a genially-abrupt man; "Utilitarian" and Democrat by creed. . .'.[5]

Strachey had left India in 1811, and was appointed an Assistant Examiner at the East India House in 1819. There he worked at the

---

[1] M.E. to S. Davis, 17.6.1819, *Elphinstone*.
[2] M.E. to Munro, 19.5.1818, *Elphinstone*.
[3] Colebrooke, *Life*, ii. 110.
[4] M.E. to Strachey, 11.3.1822, *Elphinstone*.
[5] Carlyle, *Reminiscences*, 247. On another occasion he described Strachey as 'a little bustling, logic-chopping, good-hearted, frank fellow' (Froude, *Carlyle* (*1795–1835*), i. 246).

Judicial Dispatches, which were concerned with many of the problems of social policy in which Elphinstone was interested. As
Assistant Examiner he had to read the relevant letters and proceedings of the Indian Governments and to draft replies for the approval
of the Court of Directors and Board of Control. He was thus in an
influential position.

The main principles of policy had been decided some years ago.
In 1811 the Home Government had forbidden the Bengal Government to extend the Cornwallis policy of a permanent settlement of
the land revenue.[1] Moreover, in 1814 they told the Bengal and
Madras Governments to modify their judicial systems in accordance
with Munro's principles, and in the following year they sent similar instructions to Bombay.[2] Strachey, who had served as a judge
in Bengal, was suspicious of these new tendencies. He wrote to
Elphinstone in September 1819 that

> There is in this country among the few persons who think and take
> the lead in matters of Indian domestic govt. a sort of run against the
> judicial system of Lord Cornwallis. This run was begun and continued
> by collectors & soldiers & an influence raised by them—such gentry
> don't like justice much & one must look with a jealous eye to everything
> that comes from such a quarter on such a subject. Yet I admit that the
> Collrs. and soldiers in question are in the main very able & good men &
> I believe that in most points they are in the right.[3]

But he thought that lesser men who imitated them might 'dash
into error' through a lack of understanding. This was indeed one of
the main arguments used against systems like Munro's which gave
more power and discretion to the individual Collector. The Cornwallis Regulations might be detailed and rigid; the Bengal Collector
might be surrounded by checks against arbitrary behaviour; but
these very features which to some were faults were to others safe-
guards against the folly and corruption of sinful men. Was it to be
a government of laws or of men? This was the dilemma; a man's
solution of it might well depend in large measure upon his opinion
of his fellow men.

Perhaps judges, moreover, are naturally apt to over-estimate the
value of written law. Men like Strachey who had spent their lives
in India administering the Cornwallis Regulations must surely

[1] Revenue dispatch to Bengal, 1.2.1811, S.R.J. i. 3 ff.
[2] Judicial dispatch to Madras, 29.4.1814, ibid. ii. 236 ff.; to Bengal, 9.11.1814,
P.P. 1819, xiii (533), 511 ff.; to Bombay, 10.4.1815, ibid. 795.
[3] Strachey to M.E., 18.9.1819, *Elphinstone*.

have felt better disposed towards them than diplomats like Elphinstone who had been shaped by the stresses and pressures of delicate personal negotiation.

Elphinstone certainly thought that his past career had fitted him well for his present duties. 'I think it an advantage', he told Munro in May 1818, 'not to be accustomed to the routine of civil business & to be more acquainted with the Marathas than with our own regulations.'[1] Munro was of the same opinion: 'It is fortunate that you were not trained in the usual routine of the service—The duties in which you have been employed have rendered you much more competent for the management of a broken-up Empire than you could have been by the study of all the Regulations and codes of Calcutta and Madras together.'[2]

At all events, Strachey's eventual decision was in character.

I have read & thought a great deal [this was in January 1820] since I wrote you about Munro's system—the result is a thorough conviction that M. (who by the bye is a very able & respectable & good man) is a quack—he is absolutely ignorant of the most common principles of right & wrong & law-making—He does not in the least understand the scope of his Regulations or the mischief to which they must give rise—I am speaking of him only as a Judicial man—as [a] soldier & a Collr. I say nothing against him.[3]

Strachey's career at the East India House coincided with a marked decrease in the number of Directors with any personal experience of India.[4] Directors without such experience might well be more likely to support a system of government like Cornwallis's which was so akin to traditional English ideas than one like Munro's which made such use of Indian ideas and methods. This was the situation in which, with Cumming at the Board of Control and Strachey at the East India House, the Court of Directors tended to support the Cornwallis system and the Board of Control the Munro system.[5]

James Mill joined the India House at the same time as Strachey, as Assistant Examiner in the Revenue Department, and Strachey of course came to know him well. In consultation with him Strachey in September 1819 selected some of Bentham's

[1] M.E. to Munro, 3.5.1818, *Elphinstone.*   [2] Munro to M.E., 12.5.1818, ibid.
[3] Strachey to M.E., 16.1.1820, ibid.   [4] Philips, *East India Company*, 243 ff.
[5] After Cumming had retired in 1823, Courtenay continued to press for the same policy, Philips, op. cit. 245.

works and sent them out to Elphinstone for him to read.[1] As it happened, Elphinstone's friend William Erskine had also sent him some of Bentham's works more than a year before this.[2]

Not that Elphinstone needed any such advice. As soon as the war was over, in June 1818, he was already writing to his friend John Adam at Calcutta for books to help him in the work of settling the Deccan. Among them he included Bentham:

> I wish you would get & send to me by the most speedy conveyance the Bengal & Madras Regulations, Colebrook's & Harrington's books, the 5th Report with all its appendices & any other works that some of the judicial or revenue people may suggest to you as offering good hints for settling a country. Pray—attend to this and do it speedily. Send likewise general books for I have none. Adam Smith, Montesquieu, Jeremy Bentham etc., but send the Indian books immediately.[3]

Perhaps it is easy to exaggerate Bentham's influence upon Elphinstone. Elphinstone has recently been called 'a distinguished disciple of Bentham',[4] even 'the Benthamite planner'.[5] But his friends do not seem to have thought of him in this way. Mrs. Buller, for example, writing to Elphinstone in 1829 remarked that her husband 'fears he has sunk terribly in your opinion since he avowed himself a Benthamite'.[6]

Nor did Elphinstone think of himself as a Benthamite. In a letter to an old Bengal civil servant in 1820 he wrote, for example: 'Edward Strachey will tell you of our settlement in this part of India; in those respects, if you still take an interest in such subjects, he is himself such a Jeremy Benthamist that I suppose he will think us barbarians for leaving the native institutions as we found them, & not codifying all our conquests.'[7]

On the other hand, he was often reading Bentham. And after an initial period of dissatisfaction he came to feel 'great respect and admiration' for him.[8] He was delighted when Bentham himself sent

---

[1] Strachey to M.E., 18.9.1819, *Elphinstone*.
[2] M.E. to Erskine, 4.8.1818, Colebrooke, ii. 45.
[3] M.E. to Adam, 11.6.1818, *Elphinstone*.
[4] H. M. Lambrick, *Sir Charles Napier and Sind*, 28.
[5] I. M. Cumpston, *Indians Overseas in British Territories*, 3.
[6] Isabella Buller to M.E., 23.8.1829. For Carlyle's view of the Bullers see Froude, *Carlyle (1795–1835)*, i. 142 f., 166 f. Carlyle was for a short time tutor to their sons.
[7] M.E. to Ernst, 3.8.1820, *Elphinstone*. Ernst himself was a critic of the Cornwallis system (see S.R.J. ii. 27 ff.).
[8] M.E. to Erskine, 1.11.1818, Colebrooke, ii. 51.

him some of his writings through Strachey: 'I was extremely
flattered', he replied, 'by his present of books, and know no author
from whom I should so highly have valued such a distinction.'[1]
Moreover, some of his policies were in full accordance with Benthamism. In his report on the Deccan in 1819 he suggested the
building of a Panopticon, and later when Governor of Bombay he
actually had several built. Again, when he was Governor of Bombay
he had the Regulations codified. Such measures would have delighted Bentham.

But there were also fundamental characteristics of personality
and upbringing which made it impossible for him to accept the
whole of Benthamism. His love of the past, so characteristic of
the Romantic movement, must have predisposed him to sympathy
with the traditional aspects of Indian life and to a reluctance to
tamper with them merely for the sake of utility. His aristocratic
breeding must have predisposed him to sympathy with privileged
social groups in India whose position seemed threatened by Western
methods of government. Many of his broad social policies may well
have been directed towards the greatest happiness of the greatest
number, but he was no egalitarian. He was of aristocratic birth and
proud of it. Hereditary privileges which would have seemed 'facti-
tious honours' to Bentham seemed to Elphinstone worthy of preservation both on political and on social grounds. One of the
common criticisms of the Cornwallis judicial system was that it
brought all men down to one level before the law courts. Elphinstone was determined that this should not happen in the Deccan.
In such matters he was far from being a Benthamite.

Indeed, he was far from being a Benthamite in his general
determination to maintain Maratha institutions and ways of government. He was in fact torn between two worlds. He himself realized
quite clearly the nature of this tension: 'Let me tell you', he wrote
to Malcolm in 1819, 'you are well off in having nothing to do but
war & politics & that you will not know what difficulty is till you
come to manage revenues & Adawluts & to reconcile efficiency
with economy & Maratha Maamool with Jeremy Bentham.'[2]

[1] M.E. to Strachey, 3.9.1820, *Elphinstone*.
[2] M.E. to Malcolm, 27.1.1819, *Elphinstone* (maamool = mamul = custom).
Even James Mill came to admit that 'both humanity and good policy seemed to
recommend exceptions' to the principle that all should be equal before the Courts,
'for a time at least, till the inhabitants grow more accustomed to the undiscrimi-
nating principles of our rule' (Evidence, P.P. 1831–2, v. 42 ff., Q. 354–5).

These then were the fundamental principles with which Elphinstone began. In the evolution of his policies, administrative necessity was to prove quite as important. This was no surprise to him. Nor indeed was he the man to hug the illusion that he was in complete control of events. As he recognized, the greatest difficulties in governing a newly conquered country

originate in the impossibility of standing still and of pausing while you consider what is best to be done. Our assumption of the Government is so great and radical an innovation that there is scarcely any institution in the country into which it does not necessarily introduce great changes. These require further innovations, every Collector does not consider the full effect of every measure he adopts to meet the calls that are constantly made on him. He cannot always be prevented introducing innovations, in fact he does not always [perceive] when he is innovating. One hundredth part of what he does can never be reported to me & what is reported must be instantly & hastily decided on. Thus rules are made, not deliberately & systematically, but merely in the operation of despatching current business. Many rules thus hastily made can never be retracted & we may find many years hence that we have inadvertently destroyed some institution or some feeling essential to the existence of the system we wish to preserve.[1]

The alternative would have been to fetter the Collectors with precise and detailed Regulations. Even if he had had time to draft them Elphinstone would have thought such a remedy infinitely more dangerous than the risks involved in giving the Collectors a wide discretion. In his opinion, as we have seen, one of the greatest merits of the Deccan Commission was that it enabled him to dispense with Regulations. Therefore, the dilemma remained.

He was fully convinced of the necessity of a Commission. He wrote to Munro early in May 1818:

It would be easy to get rid of an operation in which I have so little experience as the settlement of a country by making it over as soon as conquered to the Presidencies under whom it is to remain, but I am convinced this would not answer. We have never before seized on a whole country at once but have always left an independent state remaining under which those who were discontented with our Government might find a refuge. Nor have we ever in our partial acquisitions received a country so parcelled out into Jageers of military chiefs, or so swelled with districts of independent powers as the Paishwa's. These circumstances seem to me to require a provisional Govt. of some duration & a

[1] M.E. to J. Stuart, 17.8.1819, *Elphinstone.*

temporary system suited to the transition from the present state of things to that now in force in our provinces.[1]

Munro's views were similar. 'The thing is very easy', he remarked of the settling of the Southern Maratha territories, 'all that is requisite is . . . to keep them out of the hands of the Madras Government for some time. A provisional administration directed by Mr. Elphinstone, under the Supreme Government, should be established for two or three years until the mass receive its form.'[2]

Elphinstone himself found it difficult to decide how long the Commission should last. In April 1818 he was of the opinion that the rest of the year would be needed to pacify the country and that he would be able to hand it over to the Government of Bombay by the end of 1819 at the latest.[3] But he was soon disgusted by what he described to Malcolm as 'the impatience of the Bombay Government to rush into their promised land & by the plain indications they betrayed of a resolution to overturn everything they found established. If this is done it is better not to introduce any system but leave them to please themselves.'[4]

What particularly annoyed him was that as soon as Sir Evan Nepean, the Governor of Bombay, heard that Khandesh was likely to be annexed to Bombay he 'appointed a gentleman to succeed almost to supersede Briggs'.[5] On 18 June 1818 Elphinstone had written a dispatch to the Governor-General in which he recommended that the country south of Satara should eventually be annexed to Madras and that north of Satara to Bombay.[6] Two days later the Bombay Government wrote to him that they had ordered a Mr. Wilkins[7] to go to Khandesh to join Captain Briggs in order to gain any information that might be useful to him when Khandesh was put under his charge. At the same time the Bombay Government calmly requested Elphinstone to tell Briggs to give his intended successor whatever information he might need.[8] Elphinstone naturally objected to this on grounds of policy; 'the mere appearance of the avowed successor in a province not yet subdued could but

[1] M.E. to Munro, 3.5.1818, *Elphinstone.*
[2] Munro to Malcolm, 10.6.1818, Gleig, iii. 257–9.
[3] M.E. to Close, 16.4.1818, *Elphinstone.*
[4] M.E. to Malcolm, 11.7.1818, ibid.
[5] M.E. to Adam, 30.6.1818, ibid.
[6] M.E. to Governor-General, 18.6.1818, P.R.C. xiii. 394 ff.
[7] William Wilkins, Bombay writer 1806 season (*East-India Register*).
[8] Bombay Government to M.E., 20.6.1818, Bg. P.C. 31.7.1818, 65.

seriously cramp & weaken the existing authorities'.[1] As soon as the Supreme Government heard of the matter, they agreed with him that Wilkins should not be sent.[2] Briggs therefore remained in Khandesh.

Elphinstone thought with distaste of what Nepean might do next:

He will no doubt do the same here except in the case of Pottinger who is a personal friend of his. Briggs is [a] very clever, active and intelligent fellow and will certainly get on in the diplomatic line if he is thrown out of Candeish. Grant ought certainly to be provided for if he loses Sattara as he will have had a very difficult task to perform, but the person whom I shall be most sorry to see displaced on public grounds is Captain Robertson at Poona who in spite of all the affectations of his style shows an uncommon degree of good sense and even genius for civil duties united with the utmost zeal and industry and a great deal of method.[3]

Francis Warden, the Secretary to Government at Bombay, was anxious to assure Elphinstone that it was all Nepean's doing:

The Governor's plan about Candeish was entirely his own and he was obstinate upon it, it was wholly unauthorized by anything the Governor-General had written to him which went merely to be informed of the extent of our military augmentation and whether any would be necessary if Candeish and the Concan were to be annexed to Bombay and he was at once for seizing the country. I have seen also with great regret a spirit of jealousy betraying itself very unworthy of us, but this in a question where the loaves and fishes were to be divided is nothing extraordinary in one trained for so many years under the government at home where patronage seems to be the most important of state concerns—everything is a job there and it is supposed that no uninterested zeal or purity can exist in India and that a job is the ruling principle in the distribution of patronage here also.[4]

The episode made Elphinstone think of abandoning his plans for settling the Deccan. As he explained to Adam, he had hitherto thought that 'it was better for me to settle the country completely before I made it over to the Govr. of Bombay who is likely to make mistakes as well from want of knowledge of India as from want of extent of views'. But he now feared that there would be little point in this since 'anything I may settle out of the routine of Bombay

[1] M.E. to Bombay Government, 24.6.1818, ibid. 66.
[2] Supreme Government to Bombay Government, 31.7.1818, ibid. 67.
[3] M.E. to Adam, 30.6.1818, *Elphinstone*.
[4] Warden to M.E., 21.7.1818, ibid.

duty, will be done away immediately the country is given up'. He need therefore do no more than 'wind up the political arrangements'. This could be done by the end of 1818.[1]

Elphinstone wasted no time. Since the Deccan was to be yielded up to Sir Evan, Sir Evan must be prepared for it. He turned his attention to this work of education:

I formerly thought [he wrote tactfully to him] it would be long before this country could with advantage be placed under a regular Government but on a close examination I find the whole objection is comprised in the danger of a premature introduction of our regulations. If officers with extended powers are placed over the country to manage it by its old laws and gradually to reform them I hope the transfer may without inconvenience be made by the end of the year.[2]

But his pessimism did not last very long. Malcolm tried to persuade him to stay for at least another year:

Wait till August or Sept. 1819 when I pledge myself if not appointed to Bombay to go home with you. If I am appointed I pledge myself to do all you wish about the new conquests, and you can go home in two or three years, see England, marry your cousin Anne Elphinstone or Fanny Callender, both handsome, sensible and proper cast girls, and having made good acquaintances and good interest return and succeed me as Governor of Bombay.[3]

Whatever may have been his feelings upon receiving such advice from Malcolm, Elphinstone must have been reassured by the news from Calcutta. It was the Governor-General's intention to continue the provisional administration of the Deccan for another two or three years. Moreover, far from wanting to introduce Regulations into the Deccan, the Governor-General preferred a system that would make use of existing institutions—'purified as far as may be practicable from all gross abuses'.[4]

Elphinstone now looked forward hopefully to the future:

I did wish very much to get into Council [he wrote to his uncle, Lord Keith, in October 1818] but my present appointment has since been declared by Lord Hastings to be likely to last for two or three years, and in that case I would not exchange it for a seat in Council, and scarcely, if it were not in its nature temporary, for one of the subordinate governments. Those governments present no employment so interesting as

[1] M.E. to Adam, 30.6.1818, *Elphinstone*.   [2] M.E. to Nepean, 23.6.1818, ibid.
[3] Malcolm to M.E., 9.8.1818, *H.M.* 733, 331 ff.
[4] Supreme Government to M.E., 26.9.1818, P.R.C. xiii. 468 ff.

securing and regulating a new conquest with ample powers, civil and military, with plenty of troops, and the most liberal support from the Governor-General. If I get well through this duty, I do not think it at all presumptuous to look either to Bombay or Madras. If Malcolm has a chance of Bombay, as I understand is the case, I should be prevented by personal regard from any wish to interfere with him, even if his standing and services were not far superior to mine; but if he were provided for, I should hope to be considered.[1]

In short, Elphinstone thought that Malcolm's claims to be the next Governor of Bombay were stronger than his own—and Malcolm thought so too. But in the event, Malcolm was bitterly disappointed. It was Elphinstone who became Governor of Bombay and Malcolm who succeeded him in 1827.

What happened was that Canning, the President of the Board of Control, offered three names to the Directors to choose from—Elphinstone's, Malcolm's, and Munro's. Strachey assumed that the contest would be between Elphinstone and Malcolm. He wrote warningly to Elphinstone, before the Directors had made their choice, 'Malcolm is as you know indefatigable—when in England he left no stone unturned for the attainment of this object which he has long had in view. As for you—you have no such interest, you have here no friends but the public despatches and your own character.'[2] But the Directors did choose Elphinstone.

This meant that he could look ahead with confidence to the exercise of a general control over the Deccan even after its provisional government by Commission had ended, for the Supreme Government decided to transfer their control over the Deccan to the Government of Bombay with effect from the date when Elphinstone should become Governor.[3]

Even then, the Commission was continued. As Elphinstone saw it, there were two reasons for this: first, to enable the Commissioner to work out a permanent administrative system for the country, and secondly, to enable him to deal informally with the political problems of the new government. Among these he included any social evils which might drive men to rebel against it. The Commissioner's political duties, he wrote on one occasion, were

---

[1] M.E. to Keith, 3.10.1818, Colebrooke, ii. 47 ff.
[2] Strachey to M.E., n.d., *Elphinstone.*
[3] Supreme Government to M.E., 12.3.1819, Bg. P.C. 13.3.1819, 26. In accordance with Elphinstone's advice, the Southern Maratha country, destined ultimately for Madras, was temporarily attached to Bombay at the same time.

particularly important when 'such numerous bodies of men of all ranks are thrown out of their employment and when from the recent period at which their national government was destroyed even the common people are objects of political vigilance'.[1]

Elphinstone's primary task as Commissioner was in fact to meet the social problems created by the fall of the Maratha Government. They were not problems for which much guidance could be found in Bentham's philosophy.

[1] M.E., Minute, n.d., Bom. P.C. 3.5.1820, 3917 ff.

4

THE FATE OF THE OLD RULERS

BAJI RAO surrendered to Sir John Malcolm in June 1818. His fate
had already been decided. Among the fundamental principles of
the new 'arrangement' sketched out by the Governor-General in
Council in December 1817 it had been laid down not only
that Baji Rao and his house were to be perpetually excluded
from all sovereign power but also that he would be exiled from the
Deccan.

In these points Malcolm could do no more than carry out the
Governor-General's instructions. But in some of the more detailed
terms of surrender he was able to use his own discretion, and in
these respects his proceedings came to be viewed with disfavour at
Calcutta. He guaranteed that the Company would pay Baji Rao an
annual pension of at least 8 lakhs (800,000) of rupees. Moreover, he
stated that the Company's Government would give 'liberal attention' to any requests made by Baji Rao on behalf of 'principal
Jageerdars and old adherents who have been ruined by their attachment to him', and also that his recommendations 'in favour of
Brahmins of respectable character, and of religious establishments
founded or supported by his family, shall be treated with regard'.[1]

Arthur Wellesley had in 1803 guaranteed to Amrit Rao, Baji
Rao's adoptive brother, an annual pension of 7 lakhs.[2] Malcolm
thought that Baji Rao would be insulted by a pension less than, or
even equal to, Amrit Rao's, and so he now chose the figure of
8 lakhs.[3] But the Governor-General did not approve: he thought
that 2 lakhs would have been ample. Elphinstone considered this
attitude 'too rigid'.[4] As he remarked to Sir Evan Nepean, the
Governor of Bombay: 'considering Bajee Row's merits & the
manner in which he is likely to employ our bounty, eight lacks of
rupees is a large stipend for him, but it is a reasonable bargain to
purchase a quiet abdication & to put an end to the war'.[5] He wrote

---

[1] Malcolm's propositions accepted by Baji Rao (Aitchison, vii. 70).
[2] One lakh had also been assigned to Amrit Rao's adherents (Aitchison, v. 83 f.).
[3] Malcolm to Supreme Government, 19.6.1818, Bg. S.C. 24.7.1818, 22.
[4] M.E. to Munro, 21.6.1818, *Elphinstone*.
[5] M.E. to Nepean, 23.6.1818, ibid.

comfortingly to Malcolm that he was 'much annoyed' by the
Supreme Government's attitude.[1]

But Malcolm would not be comforted. He was very disappointed
at the Governor-General's attitude, and his mortification was increased when he thought that he noticed others delighting in his
discomfiture: 'your *disapproval* of my conduct', he wrote to Adam,
the Governor-General's Secretary, 'is I can assure you proclaimed
with no slight exultation, and that able Baronet who lately led your
armies thinks I saved Bajee Row from certain destruction by
General Doveton!!!'[2] His vexation was intense when he found the
same argument used in the Governor-General's official letter which
arrived a few days later. 'It was my negotiation alone', he replied
in high indignation, 'that ever allowed Genl. Doveton to come
within a hundred miles of Badjerow at the period alluded to.'[3]

While Elphinstone had no criticism of the amount of the pension
he did object to the opportunity which Malcolm had given Baji Rao
to recommend persons to the favour of the Company's Government.
This he thought would give Baji Rao an unnecessary influence. He
explained to Malcolm that 'all connection between Bajee Row &
his late subjects ought to be broken off completely & decidedly and
nothing can have so great a tendency to keep up that connection as
an idea among the thousands who are in suspense about the provision to be made for them that Bajee Row's recommendations will
be attended to'. He therefore asked Malcolm to secure Baji Rao's
recommendations as soon as possible.[4] This Malcolm did by the
end of August 1818, and the matter was then closed.[5]

Elphinstone still thought it advisable to make communication
between Baji Rao and his former subjects as difficult as possible.
Benares had been provisionally mentioned in the terms of surrender as his place of exile. But Elphinstone thought it unsuitable
because it was 'the grand resort of all Maratta pilgrims'.[6] He conceded, however, that it would have been 'well enough to carry him
there in the first instance or anywhere so as to get him in & finish
the war which I consider a great object knowing the danger of
driving anybody to despair'.[7]

[1] M.E. to Malcolm, 21.6.1818, *Elphinstone.*
[2] Malcolm to Adam, 10.8.1818, *H.M.* 733, 337 ff. The 'able Baronet' being
Sir T. Hislop.
[3] Malcolm to Adam, 17.8.1818, ibid. 344 ff.   [4] M.E. to Malcolm, 9.8.1818, ibid.
[5] Malcolm to Supreme Government, 31.8.1818, Bg. S.C. 31.10.1818, 85.
[6] M.E. to Nepean, 23.6.1818, ibid.   [7] M.E. to Malcolm, 21.6.1818, ibid.

Elphinstone realized the social consequences of the ending of the war and of the change of government—demobilized soldiers, unemployed clerks, 'Brahmins deprived of their accustomed means of subsistence by the cessation of most of the Paishwah's charities'. In all these he saw 'fine materials for an intriguing ex-Paishwah'.[1] He soon evolved policies to provide for these various groups, but at the time he felt that 'there must be a great mass of discontent in a country situated like this'. He therefore stressed the need to settle Baji Rao 'either on the East of the Ganges or as far North as may be convenient to diminish the chance of a concourse of Marratta Pilgrims'.[2]

Several possibilities were discussed. Baji Rao thought that Monghyr would be too hot. He objected to Gorakhpur because there were 'no temples of great sanctity' there. He himself suggested Mathura, but the Governor-General thought it too near the frontier. It was eventually decided that Bithur near Cawnpore and on the banks of the Ganges would satisfy both the Government's political views and Baji Rao's religious needs.[3]

These discussions were conducted while Baji Rao was on the march, every day leaving his homeland farther behind him. Malcolm relished the dignity of his own position: 'all from the lowest thief to Bajee Row come to me as a medium to obtain forgiveness'.[4] But he treated Baji Rao and his adherents as tactfully as he could: '"They have the *best water*, wherever we halt, they have tents, camels, bullocks, coolies, cash whenever required, and every species of civility, attention and respect, but all ideas opposite to their situation are crushed the moment they appear.'[5] When Malcolm was called away by more important duties he left Lieutenant John Low, his acting first assistant, with Baji Rao to escort him on his way. Baji Rao found Low congenial. Indeed, he had been 'quite in a fever' for Malcolm to appoint him.[6] Low successfully conducted his charge to Bithur and remained there with him as 'Commissioner with Bajee Row' until 1821.[7] Baji Rao himself remained there until he died.

[1] M.E. to Malcolm, 15.8.1818, ibid.
[2] M.E. to Supreme Government, 26.8.1818, Bg. S.C. 26.9.1818, 20.
[3] P. C. Gupta, *Last Peshwa*, 2–5.
[4] Malcolm to W. [F. ?] Elphinstone, 14.7.1818, *H.M.* 733, 318–22.
[5] Malcolm to M.E., 9.8.1818, ibid. 331 ff.
[6] Malcolm to Adam, 31.8.1818, ibid. 356 ff.
[7] P. C. Gupta, op. cit. 27.

Baji Rao's senior wife, Varanasi Bai, had taken shelter from the war in the historic fort of Raigarh. It was surrendered to Colonel Prother on 7 May. He found the whole in a state of decay—'we were unfortunately fifty years too late'. The gallant colonel was distressed at 'the deplorable situation in which we beheld a female of most interesting appearance, seated with the regalia of state amidst burning beams, ashes, and all the horrors of what had been a recent fire, in a place (for I was told she refused to quit the palace) cleared away on a raised terrace under the cover of a grass hut'.[1]

Elphinstone gave her an escort to Poona, where she stayed at one of Baji Rao's palaces. After some days there she went at her own request to her native village of Wai.[2] As this was within the kingdom of Satara, Grant promised to look after her. He had some misgivings from the first: 'I suspect she is no better than she should be.'[3] Early in 1819 his suspicions were strengthened by reports that she had been secretly engaging horsemen in different villages, and he sent Balaji Pant Natu to Wai to investigate. The Pant reported that Varanasi 'had numerous visitors, that she had very considerable treasure in her possession. That Bajee Row was said to carry on a correspondence with his friends through her agency. That she had entertained 40 sebundies and ten horsemen which but ill accords with her pretended poverty.' Grant therefore asked Elphinstone to send her somewhere else, adding that Balaji Pant was 'particularly earnest on the subject'.[4]

Elphinstone told Grant to send her to Bithur under escort by the most direct route avoiding Poona, and to give her at the most a month for her preparations and Rs.50,000 for her expenses.[5] Grant went to Wai and told her himself. She demanded over a lakh for expenses, but he persuaded her to agree to the Rs.50,000. She was unwilling to go, but raised no serious objection.[6] More than thirty years later Grant still remembered the scene, and maliciously related how 'she behaved *so* well when I told her how disagreeable it was for me to be obliged to tell her that the Sirkar [Government] required that she should proceed to join *Sree Munt*', her husband.[7]

[1] Prother to Adjutant-General, 12.5.1818, *Maratha War Papers*, 287 ff.
[2] M.E. to Governor-General, 24.5.1818, P.R.C. xiii. 384 ff.
[3] Grant to M.E., 20.8.1818, *Elphinstone*.
[4] Grant to M.E., 19.2.1819, Bg. P.C. 20.3.1819, 11.
[5] M.E. to Grant, 21.2.1819, Bg. P.C. 20.3.1819, 12.
[6] Grant to M.E., 13.3.1819, Bg. P.C. 8.4.1819, 39.
[7] Grant-Duff to Briggs, 28.2.1854, Bell, *Briggs*, 249 ff.

Chimnaji Appa, the Peshwa's brother, was also required to live outside the Deccan. He surrendered in May 1818 in company with Appa Desai the great jagirdar of Nipani.[1] Elphinstone wanted him to live at Ahmadnagar pending a decision upon his place of exile, and Appa Desai tried to persuade him to comply. But he insisted on coming to Poona. Elphinstone assigned him the Peshwa's palace at Phulsehr. As it was 'destitute of almost every convenience', Elphinstone supplied him with tents and other necessities. Chimnaji had been so 'harrassed by his fatigues and alarms' that both his English visitors and his own entourage suspected that 'his misfortunes had disordered his understanding'.[2]

They were mistaken: Chimnaji was certainly not a clever man, but he was quite sane; moreover, he was obstinate, and his obstinacy was soon to try Elphinstone's patience very hard. Elphinstone thought him 'much less to be feared than his brother whom he neither resembles in talent nor in disposition'.[3] This did not mean that he could be disregarded:

Appa Sahib is a man of a respectable character in private life, is of very retired habits, of an obstinate disposition and a weak understanding. He is very jealous of his dignity and bigoted to his religion, he is timid and unenterprising himself but in the hands of an active leader he might make a more formidable tool than Bajee Row as he would be less likely to derange the other's schemes by his own interference.[4]

Elphinstone told him that 'if he would immediately proceed to Hindostan and show himself disposed to meet the Governor-General's wishes, he should receive a larger allowance than he received from his brother, should have his debts paid and should be allowed to return to the Deckan' when the Governor-General thought it safe. His debts amounted to Rs.150,000. He agreed to go, but then delayed 'on various grounds some of which were not unreasonable' until the rains approached. Elphinstone made it clear that by this behaviour he had forfeited the rewards of an immediate departure for Hindusthan: Elphinstone's promises were cancelled, Chimnaji could henceforth only rely upon 'the Governor-General's

[1] Capt. E. Davies (Commanding Nizam's Reformed Horse) to Capt. Halifax (Acting Deputy Adjutant General, Brig.-Gen. Smith's Division), 7.5.1818, Bg. S.C. 31.7.1818, 173.
[2] M.E. to Governor-General, 24.5.1818, P.R.C. xiii. 384 ff.
[3] M.E. to Governor-General, 27.6.1818, ibid. 416 ff.
[4] M.E. to Supreme Government, 4.2.1819, Bg. P.C. 6.3.1819, 62.

liberality'.[1] Meanwhile the question of Baji Rao's place of exile had arisen. When Benares was suggested for him, the Governor-General announced that in that event Chimnaji had better stay at Bassein: the two brothers could not both be allowed to live at Benares, while 'the general character and moderate talents and influence of Chimnajee' meant that he could be allowed to live at Bassein without danger in spite of its nearness to the Deccan.[2] The Bombay Government did not agree. They had already protested with vigour against the possibility of Chimnaji's staying at Bassein: 'there is hardly any place where his presence would be more injurious than at Bassein where many of the adherents of his brother still remain and would be ready to show their dispositions in his favour could they do so with any prospect of success'.[3]

Elphinstone himself was convinced that Chimnaji should go to Hindusthan after the rains. His conduct at Benares Elphinstone found to be 'perfectly satisfactory'. Therefore, when he began his march, Elphinstone told Lieutenant Clarke of the Poona Auxiliary Horse, whom he had detailed to accompany him, 'to inform him that he might depend on the same liberal consideration I had first held out to him'.[4] But soon there were more arguments and delays. Elphinstone's indignation flared out: 'he is a weak, superstitious, prejudiced, touchy, obstinate, unmanageable but luckily insignificant animal'.[5]

At length Chimnaji complained that he had been invited to surrender by Madhav Rao Raste with very different prospects from those now held out before him. Reference was therefore made to Madhav Rao, who admitted that he had unfolded to Chimnaji certain prospects based upon 'his own speculations as to the probable conduct of the British Government if Appa Sahib were to come in'; he added that he had never pretended that the British had authorized these proposals, and that anyhow Chimnaji had not acted upon them but had remained with Baji Rao until later. After further investigation Elphinstone discovered that the inviting prospect which Madhav Rao had opened to Chimnaji was that the British would make him Peshwa in opposition to his brother. Before

[1] M.E. to Supreme Government, 4.2.1819, Bg. P.C. 6.3.1819, 62.
[2] Supreme Government to M.E., 14.7.1818, para. 64, Bg. S.C. 31.7.1818, 441.
[3] Bombay Government to M.E., 9.6.1818, ibid. 332.
[4] M.E. to Governor-General, 27.6.1818, P.R.C. xiii. 416 ff.; M.E. to Supreme Government, 4.2.1819, Bg. P.C. 6.3.1819, 62.
[5] M.E. to Adam, 4.8.1818, *Elphinstone*.

Madhav Rao's answer arrived, Chimnaji had shown such determination to stay in the Deccan that Elphinstone again cancelled the offers of reward which he had made, and threatened to remove him by force if necessary. He finally agreed to move to the Godaveri, to leave it by 5 February, and to cross the Narbada within a month thereafter. If he kept to this timetable, Elphinstone agreed to pay his debts: 'as those of some of his principal adherents are included in the 150,000 I conclude they will use their interest to get him to adhere to his engagement'. He reached the Godaveri by the appointed time, and thereafter his march, ably supervised by Lieutenant Clarke, proceeded according to plan.[1] In his instructions to Lieutenant Clarke, Elphinstone had told him not to use force unless it was absolutely necessary: and it seemed unlikely that Chimnaji would 'push things to extremity'.[2] In fact, Chimnaji made amends by his tractable behaviour during the rest of his journey. Lieutenant Clarke was well pleased.[3]

The Governor-General agreed to an annual stipend of 3 lakhs of rupees for Chimnaji, but he objected to Benares: 'you are aware of the objections entertained to the assemblage of natives of rank and fallen fortunes at Benares'.[4] As Lieutenant Clarke and his charge came gradually nearer to the end of their journey, a decision had to be made. Clarke was told to halt at Allahabad pending a final decision upon Chimnaji's place of exile. He was to ask Chimnaji which place other than Benares he would prefer to live in.[5] Elphinstone now intervened on behalf of Chimnaji: 'Appa Sahib though obstinate and sometimes capricious is on the whole a man of good character and of a very inoffensive disposition.' He was probably expecting to go to Benares. Elphinstone therefore recommended that he be allowed to stay there, although he himself realized 'the strong objections to any addition to the number of the Princes at that city'.[6] In consequence of this recommendation the Governor-General in Council decided after all to allow Chimnaji to live at Benares.[7]

Baji Rao's favourite, Trimbakji Dengle, whom Elphinstone

[1] M.E. to Supreme Government, 4.2.1819, Bg. P.C. 6.3.1819, 62.
[2] M.E. to Clarke, 8.1.1819, Bg. P.C. 6.2.1819, 31.
[3] Clarke to Supreme Government, 13.4.1819, Bg. P.C. 24.4.1819, 123.
[4] Supreme Government to M.E., n.d., Bg. P.C. 28.11.1818, 24.
[5] Supreme Government to Clarke, 24.4.1819, Bg. P.C. 24.4.1819, 124.
[6] M.E. to Supreme Government, 24.6.1819, Bg. P.C. 31.7.1819, 28.
[7] Ibid. Note in consultation.

regarded as an inveterate enemy of the British, suffered a harder fate. He had made a daring escape from imprisonment. Over eighteen months later Pottinger, the Collector of Ahmadnagar, heard rumours that Trimbakji was near at hand. He at once sent him a message:

You are wandering thro' the jungles in fear of your life, therefore be not mistrustful, the Hon'ble M. Elphinstone Buhadoor is expected at Ahmednuggur and without fear you may come in and visit him without any apprehensions for your life and you will be permitted to visit your family.[1]

Elphinstone was naturally annoyed by this offer:

I must say I am sorry you did not consult me before it was issued which was necessary on a matter of such general importance & so peculiarly within my province & would only have caused two days' delay. You must surely have overlooked the difference between showing mercy to a criminal after he is captured & granting him specific terms while out of your power. Besides the evil of giving up the point of honour for which we have risked so much, by making overtures in writing to Trimbuckjee you have by clear implication promised him a favourable, almost a friendly reception. When you tell a man to come in without fear & promise to restore him to his family who could possibly imagine you meant to throw him into a prison.'[2]

Elphinstone therefore told Pottinger to cancel the whole of his offer, and to announce that Trimbakji's only chance of saving his life was by unconditional surrender.[3]

A few days later Briggs, the Collector of Khandesh, heard that Trimbakji was within his own jurisdiction. He at once sent out a detachment and captured him.

Elphinstone, attentive as ever to public opinion, thought that Trimbakji's capture would have the important effect of 'showing the impossibility of escaping our power', and to point the moral with the greater force he decided to send him back to Thana Fort from which he had before escaped. 'His return to the same situation precisely in which he was before all this turmoil will show very strongly our immoveable serenity & the vanity of all attempts to disturb us.'[4]

[1] Pottinger to Trimbakji Dengle, 24.6.1818, Bg. S.C. 7.8.1818, 4.
[2] M.E. to Pottinger, 25.6.1818, *Elphinstone*.
[3] Ibid. and M.E. to Pottinger, 25.6.1818 (official letter), Bg. S.C. 7.8.1818, 5.
[4] M.E. to Briggs, 2.7.1818, *Elphinstone*.

Trimbakji was, however, soon moved to a safer distance from the Deccan—to Fort Chunar, near Benares, where he died in 1829.[1]

Only a few could be expelled from the Deccan—Baji Rao, his politically dangerous relatives, and Trimbakji Dengle. Elphinstone well realized that as Deccan Commissioner he would have the great jagirdars always with him. Their fate was more difficult to settle.

Baji Rao's relations with these overmighty subjects had never been cordial. Some years before the war Elphinstone as Resident had intervened to secure the conclusion of an agreement at Pandharpur whereby the Peshwa undertook to ignore past injuries from the jagirdars while the jagirdars undertook henceforth to render him the military service which was specified in their charters (tainat jabtas) and to surrender all lands which they had illegally usurped.[2] So long as they served the Peshwa faithfully the British Government guaranteed them in the possession of all lands to which they had a legal title.[3]

In December 1817 the Governor-General in Council laid down the main principles which Elphinstone was to follow in his relations with the jagirdars. Those who had not fought against the British or who submitted quickly were 'to be taken under the direct protection of the British Government, and to hold their lands from that Government in the same manner as heretofore from the Paishwa, with such modifications in the conditions of their tenure as may hereafter be settled on the basis of the articles of Punderpore'. Moreover, 'a proper distinction' was to be made between 'the Jageerdars whose conduct may have entitled them to favour, and those whose tardy submission may have deprived them of pretension to the consideration of the British Government'.[4]

Such a distinction was clearly necessary. In the first place, the offer of preferential treatment could be used during the war as an incentive to timely submission to the British. It would no doubt have offended against the sense of justice of those who had submitted early if in the subsequent peace those who had come in after them were preferred before them or even treated on an equality with them. Further, as the British so often contrived to find in the

---

[1] Political letter from Bengal, 15.1.1820, para. 170, Bg. P.L.R. xv. 117 ff.; Sardesai, *New History*, iii. 508.

[2] Tainat-jabta: the charter granted by the Maratha Government to a jagirdar specifying the contingent he was to maintain.

[3] Agreement of Pandharpur, 6.7.1812, P.R.C. xii. 188 ff.

[4] Supreme Government to M.E., 15.12.1817, P.R.C. xiii. 270 ff.

nineteenth century, the demands of justice were in harmony with
the precepts of economics: as Munro put it, 'if we forgive every-
body we shall not be able to pay our own civil and military
charges'.[1]

On the other hand, although some distinction had to be made
between those who had left the Peshwa early and those who had
not, no one was to be utterly cast down lest he be driven into
rebellion.

The jagirdars' importance was great. Within their own territories
they enjoyed powers of life and death, and outside them they were
inclined to pay little enough attention to the orders of the Poona
Government.[2]

The most important of the jagirdars, the Patwardhan family, had
in the space of little more than fifty years risen from comparative
obscurity to the possession of estates worth upwards of 20 lakhs of
rupees a year. One-third of the whole was owned by Chintaman
Rao of Sangli, whom Elphinstone considered to be 'a capricious
and irritable chieftain'.[3] The rest was severally owned by the six
other leading Patwardhan chiefs.[4] These Patwardhans were a turbulent family, often quarrelling both among themselves and with
Baji Rao.

At the beginning of the war Elphinstone thought that most of the
Patwardhans would probably try to be neutral for as long as they
could and eventually declare for the British.[5] Chintaman Rao, indeed, at first joined the Peshwa, but Elphinstone thought it likely
that 'his petulance and levity' would 'soon lead to quarrels between
him and Gockla[6] and to his separation from the army'.[7] On the
other hand, he saw that Chintaman was hardly suited to a British
system of government: 'he is too haughty and unruly to be pleased
with the prospect of living under our Government'.[8]

[1] Munro to M.E., 1.7.1818, *Elphinstone.*
[2] Elphinstone estimated the revenue of the Peshwa's territories at the beginning of the war to be Rs.11,500,000, of which no less than Rs.6,500,000 was in
the hands of jagirdars (M.E. to Governor-General, 18.6.1818, P.R.C. xiii. 394 ff.).
[3] M.E. to Hislop, 28.6.1817, Bg. S.C. 1.8.1817, 15.
[4] Madhav Rao of Miraj, Madhav Rao Dadaji of Chinchni, Gopal Rao of
Jamkhandi, Ganpat Rao of Tasgaon, Ganpat Rao of Shedbal, and Trimbak Rao
of Kurundwad.
[5] M.E. to Munro, 21.1.1818, Bg. S.C. 31.7.1818, 79.
[6] Gokhale, the Peshwa's Commander-in-Chief.
[7] M.E. to Supreme Government, 24.11.1817, P.R.C. xiii. 260 ff.
[8] M.E. to Munro, 21.1.1818, Bg. S.C. 31.7.1818, 79.

There was one great jagirdar, Vithal Narsing of Vinchur, whose
family had consistently served the Peshwa with fidelity. Elphinstone wrote of him in June 1817 as 'a fine young man' but 'a mere
cypher' in the hands of his minister Baloba. Still, Baloba himself
seemed to be 'a prudent, sensible old man, always inclined to
moderate measures'.[1] The Vinchur estates were thought to be
worth at least 12 lakhs of rupees a year at the beginning of the war.
Half lay in Hindusthan, and when in 1817 Baji Rao ceded to the
British all his territories to the north of the Narbada, the Vinchur
jagirdar consequently became liable to pay allegiance to the British
for that half. His position at the outbreak of war was therefore
equivocal.[2]

On the other hand, the position of Madhav Rao Raste, the jagirdar of Wai, seemed clear enough. He owed his jagir—worth some
10 lakhs of rupees a year—to British pressure upon Baji Rao. It had
been confiscated in 1814 on the ground that he had repeatedly
failed to send his contingent to serve under the Peshwa as stipulated in his charter. Elphinstone then felt unable to invoke the
Pandharpur agreement because the British had guaranteed to each
jagirdar his lands only so long as he faithfully performed the military service specified in his charter.[3] Nevertheless, he suspected
that Raste had been unjustly treated, and continued to appeal to
Baji Rao on his behalf. Nothing was done. But when he concluded
the Treaty of Poona with Baji Rao in June 1817 Elphinstone insisted upon the restoration of Raste's jagir as one of its terms. But
he doubted, all the same, whether Raste would ever be of much
help to the British: 'Rastia having been persecuted by the Paishwa
and protected by the British Government is probably well disposed
to us, but his resources are exhausted and his talents insignificant.'[4]

Sidoji Rao Nimbalkar, commonly called Appa Desai, of Nipani
was another who owed much of his position to the British. He was
a man of ability—in Elphinstone's words, 'a man of talents and a
good soldier'.[5] Beginning as the hereditary Desai, or district officer,
of a small tract of country,[6] he had risen to a certain importance

[1] M.E. to Hislop, 28.6.1817, Bg. S.C. 1.8.1817, 15.
[2] Supreme Government to Close (Resident with Sindhia), 31.7.1817, Bg. S.C.
5.9.1817, 9; abstract in Bg. P.C. 4.3.1820, 18.
[3] M.E. to Governor-General, 6.1.1814, P.R.C. xii. 310.
[4] M.E. to Hislop, 28.6.1817, Bg. S.C. 1.8.1817, 15.
[5] M.E. to Governor-General, 18.3.1813, P.R.C. xii. 233 ff.
[6] 'A little country consisting of 8 or 10 villages' (Elphinstone to Governor-
General, ibid.).

in the service of Sindhia. Then he gave valuable help to Arthur Wellesley in the war against Sindhia, and British influence with the Peshwa secured a considerable jagir for him. Baji Rao later employed him to seize Chikodi and Manoli from the Raja of Kolhapur: he seized them, but kept them for himself. He then set about securing influence at Kolhapur, and married the Raja's daughter. Elphinstone suspected that his aim was to amass supreme power there as the Raja's minister.[1] But the cup which he had laboriously filled was taken from his lips at the crucial moment, for the treaty which Elphinstone concluded with the Raja of Kolhapur in 1812 contained a guarantee of British protection for the Raja.

Appa Desai was, however, a realist: as Elphinstone put it, 'as soon as the first ebullition of his anger was over, he resumed his usual professions of devotion to the British Government'.[2] He still had his jagir, which Elphinstone estimated in 1818 to be worth $3\frac{1}{2}$ lakhs of rupees, together with Chikodi and Manoli, worth between $3\frac{1}{2}$ and 4 lakhs.[3] But Elphinstone realized that he was not a man to be disregarded: 'he is violent, oppressive and unruly, but active, energetic & much dreaded by his neighbours'. Nor was he the man to forget past injuries: 'he probably hates us & the Peshwa equally', remarked Elphinstone in June 1817.[4]

The Desai of Kittur was another jagirdar possessed of ancient hereditary office. He had lands worth about 6 lakhs of rupees, and Elphinstone thought that, unlike Appa Desai, his strength lay in them rather than in himself: 'his country is strong but he is of no consequence out of it'.[5]

But whatever a jagirdar's importance under the old government his fate under the new was to depend in large measure upon his conduct during the war.

Soon after the war had begun both Madhav Rao Raste and Appa Desai of Nipani offered to help negotiate a peace. But Elphinstone rejected the offer, as he said, 'not more from uncertainty of the Governor-General's wishes than from a conviction that the best way to command a peace is to seem indifferent to it'.[6]

On the other hand, he was anxious to win over the jagirdars from the Peshwa. Besides depriving the Peshwa of their military re-

---

[1] M.E. to Governor-General, 18.3.1813, P.R.C. xii. 233 ff.   [2] Ibid.
[3] M.E. to Governor-General, 18.6.1818, Bg. S.C. 26.9.1818, 3.
[4] M.E. to Hislop, 28.6.1817, Bg. S.C. 1.8.1817, 15.   [5] Ibid.
[6] M.E. to Supreme Government, 24.11.1817, P.R.C. xiii. 260 f.

sources he thought that this would have 'a great effect on public opinion in all parts of his dominions'.[1] He wrote to them offering terms similar to those of Pandharpur if they would return to their estates and conform to his instructions. He did not expect them actively to fight against the Peshwa, but merely to return to their homes, renounce their allegiance, withdraw their troops, and promise to obey the directions of the new government. He gave them until the end of February to make up their minds.[2]

He thought that they would be more inclined to quit Baji Rao if they knew that they would never again be under his rule or subject to his vengeance. In his letters to them promising conditions similar to those of Pandharpur as the reward for early submission, he therefore stated that they would never again be subject to Baji Rao.[3] He was, however, careful to make such promises in general terms: 'I have left it uncertain', he wrote at the time, 'whether the change alluded to will be made in their own situation alone or in that of the govt.'[4]

It soon transpired that to the Patwardhans there was something in the name of Peshwa. But Elphinstone showed no sympathy. It may be that his own intense dislike of Baji Rao as a man blinded him to the loyalty which these Maratha noblemen obviously felt for their ruler. When one chief explained his reasons for not submitting, and emphasized the dishonour of abandoning the Peshwa, Elphinstone gave a cold reply: 'I have told him that he must positively take his line.'[5] When the same argument was used to Munro he retorted that the illustrious Parashuram Bhau 'had not been so scrupulous in remaining in the Peshwah's cause'. (The analogy was hardly fair: Parashuram Bhau had supported the claims of Chimnaji Appa to the Peshwaship in opposition to Baji Rao.) The reply, however, was logical enough: the agents of the chiefs in question 'answered that he had transferred his allegiance to another Peshwah, and that if another were now set up, they could do the same'.[6]

Ganpat Rao Patwardhan was in fact the first of the great jagirdars definitely to come to terms with the British. On the night of 24

[1] M.E. to Munro, 21.1.1818, Bg. S.C. 31.7.1818, 79.
[2] Ibid. Also M.E. to Munro, 7.1.1818, Bg. S.C. 31.7.1818, 71.
[3] Compare his policy in the Deccan generally: see p. 17, above.
[4] M.E. to Supreme Government, 9.1.1818, Bg. S.C. 31.7.1818, 69.
[5] M.E. to Munro, 21.1.1818, postscript 25.1.1818, ibid. 79; M.E. to Supreme Government, 7.5.1818, Bg. P.C. 31.7.1818, 92.
[6] Munro to M.E., 21.2.1818, Gleig, iii. 308 ff.

January his agent came to Elphinstone with a firm offer: Ganpat Rao would submit if Elphinstone 'would answer for the continuance of the terms of Punderpoor, would engage that his master should be protected from all attacks on the Paishwah's part, and that he should not be obliged to fight against the Paishwah'. To all this Elphinstone agreed. After further negotiations Munro finally reached an agreement with Ganpat Rao the following month.[1]

Chintaman Rao Patwardhan answered Elphinstone's letter with what Elphinstone himself called 'a declaration in temperate language' that he would stay with the Peshwa. But he soon left the field, pleading sickness as his excuse, and then disavowed his former letter to Elphinstone and promised to withdraw his troops from combat. The rest of the Patwardhans, individualists to the end, continued to follow various and devious courses.[2] But before the proclamation of Satara was published on 20 February most of them had left Baji Rao.[3] Its publication was followed by the submission of the Pant Amatya, the Pratinidhi, and the Pant Sachiv, the three hereditary officers of the Raja of Satara who still had some importance.[4]

Three great jagirdars still remained with Baji Rao—Vithal Narsing of Vinchur, Appa Desai of Nipani, and Madhav Rao Raste. The Vinchur jagirdar prided himself upon the steadfast loyalty of his house to the Peshwa. Elphinstone had once assumed that Appa Desai would be guided by self-interest, but now that he had been faithful to the Peshwa for so long Elphinstone presumed that he would continue so until the end. For Madhav Rao Raste Elphinstone had little sympathy: 'Madhoo Row Rastia', he complained in March 1818, 'who owes his jageer entirely to the British Government has been among the most active against it.'[5]

After the Peshwa's forces had suffered further severe losses in April,[6] Madhav Rao Raste at last submitted.[7]

Appa Desai submitted early in May, in company with Chimnaji

[1] Agreement, 17.2.1818, Bg. P.C. 24.4.1819, 20.
[2] Madhav Rao Dadaji of Chinchni and Ganpat Rao of Shedbal stayed at home throughout the war. But whereas Ganpat Rao of Shedbal had no communication with Elphinstone, Madhav Rao Dadaji always seemed particularly friendly. Yet Madhav Rao's son and nephew were the last of the Patwardhans to leave the Peshwa (M.E. to Munro, 12.3.1818, Bg. S.C. 31.7.1818, 87).
[3] Madhav Rao Dadaji's son Govind Rao and his nephew and ward Gopal Rao sent promises that they would soon be withdrawing—as they did (M.E. to Governor-General, 7.3.1818, P.R.C. xiii. 313 ff.).
[4] Ibid.   [5] M.E. to Munro, 12.3.1818, Bg. S.C. 31.7.1818, 87.
[6] At the battle of Seoni.   [7] Abstract, Bg. P.C. 4.3.1820, 18.

Appa, the Peshwa's brother, and 'six elephants and sixty camels, some of them apparently laden with treasure' as one British officer reported at the time.[1]

Still the Vinchur jagirdar remained with his master. It was not until 31 May that he sent an agent to tender his submission to Malcolm. The man claimed that the Vinchur jagirdar, whose family had loyally served the Peshwa's family for five generations, 'had made a sacrifice to his sense of duty of his lands, forts and property and had at this moment that Bajee Row thought of terms for himself, no other prospect upon earth but the generosity of the British Government'. Malcolm pointed out that the Vinchur jagirdar had submitted so late in the day that to the British there was little merit in the act: however, he might yet be of service to the Company, in particular by persuading Baji Rao to submit quietly. But the agent replied that the jagirdars still with Baji Rao could not be disrespectful to him in his hour of distress: 'they had borne, he added, the daily reproach of treason without reply for two months rather than hazard the imputation of ingratitude to the family they had so long served with fidelity'.[2] Two days later, on 2 June, Malcolm decided to be more firm: he told the agents of the Vinchur jagirdar and of Aba Purandhare, a less powerful colleague,[3] that while he did not expect their masters to be harsh or to use force in order to make Baji Rao submit, yet if they failed to persuade him, 'their delicacy would be termed imbecility, and . . . they could henceforward neither expect gratitude from their Prince, nor consideration from us'. Malcolm said that there must be no more delay: 'I told them plainly that unless he came to my camp next day, I desired never to hear more of them or their claims.'[4]

Baji Rao did in fact surrender on the following day. How far this was due to any persuasion on the part of the Vinchur jagirdar, it is impossible to say. At all events, when the jagirdar's agent met Captain Briggs on 22 June he spoke of 'his master's situation not at all as one of serious calamity, but merely as an exchange of government which would not affect him in the least'. Briggs was

---

[1] Capt. E. Davies (Nizam's Reformed Horse) to Capt. Halifax (acting D.A.G. to Gen. Smith), Bom. P.C. 20.5.1818, 2958 ff.

[2] Malcolm to Governor-General, 31.5.1818, P.R.C. xiii. 367 f.

[3] Aba Purandhare: a smaller jagirdar; his jagir was thought to have amounted at the beginning of the war to some $2\frac{1}{2}$ lakhs of rupees (Abstract, Bg. P.C. 4.3.1820, 18).

[4] Malcolm to Supreme Government, 4.6.1818, P.R.C. xiii. 374 ff.

'somewhat surprised' at this and 'asked him very seriously what he meant'. He replied simply that just as his master had served the Peshwa faithfully to the end so would he serve the new government. Briggs, however, pointed out that 'with regard to serving the British Government, that must depend very much on the will of that Government to accept of those services'. The agent temporized: in Briggs's account, 'he affected at first not to understand my meaning'. Briggs soon made it clear that the British Government might not wish to follow the Peshwa's example. At this the agent's resistance collapsed: 'he said we were masters and might of course do what we chose but he confessed himself very much disappointed'.[1]

The prospects even of the Kittur Desai looked brighter than this. Elphinstone had judged him to be a person of no consequence, and he played a part of no importance during the war. But at least he had caused the British no trouble.[2]

While the fate of each individual jagirdar was thus to depend largely upon his conduct during the war, the fate of the jagirdars as a class depended in no small degree upon Elphinstone's opinion of their proper position in society. As early as January 1818 he had decided that the Pandharpur terms would have to be modified even for those jagirdars who by their conduct might prove themselves entitled to them. The Pandharpur agreement had provided that the jagirdars should supply the Peshwa with the total number of troops specified in their charters. But he suspected that in fact they had never supplied more than two-thirds of that number, 'even on the rare occasion when they exerted themselves'. It seemed a matter of course that the British Government could not countenance such laxity: the totals specified would therefore have to be reduced. On the one hand, as he pointed out, 'the nature of our offers requires us to take care that their situation is no worse than it used to be'.[3] On the other hand, 'if we force the jagirdars to keep up a large portion of their contingents we make them our enemies & at the same time put arms into their hands'.[4]

---

[1] Briggs to M.E., 23.6.1818, Bg. P.C. 14.8.1818, 87.
[2] 'He remained at home from the commencement of the war, and though he might have had a small party of horse with the Paishwa, he showed much more readiness to act with General Munro than with that Prince' (M.E. to Governor-General, 18.6.1818, P.R.C. xiii. 394 ff.).
[3] M.E. to Munro, 21.1.1818, Bg. S.C. 31.7.1818, 79.
[4] M.E. to Munro, 19.5.1818, *Elphinstone*.

In short, the size of all contingents had to be reduced. Elphinstone saw a disadvantage in thus allowing the jagirdars to maintain contingents that were small in proportion to the size of their jagirs, as he pointed out to Munro in May 1818: 'The Peshwah was entitled to call out 19 or 20,000 jagirdars' horse & in the last war I do not suppose he had more than 7 or 8,000. If we allow the same system to go on, the revenue is wasted on maintaining a few individuals in luxury & does not go as intended to pay the soldiery of the country.'[1] But this could not be helped. Besides, he was able at least to reduce the number of those whom he considered to be wasting the country's resources: this he did by depriving those who had remained faithful to Baji Rao of both the right and the resources to maintain troops. He wrote to the Governor-General on 18 June 1818: 'it is politic and humane to allow a liberal maintenance even to those who have obstinately resisted us, but it is neither required by humanity nor policy to give such persons the command of troops paid from the revenues which have fallen into our hands'.[2] He therefore allowed them to keep only that part of their jagirs which had been originally granted for their personal maintenance. The rest he took from them, and with it the right and duty of maintaining troops.[3]

Several great families suffered in this way—notably Madhav Rao Raste, Vithal Narsing of Vinchur, and the descendants of that great soldier Gokhale who had fallen at Ashti. The Supreme Government's view was that Raste's 'singular ingratitude' entitled him to no consideration at all. Of Vithal Narsing they declared, 'having adhered to Bajee Row to the last, however creditable such conduct may be to his fidelity towards his master, he can have no claim to the kindness of the British Government'.[4]

Raste's personal jagir was worth only Rs.40,000 a year. Elphinstone came to learn that in spite of his support of the Peshwa's cause during the greater part of the war, he had towards the end tried to persuade Chimnaji Appa to surrender. Moreover, the loss of his great possessions was bound to be a disappointment to him: his whole jagir had been worth some 10 lakhs of rupees at the

[1] Ibid.   [2] M.E. to Governor-General, 18.6.1818, Bg. S.C. 26.9.1818, 3.
[3] If a jagirdar's charter did not state the proportion of the jagir actually intended for the personal maintenance of the jagirdar, Elphinstone 'took the number of horse he was bound to provide, multiplied it by 300 Rs. & deducted the product from the whole annual amount of the jageer, leaving the remainder as personal to the jageerdar' (M.E. to V. Hale, 11.1.1819, *Elphinstone*).
[4] Supreme Government to M.E., 14.7.1818, P.R.C. xiii. 418 ff.

beginning of the war. In order, then, to soften the blow and to reward him for his tardy exertions, Elphinstone allowed him to keep, in addition to his personal jagir of Rs.40,000, some lands in the Carnatic worth about Rs.20,000 a year.[1]

The agent from Vinchur tried to bluff. He told Elphinstone that his master had indignantly rejected the promise, which Malcolm had conveyed, that his personal jagir would be restored and had announced his determination to stay with Baji Rao unless he was promised a more satisfactory settlement. Elphinstone thought this 'palpably false',[2] and Malcolm confirmed that it was. Malcolm, in fact, remembered that the Vinchur jagirdar had been grateful for the promise of his personal jagir. He had of course asked for more, but he had accepted Malcolm's assurance that no other promises could be given him. Finally, he had gone home quite unconditionally.[3] But his losses were indeed great. From the possession of estates worth some 12 lakhs of rupees at the beginning of the war, he was reduced to that of a personal jagir nominally worth about Rs.56,000, which was thought to be actually producing not more than Rs.36,000 a year.[4]

Elphinstone also had to consider the position of the Gokhale family. Early in the war the Governor-General had told him to imprison Gokhale if he could catch him and to annex all his lands —thought to be worth about $13\frac{1}{2}$ lakhs.[5] But Gokhale was killed in battle, leaving a widow but no son. Ramchandra Venkatesh, 'the chief leader of the Gokhale troops', subsequently asked Malcolm to send an honorary dress to one Dhondo Pant, who, he said, was Gokhale's nephew and adopted son. Malcolm rashly did so.[6] But Elphinstone was not deceived: 'Gokla', he wrote to Malcolm, 'I have every reason to believe never had a nephew and certainly never an adopted son.'[7] Malcolm looked into the matter and found that it was so: not only had Gokhale never adopted a son, but Dhondo Pant was no nephew, only a very distant relation.[8] More-

[1] His personal jagir was to remain hereditary, but not the lands in the Carnatic (Abstract, Bg. P.C. 4.3.1820, 18).
[2] M.E. to Malcolm, 18.7.1818, Bg. S.C. 31.10.1818, 81.
[3] Malcolm to M.E., 26.7.1818, ibid. 82.   [4] Abstract, Bg. P.C. 4.3.1820, 18.
[5] Supreme Government to M.E., 15.12.1817, P.R.C. xiii. 270 ff.; Forrest, *Maratha Selections*, 678.
[6] Malcolm to M.E., 9.8.1818, *H.M.* 733, 331 ff.; Malcolm to M.E., 3.10.1818, Bg. S.C. 31.10.1818, 87.
[7] M.E. to Malcolm, 29.8.1818, *Elphinstone.*
[8] M.E. to Malcolm, 12.9.1818, Bg. S.C. 17.10.1818, 5.

over, Ramchandra foolishly told Elphinstone that Malcolm had known the truth about Dhondo Pant when he sent the dress. Malcolm of course denied this.[1] Elphinstone did not regret the episode: if the British, after all these clumsy attempts to deceive them, nevertheless allowed Gokhale's widow to adopt Dhondo Pant and also continued the personal jagir to him, it would redound all the more to their credit as generous rulers.[2] This was an argument likely to appeal to the Governor-General in Council who told Elphinstone that he wished to decide in accordance with the latter's opinion of the influence which such generosity would have upon 'our power and reputation in the country'.[3] Upon Elphinstone's recommendation it was therefore decided that the widow should be allowed to adopt an heir to whom a personal jagir of about Rs.25,000 would be continued.[4]

In short, the great jagirdars who suffered most from the war were those who had been most faithful to the Peshwa.[5]

Appa Desai of Nipani was not among them. Even though he had remained with Baji Rao until early in May, Elphinstone felt that he deserved some consideration 'as he always kept up a negotiation with General Munro or with me, and certainly always counselled peace, and as he showed no particular activity against us during the war'.[6] His fate, so Elphinstone decided, was 'that he shall lose all that was promised to others, but that if he behaves well he shall keep all the rest & be entitled to consideration'.[7]

Munro soon found Appa Desai's behaviour defective. Chikodi and Manoli had been promised to Kolhapur, but even after Munro had forced him to surrender the major part of the area, he still held on to twenty-four villages which he had allotted to the support of his household troops and principal officers. Moreover, he still held in prison at Nipani a number of people belonging to districts

[1] Malcolm to M.E., 3.10.1818, Bg. S.C. 31.10.1818, 87.
[2] M.E. to Malcolm, 12.9.1818, Bg. S.C. 17.10.1818, 5.
[3] Supreme Government to M.E., 31.10.1818, Bg. S.C. 31.10.1818, 90.
[4] M.E. to Supreme Government, 10.12.1818, Bg. P.C. 19.1.1819, 40; Supreme Government to M.E., 19.1.1819, ibid. 41; M.E. to Supreme Government, 13.9.1818, Bg. S.C. 17.10.1818, 4.
[5] Aba Purandhare, who had also stayed to the end, also lost all except his personal jagir. His estates had been worth about 2½ lakhs of rupees at the beginning of the war. Now he was left with only a personal jagir worth nominally about Rs.50,000 but in fact only about Rs.26,000 a year (Abstract, Bg. P.C. 4.3.1820, 18).
[6] M.E. to Governor-General, 18.6.1818, P.R.C. xiii. 394 ff.
[7] M.E. to Munro, 5.7.1818, *Elphinstone*.

formerly under the Peshwa and now under British rule. They had been there for several years, many of them indeed for ten or twelve years. According to Munro at least, he had 'pursued a system of throwing into prison all the rich inhabitants not only of his own districts but of every district wherever he obtained a temporary authority with the view of extorting money from them and of seizing & keeping in confinement the women most remarkable for their beauty'.[1]

Munro therefore suggested strong measures:

If he does not give up the whole of the villages and prisoners within the present month, he ought to be reduced to the state in which we found him in 1800, the Dessay of six or eight villages. . . . He is a man who will never be quiet as long as he has the power of exciting disturbances. His administration is so cruel and destructive, that his fall would be a benefit to the country.[2]

Elphinstone thoroughly agreed:

As far as our interest is concerned, it would be for our advantage to crush a chief who can never be our friend & thus strike a terror into others; our faith requires us not to seek occasions for following this line of policy but it does not oblige us to submit to insults.[3]

Appa Desai eventually surrendered the twenty-four villages— but only, as Munro reported, 'with great reluctance after an interval of six weeks spent in evasion'. Munro also succeeded in persuading him to release many of his prisoners.[4] He did not suffer greatly from the war. He lost Chikodi and Manoli, worth between 3½ and 4 lakhs of rupees. He also lost his claim to tribute (chauth) from the Nizam's territories, but in compensation he was given lands worth about Rs.90,000 a year. Moreover, he was given a personal jagir and allowances worth Rs.62,000 a year, and he was allowed to keep the rest of his estates worth about Rs.270,000 a year.[5] He was still to render military service.

The Desai of Kittur had his reward. He still had to pay an annual tribute to the Government of Rs.175,000—and the Government

[1] Munro to M.E., 8.7.1818, Gleig, iii. 268 ff.; Munro to M.E., 28.8.1818, Bg. S.C. 7.11.1818, 24.
[2] Ibid.
[3] M.E. to Munro, 17.7.1818, *Elphinstone.*
[4] Munro to M.E., 28.8.1818, Bg. S.C. 7.11.1818, 24.
[5] Abstract, Bom. P.C. 27.6.1821, 4015; M.E. to Governor-General, 18.6.1818, P.R.C. xiii. 394 ff. Terms granted, Aitchison, viii. 400 ff.

continued to make him an annual present of Rs.3,955. He had, however, paid no tribute to the Peshwa's Government for the past two years. The new government excused him that payment for one of those two years: that was his reward. As a jagirdar of the Peshwa he had had to provide the service of 473 horse: the new government remitted this service and resumed an equivalent in land. According to Munro he was 'perfectly satisfied with the present arrangement & he has cause to be so'. In his comparative weakness he would gain greatly from the law and order to be enforced under the new régime. Under the old he had suffered at the hands not only of the Peshwa but also of the other great jagirdars.[1]

When Elphinstone discussed the question of a reward with Ganpat Rao Patwardhan, the jagirdar of Tasgaon, he found that the latter 'showed some anxiety for an increase in the amount but much more for a promise that none of his relations should have an equal gratification'.[2] Elphinstone finally conceded that his reward might well be in proportion to his past services to the British— which had indeed been exceptional. He was eventually given an addition of Rs.40,000 to his jagir: this was more than was given to any of the other Patwardhans, even to Chintaman Rao, whose estates were so much bigger than his.[3]

Chintaman Rao was eventually given Rs.30,000. His services during the war had not been remarkable, and Elphinstone only gave him as much as this out of consideration for his seniority in the family. The other Patwardhans similarly received rewards proportioned to their services and standing.[4]

The Patwardhans in fact were the jagirdars who gained most from the war. They all retained their jagirs, they all continued to maintain contingents,[5] and they were all rewarded with additions to the personal part of their jagirs—though some received greater rewards than others.

[1] Munro to M.E., 28.8.1818, Bg. S.C. 7.11.1818, 24.
[2] M.E. to Supreme Government, 17.[6.1819], Bg. P.C. 24.7.1819, 6. In one of Ganpat Rao's questions to Munro preparatory to his submission in Feb. 1818, he had related how in the partition of the original Tasgaon estates his two brothers had been assigned more than he, and he had asked Munro for the Company's help to rectify the matter. Munro had diplomatically replied to the effect that the Company would act justly. Ganpat Rao's questions and Munro's answers, Bg. P.C. 24.7.1819, 8.
[3] See table, p. 72.   [4] See table, p. 64.
[5] Chintaman Rao soon commuted his military service by giving up an equivalent in land. See below.

TABLE I

The Rewards for the Patwardhans[1]

	(Rs.)
Ganpat Rao of Tasgaon	40,000
Keshav Rao of Kurundwad	30,000
Chintaman Rao of Sangli	30,000
Gopal Rao of Jamkhandi	30,000
Ganpat Rao of Shedbal	20,000
Madhav Rao of Miraj	20,000
Govind Rao of Chinchni	10,000
Gopal Rao of Miraj	10,000

Elphinstone soon sketched out the conditions under which he thought that the great jagirdars should render military service:

Their contingents [he wrote in June 1818] ought only to be called out for general service, but they ought to assist in quelling any disturbance in their immediate neighbourhood. When their contingent is called out it ought not to be strictly mustered, and one fourth of the stipulated number of horse ought to be considered sufficient, if any stricter rule is observed they will be losers by their transfer to our Government.[2]

What concerned him most was not so much the jagirdars' power to render direct military assistance as their function of alleviating unemployment. As he wrote privately to Munro:

They are bound to keep up 6,000 horse. If they would keep a third or even a fourth of that number hanging on as Omedwars[3] or employed in any way that would prevent their joining insurrections it would be a great point. Keeping up horse *now* is the most important service we can ever expect of them.[4]

In these early months of peace Elphinstone was alive to the danger of disturbances by unemployed ex-soldiers. When there were rumours of an insurrection pending in the Southern Maratha country, he told Chaplin, in September 1818, to warn the Patwardhans to watch the unemployed soldiers in their jagirs and to keep enough of their contingents ready to deal with any trouble from them.[5]

---

[1] M.E. to Chaplin, 16.8.1819, Bg. P.C. 16.10.1819, 9. Chaplin carried out the allocation. The details of the lands allocated are in Chaplin to Government, 22.5.1821, Bom. P.C. 27.6.1821, 4016. Madhav Rao Dadaji died before the allocation.

[2] M.E. to Governor-General, 18.6.1818, P.R.C. xiii. 394 ff.

[3] Omedwar = umedwar = applicant for employment (lit. hopeful).

[4] M.E. to Munro, 24.6.1818, *Elphinstone.*

[5] M.E. to Chaplin, 4.9.1818, ibid.

He did not expect that the jagirdars' contingents would serve any other military purpose beyond keeping the peace within their respective jagirs. 'I would not employ them far from their own lands without some strong motive', he remarked to Chaplin, 'we must make our yoke as light as possible.'[1] In his opinion there would have been little point in doing so: 'the services of the Put-warduns', he told Chaplin on another occasion, 'will never be worth the trouble of calling for them & the only use of their contingents is to afford a receptacle for unemployed soldiers'.[2]

But he had trouble enough in arranging the details of the jagir-dars' terms of service.

In November 1818 Ganpat Rao Patwardhan of Tasgaon sent agents to Elphinstone with the claim that 'he had a promise under Munro's hand that he should not be called on to serve, and that a few horse furnished once in ten years in the way of friendship would be the most that would be required of him'. Elphinstone of course replied that he would observe any promise of Munro's that Ganpat Rao could produce.[3] It transpired that the promise referred to was contained in the agreement of February 1818, which was in fact a series of answers by Munro to questions submitted by Ganpat Rao's agent.[4] One of the questions ran as follows: 'I have served our Government and it is not in my power to serve another. Let the Company out of regard to old friendship allow me to remain in my own place without serving.'[5] This was Munro's answer: 'The Company's Government does not exact service like the constant duty you did under the Paishwa's; once in ten or fifteen years when an important event occurs it is necessary to come to the Company's assistance. Except in such times you shall not always be called on.'[6] Such vagueness invited controversy.

When Elphinstone met Ganpat Rao in 1819 to settle his terms

[1] M.E. to Chaplin, 30.9.1818, ibid.

[2] Chintaman Rao had been complaining that one of Chaplin's officials upon mustering his contingent had tried to enforce a minimum standard of height for the horses and had made other unwelcome demands. Chaplin thereupon can-celled the muster, and Elphinstone fully approved: 'we must not give up rights but there is no use in enforcing them on points that are really of very little interest' (M.E. to Chaplin, 8.11.1818, Bg. S.C. 12.12.1818, 18; M.E. to Chaplin, 9.11.1818, *Elphinstone*).

[3] M.E. to Chaplin, 8.11.1818, Bg. S.C. 12.12.1818, 18.

[4] Chaplin to M.E., 17.11.1818, Bg. S.C. 26.12.1818, 12.

[5] Ganpat Rao's questions and Munro's answers, 17.2.1818, Question 13, Bg. P.C. 24.7.1819, 8.

[6] Ibid.

of service, Ganpat Rao argued that as Munro's answer had spoken of him as coming to the Company's assistance he was to be regarded as an ally rather than a jagirdar and was therefore exempt from doing military service. Elphinstone pointed out that what had actually happened was that in answer to his demand for exemption Munro had replied by stating how he was to serve. He eventually accepted this interpretation, but demanded something more precise than the phrase 'once in ten or fifteen years'. He suggested that he should be required to serve either for not more than one year in ten with all his horse or at all times with one-tenth of his horse. Elphinstone rejected both these suggestions as entirely disproportionate to the service which the other jagirdars would have to do.[1] Ganpat Rao finally agreed to maintain at all times one-fourth of his total contingent.[2]

Chintaman Rao also raised objections. Characteristically, his were much more radical than Ganpat Rao's. He objected to serving under any government but the Peshwa's. During the war the Patwardhans had indeed continued to assert their loyalty to the office of Peshwa, though not to the person who filled it, even after they had left Baji Rao's camp. So insistent were they then, that Munro had in April 1818 seriously suggested that to conciliate their feelings the Company should itself adopt the title of Peshwa.[3] But these assertions did not outlast the war—with one exception. As late as November 1818 Chintaman Rao 'after a thousand apologies & entreaties to be forgiven put in a humble request about setting up a Paishwa'. Elphinstone always refused to listen to such suggestions, and on this occasion Chintaman Rao's agents thereupon 'made all sorts of apologies'.[4] Elphinstone asked them whether their master really expected the British to give up the conquests which they had made with all the risks and exertions of war. They replied that 'he had no such expectation but that he thought we might set up a pageant like the Raja of Sattara'. To this Elphinstone retorted that 'the Raja was not intended to be a pageant but to be as soon as he was strong enough the real and efficient head of a small state'.[5]

Elphinstone also tried to reassure Chintaman Rao about the

[1] M.E. to Supreme Government, 17.[6.1819], Bg. P.C. 24.7.1819, 6.
[2] Supplementary terms, 17.6.1819, Aitchison, viii. 265.
[3] Munro to M.E., 23.4.1818, Gleig, iii. 245 ff.
[4] M.E. to Grant, 11.11.1818, *Elphinstone*.
[5] M.E. to Chaplin, 11.11.1818, Bg. S.C. 12.12.1818, 20.

future by declaring that 'although we were resolved to permit no encroachments by the jageerdars, we were equally determined to observe all their antient privileges, that it was not intended to introduce our administration of justice (Adawlut) into their lands, and that all their old customs regarding their service should be scrupulously observed'.[1]

In December 1818 Chintaman Rao again sent his agents to Elphinstone to make the same request that a Peshwa should be set up. To the argument that it would be dishonourable for him to serve the British he added 'a very direct insinuation that our demand for such service is a breach of faith'.[2] He emphasized that it was for service to the Peshwa that his jagir had been guaranteed by the British at Pandharpur.[3] Elphinstone heard, moreover, from the agents of other Patwardhan chiefs that Chintaman Rao had made no secret of the fact that he had been asking for the restoration of a Peshwa. He decided that this must be stopped lest others might be encouraged to do likewise, and he sent Chintaman Rao a severe letter in which he included the warning that 'it is in return for service that lands and honours are conferred, and if you refuse to serve according to former custom, I can see no ground on which you can expect that you will retain your station'.[4]

Elphinstone confided to Chaplin that he thought that this letter would probably make Chintaman Rao 'sulkier than ever', but he added that the terms which he would soon send to him 'will bring his disposition to a test & either force him to break out or to be quiet for ever or at least to submit quietly to our rule & wait for some new revolution'.[5] Chintaman Rao's agent soon returned with 'a verbal answer or rather no answer but his own account of what passed'.[6] The agent described how his master's 'chagrin on this occasion joined to his grief for the recent death of his wife made him determine to relinquish his jageer and allow us to settle as we pleased with his son'. Elphinstone replied that if Chintaman Rao did not accept the terms the British Government was not bound to continue his jagir to his son but would distribute it between him and the rest of the Patwardhan family.[7] Elphinstone warned

[1] Ibid.
[2] M.E. to Chaplin, 21.12.1818, Bg. S.C. 19.1.1819, 7.
[3] Chintaman Rao to M.E., 17.11.1818, ibid. 8.
[4] M.E. to Chintaman Rao, 21.12.1818, ibid. 9.
[5] M.E. to Chaplin, 13.1.1819, *Elphinstone*. [6] M.E. to Chaplin, 19.2.1819, ibid.
[7] M.E. to Chaplin, 18.3.1819, Bg. P.C. 24.4.1819, 20.

Chaplin that 'this gentleman cannot be too closely watched',[1] and proceeded to consider how best to dispose of his jagir. He decided against resuming it: that would only create a bad impression, whereas distributing it among the rest of the family should 'convince the country that the Government has no wish to enrich itself at the expense of its dependants, and . . . prevent the bad impression that would be made by the immediate diminution of the importance of the only great family which took part with us in the course of the war with the Paishwa'.[2]

At last, in April 1819, Elphinstone formally required Chintaman Rao either to accept terms similar to those which he was offering to the other Patwardhans or to subscribe to a copy of the Pandharpur agreement in which the British Government was substituted for the Peshwa.[3] In reply Chintaman Rao refused to serve the British Government. He again made his point that at Pandharpur it was to the Peshwa that the British Government had required him to render service. To this he added the fresh argument that as the British Government had at Pandharpur guaranteed his jagir to him provided that he served the Peshwa faithfully, it could not in justice resume his jagir unless he had broken faith with the Peshwa. Elphinstone dismissed this as 'a sophistry': in fact the Pandharpur agreement had protected the jagirdars from encroachments by the Peshwa.[4]

A relative of Chintaman Rao's, one Ramji Oke, was serving under Elphinstone. Elphinstone now deputed him to negotiate. Chintaman Rao told him informally that 'he would serve without any other condition if the British Government would engage to prohibit the slaughter of horned cattle, and the pressing of Brahmins for begarrees which he said had taken place in the Concan during the war'. Otherwise, he said, neither he nor his son would serve.[5]

Elphinstone replied through Ramji Oke that he did not intend to offer the jagir to his son if Chintaman Rao himself declined to serve. Moreover, Chintaman Rao could not be allowed to live on as a private person at Sangli: he would have to live somewhere at a distance like Benares where he could not use his influence against the British Government.[6]

---

[1] M.E. to Chaplin, 19.2.1819, *Elphinstone*.
[2] M.E. to Supreme Government, 18.3.1819, Bg. P.C. 24.4.1819, 19.
[3] M.E. to Chintaman Rao, 7.4.1819, Bg. P.C. 3.7.1819, 6.
[4] M.E. to Supreme Government, 18.5.1819, Bg. P.C. 3.7.1819, 6.
[5] Begarree = begari = coolie (ibid.).   [6] Ibid.

Elphinstone also refused Chintaman Rao's invitation to an entertainment, 'declaring that I could have no satisfaction in such an appearance of cordiality when I might be required to dispossess him of his jageer on the next day'.[1]

Late one night Chintaman Rao sent a message to Elphinstone asking him where he was to live since he could not stay at Sangli and would not serve. This seemed decisive. But the next morning he had changed his mind. He agreed to serve, but begged permission to commute his service 'as his people were unfit for the strictness of English discipline'. This was just what Elphinstone wanted. He at once agreed.[2]

After this the negotiations proceeded more quickly. Chintaman Rao made several detailed modifications in the terms: they were unimportant. He also made several extravagant demands, for example, for the right of private war, or, as Elphinstone put it, 'that he should be allowed to make war on his relations'. These Elphinstone rejected. After further allusion to the dishonour of serving the British Government, Elphinstone received Chintaman Rao in his tent in the presence of Chaplin and solemnly admonished him that the prerequisite of all further negotiations must be an admission by him that the service which he had owed to the Peshwa he now owed to the British Government. Chintaman Rao 'acceded to this proposition with unexpected felicity'. There was also 'considerable altercation' about the form of the agreement: Chintaman Rao wanted it to be like a treaty between independent states.[3]

The negotiations were protracted by Chintaman Rao's arguments. 'Though otherwise rather respectable and well-intentioned', wrote Elphinstone, 'he has a narrow and crooked understanding, a litigious spirit and a capricious temper.' For example, he demanded a written guarantee of his jagir from England dated 1812 because in a letter of that date from Pandharpur Elphinstone had stated that the British Government would guarantee his jagir if he fulfilled his obligations. Elphinstone pointed out that such a document would be quite useless now, to which Chintaman Rao answered 'that it would be useless, but it had been promised and he was entitled to demand it'.[4]

Finally, on 15 May 1819, Chintaman Rao accepted the terms drawn up by Elphinstone. These terms which in fact formed the

[1] Ibid.   [2] Ibid.   [3] Ibid.
[4] M.E. to Supreme Government, 18.5.1819, Bg. P.C. 3.7.1819, 6.

model for those granted to the other Patwardhan chiefs, included on the one hand a statement of the military service actually due from the jagirdar and on the other hand a provision that while possessing independent authority in the internal administration of his jagir, he would nevertheless govern it properly: 'you will attend to the prosperity of the ryots of your jaghire, to the strict administration of justice, and the effectual suppression of robberies, murders, arsons, and other crimes'.[1] Elphinstone insisted upon the inclusion of this latter provision as an essential part of the whole agreement, even though Chintaman Rao was much opposed to any hint of interference within his jagir.[2]

The principle, it seemed, had been settled. But to enforce it in practice involved more difficulties. There were two copies of the agreement. Chintaman Rao signed only one copy and asserted in a covering letter that he did this because he had no time to refer the matter to the Government and that he really felt that he could be neither a servant nor a subject of the British Government because it was so strict. Chaplin, who had succeeded Elphinstone as Commissioner, therefore recommended that Chintaman Rao's jagir should be resumed. The Bombay Government, with Elphinstone as Governor, decided against so drastic a step since Chintaman Rao had at least signed one copy even though he refused to sign the duplicate. Some force might, however, be used. General Pritzler accordingly marched upon Sangli and Chintaman Rao thereupon signed the duplicate.[3]

The episode did not promise well for the future. 'I am glad you got on so smoothly with Chintamun Row', wrote Elphinstone to Pritzler, 'though after all I am not sure whether it would have been luckier in the end if he had held out & been dispossessed.'[4]

As Elphinstone feared, there was more trouble to follow. Chintaman Rao was required to cede lands producing Rs.135,000 a year instead of providing 450 horse for the service of the Government. But Chaplin found that the lands which he actually ceded were only worth Rs.65,000 on the basis of their accounts for the past ten years.[5] After much delay the Bombay Government finally authorized Chaplin to seize enough of Chintaman Rao's lands to cover

[1] Article 4, Aitchison, viii. 258.
[2] M.E. to Supreme Government, 18.5.1819, Bg. P.C. 3.7.1819, 6.
[3] Political letter from Bombay, 7.3.1821, para. 61 ff., Bom. P.L.R. viii. 124 ff.
[4] M.E. to Pritzler, 3.12.1819, *Elphinstone*.
[5] Political letter from Bombay, 7.3.1821, para. 74 ff., Bom. P.L.R. viii. 124 ff.

the deficiency. He did so. Thereupon Chintaman Rao sent his nephew to Poona as his special representative to settle the matter.[1] This episode was thus concluded satisfactorily, but again only after prevarication by Chintaman Rao and the use of force as a last resort by the Government. Later, in 1822, Chaplin reported that Chintaman Rao's 'ill-humour has, if possible, increased, and he has omitted no opportunity of evincing it in occasional philippics'.[2]

The other Patwardhan chiefs, however, were well pleased and Elphinstone's negotiations with them went smoothly enough. When he interviewed them all[3] at Bagalkot in June 1819 they referred to a rumour that Ganpat Rao of Tasgaon had secured from Munro complete exemption from military service. After discussion they accepted the position as Elphinstone described it to them: Munro had merely been explaining the general practice of the British Government, if by some mistake his answer could be taken as conferring exemption upon Ganpat Rao, nevertheless Elphinstone could not give the rest of them the benefit of such a mistake.

The final article of Elphinstone's draft terms stated that the British Government would maintain the rank and dignity of the jagirdar in question as in Baji Rao's time. The Patwardhans pressed him to alter this to 'in former times', because they thought that under Baji Rao their position had greatly declined. Elphinstone agreed: he thought little of this difference in wording. As he explained the article to the Governor-General in Council:

This point to which they attach so much importance involves no sacrifice on our part. It consists in addressing letter[s] to them on occasions of condolence and congratulation, going out to meet them when they pay a visit, sending a person of sufficient rank to invite them to an entertainment, presenting them with the proper number of articles of dress and of jewels (which number is regulated by a previous entertainment of the same kind given by them), helping them to perfumes and beetle in the form prescribed for persons of the highest rank and other trifling ceremonies of the same nature.[4]

Apart from this the negotiations were straightforward enough. The number of horse which the jagirdars were to maintain was reduced to one-quarter, and this they had to keep ready for service all the year round.

[1] Political letter from Bombay, 29.8.1821, para. 104 ff., Bom. P.L.R. viii. 461 ff.
[2] Chaplin to Government, 20.8.1822, para. 311, S.R.J. iv. 508.
[3] That is, all except Chintaman Rao and Ganpat Rao of Tasgaon.
[4] M.E. to Supreme Government, 7.6.1819, Bg. P.C. 24.7.1819, 5.

Elphinstone would have preferred to arrange that each jagirdar should pay an appropriate sum of money or cede some land to the Government instead of maintaining a contingent—just as Chintaman Rao decided to do. He even 'sounded' the jagirdars' representatives on the matter. With the money, he thought, the Government could maintain an efficient body of men and thus employ some of the discharged ex-soldiers as long as seemed necessary;

TABLE 2

The Settlement of the Patwardhans[1]

Jagirdars	Revenue (Rs.)	Contingent under the Peshwa	New contingent
Sangli (Chintaman Rao) . .	634,000	1,800	450 (commuted)
Miraj (Ganpat Rao) . . .	495,000	1,210	302
Jamkhandi (Gopal Rao) . .	414,000	1,146	386[2]
Tasgaon (Ganpat Rao) . . .	199,000	573	150
Kurundwad (Keshav Rao) . .	143,000	450	114
Shedbal (Ganpat Rao) . . .	143,000	450	114

their number might eventually be reduced. Whereas if the jagirdars maintained contingents, 'unremitting and invidious strictness' would be required to prevent laxity. He doubted anyhow whether the jagirdars themselves would employ very many discharged soldiers in their contingents: instead, they would probably employ relations and men with claims of long service to their families—in other words men whom they would employ somehow even if they had no contingents. He argued, in short, that if the jagirdars would agree, the Government would lose nothing but the empty right 'of calling out a contingent which when furnished would never have been of the least use and to procure the attendance of which must have constantly run the risk of a rupture with the jagirdars'.[3]

[1] Bg. P.C. 24.7.1819, 5. These figures were subsequently modified as follows:

Miraj	300 horse
Jamkhandi	300 ,,
Kurundwad	70 ,,
Shedbal	70 ,,

(Aitchison, viii. 262 ff.). The validity of these estimates of revenue is of course very small.

[2] Including Chinchni.

[3] M.E. to Supreme Government, 18.5.1819, Bg. P.C. 3.7.1819, 6.

But none of the other Patwardhans wished to follow Chintaman Rao's example. They preferred to maintain contingents rather than pay money or cede land. Elphinstone at last concluded that the reason was probably that they had 'a considerable number of stable horse and of old retainers of their families' whom they would have had to maintain in any event, so that his plan would only increase their burdens.[1] In other words, they had grasped the point of his scheme quite as clearly as he himself had conceived it.

When he drafted the agreements, however, Elphinstone left it open to the jagirdars to commute their military service in cash or land if they should ever wish to do so. In each agreement it was therefore stated that the jagirdar in question was to maintain a fourth of his contingent or alternatively to pay an equivalent in cash (or cede an equivalent in land) at the rate of Rs.300 a horse.[2]

All the great jagirdars were allowed a practical independence within their jagirs: this was in accordance with the fundamental principle of the settlement that their position should not be worse than it had been under the former government. But a saving clause was included in all the agreements. The precise wording might vary, but the substance was the same in each agreement. In the terms granted to Ganpat Rao of Tasgaon, for example, it was stated that

You will attend to the prosperity of the ryots of your jaghire, to the

---

[1] M.E. to Supreme Government, 7.6.1819, Bg. P.C. 24.7.1819, 5.

[2] Aitchison's interpretation is surely wrong: in his words, 'the number of horse they were required to furnish was reduced to one-fourth, and *in lieu of the others* land was to be assigned or cash paid at the rate of Rs.300 for each horse' (Aitchison, *Treaties*, viii. 248: my italics). But in fact the whole point of this provision was that the Government unconditionally remitted the service of the remaining three-fourths of each contingent: a jagirdar was to pay money or cede land at the rate specified only if he did not maintain the one-fourth of his contingent which was all that was now required. Take, for example, the terms granted to Keshav Rao Patwardhan, which Aitchison himself quotes (Aitchison, viii. 262): 'as the Sirdars [Chiefs] would not be able to perform the serving according to the terms of their Tynat Zabitas [Charters], it is now settled, out of consideration for them, that they shall serve with one fourth of the contingent of troops for the maintenance of which they hold lands, or that in lieu of such service they shall pay to the government in ready money, at the rate of Rupees 300 a horse, the amount of the allowance of that number of troops, or that they shall relinquish an equivalent in land'. Like the Patwardhans, Appa Desai of Nipani was granted a remission of the service of three-fourths of his total contingent of 1,107 horse, leaving him liable to provide 277. As a favour this was reduced to 250 (Terms, 14.6.1820, Aitchison, viii. 401).

strict administration of justice, and the effectual suppression of robberies, murders, arsons, and other crimes. The government will not
enquire into any trifling complaints that may arise in your jaghire. When
any complaint is made, it will be referred to you, and you are to settle it
equitably. If at any time your jaghire should fall into great disorder, and
robberies should be committed without proper investigation and redress
on your part, it will be necessary that arrangements should be made on
the part of the government.[1]

Elphinstone purposely avoided mentioning in the agreements
how the jagirs were to be inherited. The Patwardhans' custom had
been that the eldest son should inherit the whole of his father's
property. But Baji Rao had introduced the principle of dividing it
among all the sons. Which policy should be followed under the
new government Elphinstone left for the future to decide: primo-
geniture would have the effect of maintaining large estates, while
division would steadily reduce the size of each. But he declared
that if large estates were to be maintained, they could not be in
better hands than those of the Patwardhans, who were good landholders and administrators.[2]

Munro also had a good opinion of the Patwardhans' merits as
landholders: he found that their lands were well cultivated, that
they treated the inhabitants with great kindness and that they were
deservedly popular. Appa Desai, on the other hand, he found was
'detested by all the inhabitants of the jageers for his oppression &
wanton cruelty'.[3]

The new rulers reassured each other that there was no danger
from their predecessors. Their kindness, they said, would prove
itself to have been the best policy. Malcolm was convinced that
Baji Rao would never risk what was left to him: 'he places as I have
had a full opportunity of observing no ordinary value upon the
comforts and luxuries which he still enjoys . . . his is not a mind
to gain strength from difficulties'.[4] Elphinstone still suspected Baji
Rao's passion for intrigue, but he and Munro both thought that the
jagirdars had too much to lose for them to make any active resistance to the new order of things.[5]

[1] Terms granted to Ganpat Rao, 17.6.1819, Aitchison, viii. 267.
[2] M.E. to Supreme Government, 7.6.1819, Bg. P.C. 24.7.1819, 5.
[3] Munro to M.E., 28.8.1818, Bg. S.C. 7.11.1818, 24.
[4] Malcolm to Supreme Government, 31.8.1818, Bg. S.C. 31.10.1818, 85.
[5] There are many letters to this effect, for example, M.E. to Chaplin, 4.9.1818,
Elphinstone; Munro to M.E., 13.9.1818, Gleig, iii. 277 ff. But Elphinstone's

Indeed, Elphinstone was much more concerned with the dangers to the jagirdars' position which might be inherent in the new system of government than with any danger which they themselves might constitute to that government. He was convinced, as he explained to the Governor-General in Council, of 'the importance of preserving the privileges of chiefs whose friendship we have acknowledged, as well to show how much is gained by attachment to our Government as for the general advantage of having some portion of the old nobility . . . flourishing and contented'.[1]

He paid great attention to the details of the agreements with the great jagirdars and he attached much importance to them. This forms a striking contrast to his general policy of avoiding written Regulations and of guarding the living body of the Maratha people from contact with the dead hand of law. The explanation is that he feared that in conformity with the levelling tendencies of British rule there would soon arise among the Company's servants a disposition to regard the great jagirdars as 'useless encumbrances on the revenue' and as inconvenient obstacles to the spread of the Regulations.[2]

He thought that there was bound to be some friction. 'We shall have a great deal of trouble with the whims & fancies of the Patwardhans', he remarked to Chaplin on one occasion in November 1818, 'but I do not think they will ever unite in any plot against us'.[3] He urged Chaplin to bear with them: 'they certainly seem somewhat arrogant, especially Chintamun Row, but it is necessary to treat them with great forbearance as under the old govt. they used constantly to refuse to attend to orders unless communicated in a manner quite to their liking'.[4]

He had at least settled the legal position of the great jagirdars.[5] How far their written agreements would in fact protect them from the excessive zeal of Collectors and Political Agents, time alone could show.

optimism was tempered with prudence. When in Sept. 1818 he told Chaplin to warn the jagirdars to be prepared for disturbances by unemployed ex-soldiers after the rains, he pointed out that 'the delivery of this message will afford a good pretence for sending a man to observe their proceedings if you have no better reason to give' (M.E. to Chaplin, 4.9.1818, *Elphinstone*).

[1] M.E. to Supreme Government, 7.6.1819, Bg. P.C. 24.7.1819, 5.
[2] Ibid.   [3] M.E. to Chaplin, 17.11.1818, *Elphinstone*.
[4] M.E. to Chaplin, 9.11.1818, ibid.
[5] He once described them as 'little independent poligars under our protection' (M.E. to H. Russell, 21.9.1818, ibid.).

NOTE

BESIDES the great jagirdars there were others who, though less rich and powerful, may nevertheless be considered part of the ruling class. Their families were of greater antiquity, deriving their jagirs from grants made by the Rajas of Satara in the early years of the Maratha Empire, some even from grants made by the Muslim rulers of kingdoms that flourished before the Maratha Empire was born. Elphinstone offered them the choice of holding their jagirs either from the Raja of Satara or from the British Government.

Like the great jagirdars, those with military liabilities had them either reduced or abolished according to individual circumstances. They all kept the full powers of internal administration which they already had, although the new agreements also stipulated that they should govern justly.

Those who chose to live under Satara were each given two sets of terms —one from the British Government and one from the Raja of Satara. The British Government thereby guaranteed their jagirs to them so long as they served the Raja faithfully.

The following chose to serve under the Raja:

Jagirdar	Revenue (Rs.)	Former contingent	New contingent
Pratinidhi of Aundh . . .	200,000	None	None
Pant Sachiv of Bhor . . .	200,000	None	None
Raja of Akalkot	370,000	Not specified	100
Nimbalkar of Phaltan . . .	200,000	350	90
Daphle of Jath	150,000	200	50
Shaikh Mira of Wai . . .	21,000	63	10

The following chose to serve under the British:

Jagirdar	Revenue (Rs.)	Former contingent	New contingent
Venkata Rao Ghorpade of Mudhol	150,000	150	20
Venkata Rao Bhave of Nargund .	90,000	112	Cancelled
Narayan Rao Bhave of Ramdurg .	75,000	113	Cancelled

(M.E., *Report*, S.R.J. iv. 153; M.E. to Supreme Government, 17.6.1819, Bg. P.C. 24.7.1819, 6; Abstract, Bg. P.C. 4.3.1820, 18; Aitchison, viii *passim*.)

5

THE SERVANTS OF THE OLD GOVERN-
MENT AND OF THE NEW

'EVERYONE is striving hard to be taken into consideration', reported Robertson the Collector of Poona in July 1818, 'some having just claims, many none, and many with pretended claims on the new government. The chief men here retain a sullenness of humour, though they behave with an apparent cordial acquiescence in the new state of things. With the merchants and the lower classes, the popularity of government continues to increase.'[1]

Many men had been thrown out of work and many others had suffered in a lesser degree as a result of the ending of the war and the establishment of the new government. One of Elphinstone's most important tasks was to conciliate them.

He was soon receiving countless applications for employment. To military men he replied that they could have no service now, but that after the rains a small number of horsemen might be enlisted. To former civil officials he replied that they should wait until the state might require their services. In general his attitude to such applications was cold. 'It is extremely desirable', he explained to the Governor-General, 'to discourage for a time all expectation of aid from our Government that all may exert themselves to find a maintenance by other means and that those only may remain to be provided for who would be totally destitute if our bounty were withheld.'[2]

Of the servants of the former government now unemployed the soldiers were both more numerous and more dangerous to the stability of the new government than the civilians. The problem was the more acute in that the British had recently been at war not only with the Peshwa but also with Holkar, Berar, and the Pindaris. Thereafter, as Elphinstone observed, 'by far the greater part of these armies was no doubt melted into the mass of the population, but the most obstinate and untractable portion joined the Paishwa

[1] H. D. Robertson to M.E., 8.7.1818, Bg. S.C. 29.8.1818, 15.
[2] M.E. to Governor-General, 27.6.1818, Bg. S.C. 31.10.1818, 30.

and replaced the Marhatta cultivators who long since began to quit his army'.[1]

The Peshwa's troops had been deserting in ever-growing numbers after their defeat at Seoni in April 1818. Elphinstone was soon receiving reports from all over the Deccan of 'crowds of horsemen who are dispersing to their villages, worn out with hunger and fatigue'. He himself was so often asked by such men for letters of protection that he issued a proclamation guaranteeing the safety of all who would return quietly to their homes and declaring that any of them who subsequently reverted to the field or took to plunder would be treated as rebels.[2] Towards the middle of May, H. D. Robertson estimated that about 300 men a day were passing through the district of Poona bound for their homes to the south of the Nira.[3] At the same time the Patwardhans were discharging many of their troops. At Satara Grant complained that 'horse foot & dragoons are pouring in upon me from that quarter & I can now enlist 1000 men per week if I choose'. Altogether he thought that there must be between six and seven thousand horse at his disposal: 'there are thousands to be provided for—I have offers from petty Sirdars every day'. 'What is the use of the Jageerdars', he demanded, 'if not to assist in taking off a part of the burden which the late collection of ragamuffins in this country enforces upon us.'[4] From Ahmadnagar Pottinger reported that 'great numbers' of horsemen from the Peshwa's army were actually settling in his districts; he tried to ensure kindly treatment for 'the poor devils who are now coming home alarmed and tired and only anxious to get into their houses to be quiet'.[5]

Between 25,000 and 30,000 horse had served under the Peshwa.[6] What were they to do when the war was over? 'Our great puzzle', as Elphinstone remarked, 'will now be to provide for all the hungry horsemen that will be turned loose in the world.'[7] Moreover, they were in a wretched condition. 'Nothing can exceed their fatigues and their sufferings', he wrote to the Governor-General on 24 May.

[1] M.E. to Governor-General, 18.6.1818, P.R.C. xiii. 394 ff.
[2] M.E. to Governor-General, 9.5.1818, ibid. 346 ff.
[3] H. D. Robertson to M.E., 13.5.1818, Bg. S.C. 31.7.1818, 317.
[4] Grant to M.E., 17.5.[1818], *Elphinstone.*
[5] Pottinger to M.E., 1.5.1818 and 9.5.1818, *Elphinstone.*
[6] M.E. to Governor-General, 18.6.1818, P.R.C. xiii. 394 ff. For other estimates see P.C. Gupta, *Baji Rao and the East India Company*, 173.
[7] M.E. to Carnac, 11.5.1818, *Elphinstone.*

'The horses are so worn out that they can scarcely move, and the men are in rags and bear evident marks of famine on their countenances. So totally dispirited are they that there is no account of their attempting to plunder even for subsistence, but many of them are being dismounted and disarmed by the common villagers.'[1]

The enemy horsemen were not the only ones to cause him worry. In July 1817 Elphinstone had asked Colonel Skinner to send him 500 horsemen from Hindusthan. He was then raising a body of some 5,000 Auxiliary Horse in accordance with the Treaty of Poona, and at that time he needed all the recruits that he could get. Now his position was reversed. And to add to his difficulties he learnt in May that Skinner's recruits were on their way to the Deccan: 'now that the whole Maratta nation is coming on me for service I find Skinner sending me God knows how many rysallas'. He confided to Malcolm, 'I am something like the children of Israel who prayed for quails & God sent them so many that they stank in their nostrils and they were obliged to pray twice as much to get rid of them.'[2] He begged Skinner to send him no more: 'I am overwhelmed with the whole horse of the country whom I must either provide for or let them turn Pindarries & every additional man is a source of perplexity to me.'[3]

But for the time being he decided to let the Peshwa's former troops provide for themselves: 'I do not think they will stir again till after the rains, and I wish that during that interval they should remain unemployed & suffer hardship. This will drive the foreigners to their homes & the villagers to their ploughs.'[4] Those who remained would be, he thought, Marathas born and bred to a military life: these he proposed to enlist as irregular troops, for there was nothing else to do with them.

There would be time for this after the rains. Meanwhile, he had to find vacancies for these prospective recruits by discharging all his Auxiliary Horse who were not of the Peshwa's country. As early as March 1818 he had been making plans to this end. He had then asked Major Cunningham, the Officer Commanding the Poona Auxiliary Horse, to draw up lists distinguishing between those men who were to be kept in service and those who might

[1] M.E. to Governor-General, 24.5.1818, P.R.C. xiii. 384 ff.
[2] M.E. to Malcolm, 16.5.1818, *Elphinstone.*
[3] M.E. to Skinner, 16.5.1818, *Elphinstone.*
[4] M.E. to Munro, 19.5.1818, *Elphinstone.*

be discharged either because they were inefficient or because they were not of 'the military classes'.[1] Among those that he proposed to discharge at the end of the war he also included all 'foreigners' —that is, all who had come from outside the Deccan.[2]

But on further consideration he changed this part of his plan. He found that many of these 'foreigners' belonged as much to the Deccan as to any other place, for they had 'long forsaken their native villages and attached themselves to any camp that offered them a livelihood'. If he discharged them, where would they go? Perhaps they would stay in the Deccan, looking for trouble? On that view of the matter it might be more politic to provide for them than for the Marathas. As he wrote in September 1818,

the direct effect of any indiscriminate dismission of foreigners would be attended with a worse effect than the non-employment of the natives. The latter have returned to their villages where most of them have some (though perhaps very small) means of subsistence, & all have some estate in their families & relations, but the foreigners would scarcely have a choice & certainly would not have an idea but that of joining the first standard that was set up with hopes of plunder or of subsistence by any means.[3]

At the beginning of June the Auxiliary Horse numbered some 7,300. Of these nearly 1,000 were discharged upon the ending of the war. They fell into one of three classes: those who were not of military birth, those who were incompetent as soldiers, or those who had poor horses. All these could safely be discharged: those who were not of military birth would be all the more likely to take to agriculture or some other peaceful pursuit; those who were defective either in their horses or in their military ability would be so much the less dangerous if they did turn to unlawful courses. Seven hundred more of them were soon to be discharged in addition to the first 1,000. In addition Elphinstone decided to discharge 400 who had joined at the beginning of the war, many from the Madras provinces, and who were good soldiers—'perfectly faithful, well behaved, & very capable of any duty, but fit to be reduced as being unlikely to turn plunderers'. The corollary also applied. A division of about 1,000 horse recruited by Malcolm from the remains of Holkar's army Elphinstone decided to keep because he

[1] M.E. to Cunningham, 27.3.1818, Bg. S.C. 31.7.1818, 377.
[2] M.E. to Cunningham, 12.6.1818, Bg. S.C. 31.7.1818, 379.
[3] M.E. to Supreme Government, 26.9.1818, Bg. S.C. 7.11.1818, 26.

thought that if they were discharged they would be sure to join any insurrection that they could find. To temper expediency with justice gratuities of up to six months' pay were granted on discharge.[1] This was all the more necessary in that these men had invested their savings in buying their horses—'We must take care not to ruin fellows who have embarked their property in speculations of this nature.'[2] All told, his reductions brought down the strength of the Auxiliary Horse to its proper establishment of 5,000, but left no room for any large-scale recruitment of the Peshwa's former soldiers. He now thought that those who could not settle down to a peaceful life in the Deccan would probably go to Nagpur.[3]

It was easier to provide for the Peshwa's infantry. They were much more numerous than his cavalry, but Elphinstone thought that they could more easily be enlisted as sibandis or peons.[4] During the war his Collectors had already begun to enlist such men as sibandis. By the end of it there were about 17,000 of them. This was too large a number for the routine tasks of peace. Before the end of his Commissionship he had reduced it to 13,000.[5] Even this was a fair number to be restrained from sedition.

The Arab infantry who formed the backbone of the garrisons of Khandesh could not be so absorbed. They were too turbulent and impatient of discipline for Elphinstone seriously to consider it. There was only one thing to be done: 'I can think of no other way of disposing of them', Elphinstone told Briggs, 'except sending them to Arabia.' There were disadvantages to this. 'It is an inconvenient and expensive arrangement to which the Arabs will reluctantly consent and which will fill Arabia with enemies to the British name.'[6] But there was no alternative. The Arabs were therefore offered a free passage to Arabia. As an inducement to go quietly they were offered Rs.10 each as a gratuity on embarkation. Only those who had families in Khandesh or who were trading there were allowed to stay and they only on completion of a security bond.[7] There were moments of tension during their journey to the coast. On one occasion, for example, a certain Lieutenant Carr was

[1] Ibid. [2] M.E. to Cunningham, 31.5.1818, *Elphinstone.*
[3] M.E. to Supreme Government, 26.9.1818, Bg. S.C. 7.11.1818, 26.
[4] M.E. to Governor-General, 18.6.1818, P.R.C. xiii. 394 ff.
[5] M.E., *Report*, S.R.J. iv. 157.
[6] M.E. to Briggs, 11.3.1818, Bg. S.C. 31.7.1818, 89.
[7] Briggs, Proclamations, n.d., Bg. S.C. 31.7.1818, 166; Bg. S.C. 7.11.1818, 30; Briggs to Jardine, 16.6.1818, Bg. S.C. 31.7.1818, 447.

greatly alarmed to hear that an Arab, Jemadar Abdul Kadir, who thought that he had been defrauded of his pay, had declared: 'We are brave Arabs and will on no occasion be trifled with; fowls are plenty and there are but few cocks.'[1] Colonel Burr, commanding Southern Division of Gujarat, thought it 'a singular expression' and at once reported the episode to the chief of Surat as indicating trouble to come.[2] In fact, however, the operation seems to have been performed quite smoothly.

Over a year later, in October 1819, Elphinstone admitted his inability to provide for more than a small proportion of the unemployed soldiers in the Deccan. At that time, also, many who had gone to seek their fortune in the troubles of Nagpur were returning unsatisfied. He himself would have estimated their numbers at about 10,000 horse and 10,000 foot. The reports from his Collectors, however, gave a much larger total, as follows:

TABLE 3

Unemployed Soldiers in the Deccan, 1819[3]

	Horse	Foot
Khandesh	4,000	1,800
Ahmadnagar	2,500	5,000
Poona	1,800	2,000
Satara	5,000	3,500
Southern Maratha country .	5,000	3,000
	18,300	15,300

But if their numbers were large, they had no leader. Elphinstone took care that all potential leaders of revolt should still have something to lose. Baji Rao, Chimnaji Appa, the great jagirdars—all these were comfortably provided for.

In addition, Elphinstone gave pensions to many lesser men of influence. He gave pensions amounting to Rs.26,400 a year all told to distinguished military men. He gave pensions amounting to Rs.64,500 a year to 'ruined sirdars'—including some of 'the very greatest families in the country' whom the Peshwa had brought to poverty. He gave pensions amounting to Rs.26,500 a year to men who had held positions of the highest authority in the former

[1] Lieut. J. Carr to Col. C. B. Burr, 25.8.1818, Bg. S.C. 31.10.1818, 33.
[2] Burr to J. Elphinston, 26.6.1818, Bg. S.C. 31.10.1818, 32.
[3] M.E., *Report*, S.R.J. iv. 205.

government. He even gave pensions amounting to Rs.21,840 a year to men whose names had been distinguished in earlier times.[1]

From a political point of view alone, Elphinstone thought that these pensions were well worth the expense. As he put it, 'if we had deprived the civil and military servants of every means of maintaining themselves we should have forced them to intrigue and raise insurrections against us whereas we now have some hold on them all from their fear of losing the little they have left if not from gratitude [for] being permitted to enjoy it'.[2] He thought it particularly important to make some provision for the civil and military servants of the Peshwa's Government because the British had annexed almost the whole of the territories which had been subject to that government: 'while any portion of the old state is left, there is always a retreat open for those who are dissatisfied with our management, but when the whole is brought under our dominion, many must remain within our territories who are dissatisfied with their own loss of profit and consequence, and disgusted with the novelty of our institutions and manners'.[3]

He was also anxious to conciliate the Brahmans as a class. Comparatively few of them could have held office under the old government, but the majority must have benefited from the fact that Brahmans held the leading positions in it. It had encouraged their learning and done homage to their religion. However neutral the Company's Government professed to be in all matters connected with religion, the Brahmans would surely notice and dislike the change. Could neutrality either accord with their religious views or satisfy their material needs? Yet their influence over public opinion was considerable. It was therefore necessary to avoid offending them. When the Rev. J. D. Suares wrote suggesting the establishment of mission schools in the Deccan Elphinstone replied:

The Brahmins are the greatest sufferers by the change & from their temporal power & influence as well as by their control over the superstition of natives, they possess the means of creating alarm & disturbance

[1] M.E. to Supreme Government, 26.10.1819, Bg. P.C. 4.3.1820, 20; Abstract, n.d., ibid. 22 ff.; M.E., *Report*, Appendix No. 11, B.C. 697/18921, 690. Among those of high authority in the former government he included Chimnaji Narayan (Rs.3,000 a year); Rang Dikshit, Moro Dikshit's son (Rs.3,000); Narayan Dikshit, Moro Dikshit's brother (Rs.1,200); Waman Rao Apte, who had long worked in the Peshwa's secretariat (Rs.1,000). He also included men like Ramchandra Sukharam Joshi, 'a respectable Mamlutdar now poor and blind' (Rs.300).

[2] M.E. to Governor-General, 20.6.1820, *Elphinstone.*

[3] M.E. to Governor-General, 18.6.1818, P.R.C. xiii. 394 ff.

to a degree that renders the utmost prudence & vigilance necessary on our part. No engine could be put into the hands of this discontented priesthood so powerful as an opinion that we entertained even the remotest design of converting the people.[1]

It was therefore Elphinstone's policy to exclude missionaries from the Deccan. But professed missionaries were not the only ones eager to convert the heathen. Unknown to the Government, Lieutenant Jacobs, an officer of the Bombay Artillery, was making valiant attempts to do so. He entered the Deccan on military duty. When he joined his post at Sirur in 1819 he brought with him Christian tracts and school textbooks in Marathi. He subsequently reported to the Church Missionary Society that he had found many opportunities to distribute them among Brahmans and 'the very few of the other castes who could read'.[2] Again, when W. H. Mill[3] visited the Deccan in 1822 he distributed some vernacular translations from the New Testament.[4] However, it may be supposed that Elphinstone was in the main successful in discouraging missionary activity in the Deccan.

There were other ways also in which he tried to avoid offending the Brahmans. When some citizens of Pandharpur told him that liquor shops had recently been opened there contrary to the practice of the former government he at once wrote to Grant to have them closed:

This innovation which is no doubt made without your knowledge gives great offence on account of the sanctity of the place and I should on that principle alone wish it discontinued; but it is also my wish to keep up as much as possible (at least until there is time to consider the subject) all the existing prohibitions regarding the sale of spirituous liquors which give the inhabitants of this country a manifest advantage in point of sobriety over those of many of our own provinces.[5]

Besides merely avoiding the giving of offence to Brahmans, Elphinstone also took more positive steps to secure their acceptance of the new state of things.

During the war, Elphinstone's proclamation of Satara had guaranteed that the Company's authority would be established

[1] M.E. to J. D. Suares, 3.11.1818, *Elphinstone*.
[2] Jacobs to Church Missionary Society, 1.4.1822, *C.M.S. Archives*, Western India Mission Letters Received, i. 48 ff.
[3] William Hodge Mill, first Principal of Bishop's College, Calcutta.
[4] Bodleian MS. Mill 205, May 1822.
[5] M.E. to Grant, 18.1.1819, Bg. P.C. 13.2.1819, 25.

'without prejudice to the watans, inams and allowances' already in existence. But in October 1818 the Resident at Malwan urged the Bombay Government to allow him to resume all lands granted for the support of temples and substitute a cash allowance from the government treasury.[1] The question was referred to Elphinstone. He strongly opposed the idea, 'conceiving that any alteration at present would excite alarm and create doubt of the stability of the grants guaranteed by the proclamation of Sattarah'. He added that such arrangements could only be made if the parties concerned agreed and even so not until conditions were settled.[2] The Supreme Government endorsed his view.[3]

Not only did he respect temple lands, he also continued certain cash payments which the former government had made to temples of note—for example, Rs.12,000 a year to the temple of Trimbak.[4]

He also attended to the supplications of individual Brahmans of note—in this he was unlike Robertson. In July 1818 the shastris of Poona presented Robertson with a petition and told him that there were then in Poona at least 'eight thousand indigent Brahmins who had subsisted on the religious charity of Bajee Row'. They added that they hoped that the new government would also provide for them. Robertson rather tactlessly tried to persuade them that they were being unreasonable:

'I explained to the shastrees', he told Elphinstone, 'that no govt. ever exceeded the British for its impartial consideration of the rights of all men, that the principles of the govt. were founded on justice and reason, and that I was vexed to see a body of men whom it was the wish of the Government to respect, bringing me a complaint which if they themselves would calmly deliberate on the subject of it, they would acknowledge to be unreasonable.' Robertson was highly satisfied with the success of his logic: 'from one step to another we advanced in our reasoning till we agreed in the conclusion that their becoming dependant on Bajee Row had been almost entirely optional, in fact that these men had left their homes in other quarters in expectation of being cherished by him. I also proved to them from their own acknowledgement that their subsistence was as precarious as the temper of Bajee Row was capricious

[1] Hale to Bombay Government, 13.10.1818, Bg. P.C. 5.12.1818, 41.
[2] M.E. to Bombay Government, 8.11.1818, ibid.
[3] Supreme Government to M.E., 5.12.1818, ibid.
[4] Resolution, Bg. S.C. 14.8.1818, 34.

and that many of them had no certainty even had there been still a Peshwa of their ever again obtaining any pecuniary aid.'[1]

They were particularly anxious that the new government should continue the annual Dakshina festival. The money distributed to the Brahmans on this occasion used to amount to as much as 5 lakhs of rupees.[2] Of this total, from Rs.80,000 to Rs.90,000 were distributed among a relatively small number of Brahmans whose names were registered and who received their gifts at the Peshwa's Palace. These were the most learned Brahmans, and their gifts were 'handsome' and generally in proportion to the learning of each. The rest of the money was distributed indiscriminately among the other Brahmans, who assembled at the Parvati temple to receive them. These gifts were 'trifling' in size—between 7 and 20 rupees—and Robertson thought that they did 'little or no good to individuals', besides being a great expense to the Government. On the other hand, he wrote, 'I have no doubt but that if the most learned men were brought to look up to the govt. for support, they would willingly do any service the govt. should wish such as revising the laws of the Shaster or settling their doubtful and disputed meaning.'[3]

Elphinstone himself had formed the conclusion at the end of the war that 'it would be worthy of a liberal government to supply the place of the Paishwa's indiscriminate charities by instituting a Hindoo College at one or both of the sacred towns of Nassick and Wye'. The Peshwa's whole religious expenditure he estimated to have been nearly 15 lakhs of rupees. 'It would be absurd to imitate this prodigality', he thought. All told he planned to allow 2 lakhs of rupees for religious expenses. An additional amount he thought would be spent by the Raja of Satara, 'whom it would probably be impossible to restrain from this sort of expense even if it were necessary'.[4] After some reflection he decided in October 1819 to abandon the expensive idea of two colleges. Instead he kept up that part of the Dakshina ceremony which consisted in fact in the giving of prizes to the most learned Brahmans of the Deccan. In the first year of the new government these prizes amounted to Rs.50,000. The rest of the ceremony, which as he said had 'degenerated into a mere giving of alms', he abolished—although its abolition was

[1] H. D. Robertson to M.E., 13.7.1818, Bg. S.C. 5.9.1818, 2.
[2] M.E., *Report*, 56.
[3] H. D. Robertson to M.E., 13.7.1818, Bg. S.C. 5.9.1818, 2.
[4] M.E. to Governor-General, 18.6.1818, P.R.C. xiii. 394 ff.

'extremely unpopular'. He proposed, moreover, to change the nature of the prize-giving: 'most of the prizes, instead of being conferred on proficients in Hindoo Divinity, might be allotted to those most skilled in more useful branches of learning, law, mathematics, etc. and a certain number of professors might be appointed to teach those sciences. These means, with the circulation of a few well-chosen books . . . would have a better, and more extensive effect, than a regular college, and would cost much less to the Government.'[1]

He also allotted Rs.14,000 a year in pensions to 'learned shastrees selected from those on whom Bajee Row used to lavish such large sums'. Mulhar Shroti, for example, whom Robertson considered 'the most highly respected Brahmin in the country', was given Rs.800 a year; Nilakantha Shastri, renowned for his knowledge of the shastras, was given Rs.1,200 a year; Raghu Acharya, 'an eminent scholar', who later became Principal of the Poona Hindu College, was given Rs.600 a year.[2]

It was not only the Brahmans who retained some of their privileges under the new government. The proclamation of Satara had guaranteed to all their 'watans, inams and allowances' provided that they submitted within two months. That was in February 1818. When the time limit expired in April 1818 Elphinstone told his Collectors that they should resume the inams only of 'conspicuous persons or those who have been active against us'.[3] There was no general resumption. The grants thus retained by their existing holders amounted to 24 lakhs of rupees.[4]

Jagirs were not specifically guaranteed by the proclamation of Satara. In consequence, individual arrangements were made with the great jagirdars. All other jagirdars were left in possession of their lands if they had held them before the reign of Baji Rao. If not, they were given money pensions. Elphinstone tried to encourage jagirdars to commute their jagirs for money pensions by offering as a pension to all who would commute their jagirs a little more than they could have collected from their tenants.[5] The great

---

[1] M.E., *Report*, 56 f.
[2] M.E. to Supreme Government, 26.10.1819, Bg. P.C. 4.3.1820, 20, 22; H. D. Robertson to Chaplin, 10.12.1823, Bom. J.C. 4.2.1824, 754 ff.
[3] M.E. to Collectors, 12.4.1818, Bom. P.C. 6.5.1818, 2780 f.
[4] Rs.2,436,152, i.e. Rs.2,283,365 in government lands and Rs.152,787 in the Patwardhan estates (M.E., *Report*, Appendix, 18).
[5] General rules concerning jagirs encl. with M.E. to Supreme Government, 25.10.1819, Bom. P.C. 17.11.1819, 6264 ff.

majority, however, kept their jagirs. All told, the jagirs confirmed and pensions granted in lieu amounted to 7½ lakhs of rupees.[1]

The Supreme Government suggested the importance of economy in all these grants of jagirs and pensions.[2] That was in March 1820. But by that time Elphinstone was Governor of Bombay, and his government refused to reduce the grants.[3] The Supreme Government accepted the position—but they could hardly have done otherwise, for nearly all the grants had already been made. Moreover, they quite realized the political importance of the grants. All men of influence now had something to lose by open disaffection. Besides, the new government had secured some hold upon their children's loyalty in that hardly any of the grants had been specifically declared to be hereditary: 'every renewal will be a fresh act of grace conferred on the individual receiving it'. Each succeeding generation would have fresh reasons for loyalty and gratitude.[4]

There was little fear of any revolt against the new government. As Munro explained to Chaplin in September 1818, 'Men who are soldiers, and not mere thieves, in order to rise must have a leader, a fixed object and at least some hope of success. There is no respectable jageerdar who would risk his possessions on the chance of overturning our power.'[5]

The kings had departed. The captains had been pensioned off. Horsemen there might be without employment, and foot soldiers too. But what could they do without a leader?

One leader there was, a hero from the jungles of Maharashtra he might seem, a self-styled champion of the Raja of Satara. Some twenty years ago Chhatra Singh, the brother of Shahu II of Satara, had defied the Peshwa and taken refuge with Murari, a Ramusi chief. After years of hardship and adventure he had been captured by Trimbakji and imprisoned in 1811. By then his nephew Pratap Singh was Raja of Satara, but he himself remained in prison, where he died in April 1818. Some three years before this, however, an ascetic had come to Murari and persuaded the old man that he was

[1] Bg. P.C. 4.3.1820, 19.

[2] Supreme Government to Bombay Government, 4.3.1820, Bom. P.C. 17.5.1820, 4316 ff.

[3] Bombay Government to Supreme Government, 11.3.1820, ibid. 4322 ff.

[4] Supreme Government to Bombay Government, 4.3.1820, Bom. P.C. 17.5.1820, 4316 ff.

[5] Munro to Chaplin, 23.9.1818, Gleig, iii. 279 ff.

the real Chhatra Singh escaped from captivity. With the help of
Murari and his band he captured Prachitgarh; from there, so
Elphinstone heard, he 'committed the greatest cruelties in the
country within his reach'. He was still holding Prachitgarh in 1818,
still claiming to be the champion of the Raja of Satara. It was not
until 10 June 1818 that the British finally took Prachitgarh.[1]

It may have been easy enough to deceive Murari who was now
in his old age—Grant described him as 'a poor decrepit little old
man covered with rags and hacked with wounds'. It was quite
another matter for the impostor to gain a united following among
the people. Before the taking of Prachitgarh all the Brahmans
around Grant had been urging him to exterminate the man and his
followers also; on the other hand, the Marathas had been stressing
the advantages of moderation. This difference of opinion Grant
attributed to the atrocities which Chhatra Singh and his followers
had committed upon Brahmans.[2] After his capture, he still claimed
that his plan had been 'to release the Raja of Sattara from the power
of the Brahmins'.[3]

Grant thought that even Colonel Cunningham, who had taken
Prachitgarh, was 'more than half persuaded' that this was the real
Chhatra Singh. To settle the question once and for all Grant called
in 'some respectable men, the known friends & adherents of Chitoor
Singh'. They all declared that this was an impostor.[4] He was condemned to death, but the sentence was subsequently commuted to
perpetual imprisonment. Grant was glad: he thought that this
would be enough 'to ensure his being perfectly insignificant'.[5]

Grant was mistaken. Men sympathized all the more with the
hero, now that he was in prison. Moreover, there was still a general
impression that he was the real Chhatra Singh. All the officers and
men of the 2nd/9th, including Major Thatcher, were convinced that
he was. Indeed they felt so strongly that he was being unjustly treated
that Grant held a public inquiry 'in an open square in the presence
of most of the inhabitants of Sattara and of our cantonment'. At

[1] M.E. to Bombay Government, 21.2.1819, Bom. S.C. 10.3.1819, 846 ff.;
public and private correspondence in Bom. P.C. 15.4.1818, 2501 ff.; Grant to
M.E., 14.6.1818, Bg. P.C. 31.7.1818, 102; Cunningham to Grant, 10.6.1818,
ibid.; Sardesai, New History, iii. 505.
[2] Grant to M.E., 14.6.1818, Bg. P.C. 31.7.1818, 102.
[3] Grant to M.E., 25.1.1819, Bg. P.C. 6.3.1819, 34.
[4] Grant to M.E., 14.6.1818, Bg. P.C. 31.7.1818, 102.
[5] Grant to M.E., 20.6.1818, Bg. P.C. 14.8.1818, 82.

this ceremony the so-called Chhatra Singh publicly confessed that he was an impostor.[1]

Grant then sent him away to Poona to be imprisoned there. But even this did not settle the matter. The impostor's mistress went to live with one Ram Singh, a discharged Naik of the 2nd/9th, who organized a conspiracy to release him, to raise a rebellion in his name, and to overthrow British rule in the Deccan. Elphinstone thought Ram Singh 'a man of some talent and great enterprise'. But 'the plot was feeble and insignificant'. Between thirty and forty horse were engaged together with a number of Chhatra Singh's old followers. But the sepoys were unaffected.[2] Elphinstone thought little of the affair—'a number of unemployed Carkoons & starving horsemen with a few *discharged* sepoys of our own army'.[3] 'We have had a little plotting at Poona, but all among poor starving wretches & without any encouragement from the great:'[4] The reasons for their failure were obvious enough—'there being no money and no character among the conspirators'.[5]

Hitherto it had been Elphinstone's policy that offences against the state should be dealt with by a summary trial. Now that the country was more settled he thought that the trial of offences against the state should be assimilated to that of other types of offence. In other words, they should be tried according to the practice of the country before the local officer who should decide on the question of guilt and ask the Pandit of his court to pronounce sentence according to Hindu law. This sentence was always to be followed 'unless repugnant to natural reason and justice, or to the practice of the Maratta country'. But Pandits would probably declare merely that traitors should be banished, whereas in fact under the Peshwa traitors had been blown from guns. Elphinstone approved of this latter punishment in true Benthamite fashion: it contained, he said, 'two valuable elements of capital punishment; it was painless to the criminal and terrible to the beholder'.[6] He concluded that 'it seems inexpedient therefore to call for the opinion of the Pundit', and decided that traitors should be blown from guns. There was

[1] Grant to M.E., 25.1.1819, Bg. P.C. 6.3.1819, 34; M.E. to Bombay Government, 21.2.1819, Bom. S.C. 10.3.1819, 846 ff.
[2] M.E. to Bombay Government, 21.2.1819, ibid.
[3] M.E. to Newnham, 8.2.1819, *Elphinstone*.
[4] M.E. to Sir W. Keir, 15.2.1819, ibid.
[5] M.E. to Supreme Government, 21.2.1819, Bg. P.C., 8.4.1819, 8.
[6] Colebrooke, ii. 75.

another reason also for not referring to the Pandits: the fact that their lawbooks would exempt Brahmans from capital punishment. A few Brahmans were involved in this conspiracy, and on general grounds, too, Elphinstone's policy was to set aside this exemption in cases of treason and banditry, the more so because of 'the peculiar interest of the Brahmins in the re-establishment of the former government'.[1]

The affair was over by February 1819. Three of the ringleaders were sentenced to be blown from guns, two others to be transported for life.[2] Later on, the so-called Chhatra Singh was sent to Bengal to be imprisoned there. He landed at Calcutta with his family in January 1823, and was at once confined in the Fort.[3] That was the end of his adventures.

It was in keeping with Elphinstone's general policy of conciliating those likely to suffer most from the change of government that he was anxious to employ former servants of the Peshwa's Government wherever possible. A few Englishmen there had to be, as Collectors and Assistant Collectors. He had no difficulty in finding them. Indeed, he had far too many applications for posts from Englishmen. Wave after wave they rolled in upon him.[4] As early as July 1818 he was complaining to Malcolm: 'I am complete above the establishment & still have a hundred claimants.'[5] But there were to be as few Englishmen as possible. He decided, however, to bring in some Indians from the Company's old provinces, 'as well from general policy, in a new conquest, as to introduce some models of system and regularity'.[6]

In view of his sympathy with Munro's principles, and also for geographical convenience, it was only natural that he should send to Madras for these experts. Munro himself strongly urged him to employ some outside men: 'the Poona servants', he wrote, 'are the most deficient I have met with in any part of India'.[7] Besides introducing more efficiency Elphinstone hoped that the importation of

---

[1] M.E. to H. D. Robertson, 9.2.1819, Bg. P.C. 8.4.1819, 9.
[2] M.E. to H. D. Robertson and J. Lumsden, 18.2.1819, ibid.
[3] J. Vaughan (Town Major, Fort William) to Bengal Government, 22.1.1823, Bom. P.C. 26.2.1823, 1041 f.
[4] Cf. Burke's speech on Fox's India Bill.
[5] M.E. to Malcolm, 11.7.1818, *Elphinstone*.
[6] M.E., *Report*, 33.
[7] Munro to M.E., 18.6.1818, *Elphinstone*.

Madras men would reduce corruption: his plan was that they and the Maratha officials should be used by the Collector as a check upon each other.[1] In July 1818 he therefore wrote to Chaplin, who had succeeded Munro at Dharwar, and asked him to send some Madras officials. He wanted to have one Madras official and one Maratha official each holding the parallel post of Daftardar or Division Sherishtadar under every Collector. They were to be the chief Indian officials in the district. He offered them Rs.400 a month and suggested to Chaplin that each Madras man should bring with him a few dependants. One of these dependants he intended to appoint to each Collector's Treasury, either as Treasurer or as Deputy Treasurer, keeping separate accounts and serving as a check upon his Maratha superior or subordinate. This he called 'the Ceded Districts plan of having a Double Dufter'.[2]

Chaplin warned Elphinstone that 'able revenue men fit for Division Sherishtadars were 'a very scarce commodity', but he promised to do his best.[3]

Soon he sent along Hanumant Rao, who went to help Grant at Satara. Hanumant Rao had for many years held the rank of Division Sherishtadar in the Ceded Districts. He had been one of the two chief men in the office of the Collector of Bellari. Since then he had been in charge of the extensive district of Raidurg, the revenue of which was in the region of Rs.3 or 4 lakhs. His salary was then Rs.250 a month. He resigned that post to go to Satara.[4] Grant liked him at once: 'he is an old fellow, intelligent, though he shuts his eyes or looks on the ground & goes on with what I fancy are the Madras regulations without looking to the right nor the left—& when you ask him a question he repeats the last sentence of his discourse'.[5] Elphinstone soon decided that Hanumant was more needed at Ahmadnagar. Grant was sorry go see him go: 'he is a most invaluable old fellow, brimful of information, and a very Tom Munro in clear distinct answers. He has enlightened me in some things and satisfied me in many.'[6] Elphinstone decided that he and his colleague in the double daftar at Ahmadnagar should each have Rs.500 a month. Elphinstone took care to explain to

[1] M.E., Circular to Collectors, 10.7.1818, Bg. S.C. 29.8.1818, 9.
[2] M.E. to Chaplin, 9.7.1818, *Elphinstone.* Dufter = daftar = office.
[3] Chaplin to M.E., 16.7.1818, *Elphinstone.*
[4] Chaplin to M.E., 4.8.1818, ibid.; M.E. to Pottinger, 19.9.1818, ibid.
[5] Grant to M.E., n.d., ibid.
[6] Grant to M.E., n.d., ibid.

Pottinger the difficulty of Hanumant Rao's position: 'His is a very invidious dangerous office—to find fault with many things that you have approved, to accuse some of your people of ignorance, some of corruption, & to din into your ears the regulations & the practice of Madras in opposition to the much pleasanter rule of pleasing yourself & often in opposition also to the reason of the case.'[1] Hanumant Rao later rejoined Chaplin, and when the latter succeeded Elphinstone as Commissioner, Hanumant became his 'revenue oracle' and head daftardar at Poona.[2] On retirement he was given a jagir worth Rs.4,000 a year.[3] He trained up his son Krishna Rao in revenue work, and his son eventually succeeded him.[4] Altogether, Hanumant served the Company for over thirty years.[5]

Chaplin also sent Lakshman Rao, who had long been employed in revenue work under Munro 'with distinguished credit'. Chaplin thought that his qualities were more than administrative: he was 'an able & fit person to employ in negotiations with native chiefs and their wukeels, as he possesses in some perfection a degree of readiness of reply, and a talent of refuting objections, which are not often met with'. He was 'also particularly clever in giving a short intelligible abstract of long diffuse statements'. But he had 'a disposition to show favor and affection to Brahmans and other privileged personages'. He also had 'a slight inclination to intrigue'.[6] Munro, too, thought him 'very timid, and a great believer in plots'.[7] Like Hanumant, Lakshman brought some other Madras men with him. For some time he stayed at Poona, and Elphinstone, who intended eventually to send him to Khandesh, found it difficult to dispense with him. Robertson took over all the men he brought with him.[8] At last Lakshman Rao reached Khandesh in August 1819, accompanied by several Kanarese Brahmans who were relatives of his, and some other dependants as well. Many of them were at once sent out into the districts as Mamlatdars.[9]

Others there were, sons of Maharashtra, able if ambitious men, who gave useful service to the British. Balaji Pant Natu is the best

[1] M.E. to Pottinger, 19.9.1818, *Elphinstone.*
[2] Chaplin to M.E., 17.8.1823, *Elphinstone.*
[3] Chaplin to Bombay Government, 12.9.1822, Bom. P.C. 25.9.1822, 4842 f.
[4] Bell, *Briggs,* 181.
[5] Chaplin to Bombay Government, 12.9.1822, Bom. P.C. 25.9.1822, 4842 f.
[6] Chaplin to M.E., 16.8.1818, *Elphinstone.*
[7] Munro to Chaplin, 22.9.1818, Gleig, iii. 279 ff.
[8] M.E. to Briggs, 30.10.1818, *Elphinstone.*
[9] Briggs to Chaplin, 16.4.1825, para. 48, B.C. 1022/28050, 376.

known—perhaps notorious. No doubt he was wise in his generation. But he had some reason for resentment against Baji Rao. He
had been Khande Rao Raste's servant. Before his master died in
disgrace—according to rumour because he had declined to permit
his wife to kiss the threshold of the Peshwa—he had made Balaji
guardian of his children. Balaji, while attempting to interest Colonel
Close in their welfare, had himself found reasons for going often to
the Residency; Elphinstone valued his information, and for some
time he was Elphinstone's 'chief native agent'.[1] Elphinstone now
sent him to Satara at Grant's request on a salary of Rs.500 a month.
In addition, he was granted, at Elphinstone's recommendation,
three inam villages in the Poona Collectorate and two in the Ahmadnagar Collectorate; their total annual revenue was assessed as
Rs.11,981.[2] Elphinstone pointed out that such a grant was advisable 'as it is the first reward yet made to any of our immediate
dependants and as the zeal with which we are served must depend
on those rewards'.[3] Balaji was also allowed to accept two inam
villages from the Raja of Kolhapur: Elphinstone's view was that
although as a rule such grants from Indian princes should not be
accepted by anyone in the Company's service, nevertheless an
exception could be made in this instance, especially as he had
'explained to the Raja of Colapoor's vakeel that the grant of
Chikoree was determined on by Government on grounds independent of any influence that Ballajee Punt could have used, and
that this liability could not be the means of promoting His Highness's future views'.[4] That the Raja was anxious to make the grant
in spite of this assurance indicates the prestige acquired by the man
whom Elphinstone delighted to honour.

Grant thought that Balaji Pant was 'a devilish fine fellow: he
makes no difficulties and he comprehends what he is told in a
moment'.[5] Nine months later this opinion had to be qualified:
'Ballajee with all his sound judgement is easily prejudiced.' But
Grant did find him very valuable for some time. He, too, brought
with him some dependants, but after discovering certain corrupt

---

[1] Grant-Duff, *History*, ii. 470 n.; Sardesai, *New History*, iii. 450 n.; M.E. to
Grant, 8.4.1818, Bg. S.C. 31.7.1818, 131.

[2] Memorandum, n.d., Bg. P.C. 3.10.1818, 28.

[3] M.E. to Supreme Government, 5.9.1818, ibid. 25.

[4] M.E. to Grant, 27.10.1818, Bg. P.C. 28.11.1818, 27; Supreme Government
to M.E., 28.11.1818, ibid. 28.

[5] Grant to M.E., 14.7.1818, *Elphinstone*.

practices Grant told him that '*all sins* of people introduced by him are on his head'.[1]

Appaji Krishna Rao, Briggs's other Daftardar, had been 'brought up principally in the Poona Residency'; he had also served in other positions under the British. Briggs asked him to help in the taking over of Holkar's districts, and he remained in Khandesh when Briggs became its Collector.[2] Several years later, when his reputation was damaged, Briggs still remembered 'how much I owed to him, at a time when sickness and a total want of information regarding everything must have rendered me incapable of fulfilling my duties without him'.[3]

Some of the military men who helped in the initial occupation of the new territories were also appointed to civil posts. In Khandesh, Mir Fazl Ali Khan had occupied the country to the east of the Bori River with the help of 300 horsemen and Rs.10,000. Briggs looked upon his work and pronounced that 'it was well done'. He was 'a highly respectable man', related to Murtaza Yar Jang of the Nizam's Court. Briggs appointed him Mamlatdar in the same area on a monthly salary of Rs.400. He was subsequently of great help in dealing with the Bhils of the Satmala hills.[4]

Not all such appointments of military men were as successful. In particular, Elphinstone had many complaints against 'General Munro's conquering Amildars who were well chosen to annoy & disturb the enemy but unluckily continue the same practice towards their subjects & allies.'[5] But, he reflected, 'it was scarcely to be expected that the same fellows that were good to occupy a country would be good to govern it when settled'.[6] Munro himself was not surprised that Ram Rao, whom he called 'my old Lieutenant', had to be dismissed. 'I was aware that he would never be a correct Revenue Servant, and even if he were, that the regular Cutcherry men would contrive some way of removing him. I had known him for many years and therefore would not employ him in 1817 in the Cutcherry at Darwar previous to the war, but the moment hostilities commenced I was aware that he would make

[1] Grant to M.E., 10.5.1819, *Elphinstone*.
[2] Briggs to M.E., 7.12.1818, Bg. P.C. 9.1.1819, 14.
[3] Briggs to M.E., 7.2.1824, *Elphinstone*.
[4] Briggs to Hodges, 14.6.1818, Bg. S.C. 14.8.1818, 30; Briggs to M.E., 1.7.1818, ibid.; Hodges to Huskisson, 30.1.1819, Bg. P.C. 13.3.1819, 28.
[5] M.E. to Russell, 7.8.1818, *Elphinstone*.
[6] M.E. to Grant, 28.8.1818, ibid.

the best war Amildar that could be got.'[1] He was granted a jagir of
Rs.1,200 a year.[2]

Nor were all the civil officials who helped the British during the
war found fit to be employed in more settled times. At Ahmadnagar
the Kazi Shambuddin, after a brief hour of glory, was weighed in
the balance by Pottinger and found wanting. Gibbon testified that
the Kazi 'was the 1st person at Ahmednuggur that seemed cordially
to enter into the interests of the British Government on the breaking out of the war'. Gibbon employed him 'in explaining in the
Mahratta language my orders in the Cutcherry, in reading Mahratta
notes, and at that time pointing out to me the sources from whence
the Revenue was derived under the late Paishwa's Government'.
As Kazi, he was called upon by Gibbon to decide all points of
Islamic law; indeed, 'I always had him near me whenever there
was any case of dispute to settle of any consequence either by
Panchayat or otherwise.' Gibbon understood that the post of Kazi
was hereditary in his family under a charter granted by Aurangzeb.[3]
Pottinger admitted that his title was undisputed. But he thought
that he was quite unsuitable for 'any situation of the least trust
owing to his general character and on account of his neediness'.
Pottinger gathered that he and his father before him had been
'very extravagant and somewhat disreputable people'. Now Shambuddin was in great poverty.[4] When Pottinger came to Ahmadnagar
he found him drawing Rs.40 a month as Kazi and Rs.40 a month
also as Kamavisdar over three villages. He dismissed him from both
positions. But since Gibbon had promised that his successor would
continue him in a salary of at least Rs.40 a month he was granted
a pension of that amount.[5]

The Mamlatdars remained the backbone of the new administration, as they had been of the old. But their position was greatly
changed. Under the old government some had been men of wealth
and power; all had been respected by the people. There had been
little uniformity among them, however. Now both their powers and
their salaries were to be determined by the Government according
to a fixed rule upon one level, and that a low one.[6]

---

[1] Munro to M.E., 3.10.1821, B.C. 762/20696, 12 ff.
[2] Government to Chaplin, 23.10.1821, ibid. 15 f.
[3] Gibbon to Pottinger, 20.10.1818, Bg. P.C. 28.11.1818, 30.
[4] Pottinger to M.E., 27.10.1818, ibid. 31.
[5] Resolution of the Governor-General in Council, Bg. P.C. 28.11.1818, 31.
[6] For details of their new powers see Chap. 6 below.

Under the Peshwa, in some provinces there had been no one between them and the central government: in others, especially the more remote like Khandesh, a Sar Subhedar had intervened. Now in every instance there was a Collector between them and the Deccan Commissioner at Poona. Elphinstone could not find that any definite rule had existed under the old government for determining their allowances; but he thought that before the introduction of the farming system under Baji Rao 'a considerable Mamlutdar' generally received about 1 per cent. of the revenue of his district, in other words from Rs.5,000 to Rs.6,000 a year. Besides this there were large profits to be made, unauthorized but not condemned. Elphinstone concluded from his inquiries and observations that in the old days a considerable Mamlatdar 'was reckoned reasonable if his whole profits did not exceed 5 per cent on the net revenue'.[1] He could find no reliable revenue accounts for the subsequent period under Baji Rao when the post of Mamlatdar was sold to the highest bidder.[2] It was therefore a difficult task to settle the salaries of Mamlatdars under the new government.

In June 1818 Munro advised Elphinstone that the districts of Mamlatdars, or Amildars as he called them, should never be bigger than such as would produce between 1½ and 2 lakhs of rupees in annual revenue, and that until the country was properly settled and its true resources known they should be much smaller—producing from ½ lakh to 1½ lakhs. He thought this limitation essential because 'we have no information that we can depend on respecting the revenue', and there would therefore be much for every man to do; it also seemed desirable to have a good number of Amildars at first 'as it leaves room for selection hereafter'. He and Elphinstone had decided upon a scale of salaries when they met at Satara the previous month; after further consideration he now advised a higher scale: 'I mean that in place of 100 Rs. a month to a District Amil who collects a Lac I would make it 120 to 150 and below a Lac on the same scale—above a Lac and a half the former one is high enough.'[3]

Elphinstone followed Munro's advice in the instructions which he issued to his Collectors in July 1818. He told them to divide their Collectorates into taluks or districts producing between ½ and

[1] M.E., *Report*, 24.
[2] Ibid. 30.
[3] Munro to M.E., 18.6.1818, *Elphinstone*.

1 lakh; a Mamlatdar's pay should vary between Rs.150 and Rs.70 a month in proportion to the size of his taluk.[1]

To men with such heavy responsibilities the new salaries must have seemed small indeed. Moreover, under the new government they no longer had had the same opportunities as they had had in the past to make unofficial profits through the farming of the revenue. There were no doubt other ways in which they were able to supplement their lawful salaries. Pottinger in Ahmadnagar suggested that corrupt practices enabled them to increase their salaries by about a half.[2] But it may be supposed that in general the result of the new system must have been a considerable decline in their economic position.

This seems to have been accompanied by a decline in the quality of the men appointed. 'The character of our Mamlutdars', wrote Elphinstone in 1819, 'is not entirely what we could wish, as the country was occupied before the Paishwa's cause was desperate; few of his adherents would venture to join us, and we were obliged to employ such persons as we could procure, without much regard to their merit.' This did not apply to Satara, and he was satisfied that both there and in Poona the Mamlatdars were 'respectable servants of the old Government'.[3] But in general he attached great importance to the aim of 'raising our Mamlutdars to a rank which might render it creditable for Native gentlemen to associate with them'.[4] This he thought might help to bridge the gap which British governments had elsewhere set between themselves and their subjects.

As he considers this problem the realism of the utilitarian spirit gives a harsh, cutting edge to his thought:

All places of trust and honour must be filled by Europeans. We have no irregular army to afford honourable employment to persons incapable of being admitted to a share of the Government, and no Court to make up by honours and empty favour for the absence of the other more solid objects of ambition. As there are no great men in our service we cannot bestow the higher honours; and the lower, on which also the Natives set

[1] M.E., Circular to Collectors, 10.7.1818, Bg. S.C. 29.8.1818, 9. At first a taluk was not to be bigger than Rs.70,000. For the actual size of taluks see Chaplin to Government, 20.8.1822, para. 179, S.R.J. iv. 486; Ahmadnagar, Rs.81,000; Khandesh, Rs.90,000; Poona, Rs.125,000; Dharwar, Rs.150,000.
[2] Pottinger, Memorandum, n.d., enclosed with Chaplin to Government, 20.8.1822, S.R.J. iv. 723.
[3] M.E., *Report*, 32.   [4] Ibid. 45.

a high value, as the privilege of using a particular kind of umbrella, or of riding in a palankeen, cease to be honours under us from their being thrown open to all the world. What honours we do confer are lost from our own want of respect for them, and from our want of sufficient discrimination to enable us to suit them exactly to the person and the occasion, on which circumstances the value of these fanciful distinctions entirely depends.[1]

He concluded that the Mamlatdars must have higher salaries and other rewards, especially grants of land for life or even for two or three lives. Not only would this improve their conduct, it would also have the result of 'spreading over the country a number of respectable persons attached to the Government and capable of explaining its proceedings'. Indeed, the Government might well be stricter in resuming old jagirs on the death of their present holders: 'we should gain more of useful popularity by grants of this kind, than we should lose by dispossessing the heirs of many of the present Jageerdars'.[2] But he did not pursue this last idea.

He thereupon devised a higher scale of salaries for Mamlatdars and Daftardars, rising to a maximum of Rs.1,000 a month.[3] The reactions of the Governor-General in Council were mild: 'His Excellency observes that the allowances proposed for the Mamlutdars, Dufturdars and others are on a higher scale than those usually held by the native servants of our Government. This point involves general questions of great interest and importance, as well as others of a local nature.' With this comment, together with a general exhortation to economy, the Governor-General in Council left the question to be settled by the Bombay Government, because a week after he had submitted his proposals to the Supreme Government Elphinstone had become Governor of Bombay and the Deccan was at the same time annexed to that Presidency.[4]

Elphinstone postponed further discussion of the matter until the forthcoming visit of Sir Thomas Munro, the new Governor of Madras, 'whose own opinion would be of the highest value, and who must be fully acquainted with the sentiments of the authorities at home on this and similar subjects.'[5]

Munro's suggestions were all in the direction of moderation.

[1] Ibid.   [2] M.E., *Report*, 46.
[3] M.E. to Supreme Government, 25.10.1819, Bg. P.C., 18.12.1819, 18.
[4] Supreme Government to Bombay Government, 18.12.1819, ibid. 20.
[5] M.E., Minute, n.d., in Minutes of Council for 1.5.1820, Bom. J.C. 3.5.1820, 1860 ff.

Elphinstone accordingly revised his original figures, giving Daftar-dars a maximum of Rs.700 and Mamlatdars between $1\frac{1}{2}$ and 2 per cent. of the revenue of their respective districts.[1]

Of the various groups of Indians from which the new administra-tion was recruited, the Madras men must have had the greatest influence. Elphinstone drew a significant contrast between their ways and those of the old Maratha officials: 'They are more active, more obedient to orders, more exact and methodical than the Mar-rattas; but they introduce forms of respect for their immediate superiors quite unknown here, while they show much less con-sideration for the great men of the country; and are more rough, harsh and insolent in their general demeanour.'[2]

Grant drew a similar contrast when he wrote that the Maratha Brahmans were 'more civil to their inferiors, polite to their equals and less cringing to their superiors' than the inhabitants of the Company's old provinces.[3]

Chaplin was of the same opinion, and with the experience of Madras behind him suggested as a reason the fact that 'in our old territory, the nature of our institutions has in a great degree con-founded all ranks and distinctions of persons, reducing the whole to nearly one common level, with the exception of the few whom we employ in office'.[4]

It was not only the influence of the Madras officials that worked in this direction. Grant, at Satara, with so many of the old officials still in their places, found the same tendency and suggested that the reason might be inherent in the situation of British power: the position of the Mamlatdars was now secure from the influence of the 'gentry' of the country; therefore the Mamlatdars no longer troubled to conciliate them.[5]

H. D. Robertson at Poona also found that the Maratha Mamlat-dars could be as offensive towards the gentry as any new-comer from Madras. Indeed, he said, 'the Mahratta Mamlutdar has fre-

[1] M.E., Minute, n.d., Bom. R.C. 24.5.1820, 2461 ff. Circular approved by Government, 23.5.1820, issued by Chaplin, 27.6.1820. (This is the final version given in Choksey, *Aftermath*, 326 ff.) The average revenue of a Mamlatdar's district was (1822): Poona Collectorate, Rs.125,000; Khandesh, Rs.90,000; Ahmadnagar, Rs.81,000; Dharwar, Rs.150,000 (Chaplin, *Report*, para. 179, S.R.J. iv. 486).
[2] M.E., *Report*, 33.
[3] Grant, *Replies to queries*, 14.2.1822, S.R.J. iv. 674.
[4] Chaplin to Government, 20.8.1822, para. 381, S.R.J. iv. 519.
[5] Grant, *Replies to queries*, 14.2.1822, S.R.J. iv. 674.

quently too much confidence and oftener offends the gentry by a downright assumption of consequence, and an open bearing withal, than by a sly hit cloaked under public zeal'.[1]

There was a serious example of this when the Maratha Mamlatdar of Karar wrote to Chintaman Rao Patwardhan a letter which related that a Karar merchant's servant had been robbed in one of Chintaman Rao's districts and concluded with the following words: 'you will therefore enquire into the business, and send me an answer that I may communicate it to the Hoozoor. These outrages were not usual in your districts. I have now reported the present occurrence; the enquiry must be conducted without listening to the misrepresentations of any one. If you recover the Naick's money, your vigilance will be commended by the Circar.'[2]

On this occasion the insolence of office was quickly punished: Chaplin dismissed the Mamlatdar for his incivility. But the general tendency seems to have been felt everywhere. Nor was it confined to the Indian officials of the new government.

Elphinstone and his Collectors had the best intentions. Robertson, for example, tried to establish terms of friendship with his chief Indian officials. Yet his attitude seems a little patronizing: 'The Madras Mamlutdars', he wrote, 'have not the confidence of believing themselves gentlemen, and if I attempt to make them fancy they are, by offering them a chair, they commence bowing and scraping and hoping to be pardoned for presuming to take such a liberty.'[3] Elphinstone himself noted with approval the difference between the behaviour of Bengalis and Marathas towards Englishmen. Sir Henry Strachey had said that there was scarcely a Bengali in his district who would sit down in the presence of an English gentleman. 'Here', remarked Elphinstone, 'every man above the rank of a Hircarrah sits down before us, and did before the Paishwa; even a common ryot, if he had to stay any time, would sit down on the ground.' He was most anxious that friendly relations between the Marathas and English officials should continue, and he thought that the best means of securing this was 'for gentlemen to receive the Natives often, when not on business'. Yet even he wrote

---

[1] H. D. Robertson, *Replies to queries*, 10.10.1821, S.R.J. iv. 592.
[2] Chaplin to Government, 20.8.1822, para. 382, S.R.J. iv. 519 f. Hoozoor = huzur = the presence, superior authority, government; circar = sarkar = government.
[3] Robertson, *Replies to queries*, 10.10.1821, S.R.J. iv. 592.

that 'the society of the Natives can never be in itself agreeable; no
man can long converse with the generality of them without being
provoked with their constant selfishness and design, wearied with
their importunities, and disgusted with their flattery'.[1]

This may be the irritation of fatigue: the words were written in
1819 when he was working to the full extent of his powers. Yet the
allusion to flattery shows that even he with all his sympathy for
Indian customs was yet liable to be deeply offended by such a
difference in the conventions of polite behaviour—he more than
many perhaps in this one respect. Moreover, the comparative ab-
scence of social intercourse between Indians and English officials
meant that there was little opportunity for patterns of behaviour
acceptable to both to emerge. The main reason why Hindus were
unwilling to share in the Englishmen's social life was no doubt
their religious objection to eating and drinking with them. English
officials at this time may well have wanted to develop friendly
relations with Indians. But since in fact they had few Indian
friends, if any, the existence of Indian customs like sati which they
despised, together with their own position as a governing minority,
could easily give rise to feelings of contempt for Indians as
such.

Elphinstone himself was well aware of this tendency. Chaplin,
too, was so anxious to urge his Collectors to be polite towards 'the
Native Gentry' that he went so far as to quote Shakespeare in an
official report: 'Man proud man! Drest in a little brief authority',
and so on. A year later, in 1823, he even issued some circular
instructions to his Collectors on the matter, emphasizing the
anxiety of government 'that they should endeavour to conciliate
the gentry of the country'. In this letter, as elsewhere, he argued
that both from humanity and expediency 'since the change of
government has inevitably deprived the native gentry of much of
their consequence, it is more incumbent on us to continue to them
the forms of civil intercourse'.[2]

At the same time, in 1823, Elphinstone suggested to Briggs that
he should draw up a 'short code of instruction for young Company's
servants which may be put into the hands of writers and cadets on
their first arrival to dispose them to look on the Natives more
favourably than they usually do, and to point out to them the errors

[1] M.E., *Report*, 44 f.
[2] Chaplin to Collectors, 28.5.1823, Choksey, *Aftermath*, 216 ff.

most to be avoided, as well as the modes of conciliation most to be pursued'.[1]

This led eventually to the publication of a book by Briggs— *Letters addressed to a young person in India; calculated to afford instruction for his conduct in general, and more especially in his intercourse with the natives.*

[1] M.E. to Briggs, 13.1.1823, *Elphinstone.*

6

THE DECCAN SYSTEM: THE FOUNDATIONS LAID
(June 1818–October 1819)

ONCE peace had come to the Deccan, Elphinstone was able to give his full attention to the future system of government. As he wrote to Strachey from Poona in February 1819, 'All here is as settled as Benares. There are infinite details but little general politics, and my leisure (except what is wasted in eating & drinking, talking & yawning at others talking etc. etc.) is spent in considering what is to be done in judicial and revenue matters especially the former.'[1]

As Englishmen then thought, these were the main—almost the sole—functions of a government: the maintenance of law and order, the collection of the revenue, and the administration of justice. But these functions were so closely woven into the fabric of Indian village life that any change in them might not merely change its texture but even tear it apart.

Elphinstone realized the danger and sought to avoid it by refraining from changes in the existing order until he had examined its working and could judge what reforms of detail were required to improve the efficiency and preserve the integrity of the whole.

One thing he was convinced was essential: the authority and influence of the village headman must be maintained. 'Zealous cooperation of the Patails is as essential to the collector of the revenue, and to the administration of civil justice, as to the police; and it ought therefore by all means to be secured.'[2]

In order to detect existing abuses he urged his Collectors to 'move about the country', granting 'easy access to all comers, and a ready ear to all complaints'.[3] This was the classic idea of the Collector of the Munro school—the man with wide discretionary powers, constantly travelling about his district, unhampered by forms and ceremonies, always and everywhere accessible to anyone with a complaint or petition.

[1] M.E. to Strachey, 28.2.1819, *Elphinstone.*
[2] M.E., *Report*, 43.
[3] M.E., Circular to Collectors, 10.7.1818, Bg. S.C. 29.8.1818, 9.

Certainly some men seem to have lived up to this ideal—a Munro, a Metcalfe, a Lawrence—men born to rule. But the strain must have been great, and not every man could bear it.

The Deccan Collectors began in good heart. Pottinger, on tour in the Ahmadnagar district in December 1818, writes to Elphinstone: 'I am getting on very well with the ryots. They seem quite delighted and relieved by my *visitation* of them, and I find that even my best Kumavisdars have failed, though I have written them volumes, to give the ryots the explanations and assurances which they ought to have had.'[1]

Briggs also began well in Khandesh. In May 1818 he claims that 'there is hardly a Patail in the country who has not received paun from my hands'.[2] He tells Malcolm, in October 1819, 'I hold a *furyad* Kutcherry from nine to eleven daily, when all complaints are heard, verbally, or written in Mahrattee. A notice to this effect is posted up in every village.'[3]

Elphinstone, then, was relying more upon the men whom he had chosen to be Collectors than upon any comprehensive or detailed measures of policy. As he wrote to his friend Adam at Calcutta: 'The basis of my system is that nothing ought to be altered without great & apparent necessity, at all events not until we thoroughly understand the present system and see how it works. I am convinced the Maratha plan if cleaned of abuses & vigorously acted on will do very well for the people & I should dread to see Judges and chuprassis almost as much as missionaries.'[4]

This meant that the Collectors were to retain the judicial powers entrusted to them during the war in addition to their revenue and other duties. Their power of punishment was limited only by the provision that every sentence of death had to be referred to the Deccan Commissioner for confirmation before it was carried out. Elphinstone's instructions gave considerable discretion to the Collectors in all judicial matters. He authorized them to modify the existing methods and institutions of justice as they found it expedient to do so, but with the general aim of maintaining the Maratha system wherever it was not repugnant to reason and equity.[5]

---

[1] Pottinger to M.E., 31.12.1818, *Elphinstone.*
[2] Briggs to M.E., 26.5.1818, *Elphinstone.* Paun = pan = betel.
[3] Briggs to Malcolm, 17.10.1819, Bell, *Briggs,* 83 ff. Furyad = faryad = complaint.
[4] M.E. to Adam, 11.6.1818, *Elphinstone.*
[5] e.g. M.E. to Pottinger, 2.4.1818, Bg. S.C. 31.7.1818, 89.

He did not go into details. As he himself remarked, 'the language of my instructions . . . was designedly very general, as I was desirous that the original system should be pursued with as little obstruction as possible from new regulations'.[1] This also meant in practice that a Collector might without obstruction introduce almost any modifications into the existing system which he thought fit. There were, indeed, great differences in the way in which justice was administered in different Collectorates.

Although the Collector's powers were great, those of his subordinates were small. Justice and police were both to remain in the hands of 'the heads of villages and other revenue servants', that is to say, the Mamlatdars or their equivalent, the Kamavisdars in Ahmadnagar and the Amildars in the Southern Maratha country. There was no separation of powers. But 'no punishments are to be inflicted except by the Mamlutdars, and their powers are not to exceed fines of 1 or 2 rupees, or imprisonment for two days'.[2] Under the previous government their powers had stopped short only of life and death.[3] The village headmen were now deprived of all power of punishment.[4] Under the previous government there seems to have been no uniform limit to their powers: Chaplin, for instance, found that in the Southern Maratha country they had had 'great latitude of authority in inflicting summary punishments'.[5] Elphinstone was anxious, however, to safeguard the security of their position: he directed that 'Patails must never be displaced but for treason against the State' and that any fines inflicted upon them were to be 'very small, from 4 annas to a rupee'.[6]

Elphinstone's circular letter of July 1818 which contained these general principles also stated that 'the judicial business will be managed by Punchayets whose awards are not to be set aside without some glaring impropriety. Punchayets may be formed in different ways: the best seems to be to allow the parties to choose two members each, but the public officer to nominate the umpire from the most respectable of the inhabitants not in the service of the Government, and not objected to by either party.'[7] These were the panchayats which the British found in operation—ad hoc tribunals

[1] M.E. to Pottinger, 9.11.1818, Bg. P.C. 12.12.1818, 20.
[2] M.E. to Collectors, 10.7.1818, Bg. S.C. 29.8.1818, 9.
[3] Collectors' *Replies to queries*, S.R.J. iv *passim*.
[4] M.E. to Collectors, 10.7.1818, Bg. S.C. 29.8.1818, 9.
[5] Chaplin, *Replies to queries*, 25.6.1819, S.R.J. iv. 274.
[6] M.E. to Collectors, 10.7.1818, Bg. S.C. 29.8.1818, 9.   [7] Ibid.

summoned to decide judicial cases, not permanent self-governing village committees as has sometimes been supposed.[1]

In these instructions, Elphinstone was referring to civil cases, although he did not specifically say so. Grant at Satara was anxious, however, to use panchayats in criminal trials also: 'I have got', he wrote to Elphinstone, 'a large judicial establishment of *Oomedwars* with Neelkunt Shastery at the head—pray am I to establish a Criminal Court or to commence Punchayets, I myself presiding & a Hindoo Judge pronouncing the law. In a case of life and death (without any affectation of being scrupulous) I really do not like the idea of being judge & jury—I wd. much rather have the Punchayet.'[2]

Elphinstone had already given his decision shortly before this: 'the experiment of Punchayets in criminal cases is desirable and Sattara is a better place to begin at than any of our own stations but at present the most desirable of all things is to avoid experiments of every description. We will see about them a year hence.'[3]

As it happened, the experiment was made sooner than that, and elsewhere. Briggs in Khandesh misinterpreted Elphinsone's instructions: he thought that they required him to manage all judicial business, including criminal trials, by panchayat. He later explained to Chaplin that he had for many years been accustomed to assemble panchayats to try criminal offences in the army, and therefore saw nothing strange in the idea of using them to try civilians accused of crimes.[4] He might well have alluded to Elphinstone's war-time instructions to him which contained the following words: 'The Tehsildars must assist you in dispensing justice and I should think the Zemindars and Patails aided by Punchayets (or arbitrations) would be among the best instruments for its administration both civil and criminal where the case was not of sufficient importance to be referred to you.'[5]

[1] Answers to M.E.'s queries, esp. QQ. 5 and 9, S.R.J. iv, 219, 244, 257, 285 This seems to apply in other parts of India besides the Deccan, S.R.J. ii. 181 (Bombay and Gujarat); 22–93 (Bengal); 114–15, 120–1, 134, 174 (Madras). All this is not to deny the existence within particular castes of permanent panchayats exercising administrative functions. Compare *Census of India, 1911*, vol. vii, part 1, Report on Bombay by P. J. Mead and G. Laird Macgregor, especially p. 200 at para. 229, 'The "village Panchayat" fallacy'.
[2] Grant to M.E., 17.7.1818, *Elphinstone*. Oomedwar = umedwar = candidate for office.
[3] M.E. to Grant, n.d., *Elphinstone*.   [4] Briggs to Chaplin, n.d., S.R.J. iv. 906.
[5] M.E. to Briggs, 11.3.1818, Bg. S.C. 31.7.1818, 89. Compare, e.g., M.E. to Pottinger, 2.4.1818, ibid. 105.

Nevertheless, Elphinstone certainly did not intend in his instructions of July 1818 to authorize the use of panchayats in criminal trials. Yet once Briggs had started doing so, he allowed him to continue. Briggs followed no rigid rules in choosing members of criminal panchayats: he never summoned less than five members, but sometimes summoned seven or nine. He usually selected them from the hereditary district officers of the place where the case was to be tried and from other 'persons of respectability, commonly Brahmins' who might be frequenting his office at the time.[1]

The procedure of these courts was as much at Briggs's discretion as their membership, and he boasted of its informality to Malcolm, always an opponent of legal forms and ceremonies: 'This Court is formed according to no particular law, and bound by no particular form, its object being merely to ascertain the truth.' Briggs or his Assistant presided at all important trials, attended on one side by the Shastri, the Kazi, and a clerk, and on the other side by the panchayat.[2]

At first he or his Assistant decided on the punishment, but Elphinstone soon told him to take the written opinion of the Shastri (or Kazi) as to the proper punishment according to Hindu (or Islamic) legal principles and to inflict it 'unless obviously unjust or repugnant to the practice of a civilised nation'.[3] Hitherto Briggs had merely used the Shastri and Kazi to swear in witnesses. Now he found that the Kazi of Dhulia was illiterate: 'when [I] enquired of him to give the Futwa,[4] I for the first time learnt that he could neither read nor write.' Briggs was also dismayed to find that 'my present Shastry has only one law book, but he has no hesitation in reading the passages from it in Court and in explaining the letter as well as the spirit of the law'. Urgent requests issued from Dhulia for more law books and a new Kazi.[5]

There were other discouragements also. Briggs soon became critical of the attitude of panchayat members towards the trial: 'as they derive no direct advantage from it they are slow and careless in their attendance'.[6]

[1] Briggs to Chaplin, n.d., S.R.J. iv. 906 ff.
[2] Briggs to Malcolm, 17.10.1819, Bell, *Briggs*, 83 ff.
[3] Briggs to M.E., 11.12.1818, Bg. P.C. 19.1.1819, 60; M.E. to Briggs, 19.12.1818, ibid. 61.
[4] Futwa = Fatwa = judgement.
[5] Briggs to M.E., 16.1.1819, Bg. P.C. 27.2.1819, 19.
[6] Ibid.

Still, Briggs was confident of the success of the system of criminal panchayats. He thought that public opinion was increasingly
in its favour and that it did secure substantial justice: 'the investigation before a Punchayet of their own countrymen appears to me
to answer the purpose of public and fair trial'.[1]
Elphinstone himself was more concerned with the use of the
panchayat in civil suits than in criminal trials. He called it 'the
great instrument in the administration of Justice'.[2] Certainly it
seemed to have many advantages. The members would probably
have some knowledge of the matter at issue, often also of the personal characters of the parties. This knowledge they could put to
good use during the trial. Why should they restrict themselves to
the evidence produced in Court, like an English jury? Moreover,
'it was an advantage of incalculable value, in that mode of trial,
that the judges, being drawn from the body of the people, could
act on no principles that were not generally understood; a circumstance which'—and here comes a typically Benthamite hit at the
English legal system—'by preventing uncertainty and obscurity in
the law, struck at the very root of litigation'.[3] The press of litigation and the long waiting lists of suitors before the Company's
Courts were often cited as among the main evils of the Cornwallis
system in Bengal.

The panchayat itself might be very slow, but the accumulation
of suits could be avoided by holding a number of different panchayats.[4] This involved no extra expense, either to the Government or to suitors. At Dhulia, for example, as Briggs told Malcolm,
'it frequently happens that four or five Punchayuts are going on at
a time. This system ensures the following great objects of justice:
immediate investigation, full and patient hearing, least possible
expense, and the award being confirmed by an impartial superior,
who is open to complaints against corruption, the only ground of
appeal.'[5] The Company's Courts were remote from the people,[6]
but the panchayat could bring home the administration of justice
to their very doors.[7]

The system certainly seemed popular. Grant from Satara, Chaplin

[1] Ibid.   [2] M.E., *Report*, 58.
[3] M.E., *Report*, 70, corrected by reference to S.R.J. iv. 196.
[4] Ibid.
[5] Briggs to Malcolm, 17.10.1819, Evans Bell, *Briggs*, 83 ff.
[6] M.E., *Report*, 72.
[7] Judicial dispatch to Bengal, 9.11.1814, P.P. 1819, xiii. 518.

from Dharwar, Pottinger from Ahmadnagar, all reported this.[1]
Briggs in Khandesh also thought them 'on the whole popular',
but he added that 'in general the parties would prefer the decision
of an European, upon whom they seem to place much confidence'.[2]
Munro had also come across this phenomenon, at first glance so
flattering to European Judges, but he put a more cynical interpretation on it. When in charge of the Ceded Districts he had written
in 1807 that 'the native who has a good cause always applies for a
punchayet; while he who has a bad one seeks the decision of a
Collector or a Judge; because he knows that it is easier to deceive
them.'[3]

Under Elphinstone's plan the European Collector would merely
hear appeals from panchayat decisions—and then only in the event
of 'some glaring error or abuse'.[4] This finality of decision avoided
one of the defects of the Bengal system in which the facility of
appeal often greatly lengthened the duration of a case.

One of the great virtues of the new panchayat system was that
litigants would not have to wait a long time for their turn to come
before a court. As soon as the headman, Mamlatdar, or Collector
received a complaint, he was to try to reconcile the parties, and
failing that to assemble a panchayat, if he thought that the matter
was serious enough.[5] On the other hand, a panchayat often took a
long time to reach a decision. There were many complaints from
the Collectors about this. 'I cannot get them to clear *their proceedings*', wrote Grant, 'they sit day after day & talk & *kusa, kusa*, but
no decision.'[6] Elphinstone sympathized: 'I suppose the plan of not
allowing Juries to eat originated in their endless discussions. Keep
them hard at it till they agree & they will agree that they may go
about their own business.'[7] This was in September 1818. The
problem was not to be solved as easily as that. Writing to Samuel
Davis in June 1819 Elphinstone was still distressed that:

The Punchayets do not as yet answer so well which is very unlucky as
they are I think our great standby. In former times the members had

[1] *Answers to queries*, S.R.J. iv. 222 f., 261, 290 f.
[2] Ibid. 246.
[3] Munro to Collectors, Ceded Districts, 15.8.1807, para. 24, S.R.J. i. 106.
[4] Notes of instructions to Mamlatdars, 14.7.1818, Bg. P.C. 12.12.1818, 20.
[5] M.E. to Davis, 17.6.1819, *Elphinstone*.
[6] Grant to M.E., 8.9.[1818], *Elphinstone*. Italics underlined in original. Kuas
= (?) Kasa = how?
[7] M.E. to Grant, 10.9.1818, *Elphinstone*.

often the stimulus of a bribe from one or other of the parties & worked hard to earn their reward. Still they were very tedious & did not always come to any decision. Now, when a man has no inducement to serve in Punchayets but public spirit, the members cannot be got to attend & when they do meet their inexperience prevents their getting rapidly through business. The sickness of a member or the death of a relation has thus time to intervene & the Court adjourns Sine Die. The great judicial duty of the Collector & his Assistant is to keep the Punchayets moving & when by dint of constant messages & expostulations they keep a Punchayet together the danger is that the members get weary and readily sign their names to any sort of decision which one of their number (perhaps bribed into activity) may draw up.[1]

Lumsden, Robertson's assistant at Poona, was glad to find that several Brahmans regularly attended his Court every day and willingly sat on all his panchayats: 'I was pleased with this and only regretted I could not get sixty or seventy instead of six or seven of their disposition.' But he came to hear complaints about their corruption, and in a few months he 'civilly dismissed them'. Yet he had such difficulty in finding others to replace them that he took them back again. But the complaints then recurred, until in March 1819 he concluded that there was enough behind them to warrant the final dismissal of these eager administrators of justice.[2]

This was an earnest of a development which Elphinstone wished to avoid—the growth of a class of men who made their living by serving on panchayats. To have paid the members of panchayats for their trouble might have increased the number of volunteers and improved their attendance, but Elphinstone decided against it in order neither to encourage such an evil as this nor to provide a possible incentive for delay.[3]

Lumsden tried a more drastic method of securing regularity in attendance: he began to fine members who arrived very late. But the Shastri of his Court soon told him that this practice was becoming so unpopular that if he persisted in it no one would agree to serve on a panchayat at all. He therefore abandoned the experiment.[4]

It was not only the members who might delay proceedings. Briggs in Khandesh found that the party with the weaker case often

[1] M.E. to Davis, 17.6.1819, *Elphinstone*.
[2] W. Lumsden to H. D. Robertson, 18.5.1819, Bg. P.C. 27.11.1819, 6.
[3] M.E. to Davis, 17.6.1819, *Elphinstone*. The second argument against the payment of panchayat members is stated, e.g., in M.E. to Briggs, 20.1.1819, Bg. P.C. 13.2.1819, 27.
[4] Lumsden to H. D. Robertson, 18.5.1819, Bg. P.C. 27.11.1819, 6.

protracted the investigation by various devices like referring to papers or witnesses at some distance from the Court.[1] Elphinstone authorized him to collect the expenses of witnesses from the party who summoned them unless he had been forced to summon them by his opponents' 'litigious spirit or denial of the truth'.[2] Clearly, the success of the panchayat system would depend in large measure upon the ability and sympathies of the Collectors.

Pottinger, for one, hardly seemed enthusiastic about panchayats. He established a judicial system of his own devising in the Ahmadnagar Collectorate whereby either he or the Mamlatdars dealt with every case unless the parties agreed to accept the decision of a panchayat. Pottinger told Elphinstone that although in accordance with the latter's wishes he recommended suitors to make use of panchayats, he himself doubted their value and had hardly ever felt any confidence in the justice of their decisions.[3] Elphinstone accordingly told him to give more scope to panchayats.[4]

On the other hand, H. D. Robertson at Poona said that he had never come across a panchayat decision that he disagreed with. He had indeed had to decide several cases because the parties could not agree upon a panchayat. But he then found that others were thus encouraged to bring their suits to him, and so he confined his judicial hearings to criminal trials. He was soon forced to the conclusion that his organization could not cope with the amount of civil justice to be done—'I am surrounded by persons seeking redress the moment I appear in the streets.' Much of his Court's time was taken up by criminal trials. He therefore asked Elphinstone to allow him to appoint two or three learned Shastris to help him in criminal trials and in civil appeals. This he thought would 'not only prevent injustice but give a tone to our administration'. Moreover, 'the advancement of Shastrees of real merit to situations of so much dignity would please the Brahmins highly'.[5]

Elphinstone approved of the appointment of 'eminent Shastrees with handsome salaries to form a Court of cases of first importance'.[6] But Robertson could not find suitable men to appoint. Those whom he had been considering for these posts either thought themselves

[1] Briggs to M.E., 16.1.1819, Bg. P.C. 13.2.1819, 27.
[2] M.E. to Briggs, 20.1.1819, ibid.
[3] Pottinger to M.E., 29.10.1818, Bg. P.C. 12.12.1818, 20.
[4] M.E. to Pottinger, 9.11.1818, ibid.
[5] H. D. Robertson to M.E., 28.7.1818, Bg. P.C. 17.10.1818, 45.
[6] M.E. to Robertson, 4.9.1818, ibid. 46.

'too good and holy' for the work or were thought by others 'too partial, too ignorant or too corrupt'.[1]

On the whole, however, the panchayat system seemed to work quite well at Poona under Robertson and Lumsden—two able men who were both eager for it to succeed. Some supervision was essential. Two Brahmans of Maharashtra were appointed Amins in October 1818 to help in the settlement of minor suits. This meant that whenever a suit was instituted one of them had first to get the parties to nominate the members of a panchayat and secondly to supervise its proceedings. During November and December they each decided by panchayat about twenty cases a month. With Robertson's approval, Lumsden then allowed parties to waive their right to a panchayat and to submit to the adjudication of one of the two Brahmans; he also empowered them to decide any other case where either party took longer than fifteen days to nominate his share of the members of a panchayat, and to dismiss the suit of any petitioner who refrained from prosecuting it for three weeks. These reforms resulted in 'a manifest increase of decision'. In February 1819 a third Amin was appointed at Poona—a Madrasi formerly engaged in judicial work in Madras.[2]

After they had had over a year's experience of the panchayat system, Briggs, Chaplin, and Grant all reported favourably upon it.[3] Pottinger was more sceptical. He was particularly conscious of the danger of bribery. There had in fact been some unpleasant scenes in his court room. As early as September 1818 he confessed to Elphinstone, 'I have been obliged to turn apparently respectable Brahmins and Saukars [merchants] ignominiously out of the Court when it has been shown that they took a few rupees from each of the parties on whose cause I had requested them to sit. On such occasions they have acted with a great effrontery and showed no symptoms of remorse at their disgrace.'[4]

Nevertheless, even Pottinger admitted the utility of panchayats in 'disputes of castes, wuttuns, points of religion and marriages'— in other words, in matters of definite and understood custom which panchayat members would be anxious to observe for fear of being mocked at for their ignorance.[5]

[1] Robertson to M.E., 20.[5].1819, Bg. P.C. 27.11.1819, 6.
[2] Lumsden to Robertson, 18.5.1819, Bg. P.C. 27.11.1819, 6.
[3] S.R.J. iv. 222 f., 246, 261.
[4] Pottinger to M.E., 7.9.1818, Bg. P.C. 17.10.1818, 49.
[5] Pottinger, Replies to queries, 8.8.1819, S.R.J. iv. 291.

Elphinstone wanted to go much further than this. In the general statement of policy which he drew up in October 1819 before leaving the Deccan for Bombay he declared that the panchayat was to be 'our principal instrument' of civil justice. He thought that any attempt to impose rules of procedure might well deter headmen from summoning panchayats for fear of punishment if such rules happened to be broken. He therefore stated that the panchayat 'must be exempt from all new forms, interference and regulation on our part'. In Benthamite fashion he added that 'such forms would throw over this institution that mystery which enables litigious people to employ courts of justice as engines of intimidation against their neighbours, and which renders necessary a class of lawyers, who amongst the natives are the great fomentors of disputes'.[1]

The expedient of appointing Amins at Poona was to be continued: Elphinstone now formally authorized the Collector there to appoint three senior and three junior Amins who would refer suits to panchayats or decide them themselves if both parties agreed. He justified this on the ground that there had to be some way 'to make up in Poona especially, for the numerous chiefs and ministers who formerly used to assemble Punchayets'.[2] He was also considering the possibility of appointing Amins in every large town and even if necessary in every Mamlatdars' district and of giving them additions to their salaries in proportion to the number of suits decided by them or by panchayats under their direction.[3] But privately he was in some doubt about this. Only a few months previously he had written to Samuel Davis that 'it would be a remedy to have many native commissioners (you will doubtless have observed that it is by them & not by Punchayets that all the Madras files have been cleared) but commissioners without fees will be quite inefficient & with them they are certainly too active, stirring up strife and sending out emissaries to bring trials to their tribunals'.[4] In his statement of policy he therefore told the Collectors to see first of all whether their Mamlatdars could manage the business unaided.

A few rules there had to be. Definite limits were set to the

[1] M.E., *Report*, 81; M.E. to Collectors, 25.10.1819 (issued by Chaplin, 27.6.1820), Bom. J.C. 22.3.1820, 1508 ff.; Choksey, *Aftermath*, 326 ff.
[2] M.E., *Report*, 75.
[3] M.E. to Collectors, 25.10.1819, paras. 15-20.
[4] M.E. to Davis, 17.6.1819, *Elphinstone*.

jurisdiction of different types of panchayats: those assembled by village headmen could try suits up to a maximum value of Rs.150, those assembled by Mamlatdars or Amins up to one of Rs.1,000.[1] Appeals from village panchayats should be made to the Collector, not the Mamlatdar, and he should summon another panchayat only if he thought that the original one had not been freely chosen, or that it had not fully decided, or if on a summary inquiry he found 'gross error or injustice', or if he suspected corruption.[2]

Criminal panchayats as used in Khandesh were to be abandoned—'being neither consistent with former usage nor attended with any manifest advantages'.[3] The danger of caste prejudice seemed serious: 'it is obvious', he wrote in his report to the Governor-General in October 1819, 'that where a Bramin on one hand or a Beel on the other was to be tried, it would be too much to expect unprejudiced decision'.[4]

The authority of Mamlatdars and village headmen in criminal cases was to be slightly increased: Mamlatdars were henceforth to be allowed 'to fine to the extent of ten rupees, and to imprison for two days'; the village headman was to be allowed 'a similar authority to such a limited extent as may be requisite to keep up his influence in the village'.[5] All this was small enough indeed.

It was the Collector who had the power. But his authority was not to threaten the privileges of the great. Elphinstone thought that one of the great disadvantages of the British law courts in India was their tendency to act 'with a sternness and indifference to rank and circumstances very grating to the feelings of the natives'.[6] He therefore told the Collectors not to try the offences even of the smaller jagirdars without prior reference to the Deccan Commissioner.[7]

In all other judicial matters the Collectors were allowed a wide discretion.

In revenue matters also Elphinstone left a wide discretion to his Collectors after laying down a few general principles: 'For the present you will continue to collect the land revenue as has been the custom of the country through the Patel; each ryot paying him

---

[1] M.E. to Collectors, 25.10.1819, para. 25.   [2] Ibid., para. 17.
[3] Ibid., para. 7.   [4] M.E., *Report*, 53.
[5] M.E. to Collectors, 25.10.1819, para. 8.   [6] M.E., *Report*, 72.
[7] M.E. to Collectors, 25.10.1819, para. 42.

for his actual cultivation, and great care must be taken to avoid over-assessment.'[1]

But the Collectors had difficulty in finding a standard. There seemed to be no reliable village accounts. Pottinger, for example, was soon complaining of his difficulties 'in getting *true* accounts. Not one village that I have tried by individually examining the ryots has come out correct, and I fear that no common fines will put a stop to the practice.'[2] Grant in Satara was satisfied neither with the accounts nor with the men who kept them: 'The Kulkur-nees in this part of the country really do not possess correct accounts, they are by no means intelligent.'[3] Pottinger even came to doubt the very existence of accounts in some villages: 'whole districts deny having an account of any sort, and many villages certainly are so'.[4] One reason for this was no doubt the devastated condition of the country as a result of famine and political disturbances. But he later found that there had also been some concealment of such records as did exist. 'The Zemindars and Potails', he reported in 1822, 'even where they had preserved some scraps (for none have a regular series) of old accounts, were at first very backward in producing them; but latterly, as they saw our actions agreed with our declarations, they have not hesitated to show them.'[5] By 1822 Chaplin had come to the conclusion that the accountants could produce some figures if they wanted to: 'The Koolkurnees occasionally exhibit accounts of ten, twenty, thirty, or even fifty years' standing, when it suits their particular interests or purposes to do so.' But he also found that 'those who can show no ancient records, are never at a loss to furnish either a fabricated set, or to give a traditionary account of the old rates'.[6]

The Collectors had to manage as best they could in spite of the paucity and inaccuracy of the village records at their disposal. In the result, they usually decided upon a figure after consulting with the local Mamlatdar and Patel. But the village officers' lack of co-operation could not have predisposed the Collectors in their favour.

From the first the Collectors tried to reach behind the headman to

[1] M.E. to Collectors, 10.7.1818, Choksey, *Aftermath*, 239 ff.
[2] Pottinger to M.E., 17.7.1818, *Elphinstone.*
[3] Grant to M.E. 4.12.1818, ibid. Kulkurnee = kulkarni = village accountant.
[4] Pottinger to M.E., 15.10.1818, *Elphinstone.*
[5] Pottinger to Chaplin [1822], S.R.J. iv. 723 f.
[6] Chaplin to Government, 20.8.1822, para. 71, S.R.J. iv. 466.

the individual peasant. After different experiments in the different
Collectorates there emerged the policy of giving to each ryot a
certificate stating the revenue due from him.[1] None of the Collectors managed to see each ryot personally. What happened seems
to have been that they generally tried to settle as many villages
as they could, and that their Mamlatdars had to settle the rest. In
either event, the intention was to strengthen the position of the
individual ryot as against the village headman.

How far and how quickly this actually happened it is difficult to
say. Robertson was surprised by one instance which came to his
notice. In the revenue year 1817–18 the Patel of one of his villages
had been allowed special terms by the old government's Mamlatdar
because of the wretched state of the village. The Patel himself then
arranged special terms with his ryots, whereby they were to pay a
small amount of revenue in the first year and more in each succeeding year until in the sixth year they would be paying the
maximum rate. Robertson agreed to respect these arrangements,
but unknown to him in the very next year the Patel demanded the
maximum rates from the ryots while handing over to the Government the reduced revenue allowed by the special terms and keeping
the difference for himself. It was not until 1821 that Robertson
discovered what had been happening. The revenue certificates
which he had given to the ryots had not in fact encouraged them to
stand up against their Patel: 'not one Ryot complained to me',
he wrote, 'although I gave in 1229 (1819–20) every Ryot his pottah
with my own hands. I hope my cutcherry servants were ignorant
of the truth, but I cannot help suspecting their connivance, from
the silence of the Ryot.'[2]

On the other hand, Briggs in Khandesh noted that several
attempts to extort too much money from the ryots had been reported to him by the victims themselves and redressed by him. He
thought that the certificates had definitely encouraged the ryot to
stand up for himself: 'the ready reply which every cultivator now

[1] For the experiments of the different Collectors see S.R.J. iv. 550 (Poona),
651 (Satara), 695 (Khandesh), 738 (Ahmadnagar), and 794 (Southern Maratha
country). The methods of assessment also varied from place to place. There
was no uniform level for the government demand. After several years' experience
of the working of the system, however, Chaplin concluded in 1822 that the
average government demand upon 'a ryot of middling circumstances' was for
35 per cent. of the gross produce (ibid. 472).
[2] Robertson to Chaplin, 10.10.1821, para. 78, S.R.J. iv. 560. Cutcherry, the
Collector's office. Pottah = patta = revenue certificate.

gives, if he is asked whether any extra levies have been made, by referring with a smile to his pottah, tend[s] to prove that such levies are but seldom practised'.[1]

No doubt the usefulness of the certificates in this respect depended in large measure upon local circumstances, particularly the strength of the Patel's personality. Pottinger, who thought that the Patel's authority had already been shaken under the old government by the appointment over them of revenue farmers who cared only for their own profit, testified in 1819 that 'Potails, however, where they are shrewd and well-informed, have still great influence amongst their Ryots; whilst in different cases they are reduced to the most abject pitch of contempt, and are often lorded over by the Koonbees.'[2] In general, as the Patel's authority was progressively undermined and his power reduced by one after another of the new government's policies, the ryots may well have become more ready to stand up to him because they had less to fear from his hostility.

Under the old government the Patel seems to have had a considerable discretion to alter the expenses of his village. Briggs estimated that in Khandesh these expenses used to amount to as much as 50 per cent. of the gross revenue of large villages and at the least 25 per cent. of that of small villages.[3] Chaplin, however, thought such calculations 'greatly over-rated'. His own estimate was that in Baji Rao's time village expenses in the Deccan amounted on an average to Rs.17 As.12 for every Rs.100 of gross revenue.[4] The inadequacy of the available figures precluded any approach to accuracy. But whatever may have been the amounts actually spent in the different Collectorates, the Collectors soon set to work to limit them.

These expenses included the customary dues of the hereditary district and village officers. These dues were respected. What was in question was the variable provision made for extraordinary expenditure—on matters of charity, village entertainments and festivals, and so on. Chaplin thought that such extra expenses had amounted on an average to Rs.12 As.5 per cent. in the Deccan

---

[1] Briggs to Chaplin, 31.10.1821, ibid. 346 f.
[2] Pottinger, *Replies to queries*, 8.8.1819, ibid. 288 f. Koonbee = Kunbi = cultivator, peasant.
[3] Briggs, *Replies to queries* [1822], S.R.J. iv. 701.
[4] Chaplin to Government, 20.8.1822 (the 1824 version), para. 29 and table.

under Baji Rao.[1] Briggs, for example, tried to restrict them to 4 per cent. of the gross revenue for the year 1818–19. But he was too late in making the attempt, and had to report that in two of his parganas the total village expenses were in fact more than half the gross revenue.[2] When Pottinger tried to fix a similar maximum he experienced 'great difficulty' in restraining his headmen from exceeding it; 'a vast number' of them in fact did so, and he decided to resume their livings until they had made good the effects of their extravagance.[3] In the general statement of policy which Elphinstone drew up on leaving the Deccan he told the Collectors to 'institute a strict enquiry' into these extra expenses but not to lay down any sweeping general rules limiting them to a particular amount:

the ancient practice of the village in good times should be enquired into, and the real interest and wishes of the ryots regarding all expenses of this sort, that are not in their nature fixed, being ascertained, a standard may then be adopted for future observance: care however must be taken in this operation not to trench too much on the influence and consequence of the Patail for it must always be remembered that he is the keystone on which the whole village system so essentially depends.[4]

In the result, there seems to have been a considerable reduction in village expenses. According to Chaplin's calculations the average total for the Deccan, which had been Rs.17 As.12 per cent. of the gross revenue in Baji Rao's time, was reduced to Rs.9 As.3¾ in 1820–1.[5] In human terms the result seems to have been at least in some places to make village life a little more austere. Robertson, for example, felt sure that 'even the people, who alone benefit by this measure, would rather I had not been so strict'. In his Collectorate the village headmen gave 'no holiday feasts now as formerly', and he thought that this was because they simply had not the money to do so. He therefore decided to allow 'a little sum' for such festivities.[6] But looking at the Deccan as a whole, Chaplin's general conclusion in 1822 was that many of the charges which had been

[1] Ibid.
[2] Briggs to Chaplin, 31.10.1821, S.R.J. iv. 343.
[3] Pottinger to Chaplin, 29.5.1821, ibid. 385.
[4] M.E. to Collectors, 25.10.1819, para. 3, Bom. J.C. 22.3.1820, 1508 ff.
[5] Chaplin to Government, 20.8.1822 (the 1824 version), 13, table. Extra expenses had been reduced from Rs.12 As.5 to Rs.4 As.4¾ per cent.
[6] H. D Robertson to Chaplin, 10.10.1821, S.R.J. iv. 581; he had through a misunderstanding increased the severity of the restriction in the revenue year 1819–20 by not allowing for village expenses in the revenue which he collected for the Government.

abolished had merely gone in the old days 'to satisfy the rapacity of the native functionaries', and he added: 'I do not find that any legitimate ceremonies have been abolished, nor any festivities abridged, by our economy in the article of village charges. There is of course less extravagance, but no just source of amusement or rejoicing has been retrenched.'[1]

Perhaps the tendency noticed by Robertson was only temporary. But in spite of Elphinstone's instructions that the headman's position should not be undermined, it nevertheless remained that the regulation of the village expenses was another respect in which his previous freedom was now curtailed.

Under the old government the headman had been free to dispose of waste land by giving special terms providing for a progressively increasing rental. The British Collectors, however, required their headmen first to obtain the Mamlatdar's permission. They assigned various advantages to this procedure. Pottinger, for example, thought that it prevented disputes among the villagers, for 'no Potail can now assign ground to a Koonbee till the possible right of another to it is fully discussed'.[2] Grant thought that it gave a 'general protection' against exaction on the part of the village officers[3]—presumably on the assumption that in the old days they had demanded some illicit reward from the peasant to whom they granted special terms. Characteristically, H. D. Robertson was more sceptical: he thought that what happened now was that the Mamlatdars and Collector's Daftardars themselves exacted an illicit reward for any special terms that were granted, and were contriving 'to cheat both the Government and the people out of a good deal of money'.[4]

---

[1] Chaplin to Government, 20.8.1822, para. 35, S.R.J. iv. 461.
[2] Pottinger, *Replies to queries*, 31.7.1822, ibid. 740 f.
[3] Grant, *Replies to queries*, 17.6.1822, ibid. 652 f.
[4] Robertson to Chaplin, 10.10.1821, para. 77, ibid. 560. I presume that Briggs similarly restricted the headman's powers in Khandesh. This seems implied in Briggs to Chaplin, 31.10.1821, ibid. 349 f., but I have nowhere found it definitely stated. Robertson's solution was 'to plant guardians between the mass of the people and these our servants' (the Mamlatdars and Daftardars)— in other words, to foster and protect the rights of landholders like the mirasdars who would themselves let land to the poorer peasants and stand between them and the government officials. Chaplin drew the moral that a revenue survey would enable the Collectors to check abuses and protect mirasdars by stabilizing the Government's revenue demand upon them. In fact, however, the survey was so protracted that its results lie outside the scope of this book. At this time, Chaplin estimated the proportion of mirasdars to tenants-at-will as 3 to 1 in Poona, 2 to 1 in Satara, and equal in Ahmadnagar (there seemed to be none in Khandesh).

In all these ways the authority and consequence of the village headmen were reduced. This happened in spite of Elphinstone's wishes. It came as the incidental but cumulative result of diverse policies of the new government.[1]

The new government's revenue policies also had important effects upon the position of the hereditary district officers—the Deshmukhs or Desais and the Deshpandes. They had already been largely superseded by the Mamlatdars appointed by the Maratha Government. They had come to be used merely as a check upon the Mamlatdars, whose accounts they had to countersign.

Elphinstone at first thought of restoring them to their old position, and he asked Munro for his advice:

I think they would make good justices of the peace [he wrote in April 1818] & ought to be made much of for the sake of having a gentry the want of which is so much complained of in other parts of India, but I am in doubt whether we ought to employ them at all in the revenue, whether it is worth our while to restore their allowances in cases where they have been seized & also whether there is any danger in bringing them forward & giving them influence with the people which their Marratta feeling may lead them to employ against us.[2]

Munro advised against restoring them to their old position in the collection of the revenue: 'Though the people of India have not what we call gentry they have what they respect as such themselves.' Here no doubt he was referring to the popular respect for Patels, Mirasdars, and men of high caste. 'It will not therefore I think merely with a view to the establishment of this class of society be necessary to restore the Desmooks and Dessoys who have been removed to make way for the Mahrattah revenue servants.' Those whose allowances had been taken away but not given to anyone else might well have them restored, as this would not disturb the existing order of society. But there was no need to fear that they might stir up Maratha feeling against the British: 'I do not apprehend the smallest danger from their influence—good treatment

---

[1] Only in the Southern Maratha country could it be said that the Patel's position had been improved by the new system of government. In the old days there had been a Kamavisdar in almost every village there who had carried out the duties normally performed by a Patel, while the actual Patel merely carried out his orders. But the British dispensed with these village Kamavisdars, and the Patels' importance therefore increased. This, however, was a situation peculiar to this area (Thackeray, *Replies to queries*, n.d., S.R.J. iv. 794, 797 f.).

[2] M.E. to Munro, 2.4.1818, *Elphinstone*.

will reconcile them all to our Government [and] lead them to employ whatever influence they have in its favour.'[1]

The Collectors, however, were generally hostile towards them. The least of their objections was that the hereditary district officers were a parasitic class: as Pottinger wrote in 1822, 'I look on them at this time as merely a class of men who add to the burthens of the Ryots, without bringing any equivalent in the scale, either as regards the people or the Government.'[2]

Not that when the British took over the Government they found the hereditary district officers without anything to do at all. They had indeed been generally displaced by the Mamlatdars, the agents of the central government. But where the central government was weak, as in Khandesh, their influence was much stronger than in the rest of the Maratha dominions. This was Briggs's experience: 'When I arrived in Candeish, I found the district Zemindars possessed of unlimited powers; they had been the agents of extortion made use of by all the plunderers, of whom no less than 181 independent leaders are stated to have desolated this country within the period of twenty years preceding our rule.'[3]

Elsewhere in the Deccan, too, the laxity of the farming system had enabled many of them to regain a little of their lost influence.[4]

It was their duty to keep the accounts of their districts. Yet when the Collectors began to investigate the economic resources of their collectorates these men were of little help to them. Pottinger, for example, found those of Ahmadnagar as little inclined to help as were the village officers. 'I have had Daishmookhs, Daishpandies, Potails and Coolkurnees from all parts of the country in confinement', he wrote to Elphinstone in September 1818, 'and when they saw they could not carry their roguery through, and confessed it, there were always others ready to take their places.'[5] Again, Briggs found that 'they not only withheld their own papers, but urged the village officers to conceal theirs'.[6] Such records as they did produce were often found to be false, because they themselves were either corrupt or incompetent.[7]

[1]   Munro to M.E., 8.4.1818, *Elphinstone*.
[2]   Pottinger, *Replies to queries*, 31.7.1822, S.R.J. iv. 757.
[3]   Briggs to Chaplin, 30.12.1822, ibid. 714.
[4]   Chaplin to Government, 20.8.1822, ibid. 486.
[5]   Pottinger to M.E., 3.9.1818, *Elphinstone*.
[6]   Briggs to Chaplin, 30.12.1822, S.R.J. iv. 715.
[7]   Ibid., also Thackeray (Dharwar), *Replies to queries*, 1822, ibid. 799.

Pottinger could find nothing useful for them to do: 'the more we limit the authority of the Zemindars the better'.[1] Not all the Collectors were as hostile to them as that. Grant admitted in 1822 that he had 'sometimes obtained very useful information from the Daismooks and Daispandees on general subjects'. At first he often consulted them. But 'the only discoveries of frauds have come from some of their dissatisfied relations'. He soon concluded that he could not depend upon them and by 1822 he did not even allow the Mamlatdars to consult them without express permission.[2] Robertson had a higher opinion of their value: 'I think they are a useful class of men, if precluded from the power which any Government agency in their hands would enable them to exercise.' Their duties were only advisory—'sitting in the cutcherry, and acting as umpires' between the Collector's office staff and the headmen when the revenue settlement was made with the villages. This duty he thought they did well: 'they seem to moderate the demands of my cutcherry and to influence the Potails in the admission of rightful demands, and as far as I can judge, I think their services in this way are very beneficial to the interests of the people; they are their representatives, and there is great need indeed that the people should have honest persons of this description'.[3] Briggs, who had lost all faith in their usefulness in revenue matters, nevertheless made great use of them as members of panchayats in criminal trials.[4]

In general, however, the new government continued the policy of the old, which had been somewhat interrupted under Baji Rao, to exclude the hereditary district officers from all effective power. At the same time, their existing emoluments were continued to them, although with their loss of power they no doubt tended to lose also the illicit perquisites which had been the natural accompaniments of power. As in the case of the village headmen, these changes were the incidental result of the administrative reforms of the new government.

In one area, at least, the administrative requirements of the new government also produced some changes in the social structure of

---

[1] Pottinger, *Replies to queries*, 31.7.1822, ibid. 757.
[2] Grant, *Replies to queries*, 17.6.1822, ibid. 667.
[3] Robertson to Chaplin, 10.10.1821, ibid. 582 f.
[4] See above, p. 108.

the village police system and raised fundamental questions concerning the proper social policy to be adopted towards the wild tribes of the hills.

Each village had its own watchmen—low caste men like the Dhers or the Mangs or tribesmen like the Ramusis or the Bhils. They were usually paid in kind; in some places they might be allotted a piece of land to cultivate, or they might also be given a small sum in cash. Robertson in Poona, Grant in Satara, and Pottinger in Ahmadnagar had little difficulty in maintaining this system and in coming to terms with the Naiks or chiefs, each of whom had charge of the Ramusis or Bhils of a number of villages.[1] But in Khandesh Briggs had a much more difficult task.

In Khandesh the village police system had broken down. In the distress and disorder which prevailed there during the first two decades of the century, great numbers of Bhil watchmen had left their villages for the surrounding hills where they either formed gangs of their own or joined the following of existing hill chiefs. From the hills these gangs made sporadic raids upon the peaceful villages of the plains.

The volatile Briggs was at first sympathetic towards the Bhils. Even in retrospect his memory of his early meetings with the hill Bhils of Baglana[2] in the west of Khandesh dwelt upon the freshness and simplicity of their ways:

Upon my arrival among them they brought flowers, fruits and sugar cane, to propitiate an elephant which I had with me (never having seen one before) and they sang and danced round him. Their music is an extemely melodious pipe, with a base drone accompaniment produced from a gourd, and a small drum. The men and women danced together in a circle keeping time with their feet, around which they wore bells. The dance and the tune were unlike anything I had ever seen or heard in the East during a sojourn of 24 years in many parts of India, Arabia and Persia.[3]

These were the true hill Bhils. Those Bhils who had once been village watchmen and had shared in the common life of their villages before they took refuge in the hills were much less outlandish in their culture. According to Briggs the only characteristics which

[1] Pottinger to M.E., 14.8.1818, Bg. P.C. 17.10.1818, 38; Robertson to M.E., 1.8.1818, Bg. S.C. 31.7.1818, 306; Grant, *Replies to queries*, 30.4.1819, S.R.J. iv. 236.
[2] Later Satana taluk, Nasik Collectorate.
[3] Briggs to Chaplin, 16.4.1825, para. 10, B.C. 1022/20850, 314.

they shared with the hill Bhils of Baglana and Rajpipla were the name of Bhil and a strong propensity for drunkenness.[1]

Altogether the number of Bhils in Khandesh was estimated in 1833 to be 55,000—one-eighth of the total population.[2] They constituted a formidable problem for Briggs at the beginning of his administration there.

The main lines of future policy had been laid down in the instructions which Elphinstone gave him during the war. The village Bhils were to be encouraged to help the headman to preserve law and order and generally to do their customary duties as village watchmen. The chiefs of the hill Bhils were to be conciliated either by allowing them their customary dues or by arranging some equivalent. Elphinstone referred Briggs to the example of Augustus Clevland, Collector of Bhagalpur some forty years before: 'I beg to call your attention to the policy of pensioning the more powerful chiefs on condition of their answering for the conduct of their tribes according to the plan formerly practised with so much success by Mr. Cleavland with the mountaineers of Baglepoor.' If these expedients failed, then force might have to be used.[3]

Much of the disorder in Khandesh had been caused by the harsh policy of the old government. The jagirs of many of the ancient chiefs of Baglana had been resumed by Baji Rao's officers—in intention, though not in fact, for the chiefs had at once roused the neighbouring Bhils, ravaged the plains, and refused to yield up their lands. Briggs asked permission to restore these jagirs.[4] 'To these Jageerdars I think it politic to restore what the Peshwa *could never usurp* altho' he directed its resumption; the value of the lands is trifling the purchase of their good will & local knowledge & restoring them to peaceful habits is important.'[5] Elphinstone fully agreed. Briggs could restore resumed lands wherever he thought fit.[6]

The Bhils in the Satpura mountains presented the most difficult problem, for that range, in Elphinstone's words, was 'deep and strong and so unhealthy that no stranger can long remain in it'.[7] Briggs was confronted with accounts of vast numbers of Bhils there,

[1] Ibid., para. 26.
[2] W. S. Boyd to Bombay Government, 30.4.1833, B.C. 1467/57760, 12.
[3] M.E. to Briggs, 11.3.1818, Bg. S.C. 31.7.1818, 89; *Imperial Gazetteer of India* (1908), viii. 28.
[4] Briggs to M.E. 18.4.1818, *Elphinstone*.
[5] Briggs to M.E., 4.6.1818, *Elphinstone*.
[6] M.E. to Briggs, 4.5.1818, *Elphinstone*.   [7] M.E., *Report*, 4.

but he soon concluded that these were much exaggerated: his own estimate was that there were never more than 2,000 men there.[1] Only two or three of their chiefs had been born in the hills, and only about 300 of their followers. The rest of the chiefs and followers came from the plains—in other words they were originally village watchmen. Moreover, they still kept up relations with the village Bhils, sometimes, even returning to their villages for a while. There was, in short, nothing outlandish about them. Briggs found that the Satpura Bhils were 'by no means a wild race of people, their language and their habits are the same as those of the towns who resemble the ordinary inhabitants of the country as nearly as the state of society to which they belong admits, and it need hardly be mentioned that that is of the very lowest class'.[2] Elsewhere the problem was similar in kind, if less serious in degree.

The privileges of the hill chiefs were objectionable to the new rulers.

Among all my Bhil friends here [noted Briggs] each fellow has the privilege of taxing a particular ghaut, some rent the privilege at two hundred Rupees annually from the Sircar, while others have a fourth of the government customs. These are the . . . privileges of their birth and they relinquish them with extraordinary reluctance, but it is a point on which I am disposed to give liberal equivalents to gain an object so important to an economical revenue.[3]

This privilege of taxing all goods and travellers going through a specified mountain pass must have been lucrative and was likely to become even more so as peace and a relative prosperity returned to Khandesh. But to give such discretionary power over trade to an individual chief was quite contrary to the principles of the new government.

The privilege of collecting tolls on goods and travellers implied that the chief in question had a corresponding duty to protect all goods and travellers paying his tolls. Briggs therefore made agreements with the chiefs, promising to pay them the value of their tolls if they in return fulfilled their responsibility of protecting all goods and travellers passing through their jurisdiction. The tolls were still levied, but by agents whom he himself appointed.[4]

[1] Briggs to M.E., 19.11.1818, Bg. P.C. 19.1.1819, 22.
[2] Briggs to M.E., 8.1.1819, Bg. P.C. 17.4.1819, 8.
[3] Briggs to M.E., 21.8.1818, *Elphinstone.*
[4] Briggs to Gerald Wellesley (Resident at Indore), 3.1.1819, Bell, *Briggs*, 79 f.

He also required the chiefs on the one hand to provide watchmen for every village under their protection and on the other hand to expel all village Bhils from their own camps in the hills.[1] This of course would considerably reduce the number of their followers. Briggs hoped for wider benefits as well: 'by making it appear to them that their vigilance is necessary in protecting the villages it gives them a degree of consequence among themselves, a kind of self-importance, teaches them confidence in us and at length will draw the hill population altogether into the town and they will mix at last in the mass of civilised people'.[2]

If any chiefs were unwilling to come to terms, Briggs had no hesitation in using force and inflicting summary punishments. As he wrote on one occasion in June 1818, 'now the war with Bajee Row has ceased, all persons guilty of plundering the country or acting hostilely are to be treated as rebels and to be executed forth-with'.[3] The Governor-General in Council, however, objected to such summary measures: even where immediate punishment was necessary, it should not be inflicted without some previous investigation like a Drum Head Court Martial wherever possible, and a short minute should always be written to certify that the identity and guilt of the criminal had been carefully ascertained; moreover, where circumstances permitted delay, capital sentences should not be carried out until the confirmation of the commanding officer or chief civil or political officer in the district had been obtained.[4] But Briggs was a difficult man to teach, and the Governor-General in Council found it necessary to administer similar rebukes to him on subsequent occasions of crisis.[5]

His arrangements with Gumani, the chief of the Sindwa pass, were typical of his general policy towards the chiefs. Ever since his arrival in Khandesh in February 1818 he had been in contact with Gumani. Indeed, Gumani was clearly a power in the land. Only the previous year, at the head of a gang of 500 Bhils, he had stolen 400 head of cattle from the Malegaon area. In return for his promise to protect the Sindwa pass Briggs allowed him a pension of Rs.2,000 a year. Even after he had sent away all the village Bhils among his

[1] Briggs to M.E., 11.7.1818, *Elphinstone*; Briggs to M.E., 8.8.1818, ibid.
[2] Briggs to M.E., 11.7.1818, ibid.
[3] Briggs to Major Watson (concerning Gangthadi area, in the south), 22.6.1818, Bg. S.C. 7.8.1818, 67.
[4] Supreme Government to M.E., 7.8.1818, ibid.
[5] e.g. Bg. P.C. 17.10.1818, 35; Bg. P.C. 13.2.1819, 30.

following, he still had twenty-five horse and 200 Bhils under his authority in the hills.[1]

Briggs seems to have tried not to be a hard taskmaster. In September 1818 he told Captain Leighton, an officer engaged in operations in the neighbourhood, 'to distinguish clearly between Bheels molesting persons belonging to the British Government and those connected with Holkar', and explained that he was anxious to prevent Leighton from attacking any of Gumani's Bhils, 'who I am afraid still continue to infest Holkar's territory beyond Sindwah, though he has most rigidly adhered to the agreement he made with me in February last'. In other words, Briggs at first tried to limit his protection to the area of the Company's territories.[2]

He was quickly taught the utility of doing as he would be done by. When he complained to Ganpat Rao Vithal, the Kamavisdar of the neighbouring district of Chopra belonging to Sindhia, that some of the villagers in that district were known to be in possession of goods stolen by Bhils from subjects of the Company, Ganpat Rao in return complained that Gumani, who was in the Company's service, had been plundering one of Sindhia's villages.[3] The moral which Briggs drew was that to avoid such troubles in the future Sindhia should be persuaded to relinquish his territories in this area.[4] Elphinstone, however, drew the more logical conclusion: Gumani, he told Briggs, 'must not be permitted to pursue towards Sindia the course which we so justly complain of when adopted towards ourselves'.[5] Briggs accordingly admonished Gumani, and threatened to withhold his pension if he offended again—'if you are allowed to plunder other people, they will of course retaliate on this Sircar'.[6]

By the end of 1818, Briggs's policy was seen to be inadequate. He claimed that it had stopped the old attacks by large Bhil gangs who would carry off the cattle of a whole village. Instead there were many small gangs, each of a dozen or so Bhils, robbing where and when they could. But that was serious enough, as he realized. 'The

[1] Excluding perquisites from villages in Thalner pargana. Briggs later increased Gumani's pension to Rs.4,380 a year (Briggs to M.E., 9.11.1818, Bg. P.C. 19.1.1819, 22; Briggs to M.E., 16.1.1819, Bg. P.C. 6.3.1819, 29).
[2] Briggs to Leighton, 3.9.1818, Bg. P.C. 17.10.1818, 35.
[3] Briggs to Ganpat Rao Vithal, n.d., Bg. P.C. 19.1.1819, 24; Ganpat Rao Vithal to Briggs, 30.11.1818, ibid.
[4] Briggs to M.E., 2.12.1818, ibid.
[5] M.E. to Briggs, 10.12.1818, ibid.
[6] Briggs to Gumani, 11.12.1818, ibid. 43.

distress occasioned by these robberies to the inhabitants is not to be imagined', he wrote in January 1819. A few districts even declined the advances of money in aid of cultivation which he told the Mamlatdars to offer. They were afraid of accepting the obligation to repay such advances until their property could be better safe-guarded from the Bhils.[1]

To deal with the chiefs was, after all, a straightforward prob-lem—at least in principle. They could always be pensioned. What was more difficult was to provide for the village Bhils who had fled to the hills. The chiefs were told to send them back to their villages. But it was not enough merely to restore the old village system in this way. The inadequacy of their customary village dues was the very reason why they had taken to the hills. Briggs admitted that the condition of the village Bhils was often 'truly miserable'. The peasants lacked the resources adequately to maintain the Bhils then in the villages, much less those who had taken to the hills. Some villages were half deserted: there were simply not enough inhabitants in them to maintain the traditional number of Bhils. Many villages were completely deserted. On the other hand, the Bhils who could not be maintained as watchmen had no other means of livelihood except robbery. Despised by the peasants as outcasts, they had no knowledge of agriculture or any other occupa-tion.

Briggs concluded that since the customary dues were inadequate a general tax should be levied throughout Khandesh, 1 rupee a month on every village. This he thought would be enough to provide every watchman with 2 rupees a month—'a sum which in Candeish will not support more than one person of the very lowest order with food'. To maintain their families the Bhils would have to turn to subsidiary occupations like cutting wood or grass. He thought that Khandesh could well afford such a tax, assuming that more than half of its population paid no tax at present.

He also suggested that a Bhil Naik should be appointed under every Shaikdar (the local official in charge of groups of between eight and fifteen villages) and a chief Naik under every Mamlatdar, each Naik being paid ½ rupee a month for every village under his charge.[2]

Elphinstone agreed with Briggs's diagnosis: 'it is obvious that the villages are not populous enough for the fees to maintain the

[1] Briggs to M.E., 8.1.1819, Bg. P.C. 17.4.1819, 8.   [2] Ibid.

Beel watchman and he is obliged to rob for bread'. But he dis-agreed with Briggs's remedies. He denied the expediency of fresh taxation: 'the present state of Candeish requires that additional population and capital should be drawn into it by lightening the taxes rather than that they should be repelled by heavier imposts'. And he disliked the idea of appointing Naiks and chief Naiks throughout Khandesh: 'such a system would have a tendency to keep up a spirit of cast among the Bheels, to withdraw their atten-tion from the village authorities and to throw a power into the hands of their chiefs which is as likely to be employed against society as for it'. The danger of weakening the village system was also his reason for rejecting the idea that the Government might pay the watchmen from its own resources without levying any fresh tax. 'The great excellence of the village system of police', he thought, 'arises from the intimate connection of the watchman with the village, his dependance on the Patail and even on the contributions of individuals.'[1]

Instead, Elphinstone proposed to revise the customary dues paid by the villagers to their watchmen, to fix a sufficient amount to be paid in grain by each villager, and to deduct this from the public revenue demand upon the village.[2] The Supreme Government agreed.[3]

Elphinstone also wanted Briggs to follow the example of Augus-tus Clevland and form an irregular corps of Bhils, 'like the Baugle-poor hill rangers'.[4] During 1818 Briggs had in fact ventured a cautious step in this direction: he had enlisted some Bhils of a few encampments at a cost of Rs.700 a month.[5] But, he reported in January 1819, 'they were constantly in a state of intoxication, never capable of any exertion themselves, and the rest of the Bhils who were more active [were] constantly calling out for a similar provi-sion'. If the system were continued he foresaw that all the village Bhils in Khandesh would make trouble and consequently have to be enlisted, with the result that 'instead of being useful and active members of society in that class to which they belong', they 'would become drones on the state'.[6]

By now Briggs had apparently lost some of his affection for the

[1] M.E. to Briggs, 13.1.1819, Bg. P.C. 17.4.1819, 7; M.E. to Briggs, 5.11.1818, Elphinstone.
[2] Ibid.
[3] Supreme Government to M.E., 17.4.1819, Bg. P.C. 17.4.1819, 10.
[4] M.E. to Briggs, 1.9.1818, Elphinstone.   [5] In Rawer pargana.
[6] Briggs to M.E., 8.1.1819, Bg. P.C. 17.4.1819, 8.

Bhils, and he solemnly declared that 'any military organisation of the Bheels would be at best difficult. That it would be elevating them from thieves to soldiers for which they are in my mind wholly incapacitated from their licentious habits and their grovelling ideas. . . .'[1] The project was abandoned.

Early in 1819 large-scale plundering began again. The chiefs who thus broke their agreements usually claimed that their rights had been violated. They may well have misunderstood the terms of their agreements. On the other hand, they may have been bluffing—inventing grievances to serve as excuses. The truth seems in most instances to have been obscure at the time. Briggs tended towards a cynical attitude. Viewing matters from London, the Court of Directors were sometimes more charitable.

Chil Naik's sudden revolt was typical of many. He was a chief in the Satmala range. He had accepted an annual pension of Rs.648 as recently as November 1818, but on 19 January 1819 he suddenly plundered a village, stole its cattle, and generally caused damage to the extent of some Rs.1,500. Briggs's Assistant Hodges at once told Chil Naik to return the cattle on pain of forfeiting his pension.[2] In reply Chil Naik asserted that he had not been paid his full pension which, he claimed, amounted to Rs.2,200: 'you have not performed your engagement', he wrote, 'on which account we attacked the village; if you will now provide for us, we will refrain from plundering. Is it right in you to desire us not to plunder and yet to make no provision for us? First cause to be paid to us our just claims and then call us to account for any robberies committed.' At the same time, he admitted that he had received Rs.175.[3]

Briggs thought that this was 'an insolent letter'. He dismissed Chil Naik's arguments as 'wholly unfounded', and sent a detachment to the Satmala hills with instructions to 'humble the Bheels' by cutting off their supplies of food from the plains. If it appeared that Chil Naik had actually written the offending letter, Major Hall, who commanded the detachment, was told by Briggs to 'execute him on the spot'. His followers were also to be sternly treated: 'severe examples should be made, all prisoners taken should be kept in irons'. A reward of Rs.500 was to be offered for Chil Naik himself.[4]

[1] Ibid.   [2] Hodges to M.E., 31.1.1819, Bg. P.C. 13.3.1819, 28.
[3] Chil Naik to Collector of Khandesh, n.d., ibid.
[4] Briggs to Hall, 4.2.1819, ibid.

As it happened, Chil Naik gave himself up voluntarily. In these circumstances, Hall deferred his execution pending fresh orders from Briggs.[1] But Briggs was adamant: 'his punishment on the spot appears to me absolutely necessary as an example to check the licentious spirit of the Bheels who are in the habit of throwing themselves readily on our mercy whenever their means of subsistence is straitened and reverting to their former malpractices the instant this inconvenience is removed'. Hall was therefore to make inquiry whether Chil Naik had actually plundered the village and written the letter, and if so he was to 'cause him to be executed in front of the other Bheels who have been taken'.[2] Chil Naik himself admitted that he had done these things, and so at five o'clock one afternoon he was executed in the presence of his comrades.[3]

Briggs directed other campaigns also in 1819 with the aim not only of punishing chiefs who had broken their agreements but also of forcing to terms those who had hitherto evaded all negotiation. The campaign against Dasrat Naik illustrates one of the great difficulties which the new rulers had to face—the unwillingness of the inhabitants to co-operate against the Bhils until they could be assured of protection against their revenge.[4]

Colonel Jardine, the officer commanding the detachment, was only able to find the village where Dasrat had been hiding because he was given information by the son of a peasant whom Dasrat and another chief had killed. The local Deshmukh 'denied to the last moment that any Beels were in the village, even after we had surrounded it, and he quitted it with us from an apprehension of being killed or carried off for his supposed connection with us'.[5] As it happened, Dasrat was away at the time, but Jardine captured among others his uncle and his uncle's wife and child. Dasrat eventually submitted to Malcolm.

Like many of the Bhil chiefs, Dasrat was of humble origins: he had himself been a village watchman. But he later acquired so much power that not long before the campaign against him he had successfully carried off 170 head of cattle in a single raid.[6] Lieu-

---

[1] Hall to Briggs, 19.2.1819, Bg. P.C. 17.4.1819, 15.
[2] Briggs to Hall, 21.2.1819, ibid.
[3] Hall to Briggs, 26.2.1819, Bg. P.C. 3.4.1819, 8.
[4] Dasrat's daughter was Gumani's wife (Briggs to M.E., 19.11.1818, Bg. P.C. 19.1.1819, 22).
[5] Jardine to Steele, 28.2.1819, Bg. P.C. 24.4.1819, 22.
[6] Briggs to M.E., 19.11.1818, Bg. P.C. 19.1.1819, 22.

tenant-Colonel Smith, one of the officers engaged in the operations against him, learnt from 'tolerable good authority' that he had been helped by influential men like Kamavisdars in the neighbouring districts ruled by Sindhia and Holkar. 'When such fellows as Dusrut are encouraged by the higher classes to plunder', observed the colonel, 'there is certainly some excuse to be made for them.'[1]

Years might well pass before the new government could convince men that it had the power to protect those who helped it against the Bhils. Meanwhile Briggs continued his strategy of forcing the chiefs to make agreements and to keep them. He made no great change in his tactics: the villages from which the gangs obtained food were occupied; their encampments were destroyed; the need for food alone might force them to submit; if a chief proved elusive a reward would be placed upon his head, and this might set other chiefs against him.[2]

Briggs's policy towards the Bhils was summed up in a proclamation which he issued in 1819. The only Bhils who would be allowed to live in the hills were those in the service of the Government—in other words, hill Bhils employed by chiefs who were paid by the Government to protect the passes. Village Bhils who had taken to the hills must return to the plains. The Government would allow village headmen to issue a seer of grain a day to every Bhil who came to live in their villages. But, the proclamation continued, the Government did not intend 'to maintain a useless class of people or to encourage idleness'. The village Bhils must perform the police duties of their villages. This was in accordance with the policy sanctioned by the Governor-General in Council: for every seer of grain issued the Government would make a corresponding allowance in its revenue demand upon the village concerned; the inadequacy of the established customary dues would thus be rectified without lessening the headman's authority or the Bhil's dependance upon the village.[3]

The old system, in short, had to be altered before it could work at all. But fundamentally it was the traditional system of village police which Elphinstone hoped would be enough to keep the village Bhils occupied and fed. The hill Bhils, he hoped, could be

---

[1] Smith to Malcolm, 16.3.1819, Bg. P.C. 1.5.1819, 26.

[2] For example, when Ramji, a Satpura chief, fled after having surrendered, Briggs offered a reward of Rs.1,000 for his capture. He was captured by Gumani and another chief (Briggs to M.E., 9.6.1819, Bg. P.C. 31.7.1819, 22).

[3] Proclamation, n.d., Bg. P.C. 11.9.1819, 16 (compare Bg. P.C. 31.7.1819, 22).

left in peace in their hills under the rule of their chiefs for whom permanent pensions from the Government would replace the erratic profits of plunder. To govern the hill Bhils through their own chiefs, he wrote in October 1819, was the only practicable plan 'until the gradual effects of civilisation shall have undermined the power of the chiefs, at the same time that it removes the necessity for their control over the people'.[1] That was a matter of expediency. To govern the village Bhils through the headman, on the other hand, accorded well with the policy of maintaining the headman's general authority, which was one of Elphinstone's principal aims.

[1] M.E., *Report*, 49.

PART TWO

7

ELPHINSTONE, THE GOVERNOR
OF BOMBAY
(1819–27)

WHEN Elphinstone first heard that he was to succeed Sir Evan Nepean as Governor of Bombay he recorded in his journal that 'It gives me no great delight. It strikes out all hope of seeing England for five years at least; and I look with some dread to so protracted a residence in India. Besides, I leave a new, interesting, active office, for an old-established and regulated appointment; and I quit the field of expectation and popularity for the difficulties of performance and the envy of possession.'[1]

Other forebodings soon began to trouble him. As he lay awake one night he reflected that

the climate will certainly not agree with me, and I shall have the languor and the irritability which made me so uncomfortable in Candeish. The society will be new and awkward to me—lawyers, merchants, sailors, etc., etc., instead of officers whom I am used to, and with whose ideas I sympathise; numbers of strangers, and new intimacies. I shall not be able to keep up the constant entertainments I have here, even on a much more limited scale. I shall exceed my means without having much real comfort. My business will be complicated without being interesting. I shall have constant occurrence of business of which I am ignorant, without any being so important or lasting as to compel me to master the subject. To aid me, instead of a staff of my own choosing, and forming part of my own family, I shall have secretaries who will each have his own views, interests and dependants; and councillors, who will start objections, point out difficulties, or at least require confirmations, and create delay.[2]

However, as the time approached for him to go to Bombay, he came to feel more optimistic: 'I go to Bombay in good spirits. The novelty, the bustle, the new scenes and new faces, all prevent

[1] Journal, 12.2.1819, Colebrooke, ii. 39.
[2] Ibid. 23.2.1819.

any apprehension of depression and ennui; and if I expected to retain my health, I should not despair of becoming attached to the new life on which I am entering.'[1]

His first impressions of Bombay were mixed. He liked the informality of his position: 'The Governor, . . . by the custom of Bombay, constantly drives out, and is quite a private gentleman, which suits well with my habits and tastes.'[2] On the other hand, he strongly disliked the shabbiness of his immediate surroundings: 'The Govt. houses & furniture at Bombay are worthy of the worst days of Mr. Duncan (all of which as well as those of Mr. Hornby etc. etc. they have witnessed) and contribute in no small degree to bring that Govt. into contempt. They are really inexpressibly bad.'[3] Part of the blame for this he assigned to the frugality of his immediate predecessor, Sir Evan Nepean: 'Among other effects of Sir Evan's thrift he has left more ruined houses to repair & ruined furniture to replace. The latter was declared by a Committee ordered by Sir Evan to be "too mean to be admitted into any private house in the settlement".'[4]

He liked what he first saw of the social life of Bombay. 'The society is pleasant and easy', he told Adam, in December 1819, 'at least as much so as Calcutta. People either always dance or have a good deal of music and singing when there is a party, and no stiff private circle.'[5] Perhaps in these early months he was too favourably impressed by the bustle and catholicity of Bombay after the comparative solitude and austerity of his life in the Deccan. Or perhaps it was that some of the more cultured English people in Bombay left soon after this. Whatever the explanation, he soon came to feel some dissatisfaction with the tastes of English society there. When in 1822 he asked Adam to thank a lady who had sent him some music he added, 'Nobody here ever plays, indeed music is voted such a bore that I never like to ask them. To say the truth, nothing could be stupider than our Government House parties.'[6] And two years later he was writing, 'I believe I keep the quietest house in the Island, except giving a large dinner once a month.'[7]

[1] Journal, 23.10.1819, Colebrooke, ii. 98.
[2] M.E. to J. Adam, 3.12.1819, ibid. 108.
[3] M.E. to J. Adam, 23.3.1819, *Elphinstone.*
[4] M.E. to W. F. Elphinstone, 31.12.1819; *Elphinstone.*
[5] M.E. to J. Adam, 3.12.1819, Colebrooke, ii. 108.
[6] M.E. to J. Adam, 15.2.1822, *Elphinstone.*
[7] M.E. to R. Jenkins, 8.10.1824, *Elphinstone.*

There was one aspect of Bombay's social life which he disliked from the first: 'What I dread, detest, and abhor, to a degree which I fancy never was equalled, is making speeches, and ceremonies of that nature. I avoid them as much as I can by avowing my horror of the practice; but sometimes they occur. All the other people of Bombay harangue to such a degree that if I were Charles Fox I should hold my tongue on purpose to put down the fashion. No party of thirty meets without thirty regular speeches.'[1] Nor did he grow more accustomed to speech-making. In 1821 he remarked to Malcolm, 'I cannot say thank you when my health is drunk.'[2]

He retained his old suspicions that he did not mix well. For example, when Bishop Heber visited Bombay in 1825, Elphinstone noted in his diary that 'My shyness and awkwardness prevent my getting so well acquainted with him as I could wish.'[3] The Bishop, on the other hand, was full of praise for his amiability and popularity, as well as for the exceptional depth and width of his reading and knowledge.[4]

He was abstemious for his health's sake—'no wine, not a drop of wine, spirits or beer; moderation in the use of them did no good, but absolute renunciation was effectual'.[5]

Whether on tour or in the capital, he still led the same strenuous life. Up at dawn; then an hour and a half of riding, 'principally at a hard gallop'; a public breakfast; work until lunch; after lunch a short siesta; then Greek or Latin; sometimes work in the evening; dinner at eight; at ten he retired, to read for a short time before going to bed. He was, however, always ready to abandon this programme for the chance of some pigsticking.[6]

To one of his studious nature, the weakness which developed in his eyesight must have been particularly distressing. By 1822 he had to use blue spectacles for reading.[7] Towards the end of his period of office he was glad to acquire a Church Bible in large print —'I find I can read my Bible by candlelight, which is an immense point gained.'[8]

[1] M.E. to J. Adam, 3.12.1819, Colebrooke, ii. 108.
[2] M.E. to Malcolm, 31.1.1821, Elphinstone.
[3] Journal, 3.5.1825, Colebrooke, ii. 169.
[4] Heber, Journal, ibid. 169 f.
[5] M.E. to J. Adam, 30.12.1822, Elphinstone.
[6] John Warden to T. E. Colebrooke, Colebrooke, ii. 174.
[7] M.E. to Major Close, 5.5.1822, Elphinstone.
[8] Journal, 26.4.[1827], Colebrooke, ii. 197.

His official duties were lighter than at Poona: 'though I have not near so much to do here as in the Deccan', he confided to Chaplin in December 1819, 'I have a great deal to learn and two entire days in every week going to Church and Council & the other avocations to which they lead.'[1]

He took to his duties much better than he had expected.[2] But he thought that there were considerable defects in the system of government. 'There is a great deal of trifling business and details with which a government ought not to be plagued, because they bind it down to particulars, and prevent the general and constant superintendence, and the consideration of the past, the present, and the future, which ought to be its essential duty.'[3] He disliked, moreover, the methods of government by Council. 'It is however a great annoyance', he explained to Malcolm in December 1819, 'to a person who is used as we are (or rather as we *were* and *you are*) to have his word law and to have no body to satisfy of the propriety of a measure but himself, to be obliged to explain his motives to a Council. Ours is perfectly cordial & harmonious but 9 times out of ten one can settle a question without exactly stating the reasons even to oneself & on the Council plan you are not only obliged to state your reasons but sometimes to enter into long arguments about matters not worth the pains of saying two words about.'[4] To Adam he made a similar complaint—one indeed that has often been made by administrators in India: 'Much time is lost in minute writing. For instance, if a Collector in a new district applies for tents for his native establishment on a circuit of his district, I say "Granted", but another member of the Government writes a minute to show that his case differs from Mr. So-and-so's case, in which tents were formerly allowed, and it takes half an hour to reply.'[5]

When in August 1818 he had been considering his chances of an appointment to the Council of one of the Presidency governments, he had given the preference to Madras rather than Calcutta, adding as an aside, 'about Bombay I know less but I fear they are narrow and greedy'.[6]

[1] M.E. to Chaplin, 13.12.1819, *Elphinstone*.
[2] M.E. to Malcolm, 4.12.1819, *Elphinstone*.
[3] M.E. to J. Adam, 3.12.1819, Colebrooke, ii. 108–9.
[4] M.E. to Malcolm, 4.12.1819, *Elphinstone*.
[5] M.E. to J. Adam, 3.12.1819, Colebrooke, ii. 109.
[6] M.E. to J. Adam, 15.8.1818, *Elphinstone*.

In fact, however, he was well satisfied with his first Council—
'perfectly well-intentioned, good-humoured, and unanimous on
great points', although often at variance with each other in matters
of detail, as was only to be expected. Sir Charles Colville, the
commander-in-chief, he considered to be a 'plain, gentlemanly,
good sort of fellow—a most distinguished officer, and quite free
from all sort of fuss and military affectation'. The third and fourth
members, Bell and Prendergast, were old Bombay civil servants of
experience. He found, at least at first, that 'the Councillors save a
good deal of trouble, as I am able to refer to them matters which I
do not understand myself'.[1]

In the early months he was also glad of the help of Francis
Warden, who had been Secretary to Government since 1805. 'New
and unknown details', he told Adam, gave him little trouble: 'I
have always Warden to tell me what is usual.'[2] But Warden was in
fact alien to many of his beliefs and sympathies. Warden had spent
the whole of his official career at Bombay; he had had no experience
of the districts at all, and it later transpired that he had little interest
in Indian culture.[3] In 1823 he became a Member of Council, and as
such proved a formidable opponent of many of Elphinstone's
policies. Even his wife seemed to Elphinstone to lack sympathy for
India: 'her only fault is her rooted dislike to the country into which
her lot has thrown her'.[4]

Elphinstone still had control of the Deccan, for it was annexed to
the Bombay Presidency on 1 November 1819—the day on which
he became Governor. But he also had to deal with the problems of
territories widely different from the Deccan both in their past
history and also in the men and measures by which they were then
being administered.

M.E. to J. Adam, 3.12.1819, Colebrooke, ii. 108 f. Guy Lenox Prendergast,
Bombay writer 1792 season; 1805, Judge and Magistrate Broach, subsequently
Acting Chief Judge Surat, Chief Judge Surat Court of Appeal (*Personal Records*,
v. 651 f.). Alexander Bell, Bombay writer 1789 season; 1796, Assistant to Com-
mercial Resident Malabar; 1807, Commercial Resident Malabar (*Personal
Records*, viii. 693 ff.).
    [2] Ibid.
    [3] Francis Warden, writer 1793, Assistant to Military Board 1796, Acting
Secretary to the Military Board 1798, Deputy Secretary to Government 1802,
Secretary to Government 1805 (*Personal Records*, v. 637 ff.).
    [4] M.E. to General Smith, 6.5.1822, *Elphinstone*.

8

THE OLD BOMBAY TERRITORIES
(1819–27)

BEFORE the annexation of the Deccan the Bombay Government was already in possession of considerable territories in Gujarat and the Konkan.

A large part of those territories in Gujarat had been acquired from the Peshwa and the Gaikwar at the beginning of the century, and the Bombay Government had then appointed a certain Major Walker to administer them. He seems to have been both efficient and idealistic, and he trained up a number of able assistants, both soldiers and civilians. There was therefore a reserve of knowledge and experience available when the Treaty of Poona in 1817 and the end of the war in 1818 brought further acquisitions in the same area.

The whole was divided into four Collectorates—Surat, Broach, Kaira, and Ahmadabad. Three of the four Collectors were civilians —Morison at Surat, Shubrick at Broach, and Dunlop at Ahmadabad. Morison and Dunlop both seem to have been competent enough. Shubrick, however, was a man of independent mind and ungovernable spirit: whenever his principles or his policies were criticized, he was apt to be outspoken to the point of insubordination in their defence. It was the soldier, Captain Archibald Robertson of Kaira, who stood out as an administrator of unusual ability.[1]

When Elphinstone visited Surat in 1821 he found the peasants 'ill-clothed and ill-lodged', and concluded that the condition of the people was 'very much depressed'. Nearly one-third of the district lay waste.[2] However, Morison had under his charge no less than 684 villages, with a population of 360,000 souls.[3]

Broach had only 417 villages, with a population of 229,000.[4] But

---

[1] John Morison, writer 1796 season: Charles Shubrick, writer 1794 season; John Dunlop, writer 1806 season (*East-India Register*). Archibald Robertson, Cadet 1800, Lieut. 1801, Capt. 1811, Major 1822; employed in revenue work since 1804. He was the brother of H. D. Robertson the Collector of Poona (*Personal Records*, xx. 209 ff.; *D.N.B.*).

[2] M.E., Minute, 6.5.1821, S.R.J. iii. 697 ff.

[3] 360,323 is the exact figure given (Revenue letter from Bombay, 5.11.1823, para. 219, Bom. R.L.R. vi, 872 f.).

[4] 229,527 is the exact figure given (ibid.).

Elphinstone was better pleased with conditions there. The land seemed well cultivated, and the inhabitants generally in comfortable circumstances. Nevertheless, he thought that the villages, 'though good compared to most in India', had 'nothing of the comfort and solidity of those beyond the Myhee'.[1]

Of the two Collectorates beyond the Mahi, Kaira seemed the more prosperous. Elphinstone paid it a remarkable tribute. 'In the fertility and improvement of the fields, there are many parts of the Bengal provinces which cannot be surpassed; but in the abundance of trees and hedges, in handsome and substantial well-built villages, and in the decent and thriving appearance of the people, I have seen nothing in India that can bear a comparison with the eastern zillah of Guzerat.'[2] It contained 561 villages, with a population of 371,000.[3] Ahmadabad was larger, with 1,077 villages and a population of 550,000, but much of it was occupied by important chiefs like the Girasias.[4]

The British had had possession of a few isolated places in the Konkan since the eighteenth century.[5] When the cession of some territory was about to be required of Baji Rao in 1817, Elphinstone had told Nepean that the Konkan was the most desirable area. Geographically it was convenient for Bombay; it would supply recruits for the Bombay army; it was the strongest part of the Peshwa's territories and his refuge in time of trouble; moreover, its possession would give the Company control of the whole of the western coast of India. But he thought that Baji Rao would be most reluctant to part with 'the cradle of his family and of the Maratha Empire'.[6]

Nepean agreed. The advantages of Khandesh—in particular the separation of the Peshwa from Hindusthan—seemed slight indeed compared with those of the Konkan. 'I should be inclined to sacrifice a good deal', he replied, 'to obtain possession of all the coast even down to Goa.'[7]

But Elphinstone soon had to report that 'I cd. not take the lower

[1] M.E., Minute, 25.4.1821, S.R.J. iii. 661 ff.
[2] M.E., Minute, 6.4.1821, S.R.J. iii. 677.
[3] 371,504 is the exact figure given (Revenue letter from Bombay, 5.11.1823, para. 219, Bom. R.L.R. vi. 872 f.).
[4] Ibid.
[5] Bankot since 1755, Karanja and Salsette, Elephanta and Hog Islands since 1774, and Malwan since 1812.
[6] M.E. to Nepean, 21.5.1817, Bom. S.C. 25.6.1817, 338 ff.
[7] Nepean to M.E., 26.5.1817, ibid. 343 ff.

Concan without giving great pain to the Paishwa, & what is worse, great disgust to every man about the Government. I have therefore contented myself with the part North of the road to Bombay, wh. I reckon at 1000000 Rupees.'[1] In justifying such moderation to the Court of Directors, Lord Hastings explained that 'almost all the principal Bramin families connected with the Poona government' came from the Southern Konkan and argued that since so many of its inhabitants were Brahmans there was considerable loyalty there to the Peshwa's Government.[2]

Consequently, it was not until 1818, after the war, that the British gained possession of the whole of the Southern Konkan.

The first Collector of the Northern Konkan was Saville Marriott[3]—an able man, but ponderous in expressing his views, and, some thought, a slow worker. Later, in 1838, Sir Robert Grant made what seems to have been a fair assessment—'very patient and painstaking, a little formal and punctilious perhaps, but eminently upright, conscientious and independent'.[4] He made a good impression upon Elphinstone when he visited Bombay in 1820: 'Marriott is here trying himself among all the ladies after the fatigues of war. He is an uncommonly gentlemanlike, fine young man.'[5]

With headquarters at Thana Marriott had charge of a Collectorate of 2,111 villages and some 420,000 souls. He found general poverty except in the Bassein area.[6]

The first Collector of the Southern Konkan was John Pelly.[7] He seems to have been a humane man: at least, he praised his executive engineer on one occasion for having treated his Indian labourers as 'something more than mere machines, formed to administer to our pleasure and convenience'.[8] Grant wrote to Elphinstone in 1819 that Pelly was 'a very gentlemanlike, sensible sort of personage— a little stiff at first but that is mere *mannerism*. I think he would have

---

[1] M.E. to Nepean, 7.6.1817, ibid. 357 ff.
[2] Governor-General to Court of Directors, 4.9.1817, para. 11, P.P. 1818, xi. 369, 45–49.
[3] Minutes of 19.6.1817, Bom. S.C. 25.6.1817, 312 ff. Bombay writer 1806 season.
[4] *Personal Records*, xx. 273 ff.
[5] M.E. to Sir W. Keir, 29.2.1820, *Elphinstone*.
[6] Marriott to Government, 11.7.1821, para. 44, Bom. R.C. 22.8.1821, 3802 ff.; Revenue letter from Bombay, 5.11.1823, para. 219, Bom. R.L.R. vi. 872 ff.
[7] John Hinde Pelly, Bombay writer 1806 season.
[8] Pelly to T. B. Jervis, 5.12.1820; W. P. Jervis, *T. B. Jervis*, 13.

made a good Collector by this time if they knew how to direct him in Bombay, but this is not the case. Pelly fritters away his time in writing speculative letters to Govt. when he ought to be acquiring information.'[1] Speculation seemed a waste of time to Grant, who was more interested in people than ideas and in detailed facts than general tendencies.

With headquarters at Bankot until 1820, and thereafter at Ratnagiri, Pelly had charge of a Collectorate of 2,291 villages and some 632,000 souls.[2] The standard of living he thought low; people went about 'almost naked'; a man with a turban or dress attracted attention as a person of some consequence.[3]

As in the Deccan, the new rulers had to find men to serve them: those who collaborated were naturally the gainers.

When Marriott took charge of his Collectorate in 1817 he found 'a general impression' among the people that the new government would not long endure and a consequent reluctance to serve it for fear of Baji Rao's vengeance upon his return to power there. 'Respectable men' of sufficient ability and fidelity were difficult to find. In the troubled months that followed, Marriott therefore tended to look first for fidelity. Three whom he made Kamavisdars, or district officers, had served the Company for twenty years as Karkuns, or clerks, at Karanja.[4] Even so, he was soon employing many officials of the former government.[5] In the early years, indeed, the majority of his clerks were men who had served the Peshwa, though few of his district officers had done so.[6]

At first he nursed a prejudice against appointing Brahmans as Kamavisdars. But by 1820 he had overcome it, and in his systematic way he then drew up for Elphinstone a memorandum entitled 'Brahmin Comavisdars'. On the one side he argued, 'if we give encouragement to Brahmins, shall we not make the Mussulmans & lower castes of Hindoos our enemies?' On the other side, he argued that Brahmans were of all social groups the best informed and the most respectable, that if they were not conciliated by

[1] Grant to M.E., 13.1.1819, *Elphinstone.*
[2] The exact figure was 632,337, but such statistics have no claim to accuracy (Revenue letter from Bombay, 5.11.1823, para. 219, Bom. R.L.R. vi. 872 f.).
[3] Pelly to Government, 18.12.1820, para. 37, Bom. R.C., 24.1.1821, 655 f.
[4] Marriott to Government, 17.4.1824, Bom. R.C. 28.4.1824, 2409 ff.
[5] Marriott to Government, 11.5.1821, Bom. R.C. 6.6.1821, 2641 ff.
[6] Marriott to M.E., 5.6.1820, *Elphinstone.*

office they might try to thwart all the new government's plans, and
that to impoverish them would eventually destroy the only learning in the country.[1]

When Grant, the Resident at Satara, visited the Southern Konkan he noted with disapproval that Abdul Ghaffar, who had long
been the Company's 'head native agent' at Bankot, had so used his
influence in the distribution of posts in the new Collectorate that
most of the officials there were Muslims. 'This is very impolitic',
wrote Grant to Elphinstone in January 1819. 'They are illiterate,
ignorant & overbearing. In place of using the Brahmins who are at
present the only men who possess information regarding the
revenue & the modes of administering justice, they complain of
being insulted & abused by the Mussulmen on every occasion.'[2]

When Pelly reported, in August 1820, the murder of a Brahman
and his family by a body of Muslims, he added that because the
local police officer, who happened to be a Muslim, seemed to have
been neglecting his duties in the case, he had been forced to depute
a European to handle it.[3] This prompted the Governor in Council
to tell him that 'as the Southern Concan is so much inhabited by
Bramins who have been unused to the rule of Mussulmans and
whose prejudices against that persuasion are very strong it would be
extremely desirable to take advantage of every opening to introduce Brahmins into the chief offices of the district'.[4]

In December 1820, however, Pelly reported that his officials
were drawn from three different social groups—Brahmans, Prabhus, and Muslims—for the reason that 'it has always been considered a desirable arrangement to mingle these castes as much as
possible in each mehaul [district] in the hope of thereby checking
the prevalence of abuses'.[5] This doctrine seems to have received
official approval, for in 1822 the Government were reporting to the
Court of Directors that Brahmans, Muslims, and Prabhus had been
'mingled as much as possible' in the government services in every
district of the Southern Konkan.[6]

John Dunlop, an experienced Bombay civil servant, who succeeded Pelly in the Southern Konkan in 1822, soon realized how

[1] Marriott to M.E., 5.6.1820, *Elphinstone.*
[2] Grant to M.E., 13.1.1819, *Elphinstone.*
[3] Pelly to Government, 15.8.1820, Bom. J.C. 30.8.1820, 3593 f.
[4] Minutes of Government, 28.8.1820, ibid. 3595.
[5] Pelly to Government, 18.12.1820, Bom. R.C. 24.1.1821, 665 ff.
[6] Revenue letter from Bombay, 23.2.1822, para. 45, Bom. R.L.R. vi. 1 ff.

much the Brahmans there had suffered from the change of government: the Peshwas themselves, he pointed out, had been Konkan Brahmans; much of their patronage and also of their charity had flowed thither; the number of influential men who had lost office was greater there than elsewhere. He therefore reported, in 1824, that he had 'tried to select persons who had held responsible situations under the former government, or whose families were respectable' for the post of Sar Kamavisdar, or senior district officer. But he added regretfully that he had had no success: 'the advantage of respectability has been counterbalanced by want of intelligence'. Indeed, he stated as a general principle that 'natives of the most respectable families' were 'seldom qualified for our best situations'. Such posts, he concluded, 'necessarily fall to their more intelligent inferiors, who are content to learn their duty in subordinate situations'.[1]

Elphinstone was in fact unable to do much to improve the status or prospects of the Company's Indian officials. In the Deccan he had arranged their salary scales with some reference to the maxim that where there was 'considerable trust' there ought to be 'liberal pay'.[2] He wanted to apply the same principle to the salary scales of Indian officials on the Bombay establishment. In 1820 he recommended that the salaries of the Hindu and Muslim law officers of the Sadr Adalat—the highest of the Company's law courts—should be increased to 400 or 500 rupees. But the civil service members of his council declared that 200 rupees would be ample.[3] The matter was accordingly referred to the Court of Directors, who in due course decided that 300 rupees should be the limit.[4] The episode is significant. There seems to have been a general assumption among the Englishmen employed in the Company's civil administration that to pay their Indian subordinates substantial salaries would have been a needless extravagance. At the same time, and in the reaction against the zamindari settlement of Bengal, there was a tendency to look with suspicion upon any claims to a privileged position in the revenue system. Both these tendencies contributed towards the levelling effect of the Company's rule, and Elphinstone was as much opposed to the one as to the other.

[1] Dunlop to Government, 15.8.1824, para. 169 f., Bom. R.C. 12.1.1825, 44.
[2] M.E., Report, 46.   [3] Minutes, 7.11.1820, Bom. J.C. 8.11.1820, 4891 ff.
[4] Judicial dispatch to Bombay, 12.4.1826, para 9 ff., Bom. J.D. i. 380 ff.

In the Southern Konkan, for example, Pelly was disturbed to find that it was a custom in one of his districts for the Mamlatdar, unknown to the Government, to levy an extra cess from certain classes and to give part of this in charity to some of the local Brahmans. He duly recommended that the practice should be prohibited, 'as this exaction is without a parallel in the whole Zillah, and is levied exclusively on those classes who are least able to bear it'.[1] In this matter Elphinstone seems to have carried his colleagues with him. In the minutes of the Governor in Council it was resolved that 'it is desirable that Mr Pelly should be cautious in recommending the abolition of taxes of this sort merely because they seem irregular since the whole of the native system is irregular and one part of it makes up for the other'.[2]

On the other hand, as in the Deccan Elphinstone was careful to restrain the overweening zeal of Collectors eager to make all things new. Marriott, for example, far from wanting a ryotwari system had been proposing to raise up landlords after the English style in the Northern Konkan. Elphinstone nevertheless preferred caution.

Before Elphinstone became Governor of Bombay, Marriott had been blaming the Maratha revenue system for the widespread poverty which he found in his Collectorate. He thought that the multitude of cesses gave local officials safe opportunities to squeeze as much as they could from the peasants. Moreover, there were no great landlords to foster cultivation and improved methods. He studied the Fifth Report of 1812, but drew from it the singular conclusion that the main defect of the Bengal revenue system was not that the zamindars had too much power over their tenants but that they had too little—that they were not more like English landlords. If the peasants of the Northern Konkan were freed from their burdens, however, the most efficient of them might become improving landlords.[3]

Both in official correspondence and in private conversation with Sir Evan Nepean, Marriott had argued that the cesses must be abolished, a survey begun, and the revenue demand restricted to a

[1] Pelly to Government, 30.5.1820, Bom. R.C. 14.6.1820, 2627.
[2] Minutes, 9.6.1820, ibid. 2629. This declaration was qualified by the suggestion that if Pelly found that the cess was 'really oppressive' the Government would sanction its abolition.
[3] Marriott to Government, 22.6.1818, S.R.J. iii. 768 ff.; Revenue letter from Bombay, 19.4.1822, esp. paras. 249–51, ibid. 765 f.

third of the gross produce. He was so persuasive that in December 1818 the Government authorized him to carry out his proposals.[1]

Elphinstone, however, was more sceptical. He thought that it was too early for such drastic changes. Besides, Marriott could hardly have the time for a survey accurate enough to be the basis of a new assessment within the coming revenue year. But it soon transpired that Marriott had already issued a proclamation in which he explained the main features of his policy, and in particular promised a remission of the obnoxious cesses.[2]

Elphinstone finally decided that what Marriott had promised in his proclamation he must be allowed to perform. He had promised to abolish the cesses: they must be abolished, the assessment being increased at the same time to compensate Government for the loss. In future, Marriott must be careful not to move until he had first obtained the Government's permission for every step which he intended to take.[3]

The home government delivered a crushing verdict upon Marriott's plan to establish a landlord system. 'On this subject his ideas are somewhat crude', they wrote in 1822. 'This momentous conclusion is established upon an opinion which Mr. Marriott has taken up, that the people of Bengal were happy and prosperous under a zemindarry system before the period of the British rule. Mr. Marriott may rest assured that this opinion of his is founded upon very unsatisfactory evidence.' And they went on to declare that any 'intermediate agency' between the Government and the cultivators was always undesirable, and as a principle of general policy to instruct the Bombay Government to consider how best to remove it wherever it occurred and 'where the removal of it may not be precluded by a regard to existing rights, or what may be due to the feelings of individuals'.[4]

They approved, however, of Marriott's abolition of petty cesses and the substitution of a higher rate of assessment upon the land.[5]

Another attempt of Marriott's to introduce Western ideas into the system of land tenure also came to grief. When, indefatigable

[1] Ibid.

[2] M.E. Minutes, n.d., Bom. R.C. 1.12.1819, 4104 f., 4108 ff.; Proclamation by S. Marriott, Bom. R.C. 22.12.1819, 4464 ff.

[3] M.E., Minute, n.d., ibid. 4476 f.; Minutes of Council, 16.12.1818, ibid. 4477 ff.

[4] Revenue dispatch to Bombay, 13.2.1822, para. 138 f., S.R.J. iii. 771 f.

[5] Ibid., para. 140.

in his inquiries, he asked inhabitants of his Collectorate 'To whom does the soil belong?', he found that his question was always met with 'an air of surprise mixed up generally with a sarcastical kind of look'. All the Indians whom he asked replied that it belonged to the sovereign. There was, however, a superior type of tenure[1] according to which the cultivator enjoyed a virtually guaranteed occupancy so long as he paid the revenue demanded by the Government. Some Maratha officials had tolerated without authorizing the transfer of such rights in the land by the holder to anyone else. Marriott asked the Government to announce that it formally recognized the right of such ryots to sell, mortgage, or otherwise alienate their lands, on the ground that this would raise land values—an important consideration for a government 'whose exigencies require so large a share of the produce of the land as ours do'.[2] The Government, however, decided against such a change in present circumstances. This was the sort of change in the direction of a Western social system which Elphinstone was anxious to postpone.

In spite of Marriott's early proposals to establish a landlord class with full private property rights in the soil, his subsequent activities carried him in the opposite direction.

When he came to consider the traditional claim of the Pandharpeshas,[3] mainly but not entirely Brahmans, to a lighter assessment than other cultivators his immediate reaction was to reject it on the ground that 'the first principles of Political Economy require that each member of the community should contribute to its support according to his respective abilities; and I presume it to be clear that nothing can more militate against natural justice, from which the above principles emanate, than that one class of the community should be burthened with taxes merely to lessen those which would otherwise be equally assessable on the favoured few'. In theory, however, there was no inconsistency between the levelling tendency of his attitude towards the Pandharpeshas and his wish to establish a landlord class, for he thought that it was only by means of the Government's revenue demand being light enough to allow the cultivators an economic rent that a landlord class could

---

[1] The suti tenure, resembling the mirasi tenure of the Deccan.

[2] Marriott to Government, 11.7.1821, Bom. R.C. 22.8.1821, 3802 ff.

[3] They claimed special rates as being the descendants of the original founders of the village, probably deriving their name from pandhar (Mar.) = village community and peshan (Pers.) = profession or occupation (Rogers, i. 229).

develop by the rise of the most efficient[1]—on the principles of
economics and natural justice which happily seemed so harmonious
in the early nineteenth century.

Besides attacking the Pandharpeshas' privileges as 'a gross viola-
tion of the first principles of general political economy' he also
suggested a cruder reason for their abolition—that 'the common
principles of humanity will occasion by far the major part of the
people to become more attached to a Government when they see an
unjust distinction abolished in their favour'.[2]

The Governor in Council, however, decided that the Pandharpeshas' privilege of a light assessment should be continued to them.[3]

Marriott returned to the attack in 1823. The Pandharpeshas had
no official charters (sanads) from the Maratha Government: their
privileges originated in concessions made by Maratha officials and
revenue farmers, particularly after Baji Rao's return to Poona after
the Treaty of Bassein. How were the Pandharpeshas' claims to be
judged? Marriott suggested that only those should be recognized
who could prove that their claims originated before that time.[4]
The Governor in Council approved of the principle, but pointed
out that it had also been customary to grant lands at a favourable
rent to classes supposed to have special disadvantages in undertaking agriculture—because their women did no work in the fields
and they had to employ labourers, and so on. If there were Pandharpeshas in this category, 'the exemption must depend on the
circumstances of the persons and not on prescription'.[5]

In the Southern Konkan the privileged class of Khots attracted
as much unfavourable attention from some at least of the new
rulers as the Pandharpeshas in the north. When Grant visited the
area he found much discontent. 'The Concan ryots are not a bit
bettered by the change of Govt.', he wrote privately to Elphinstone
in January 1819. 'They appear exceedingly dissatisfied and every
man I assure you that I have conversed with contrasts his situation
with that of the ryot in the Deccan.' Their complaints to him were
always directed against the Khots.[6]

[1] Marriott to Government, 29.1.1820, Bom. R.C. 9.2.1820, 861 ff.
[2] Marriott to Government, 12.5.1820, Bom. R.C. 19.7.1820, 3614 ff.
[3] Minutes of 14.7.1820, ibid. 3624.
[4] Marriott to Government, 13.6.1823, Bom. R.C. 8.7.1823, 6138 ff.
[5] Government to Marriott, 5.7.1823, ibid. 6140 f.
[6] Grant to M.E., 13.1.1819, *Elphinstone*.

In fact, not more than about half the villages in the Southern Konkan were entirely managed by Khots. In the rest the Khots were either absent or had their power restricted by the presence of a superior class of cultivators—the dharakaris, who enjoyed hereditary occupancy rights.[1] Most of the Khots' tenants, however, were less fortunate, for they seemed to have no rights of any practi-

TABLE 4

Khoti, Dharakari, and Mixed Villages in the Southern Konkan[2]

Villages worth less than Rs.1,000 annual revenue

Khoti	1,062½
Dharakari	337
Mixed	525½
Total	1,925

Villages worth more than Rs.1,000 annual revenue

Khoti	38
Dharakari	133
Mixed	106
Total	277

cal importance.[3] This class—the ardhelis[4]—naturally attracted the sympathy of the new rulers.

The Khots, on the other hand, were never very popular among British administrators.[5] As the years passed the trend of opinion turned ever more strongly against them. As long ago as 1887 it was suggested that the British had intended in 1818 to establish a ryotwari system and hence to abolish the Khoti tenure, but that they were misled: their informants, so the argument runs, were either Khots themselves or had some interest in the preservation of the tenure and therefore gave them an exaggerated impression of the stability and importance of the Khots' position under the Peshwa's Government.[6]

---

[1] Dhara = a holding.
[2] Bom. R.C. 12.1.1825, 46 f.
[3] Pelly to Government, 18.12.1820, Bom. R.C. 24.1.1821, 665 f.
[4] Ardheli = paying half one's crop as rent.
[5] Or among Indian nationalists. The tenure was abolished by Bombay Act VI of 1950.
[6] Achyut Rao Bhaskar (Deputy Collector) to Collector of Ratnagiri, 22.10.1887, S.B.R. (N.S.) ccccxlvi. 25.

But Elphinstone for his part never determined upon a wholesale introduction of the ryotwari system. Moreover, while he was anxious to make no unnecessary changes, his policy towards existing institutions was never shaped solely by reports of what had been the practice under the Peshwas.

The Collectors certainly had great difficulty in ascertaining the rights of the Khots. At the least, they had the right to collect the revenue on behalf of the Government and incidentally to enjoy whatever profits they could make by extending the area under cultivation in their respective villages.[1] But before their fate could be determined it was necessary also to consider their utility under the new government.

Elphinstone asked Chaplin for his opinion. Chaplin replied that 'the office seems to be of little use under our Government', and drew the conclusion that on general principles the Khots should be treated in the same way as the Deshmukhs, Deshpandes, 'and other superfluous officers' of the Deccan.[2] In other words, they should be deprived of their duties and powers but left with their customary emoluments. This solution would have accorded with Elphinstone's guiding principle that men of influence who lost office because of the change of government should nevertheless retain some suitable means of subsistence and thus some substantial reason for loyalty. But as Chaplin himself realized, the analogy between the Khots and the 'superfluous officers' of the Deccan was defective in one fundamental respect: the Khots had no official emoluments, 'their profits'—in Chaplin's words—'being entirely derived from what they could squeeze from the villager'.[3]

Pelly, the first Collector of the Southern Konkan, did find some virtue in the Khots: they paid the revenue promptly, he reported, and 'the more respectable of them' he described as 'capitalists, who lay out money in bringing new lands into cultivation, and may be considered as a description of yeomanry'. However, far from being so misled by his informants as to countenance all the Khot's pretensions, he soon began to set some limits to their powers. Each inferior (ardheli) tenant was by custom bound to labour for his Khot for one day in every eight. Pelly found that the Khots had

[1] Ibid. 6. The Khots apparently arose as government revenue contractors as early as the seventeenth century.
[2] Chaplin to Government, 18.11.1820, Bom. R.C. 28.2.1821, 1401 ff.
[3] Ibid.

been exacting similar service from their superior (dharakari) tenants. This he strictly forbade.[1]

What he thought was the great disadvantage of the system was the fact that it left him in ignorance of the real relations between the Khots and the inferior tenants. Few of the Khoti villages had accountants. Such accounts as there were the Khots kept themselves. But according to custom a survey should be made every seven years, and he therefore recommended one.[2]

The Governor in Council agreed. And although there was no intention to introduce a ryotwari system everywhere, it must be admitted that one of the presuppositions of the ryotwari system had found general acceptance—the idea, namely, that the Collector should know exactly how much produce was being grown by each cultivator and how much he had to pay as rent or revenue; otherwise, it was thought, there might be oppression. Village accountants must therefore be appointed, and an 'early and minute enquiry into the tenures' must be made. 'Should you for any length of time content yourself with settling with the Khotes it is much to be feared that the rights of all the other persons of the agricultural classes may fall into oblivion as they have done in Bengal.'[3]

Pelly and his successors, however, found it very difficult to determine what were the rights of the other agricultural classes as against the Khots. The new rulers might well have expected the hereditary district officers—the Deshmukhs and Deshpandes—to be the proper source of unbiased information on such points. But most of these were Khots themselves.[4] In order to curb the power of the Khots, Pelly's successor Dunlop suggested that more of the superior class of tenants (the dharakaris) should be established in Khoti villages wherever the Khot could be persuaded to agree. If this were done gradually, he hoped that in time the Khots might 'become much the same sort of agents as Patells in other parts of the country'. He also wanted to press on with the measures which had already been begun. A revenue survey should give enough information to enable him to draw up a scale of pay for the Khots proportionate to the produce of their respective villages. Accountants should be appointed in every village or group of nearby

[1] Pelly to Government, 18.12.1820, Bom. R.C. 24.1.1821, 665 f.
[2] Ibid.
[3] Resolutions of Government, Bom. R.C. 24.1.1821, 856 ff.; Government to Collector, Southern Konkan, 28.6.1821, Bom. R.C. 4.7.1821, 2911 ff.
[4] Dunlop to Government, 31.12.1822, para. 22, Bom. R.C. 26.3.1823, 4310.

villages in order to give correct information about the produce to government. An incidental advantage of this he thought would be to absorb 'the crowds of discontented Brahmins, who are so numerous'.[1]

But all such reforms would have to be carried out with caution. The ardheli tenants were in general deeply in debt to their Khots, and many of them were consequently 'little better than abject slaves'. If the Khots took alarm at the intentions of government and tried to recover these debts by prosecuting their tenants in Court, the tenants would be ruined. Caution was the first essential.[2] Dunlop's forebodings were soon justified.

When Elphinstone visited the Southern Konkan in 1823 he came prepared by the Collectors' reports to find 'an impoverished, dispirited and degraded population'. In fact he did not consider them much worse housed or clothed than in the Deccan. On the other hand, 'they all seemed very much dissatisfied and all seemed to prefer the Paishwah's Government to ours. I have in no district that I ever visited received so many and so loud complaints.'[3]

Numbers of these complaints were directed against the Khots: it was said that they levied heavy and arbitrary taxes upon their tenants, and there was also opposition to the system of compulsory labour service. The Judge's Court was very unpopular, for the Khots had taken advantage of what Elphinstone considered 'the best part of the Adawlut system', namely 'the regularity with which it enforces the payment of debts, by means of which the interest of money is diminished, trade is encouraged and in time people learn to avoid borrowing money which they are not likely to pay'. The Khots were even extending their power over the superior (dharakari) tenants to whom they had lent money, by suing or threatening to sue them in the Court at Ratnagiri which might be 150 miles away. If such a tenant were sued, and could not afford to go to Ratnagiri, judgement would be given against him in his absence, his house and cattle would be sold, and he himself left destitute. 'The power of the Brahmins', one ryot told Elphinstone, 'is doubled since they lost the country.'[4]

It was not to be expected that the Brahmans should congratulate

---

[1] Ibid.   [2] Ibid.
[3] M.E., Minute, n.d., Bom. R.C. 26.3.1823, 4337–8.
[4] Ibid. 4338 ff.

themselves on this account—least of all the Brahmans of the Southern Konkan. The Peshwas had taken 'almost all the civil officers employed under their government with many of the military' from Brahmans of that area. Elphinstone had heard, moreover, that Baji Rao's charities to them amounted to as much as 5 lakhs of rupees a year. On the other hand, although they had lost much as a result of the change of government, they still enjoyed great influence over public opinion. 'As they still retain almost an unlimited power as Khotes, and an ascendancy derived from religion, and [as] their habits of business and intrigue [are] sufficient to influence the ryots even in points the most opposite to their own interests', Elphinstone reflected, 'we have some reason to wonder that they occasion us so little disturbance, and that we do not feel more sensibly the effects of their power over the people.' No doubt their influence was one great reason why there was so much discontent in the Southern Konkan.

Like Dunlop, Elphinstone put much faith in the appointment of village accountants and the completion of a survey.[1]

After further discussion it was finally decided in 1825 that whatever their origin the Khots 'appear now to have acquired a right with which it would neither be just nor politic to interfere'. It followed from this that 'our improvements should be confined to ascertaining and securing the rights of the other classes without setting aside the established claims of the Khotes'. By 'the rights of the other classes', the Governor in Council meant those of the superior tenants: their rights should be discovered 'during some good period of the Maratta Government such perhaps as that of Nana Furnavees'; if that were impossible then it should be discovered what they were paying in recent years. The inferior (ardheli) tenants, on the other hand, seemed to have no rights. The Governor in Council concluded that 'the competition among the Khotes themselves will always secure them the requisite remuneration for their labour, and if there appears to be a combination among the Khotes to depress them it can be counteracted by the grant of liberal terms on the part of Government' in the other villages—'which would soon draw off the ardelas from the Khotes or force them to grant reasonable terms.'[2]

These tenants at will could be left to the operations of the market.

[1] Dunlop to Government, 16.8.1823, para. 4, Bom. R.C. 17.9.1823, 7416 ff.
[2] Government to Collector, 10.1.1825, Bom. R.C. 12.1.1825, 47.

As for the rest, the forthcoming survey should fix the dues of all parties and reconcile conflicting rights and interests, in particular by the establishment of a record of the rents payable by the superior tenants and by the appointment of village accountants.

No doubt the survey would discover concealed cultivation and under-assessed lands. But the Governor in Council told the Collector that 'no advantage should be taken of these openings, for the Khotes must unavoidably be great losers by the proposed strict enforcement of the rights of the Ryots and must be ill prepared to meet any new impost by the Government'.[1]

But the survey was to be a lengthy operation. Meanwhile the Khots flourished.

Not all privileged classes were so fortunate. When the British took charge of Surat they found that the most influential men there were the hereditary district officers, the Desais. The only way in which the Collector could settle the revenue of a district was, as Elphinstone put it, 'to send for the Dessaye and make as good a bargain as he could with him'. The Collector had no idea of the productivity of the soil or of the condition of the peasants: he 'made his assessment entirely in the dark'.[2]

But in 1817–18 the Bombay Government under Nepean introduced the ryotwari system there. Henceforth every peasant went to the Kamavisdar to arrange how much revenue he was to pay for the coming year; the account was recorded on a certificate which the Kamavisdar sealed and gave to him. This was the ruin of the Desais.

It was none of Elphinstone's doing. Yet he did not disapprove. His main objection to the ryotwari system was that it weakened the influence of the village headman in that the officers of government went behind him to the peasants themselves. In Surat, however, it was not the headman but the Desai who was weakened by this arrangement: the headman had already been reduced to insignificance by the past encroachments of the Desai.[3] In Kaira and Ahmadabad the Desais had also lost their old importance: they had in fact been almost superseded by their assistants, the Amin Patels, whose posts were hereditary, but not permanent.[4] Elphinstone

---

[1] Ibid.   [2] M.E., Minute, 6.5.1821, S.R.J. iii. 697 ff.   [3] Ibid.
[4] They were selected from particular families, but were only paid if the Collector decided to employ them (Dunlop to Government, 5.12.1820; Bom. R.C. 20.12.1820, 7179 ff.).

found in 1821 that the Desais were 'scarcely ever now employed' there.[1] What, then, was to become of the Desais? Elphinstone thought that they were 'still not without their use as checks on the Camavisdar whom they always look on as an intruder, and against whom they are always ready to bring forward or to instigate information'.[2]

But there was no positive function for them. In the 'final instructions' issued by the Governor in Council in July 1821 the Collectors were told that they were not to revive the functions of the Desais where they were now dormant and 'that in cases where they may be still employed it is advisable for you to allow that branch of their office to fall into disuse by forming your own assessment without their intervention'. But the process should be gentle: 'it should be done gradually in the manner best suited to your own convenience and least likely to create disgust or opposition'. The Collectors were still to make use of the Desai's local knowledge, to use them in matters like the adjustment of boundary disputes, the arbitration of disputes about succession to land, and so on. But they were to have no power, and though their allowances were to be continued they were not to be increased.[3]

It seems that the way in which these orders were carried out differed from one Collectorate to another: in Surat, the Desais henceforth had no further part in the administration, except that some were later appointed Shaikdars; elsewhere, however, the Collectors continued to make some use of their services, as had been suggested by the Governor in Council.[4]

The Majmudars or hereditary district accountants met with more favour in their new rulers' sight. Dunlop, for example, as Collector of Ahmadabad, commented appreciatively that they were the only dependants of former governments whom he had found to be at

[1] M.E., Minute, 6.4.1821, S.R.J. iii. 677 ff.

[2] M.E., Minute, 6.4.1821, S.R.J. iii. 681. Prendergast thought that the hereditary district officers, Desais as well as Majmudars, &c., should be restored to an active part in the administration (Prendergast, Minute, 8.7.1821, S.R.J. iii. 711).

[3] Government to Collectors, 6.7.1821, Bom. R.C. 1.8.1821, 3361 ff.

[4] S.B.R., N.S. clxxiv, 317 f. In Kaira, in particular, the Desais continued to do important revenue work. In 1859 the Collector described their 'ordinary duties' together with those of the Majmudar as 'both onerous and responsible'— e.g. helping to prepare genealogical tables, measuring land, making out returns of cultivation, &c. (ibid. 212).

How far these differences in the execution of the Government's orders were due to local circumstances and how far to the personal views of different Collectors will be a fruitful problem for future research.

all anxious to help. Their work was useful but laborious—they kept abstracts of the papers of the village accountants.[1]

Morison, while admitting the usefulness of the Majmudars, wanted a complete reform of their position. In 1818 he submitted a draft for a Regulation which he had drawn up, providing that while the Collector should where possible appoint from the same family, the post should no longer be hereditary, and substituting payment from the government treasury for the traditional system of allowances from the villages. The latter provision he recommended 'as rendering the Mujmoodars completely independent of the village managers'.[2] He thought that while the Majmudars were paid by the villages 'we must expect that great collusion will exist between the Mujmoodars and the persons in charge of the village collections, and that the accounts furnished under these circumstances are not much to be relied on'.[3] The fifteen Majmudars in his Collectorate were paid a total of Rs.4,752 a year: this the Governor in Council considered inadequate.[4] Morison recommended a new scale of pay related to the revenues of their respective districts and ranging between Rs.30 and Rs.75 a month.[5] But the Governor in Council then experienced 'the greatest distrust of sweeping reforms of the nature proposed by Mr. Morison and finds it difficult to be satisfied, when any of them is proposed, that we really see the full extent of the alteration'. The matter was referred to Chaplin for his opinion.[6]

Chaplin had no need of Majmudars in the Deccan, but he conceded that where they had long existed upon an hereditary footing, as in Gujarat, it might be useful to keep them in a state of efficiency.[7]

When Elphinstone visited Kaira and Ahmadabad in 1821 he noted that 'the Muzmoodar has still much employment'.[8] Prendergast hoped that this would continue, for he was a strong advocate of the employment of the old hereditary officers on account of their experience and knowledge.[9]

[1] Dunlop to Government, 5.12.1820, para. 2, Bom. R.C. 20.12.1820, 7179 ff.
[2] Morison to Government, 17.4.1818, Bom. R.C. 13.5.1818, 2236 ff.
[3] Morison to Government, 3.8.1818, Bom. R.C. 30.9.1818, 4609 ff.
[4] Government to Morison, 29.9.1818, ibid. 4619 ff.
[5] Morison to Government, 6.6.1820, Bom. R.C. 6.9.1820, 4853 ff.
[6] Minutes of Government, 5.9.1820, Bom. R.C. 6.9.1820, 4867.
[7] Chaplin to Government, 18.11.1820, Bom. R.C. 28.2.1821, 1401 ff.
[8] M.E., Minute, 6.4.1821, S.R.J. iii. 681.
[9] Prendergast, Minute, 29.6.1821, ibid. 704 f.

The Governor in Council finally decided, in July 1821, that the district accountants should be maintained in a state of efficiency, and revived or established where there was none already. The Collectors were told to leave the emoluments of the post to the family then enjoying them, to entrust the duties to one of the family and to reward him with a larger allowance than the others received.[1]

How much larger this sum should be and from whom it should be taken aroused lengthy discussion and a final solution was not reached until 1826. The Collectors made many different suggestions. One suggested that the officiating Majmudars should receive three-quarters of 1 per cent. of the gross revenue of their respective districts, another one suggested 2 per cent., another suggested that some minimum be fixed instead of a percentage. The Collectors also differed in their opinions of the best way of finding the money: one thought that the officiating Majmudar's payment should be taken from the inactive members of the family; another thought that the inactive sharers should not have to contribute at all.[2]

Clearly, much depended upon circumstances. If the family were large and the allowances small the inactive members might well suffer hardship if they were forced to pay the salary of the officiating Majmudar. It was therefore decided that where the allowances were 'considerable' and the shares nearly equal, the Collector might levy a suitable amount from the inactive members. Otherwise, the Government would pay the salary of the officiating Majmudar. Further dissipation of the allowances attached to the post was to be stopped.[3]

In short, the position and pay of the district accountants were both stabilized, while uniformity was not attempted.

In Broach as elsewhere in Gujarat the new rulers found a barrier between them and the peasants. For some time they had been trying to secure adequate information to enable them to regulate the

[1] Government to Collectors, 26.7.1821, Bom. R.C. 1.8.1821, 3361 ff.
[2] Summary of replies to queries of 22.12.1825, Bom. R.C. 20.9.1826, 50; L. R. Reid (Acting Secretary to Government), Report, 18.9.1826, ibid. 54.
[3] Government to Collectors, 18.9.1826, Bom. R.C. 20.9.1826, 56 ff. All emoluments whether in cash or in kind were declared to be henceforth inalienable and indivisible. If any member of the family died without lineal heirs his share was to be devoted to the payment of the officiating Majmudar, provided that widows were to receive a suitable maintenance during life.

assessment according to actual circumstances. For this reason, a survey had been instituted in 1811.

But in spite of the survey, the particular village system that predominated in Broach made it, in Elphinstone's words, 'utterly impossible' for the Collector 'to guess whether the assessment is light or heavy'. When he visited Broach in 1821 he was troubled to find that the assessment had recently been raised by 4½ lakhs of rupees. Yet there was no evidence by which he could judge whether this was too large or too small an increase.[1]

Considerably more than three-quarters of the villages in Broach were managed according to the bhagdari system. The land of each village was divided into shares (bhags), and the revenue due from the village was paid by the sharers (bhagdars) collectively according to the value of their shares. It was calculated by the Collector from crop estimates made by the hereditary district officers. The general principle was for the Government to demand half the estimated market value of the gross produced. But there was no means of telling either how much the sharers took from the peasants who cultivated for them as their tenants, or how heavy was the actual burden of the Collector's assessment.[1]

Elphinstone had on his Council a staunch defender of the bhagdari system in Prendergast who had himself served in Broach. Prendergast painted an idyllic picture of its advantages:

Every share of the government lands possessed by a Patell or other cultivator, down even to the smallest Patteedars, is known, and is denominated a four-anna share, or a three-hundred-and-one anna, or a half-anna share. Supposing then that the Government assessment is fixed (say at 1,000 rupees) the Patells with whom the amount has been adjusted by the Collector return to their village, all persons interested meet them at the public meeting place in the village, the amount is declared, and every man by the simplest process instantly knows precisely what he has to pay. The Patell who has a four-anna share has to pay 4,000 annas; the Patteedar who has a half-anna share has to pay 500 annas.[2]

Elphinstone agreed that this was an excellent way of distributing the assessment. But it only applied to the sharers (bhagdars), not to their tenants. Where the sharers were many, the system was no doubt equitable. But where they were few, the system might well permit the exploitation of the tenants. Moreover, he had noticed

[1] M.E., Minute, 25.4.1821, S.R.J. iii. 661 ff.
[2] Prendergast, Minute, 29.6.1821, ibid. 701 ff.

that it was only in half the villages of Broach that nearly all the cultivators were sharers.[1]

Elphinstone had also complained that the Collector of Broach was left in ignorance of the real weight of his assessment. To this Prendergast replied that the survey recently carried out in Broach had provided more information about 'the sources and principles of revenue' than was available anywhere else in India.[2] Elphinstone, however, pointed out that much of the information necessary for any judgement of the fairness of the assessment varied from year to year and therefore could not be found in the pages of survey reports.[3]

Prendergast also argued that if the Collector demanded too much, the head of the village was by custom allowed to reject his assessment and instead to require him to take as the Government's revenue one-half of the gross produce from the actual crops at the harvest when they lay stored in the village barnyard.[4]

But even if that was an effective safeguard against too heavy an assessment upon the village as a whole, there still remained the objection that the distribution of the revenue demand among the sharers' tenants might be unjust. Prendergast's argument here was that since the sharers were themselves villagers they would be anxious to avoid injustice lest they should become hated by the rest of the community.[5]

Underlying these discussions was surely the assumption that the ideal was a village in which all the cultivators were sharers.

In general, both Elphinstone and Prendergast agreed that it was desirable to continue the bhagdari system. But there were signs that it was disappearing before their very eyes. In Broach it was certainly flourishing. It had also prevailed in the Olpar pargana formerly owned by the Vinchur jagirdar and now annexed to Surat. But there Prendergast feared that the Collector, Morison, had been deliberately subverting it: in 1817–18 he had settled the revenue of no less than 138 of its 139 villages with the bhagdars themselves, but in 1820–1 he settled with the bhagdars in only three villages and with the ryots in the remaining 136.[5] Elphinstone agreed that Morison had destroyed the bhagdari system in his eagerness to

---

[1] M.E., Minute, n.d., ibid. 706 ff.
[2] Prendergast, Minute, 29.6.1821, ibid. 701 ff.
[3] M.E., Minute, n.d., ibid. 706 ff.
[4] Prendergast, Minute, 29.6.1821, ibid. 701 ff.
[5] Prendergast, Minute, 8.7.1821, ibid. 709 ff.

spread the ryotwari system there.[1] The Collector was accordingly ordered to leave untouched any bhagdari villages that might still exist in Surat; he was also, however, to maintain the ryotwari system introduced by Morison. The latter provision was in accordance with Elphinstone's leading principle of avoiding all unnecessary change at least for the present: although he might not agree with all the changes that had been made under the authority of his predecessor Sir Evan Nepean, he did not want to make further changes by reversing them.[2]

Similarly he tried to preserve any bhagdari villages that might still exist in other Collectorates. Before the formation of the Collectorate of Ahmadabad in 1818 the British possessions to the north of the Mahi had all been administered by the Collector of Kaira. In the early years of British rule that official had tried a succession of different methods of collecting the revenue, first following the Maratha system of farming it out to the hereditary district officers, the Desais, and Amins, then farming it out to the Patels, then to the highest bidders, and finally from 1816 onwards introducing the ryotwari system. This procedure had incidentally reduced the number of bhagdari (and narwadari)[3] villages in the Ahmadabad Collectorate from twenty-six in the year before the British took possession to three in 1821.[4] The Collectors were now told that this was the most desirable system of all so long as the sharers outnumbered the other cultivators. Several years later, in 1825, the Collector came across eleven villages in the Daskrohi district where the Patels were very anxious for the Narwadari system to be restored.[5] In 1821 the Government had refrained from ordering a change like this in Surat. But now the initiative had come from the Patels themselves, and the country had been under British rule for a number of years. The Collector was accordingly authorized to restore the narwadari system in such circumstances.[6]

---

[1] M.E., Minute, n.d., ibid. 712.

[2] Government to Collector of Surat, 11.8.1821, Bom. R.C. 15.8.1821, 3729 ff.

[3] Narwadari villages differed from Bhagdari in that they lacked any field assessment. In social structure they were similar to each other (Gordon, *Survey and Settlement Manual*, i. 272 f.).

[4] M.E., Minute, 6.4.1821, esp. para. 43, S.R.J. iii. 677 ff.; M.E., Minute, n.d., ibid. 709; Prendergast, Minute, 8.7.1821, ibid. 709 f.; M.E., Minute, n.d., ibid. 712.

[5] Crawford (Collector Ahmadabad) to Government, 24.10.1825, Bom. R.C. 9.11.1825, 143.

[6] Government to Collector of Ahmadabad, 9.11.1825, ibid. 144.

But it was seldom easy to preserve the past. In general, the Government's revenue policy was bound to have important social consequences if only because the man with whom the Collector made a settlement gained in importance and influence from that very fact. Moreover, if the settlement were made for several years instead of merely for one, its social importance would be all the greater because it would be cumulative.

Elphinstone soon found that 'all gentlemen on the spot' were in favour of granting leases for a term of years on the ground that if the lessee knew that the Government would not raise the assessment of his lands for some time, he would be encouraged to undertake improvements. Elphinstone distinguished four types of man to whom such leases might be given—strangers, village headmen, village sharers (bhagdars or narwadars), or, finally, the peasants themselves.[1]

The idea of farming the revenue of villages to strangers seemed to Elphinstone to be 'the worst of all', especially if the strangers were chosen from the highest bidders, for under such a plan the only interest of the revenue farmer would be to squeeze as much as he could from the peasants. On the other hand, he thought that such a system had 'the advantage of inducing monied men to embark their capital in agriculture and to assist the ryots with money'. Strangers might therefore be given the leases of depopulated or new villages for a term of years at a gradually increasing rent, 'for as the success of the undertaking depends entirely on getting new ryots there is no chance of ill-treatment to that class for the first years'.[2]

Anxious as he was to safeguard the position of the village headman, Elphinstone nevertheless thought that if he were given the lease of his village for a period of years he might well oppress the ryots while using his powers as headman to 'stifle complaints'.[3]

The Collectors were accordingly told not to grant leases to strangers or headmen—except for new or depopulated villages at a gradually increasing rental.[4]

The main objection to the giving of long leases to individual ryots was that they lacked the capital to tide them over bad seasons: in

---

[1] M.E., Minute, 6.4.1821, S.R.J. iii. 677 ff.
[2] Ibid.   [3] Ibid.
[4] Government to Collectors of Ahmadabad and Kaira, 6.[8].1821, Bom. R.C. 15.8.1821, 3706 ff.

the result, 'the losses of unsuccessful cultivators must fall on the government, while the gains of successful ones remain to the individual'. Moreover, there was the disadvantage of the ryotwari system as such—that 'combined with our general revenue and judicial system, it has a great tendency to annihilate the power of the Patell and to dissolve the village government'. But where it had already been established, to remove it would involve drastic change of the sort which he wished to avoid. The Collectors were accordingly allowed to grant five-year leases to ryots in all villages where the ryotwari system had already been established.

Long leases seemed best suited to bhagdari (or narwadari) villages where the sharers were much more numerous than the other cultivators. They involved the least possible interference with a village system that seemed the best possible. The Collectors were accordingly authorized to grant five-year leases to the sharers of such villages.[1]

When the leases granted under this scheme would soon have been due to expire, Elphinstone raised the matter again, and a letter was sent to the Collectors in Gujarat requesting their views.[2]

From the Collectors' replies it appeared that the authority conferred in 1821 had not been generally acted upon. But they made a number of constructive suggestions for the future, and some of these were incorporated in the new rules for granting leases which were issued by the Government in October 1826.

Elphinstone had suggested that security should be provided for levying a penalty from the lessee if the village was not prospering at the end of his lease. But Stubbs, the Collector of Surat, pointed out that when such security was demanded it was in accordance with Indian custom for the person furnishing it to demand in his turn some consideration for the risk which he had borne—say one-third of the profits. The lessee would, however, make sure that he himself did not bear the loss. Stubbs also pointed out that merely to stipulate that the village was in a prosperous condition would be too vague a provision to be inserted in the terms of a lease. He suggested that instead the lease should provide that the farmer should give it up at any time if a panchayat appointed by the

---

[1] M.E., Minute, 6.4.1821, S.R.J. iii. 677 ff.; Revenue letter from Bombay, 23.2.1822, paras. 195, 199, ibid. 665 ff.
[2] M.E., Minute, n.d., and draft letter to Collectors (which was sent on 7.9.1825), Bom. R.C. 7.9.1825, 80 ff.

Collector decided that his system of management was injurious to the interests of the Government.[1]

Dunlop, who had been Collector of Kaira before the creation in 1818 of the separate Collectorate of Ahmadabad, pointed out another use for panchayats: he recalled that Rowles, his predecessor there, had granted many villages on lease, mainly to merchants, and with excellent results. One of the conditions of these leases had been that any dispute between the lessee and the ryots about the rate of assessment should be settled by a panchayat nominated by both sides. Dunlop himself had had experience of the system, and he bore witness that he had scarcely ever found that any of these panchayats had under-assessed anyone's land—indeed, he had often reduced the rates which they had fixed. He therefore suggested that this system should be continued.[2]

In the new rules for leases it was accordingly provided that disputes between lessees and ryots should be decided by panchayats nominated by the parties concerned or by the Collector if they themselves refused to nominate anyone. It was also provided, as Stubbs had suggested, that a lessee should surrender his lease if a panchayat nominated by the Collector declared his management to be injurious to the Government or vexatious to the ryot.[3]

The rules of 1821 had contained restrictions upon the type of person to whom leases could be granted. The Collectors were then authorized to grant leases to the sharers in bhagdari (or narwadari) villages if they were much more numerous than the other cultivators, and to ryots in villages where the ryotwari system was already established. They were forbidden to grant leases to headmen or to strangers except for new or depopulated villages.

The Collectors were now advocating some relaxation of these restrictions: one thought that wealthy merchants were the best persons to hold leases; another thought that headmen were the best.[4]

In the light of these various suggestions Elphinstone modified his previous opinions, and decided that a village should be leased to the whole community where possible, and otherwise to the

[1] Stubbs to Government, 3.7.1826, Bom. R.C. 5.8.1826, 15. William Stubbs, writer 1815 season (*East-India Register*).
[2] Dunlop to Government, 8.3.1826, Bom. R.C. 11.10.1826, 52.
[3] Rules for giving villages on lease, enclosed with Government to Collectors, 9.10.1826, Bom. R.C. 11.10.1826, 55.
[4] Remarks, Bom. R.C. 11.10.1826, 55.

headman. If, however, there was no substantial headman, the village might be leased to a stranger, but the Collector must make sure that he was a suitable person. When granting leases in such circumstances the Collector should look for 'men of capital and character who will make immediate sacrifices for eventual profit. We must particularly guard against needy adventurers who take a lease in the hope of immediate profit by extortion.'[1] If the ryots themselves were prosperous and enterprising enough to undertake improvements, leases might be granted to them.[2]

The final results of these policies lie outside the scope of this analysis. It seems that leases for terms of years were in fact generally given to headmen.[3] But whoever actually held such leases must surely have suffered greatly in the disastrous price falls of the 1830's. In this instance, at least, economic forces may well have been a more effective levelling influence than any measures of government.

Those who had suffered most severely from the levelling tendencies of British rule were perhaps the great chiefs.

British revenue policy in Gujarat had weakened the position of the Girasia chieftains in three main respects. In the first place, from 1811 onwards the Collectors steadily persevered in the task of persuading them to abandon the right to levy their traditional dues upon government villages and to accept instead a guaranteed payment by government of an equivalent amount from its treasury. Government gained by this policy in two main ways: its villages were freed from their interference, and the fact that it became responsible for paying them their dues gave it a hold over them.[4] The chiefs also gained, at least in the short run, for they saved themselves money and effort—for according to Captain Robertson, the Collector of Kaira, 'they generally consumed as much in victuals while making the collection, and their quarrels in the prosecution of their object often ended in running the village

---

[1] M.E., Minute, n.d., Bom. R.C. 11.10.1826, 53. Rules for granting leases, ibid. 55. Since the longer the lease the greater the incentive to spend money upon improvements, the maximum term was now increased from five years (as in 1821) to seven.

[2] Since their capital was likely to be less than that of any other class of lease-holder, their leases might be granted for nine years or even longer at the Collector's discretion.

[3] At least in Kaira (*Bombay Gazetteer*, iii. 103).

[4] Revenue letter from Bombay, 28.5.1817, S.R.J. iii. 717 ff.

entirely [to] waste'.[1] On the other hand, in the long run they lost much influence. In view of 'the various acts of authority which they exercise in the course of collecting their dues, and the respect which, as a matter of course ensues', the Bombay Government prophesied that 'the consequence of the grassias, by becoming fixed pensioners of Government, would greatly diminish'.[2]

In the second place, the Girasias' authority within their own villages was weakened. Under a Regulation of 1814, village accountants were appointed by the Collector to their villages. Moreover, those Girasias who had more than one village were required to appoint an effective headman in each, and this headman was thereafter responsible to the Collector; those Girasias who each had only one village were themselves appointed headmen. When Elphinstone visited Gujarat in 1821 he found great resentment against this policy: the chiefs of Dholka told him that the village accountant 'assumed the character of a representative of government, received complaints from their ryots, threw their whole village into confusion, and utterly destroyed their consequence among their people'. Elphinstone therefore decided to remove the accountants.[3]

In the third place, the Dholka Girasias' relations with Government had changed for the worse. They had been paying tribute as dependant chiefs. But from 1815 onwards the Bombay Government had been increasing the amount due from them to accord with improvements in prosperity. This was to turn the tribute of a chief into the rent of a landholder. Elphinstone decided to fix their payments for five years at a time for such an amount as would leave them 30 per cent. of the revenue instead of the 20 per cent. which was all that they seemed to have been left hitherto.[4] This measure may have improved their economic position but it did not change their new status: they were still leaseholders on a five-year term and not dependant chiefs. But the measure had nevertheless been dictated by a respect for their feelings.

The smaller Rajput chiefs, or Gametis, who each held single villages in the Dhanduka, Rampur, and Gogha districts, were also

[1] A. Robertson to Government, 10.10.1819, para. 48, Bom. R.C. 19.1.1820, 311 ff.

[2] Revenue letter from Bombay, 28.5.1817, para. 99 (paraphrasing a report by Diggle), S.R.J. iii. 726.

[3] M.E., Minute, 6.4.1821, esp. paras. 30, 32, 34–35, S.R.J. iii. 682 f.

[4] M.E., Minute, 6.4.1821, paras. 31–34, ibid.

treated with some respect for their feelings. Until 1821 the British had followed the traditional system of allowing them to manage their villages as they thought fit, and collecting from them a fixed amount every year as revenue. But on the ground that the precariousness of their cotton and other crops was liable to involve them in difficulties, Williamson the Assistant Collector suggested in 1821 that they should henceforth be made to pay a proportion of the gross produce. This aroused general opposition among them: as he admitted, his plan 'did not appear to correspond with their ideas of independence'; in particular, 'the interposition of a Tulatee' was 'above all things what they dislike'.[1]

Several of those whom Williamson regarded as the most respectable Gametis said that they wanted leases of their villages. He thought indeed that this was what they all wanted.

The Governor in Council concluded that 'to fix the assessment by the value of the produce would be odious to the Gametees, in principle as inconsistent with the footing of tributaries on which they have hitherto been allowed to remain and in practice from the scrutiny into their affairs to which it leads'. The Collector was accordingly authorized to grant leases for six or seven years to them.[2]

As a general principle, it was also laid down that henceforth no Girasia or Gameti should have to pay more than two-thirds of the amount demanded from a cultivator.[3] These provisions might seem enough to preserve some differentiation. But since the accountants had been excluded from the estates of these chiefs, the Collectors had no information upon which to base their quinquennial assessments. With their customary zeal they therefore tended to increase the assessment every five years. But at the same time, in the absence of wars and disturbances, the chiefs' dependants were multiplying faster than their means of subsistence. Nor did they practise economy: it had never been their habit to do so. They had been accustomed to borrow money lavishly and to repay it more or less at their own convenience: but now the moneylender could go to the Courts and enforce payment of both premium and interest. The Collectors and the Judges combined to threaten the

[1] Williamson (Assistant Collector Ahmadabad) to Collector, 1.5.1821, Bom. R.C. 4.7.1821, 2943 ff.
[2] Minutes, 29.6.1821, ibid. 2972 ff.
[3] Revenue letter from Bombay, 23.2.1822, para. 151, S.R.J. iii. 671.

chiefs with ruin. It was only special legislation in 1862, combined
with the sudden rise of cotton prices at the same time, that enabled
the chiefs to pay off their debts.[1]

The Company's judicial policies, in fact, were liable to have
social consequences as serious as those of its revenue policies.

In 1815, soon after their conversion to a belief in the benefits of
the Munro system, the home government declared to the Bombay
Government their acceptance of the maxim that 'in the dawning of
civilization our Regulations should be few and simple'. Equating
the dawning of civilization with the introduction of British rule
into a newly conquered territory, they explained that the establishment of the usual Regulations in such a country should be a
slow and cautious process.[2]

Ignoring this advice, the Bombay Government under Sir Evan
Nepean in 1817 introduced their Regulations and their judicial
system into the territories which had just been ceded in the Konkan and Gujarat.[3] They were duly rebuked for their precipitancy.[4]
Undeterred, in 1819 they introduced their Regulations and judicial
system into the territories in the Konkan and Gujarat which they
had acquired in 1818.[5]

With the Regulations came Judges to administer them. The
office of Magistrate was transferred from the Judge to the Collector
in 1818, in obedience to the home government's orders of 1815.
Nevertheless, the Judge was still the possessor of formidable
authority.[6]

Marriott, for example, in the Northern Konkan, thought that
the introduction of the Judge's Court and the Regulations had had
disastrous results:

It is difficult to conceive the laborious duties, & I may safely say evils
too, which have resulted & will result from the Govt. having within
three months of the acquisition established our Courts & Code of Regulations in a country whose system of administration was as diametrically

[1] Bombay Act VI, 1862, S.B.R., N.S. cvi, esp. 14 ff.; Rogers, i. 21.
[2] Judicial dispatch to Bombay, 22.12.1815, Bom. J.D. i. 73 ff. The maxim
seems to have been formulated by Keate, a Bombay civilian, then Judge and
Magistrate of Kaira.
[3] Bom. Regs. I and VI, 1817.
[4] Judicial dispatch to Bombay, 19.2.1819, Bom. J.D. i. 263 ff.
[5] Bom. Reg. III, 1819.
[6] Bom. Reg. III, 1818; Judicial dispatch to Bombay, 10.4.1815, P.P. 1819,
xiii (533), 795 (317).

opposite to our forms of justice & of revenue affairs as any could possibly be in respect to the genius of the people within its control.[1]

In the Southern Konkan, as we have seen,[2] the Khots had made use of the new judicial system to improve their own position at the expense of their proprietary tenants. In Gujarat, on the other hand, the new Courts had begun to threaten the position and influence of men of rank from the headmen to the chiefs.

The chiefs of Gujarat were in fact suffering on the one side from the new government's revenue Collectors and on the other side from its Judges and Magistrates. Elphinstone realized that they needed protection from the Courts. One of the main reasons for his reluctance to introduce Judges and Law Courts into the Deccan had been his belief that they tended to act 'with a sternness and indifference to rank . . . very grating to the feelings of the natives'.[3]

He soon found that some of the chiefs of Gujarat had already encountered the insolence of office that he and Chaplin were so anxious to prevent in the Deccan.[4] The Raja of Koth, for example, the leading Girasia chief, who in the early years of the century had paid an annual tribute of Rs.48,000 and maintained 150 horse and 2,000 foot, had on one occasion been sent to prison for neglecting a Magistrate's summons.[5]

Even though the chiefs were at least spared such humiliation during Elphinstone's period of office, their position was anomalous, 'subject to the Regulations in law but exempt in fact'.[6] It was therefore decided to bring a new Regulation into existence to temper the harshness of the old ones. It was explained in the preamble that the measure had two purposes, the one negative—to avoid giving offence to Indians of rank in criminal trials—the other positive— to invest them with police authority.

In the Deccan the great jagirdars had powers of life and death within their own territories, and the lesser jagirdars had police authority within theirs, reporting serious offences to the Magistrate and accepting the concurrent police authority of the Government. It was now proposed to treat the chiefs of Gujarat in broadly the same way as the lesser jagirdars of the Deccan. They

---

[1] Marriott to M.E., 19.11.1818, *Elphinstone.*
[2] p. 153, above.
[3] M.E., *Report*, 72.
[4] It was Chaplin who made this Shakespearian allusion.
[5] M.E., Minute, 6.4.1821, S.R.J. iii. 682 f.
[6] M.E., Minute, n.d., Bom. J.C. 1.3.1826, 32.

were to be given police authority and divided into two classes: the
first class were to be given charters (sanads) in the name of the
Governor in Council defining their powers, and to be authorized
to inflict up to two months' imprisonment and a fine of up to
Rs.30; the second class were to be given charters from the zilla
Magistrate, and to be authorized to inflict up to eight days' imprisonment and a fine of up to Rs.5.[1]

Both Goodwin and Sparrow were convinced, in spite of Elphinstone's opposition, that every chief should be required to keep a
register of his sentences as a safeguard against abuses of power. It
was accordingly provided that such registers should be kept, that
whenever a punishment exceeded 3 rupees' fine, five days' imprisonment, or six hours in the stocks 'the whole of the proceedings'
was to be recorded, and that all such records were to be open to
inspection by the zilla Magistrate.[2]

Besides investing the chiefs with these powers, the Regulation
had the further purpose of 'screening them, when charged with
misconduct, as much as possible from the public eye'—as Norris,
one of the members of the Regulation Committee, put it. It was,
therefore, provided that complaints against landholders invested
with police powers might be heard by the zilla Magistrate. The
Magistrate was a more suitable person than the Judge, for in his
capacity as Collector he was often in contact with the chiefs. If a
chief had to go before the Judge or the Court of Circuit on any
matter, 'the whole world knows', wrote Norris, 'that it must be of
a [purely] criminal nature, whereas when the case is before the
Magistrate no such unpleasant disclosure necessarily takes place'.
Nowhere could an inquiry into the conduct of a chief be held 'with
so little noise and violence to his feelings as in the Magistrate's
office'.[3]

Moreover, to protect the chiefs against frivolous complaints it
was provided that the Magistrate need not investigate any complaint 'which shall not bear upon the face of it appearance of probability that injustice has been done to such an extent as to call for
his notice and intervention'. The Magistrate could not sentence a
chief to more than a year's imprisonment: offences requiring a

---

[1] Bom. Reg. XV, 1827, chap. i.
[2] M.E., Goodwin and Sparrow, Minutes, n.d., Bom. J.C. 1.3.1826, 28 ff.
[3] Norris, Minute, n.d., ibid. 27. Charles Norris, writer 1808 season (*East-India Register*).

heavier punishment must go before the Court of Circuit or a Special Court. Such Courts were directed to conduct the trial of a chief in accordance with the ordinary Regulations 'except that it may, if the Court shall see fit, be conducted privately, provided always, that no one be excluded whom the landholder should wish to be present: any form of courtesy and consideration due to the rank of the accused shall also be observed'.[1]

There was one strong cry of dissent: 'The Judge of the Southern Concan with respect to criminal procedure against chieftains has no objection to preliminary forms of courtesy, but in regard to crimes subjecting a man to heavy punishment protests against there being one law for the rich, and another for the poor.'[2]

It was not wealth, however, but social position which it was the purpose of the Regulation to protect. Nor was such care confined to chiefs and landholders invested with police powers. When another draft Regulation for the Code was being considered, and a clause was submitted to the Governor in Council to the effect that respectable women might either be excused attendance at Court or protected by screens from the public gaze, Elphinstone suggested that 'persons whose rank in life renders their attendance in Court improper should be exempted in the same manner as females'.[3] The Regulation as finally passed accordingly provided that the Court might 'at its discretion dispense with the attendance in Court of a man of rank, and may cause his evidence to be otherwise taken'.[4]

Elphinstone included the village headmen in the aristocracy of the country, and was determined to maintain them in their social position. Nevertheless they were weakened by the new government, both in its judicial and in its revenue policies.

The headman's powers of punishment had been defined by Regulation in 1818.[5] Defined and also limited: limited not only in that hitherto they had been undefined but also in that the powers conferred by Regulation were in fact, as the Circuit Judge wrote in 1819, 'most trifling compared to what Patels etc. often exercise under native Governments'.[6]

[1] Bom. Reg. XV, 1827, chap. ii.   [2] Bom. J.C. 1.3.1826, 25.
[3] Draft Regulation submitted 21.12.1825, sec. xxxiv, cl. 6, Bom. J.C. 11.1.1826, 48; M.E., Minute, n.d., ibid. 52.
[4] Bom. Reg. XIII, 1827, sec. xxxiv, cl. 6.
[5] Bom. Reg. IV.
[6] Sutherland to Bax, 20.7.1819, B.C. 768/28072, 110 ff.

The headman was not to detain a suspect in custody for more than twenty-four hours. He was not to inflict more than twelve hours' imprisonment as a punishment, and he was authorized as an alternative, 'if the offending parties shall be of any of the lower casts of the people, on whom it may not be improper to inflict so degrading a punishment, to order them to be put in the stocks for a time not exceeding six hours'.[1]

Such was the law. But Shubrick the Collector of Broach thought that the headmen could not be trusted to use these powers properly. As was his wont, he therefore ignored the Regulation. It was only after a direct order from the Government in November 1819 that he reluctantly carried it out.[2]

It soon transpired that Shubrick was not alone in his neglect of this Regulation. Morison the Collector of Surat had not troubled to inform the headmen in his Collectorate of their new authority for the curious reason that few offences were committed that could be punished in the trivial way which was all that the Regulation allowed them.[3] In his turn he was duly rebuked and ordered to carry out the Regulation.[4]

In the Southern Konkan, too, Pelly the Collector thought that the Khots were not to be trusted with these powers, at least for the time being.[5] The Government decided that wherever there were Patels capable of exercising these powers they should be entrusted with them, but that otherwise the Khots were the only suitable men.[6] When Pelly had left the Southern Konkan, his deputy Reid also proved reluctant to invest the Khots with these powers.[7] But when Elphinstone went there in 1823 he decided that it must be done, for there were no efficient Patels left in Khoti villages.[8]

Even when these powers had been given to them the headmen

[1] Bom. Reg. IV, secs. iv, v and ix.
[2] Circuit Judge to Zilla Magistrate Broach, 1819, B.C. 768/28072, 96 ff.; Shubrick to Government, 28.12.1819, Bom. J.C. 12.1.1820, 72 f.; Minutes of Government, 8.1.1820, ibid. 74.
[3] Morison to Government, 10.5.1820, Bom. J.C. 24.5.1820, 2018 ff.
[4] Minutes, 5.10.1820, Bom. J.C. 11.10.1820, 4285 f.
[5] Pelly to Government, 11.5.1820, Bom. J.C. 7.6.1820, 2125 ff.
[6] Resolutions of Government, Bom. R.C. 24.1.1821, 856 ff.
[7] Reid (Assistant Magistrate) to Government, 4.7.1821, Bom. J.C. 25.7.1821, 2223 f.
[8] M.E., Minute, n.d., Bom. R.C. 26.3.1823, 4349 f. Dunlop proposed in 1824 to appoint Patels to Khoti villages, but the Government rejected the proposal on the ground that it would only lead to a 'clashing of authority' (Government to Collector, 10.1.1825, Bom. R.C. 12.1.1825, 47).

often seemed reluctant to use them. Morison the Collector of Surat pointed out a sufficient reason for this: he thought that they were afraid of having to go to the Court at Surat and neglect their crops for an indefinite period.[1] This was no doubt partly a matter of time and partly one of tactful management by the Collector. By 1825 the Collector of Kaira could report that ever since the passing of the Regulation of 1818 the headmen had been using their powers sensibly and hardly ever abusing them.[2]

Even so, when the Code of Regulations was being drawn up and the Regulation Committee submitted a draft specifying slightly larger powers for the headmen than had been authorized by the Regulation of 1818, the Governor in Council rejected part of the proposal. The 1818 Regulation had empowered the headman to inflict punishments of twelve hours' imprisonment or six hours in the stocks. The new draft increased the period of imprisonment to twenty-four hours and retained the punishment of six hours in the stocks.[3] Elphinstone, with the agreement of his Council, decided that the headman might be allowed to punish offenders by twenty-four hours' imprisonment but that 'placing in the stocks is too great a power for a Potail'.[4] The final draft, which became Regulation XII of 1827, therefore left the headmen with only the power of punishing by twenty-four hours' imprisonment.[5]

Elphinstone was nevertheless anxious to preserve the social status of headmen. When, for example, some Kunbi Patels of Kaira were sentenced to a year's imprisonment with hard labour for taking the leading part in an affray between two villages one Sunday morning, they petitioned for a remission of that part of the sentence 'which condemns us to hard labour and irons otherwise we shall not be able to marry our children among people of our own class, and we shall sustain a great loss of character'.[6]

The Collector himself sympathized with their complaint: 'they are not themselves accustomed to manual labour, and may therefore be looked upon as Gentlemen Farmers. In fact they are the

[1] Morison to Government, 27.3.1821, Bom. J.C. 18.4.1821, 907–11.
[2] Williamson (acting Collector) to Government, 8.1.1825, Bom. J.C. 26.1.1825, 18.
[3] Draft Regulation submitted 21.12.1825, sec. xlix, cl. 1, Bom. J.C. 11.1.1826, 46.
[4] M.E., Minute, n.d., ibid. 51.
[5] Bom. Reg. XII, 1827, sec. xlix, cl. 1.
[6] Petition, 25.4.1823, Bom. J.C. 11.6.1823, 2741 f.

gentlemen of this part of the country, and therefore to subject them to a degrading punishment without a very strong reason appears to me unjust, and is certainly very impolitic.'[1]

At Elphinstone's suggestion the petition was complied with, 'the Governor in Council being anxious to show consideration for the rank in life which may be occupied by a criminal except in cases where the nature or the magnitude of their offence may degrade them to a level with ordinary felons'.[2]

The Regulation Committee were also told that when drawing up the criminal part of the new code they should 'guard as much as possible against punishments inconsistent with native·manners, and with the customs of casts, an [in]attention to this point may lead to a great inequality of punishment extending in some case[s] even to the posterity of the prisoners under sentences' [sic].[3]

As in the Deccan, the headman's perquisites were restricted. He was no longer to be allowed to levy extra assessments without the Collector's permission.[4] But in some areas this meant that his allowances were less than those provided for the accountant in the 1814 Regulation. Morison the Collector of Surat, for example, recommended in 1820 that his headmen's allowances should be increased so that they should not receive less than their accountants, and he suggested 2½ per cent. of the gross revenue of the village as a suitable standard.[5] But local customs were various; moreover, the emoluments of the headman's office might be shared among a number of relatives while one did the work. It was therefore difficult for anyone to say how much the headmen of any area were receiving at the time. Shubrick thought that in Broach the headmen were already receiving in all probability more than Morison suggested that those of Surat should receive in the future.[6] At length the Governor in Council directed that henceforth whenever a headman's income from all sources was less than that assigned to his village accountant by the 1814 Regulation, the

[1] G. More (Collector, Kaira) to Government, 8.5.1823, para. 4, Bom. J.C. 11.6.1823, 2737 ff.
[2] Government to Sadr Faujdari Adalat, 23.7.1823, Bom. J.C. 23.7.1823, 3189 f.; M.E., Minute, n.d., ibid. 3187 f., suggested the wording of this letter.
[3] Government to Regulation Committee, 5.6.1823, Bom. J.C. 11.6.1823, 2742 f.
[4] Government to Collector of Broach, 9.2.1821, Bom. R.C. 21.2.1821, 1319 f.; More (Kaira) to Government, 15.2.1821, Bom. R.C. 14.3.1821, 1575 ff.
[5] Morison to Government, 6.6.1820, Bom. R.C. 6.9.1820, 4853 ff.
[6] Shubrick to Government, 27.11.1820, Bom. R.C. 20.12.1820, 7174 f.

difference should be made up to him in equal proportions of money and waste land.[1]

But the matter could not be decided as simply as that. In Kaira, for example, where the emoluments of the office of headman were divided among a number of relatives, Robertson chose one to be the officiating (mukhi) headman. But he pointed out that his allowances could hardly be compared with those of the accountant because the accountant worked full time at his figures whereas the headman spent only part of his time in transacting the duties of his office, and devoted the rest to agriculture, from which he probably derived most of his wealth. Two and a half per cent. of the revenue of villages worth more than Rs.4,000 or 5,000 a year would enable him to live without agriculture.

Placing the Mookhee Patel in such a situation, might altogether alter the character of his office. He might as a stipendiary officer of the Government cease to consider himself a member of the village society and in some respect their municipal officer. He might also cease to have a community of feeling with his brethren—and hence, in the discharge of his duty, be less inclined to conciliate and more apt to give offence and disgust.[2]

The Governor in Council agreed that although the accountant had to spend all his time at his books it was not only possible but essential for the headman to be a practising cultivator, certainly not 'a stipendiary officer of Government'. The headman's 'connection with the village community' must be maintained. As a general principle it was also declared that there should be one man to do the work permanently and to draw an additional allowance for doing so.[3]

In some villages, however, there were no allowances at all for the headman.[4] The Collector of Ahmadabad reported in 1825, for example, that in 356 of the 852 villages under him no provision at all was made for the officiating headman.[5]

Two inquiries were instituted by the Government, one in 1821 and one in 1825, to elicit from the Collectors how much they

[1] Circular, n.d., Bom. R.C. 28.2.1821, 1441 ff.
[2] Robertson to Government, 3.7.1821, Bom. R.C. 1.8.1821, 3346 ff.
[3] Government to Collector, 26.7.1821, ibid. 3361.
[4] More (Acting Collector, Kaira) to Government, 5.7.1821, Bom. R.C. 25.7.1821, 3319 f.
[5] Crawford (Collector, Ahmadabad) to Government, 26.5.1825, Bom. J.C. 31.12.1825, 25. He does not include mehvasi or unsettled villages.

thought the officiating headman should be paid and whether he was
actually receiving enough at the time. On both occasions Elphinstone was much dissatisfied with their replies: their information
and their recommendations both seemed inadequate.[1] No definite
changes in the headman's allowances seem to have resulted from
these discussions.

The main result of the change of government upon the economic
position of the headmen in Gujarat, as in the Deccan, seems to have
been to confirm those parts of their allowances which were fixed by
custom but to abolish the perquisites of office which the headmen
used to enjoy at their discretion.

When Dunlop went to the South Konkan, however, he did reform the headmen's allowances, although he could not of course
interfere with those of the Khots. The accountants of very small
villages could deal with the accounts of several villages and so increase their allowances. But the headman of a village, however
small it might be, was confined to it. Therefore, although he fixed
the allowances of headmen on a scale proportioned to the revenue
of their villages in order to give them an incentive to encourage
cultivation, he assigned a larger proportion to the headmen of
small villages than to those of large ones, with the result that the
headman of a small village drew more than his accountant while
the headman of a large village drew less.[2]

In determining his social standing in the village, however, what a
headman was paid no doubt mattered less than what he could do.
The changing position of the village accountant was crucial in this
respect.

In the early years of British rule in Gujarat and the Konkan, the
Collectors had much difficulty in finding out the real resources of
their new territories. The village accountants might well have been
expected to give valuable help. Many villages in Gujarat, however,
had no accountants. Where accountants did exist, they often

---

[1] M.E., Minute, n.d., Bom. R.C. 31.12.1825, 20.

[2]

Revenue of village	Headman's allowance as percentage of village revenue
Under Rs.500	6
Rs.500–1,000	4
Rs.1,000–2,000	3
Rs.2,000–3,000	2
Above Rs.3,000	1

(Dunlop to Government, 15.8.1824, para. 101, Bom. R.C. 12.1.1825, 44;
Government to Dunlop, 10.1.1825, para. 19, ibid. 47.)

seemed unreliable to the new rulers, either because they were thought to be too dependent on their headmen, or because they were judged incompetent.[1]

In 1814 the Bombay Government had passed a Regulation bringing the village accountants under the direct control of the Collector. This Regulation provided that they could be dismissed for disobeying his orders, for incapacity, or for falsifying the village accounts. They could be appointed to every village with an annual revenue of at least Rs.1,000. Villages poorer than that could share an accountant among several. The accountants of villages richer than that were to be paid according to a sliding scale proportionate to the revenue and in amount ranging from Rs.50 to Rs. 300.[2]

The measure aroused great opposition among hereditary district officers, village headmen and others who saw in the new accountants a grave threat to their own interests.[3]

Robertson thought that the opposition raised against this policy was 'sufficient in itself to stamp its value as an aid to the Government'—a dangerous criterion. By 1819 he considered that all classes accepted the new system. 'The body of the people', he thought, had always welcomed the measure as a safeguard against the oppression of their headmen. An experienced administrator, he expatiated at length to government upon the wisdom of its policy. Even the headmen now realized that 'what they have gained by uninterrupted industry has more than compensated for the corrupt advantages which they have lost which cost them the greatest exertions and anxiety as well as expenses to maintain'. The accountants were a positive help to the headmen—they acted as their clerks and took care that everything of importance was reported to the Collector. Great and manifold were the benefits which Robertson found in the new system. Not only were the accountants helpful

[1] Morison to Government, 3.2.1820, Bom. R.C., 23.2.1820, 1084 ff.; Dunlop to Government, 11.8.1820, Bom. R.C. 18.11.1820, 6622 ff.

[2] Bombay Reg. II, 1814, sec. xiii gives the scale:

Revenue of village (min.)	Accountants' pay
Rs.1,000	Rs.50
Rs.2,000	Rs.90
Rs.3,000	Rs.120
Rs.4,000	Rs.140
Rs.5,000	Rs.150
Rs.10,000	Rs.200
Rs.15,000	Rs.250
Rs.20,000	Rs.300

[3] S.R.J. iii. 736 ff.

to the people, 'a shield to the industrious and honest against the plots of the wicked', but they were also proving themselves fruitful servants of the Government by revealing hidden sources of revenue and enabling the Collector to revise the assessment in the most productive way.[1]

The irrepressible Shubrick, on the other hand, made no secret of the fact that as Collector of Broach he found it impossible to carry out the Regulation of 1814. The Regulation provided that it was for the Governor in Council to dismiss an accountant. But Shubrick declared that neither he nor his predecessor had troubled to request the Governor in Council to do so. He often dismissed them himself. 'Many are discharged every year, . . . for giving false accounts, keeping back money they have recovered', and so on. How could he manage his villages if, whenever he wanted to dismiss an unsatisfactory accountant and appoint another in his place, he had to wait for the decision of the Government?[2]

Shubrick was duly rebuked by the Government: 'it would appear that the removal of Tullatees were an almost every day occurrence within your Collectorship'. In future, he must prosecute a dishonest accountant in the Judge's Court, meanwhile suspending him from his duties and appointing a provisional successor upon the headman's recommendation.[3]

It transpired later that Robertson had met with the same problem. He had often dismissed accountants without informing the Government. But he tactfully explained that he had only appointed them *temporarily*. Indeed, only 14 accountants out of a total of 568 had he considered suitable for permanent appointments.[4] Morison at Surat had also dismissed some of the accountants whom he had appointed under the Regulation. But he explained that they were all 'employed experimentally'.[5]

Shubrick also had the temerity to criticize the rule that accountants should be appointed on the headmen's recommendation: 'the tulatee being chosen by the Patells it becomes his interest to be their friend'.[6] The Government's view was that a Collector could never know enough about the local inhabitants to be able to make

---

[1] Robertson to Government, 10.10.1819, Bom. R.C. 19.1.1820, 311–444.
[2] Shubrick to Government, 19.11.1819, Bom. R.C. 8.12.1819, 4257 ff.
[3] Government to Shubrick, 18.1.1820, Bom. R.C. 19.1.1820, 306 ff.
[4] Robertson to Government, 10.6.1820, Bom. R.C. 28.6.1820, 3363 ff.
[5] Morison to Government, 3.2.1820, Bom. R.C. 23.2.1820, 1084 ff.
[6] Shubrick to Government, 18.12.1819, Bom. R.C. 19.1.1820, 305 f.

a proper choice. All that he could do would be to ask the Indian officials on his staff: 'they recommend their dependants and are from their situation near the Collector's person able to prevent complaints against their favourites reaching him'.[1]

Shubrick was rebuked for implying that the accountant should be in a state of hostility to the headman: 'The Tullatee is more the servant of the Patells and cultivators than of the Collector or Government and your idea of the advantages to be expected from the Patells and Tullatees being at variance is pregnant with serious evil; your making the Tullatee exclusively your own will force the Patells to have another upon whom they can rely, and the villagers will thus become doubly burdened.'

On one of his visits to Broach, the Circuit Judge found that Shubrick was allowing the accountants to leave their villages for several months every year, although the 1814 Regulation had provided that they should live permanently in the villages to which they were appointed.[2] But as he himself admitted this was no doubt due to the repeal in 1816 of that part of the 1814 Regulation which laid down a new salary scale for village accountants.[3] Their traditional allowances, varying between Rs.100 and Rs.50, were not large enough to induce them to devote their whole time to the concerns of the village and to live there permanently. The Circuit Judge therefore recommended the restoration of the larger allowances sanctioned in 1814, both for this reason and also because 'the policy of paying Tulatees of villages by a percentage on the revenues of the village, when it fluctuates as in Broach, is obvious, they become independent of the Patels and feel an interest in the amount of the revenue, and are desirous of increasing it'.[4]

This resembled Shubrick's argument against deferring to the recommendation of the headman when appointing an accountant. Both were contrary to Elphinstone's wish to maintain the headman's authority. Revision of the accountants' salaries was deferred, but Shubrick was frequently told to make sure that his accountants lived permanently in their villages.

The Governor in Council even suggested that one reason why Shubrick was finding it necessary to dismiss accountants was that

[1] Government to Shubrick, 18.1.1820, Bom. R.C. 19.1.1820, 306–10.
[2] Bom. Reg. II, 1814, sec. xiii.
[3] Bom. Reg. II, 1816.
[4] J. Sutherland, Minute, 19.12.1818, B.C. 768/20872, 101 ff.

he had been appointing strangers from the towns instead of villagers.[1] If he appointed villagers, moreover, they would be satisfied
with small salaries:

The permanent residence of the Tullatee is even more indispensably
necessary than that of the Patell, he is the accountant, notary public,
registrar and writer not only in every transaction in which the Government is interested, but in those of individuals also, though townspeople
may object to the practice and find the fixed allowance insufficient to
maintain their town and village establishments, the Government is persuaded that neither the permanent residence nor the allowance attached
to the situation will be objected to while the Tullatee is, as he ought to
be, one of the inhabitants of the village.[2]

It soon transpired that the other Collectors had been having
similar difficulties.

All had had difficulty in finding suitable men. Dunlop, for
example, had issued proclamations specifically inviting those who
had held office under the traditional system to apply for posts under
the 1814 Regulation. None agreed to accept office on the new
terms.[3] Robertson testified that 'it was not until some time in 1815
that after the most pressing invitations, I may say solicitations,
a few individuals who had been occasionally engaged in village
scrutinies by the former Governments, were induced to undertake
the duty'.[4] Dunlop in Ahmadabad was particularly conscious of the
scarcity of competent men of sufficient education: only the towns
in the more developed Collectorate of Kaira could supply recruits,
he complained, and 'we of course only get the refuse who cannot
procure employment there'.[5]

The Collectors all shared Shubrick's view that it was impolitic
to ask the headman to recommend candidates. As Robertson
pointed out, 'The Patells were the greatest opponents to the
introduction of the new system, and consulting them on the
subject of Tullatees would have only tended to impede its
establishment.'[6]

Shubrick had also recommended the restoration of the 1814 scale
of accountants' allowances on the ground that they could not

[1] Government to Shubrick, 6.12.1819, Bom. R.C. 8.12.1819, 4262 ff.
[2] Government to Shubrick, 18.1.1820, Bom. R.C. 19.1.1820, 450 ff.
[3] Dunlop to Government, 11.8.1820, Bom. R.C. 18.11.1820, 6622 ff.
[4] A. Robertson to Government, 10.6.1820, Bom. R.C. 28.6.1820, 3363 ff.
[5] Answers to Sutherland's queries (1819), B.C. 768/28072, 137 ff.
[6] Robertson to Government, 10.6.1820, Bom. R.C. 28.6.1820, 3363 ff.

otherwise afford to build themselves houses in the villages suitable for the monsoon and live there all the year round.[1] The Circuit Judge also recommended the restoration of the 1814 scale, and on forwarding his report to the Government the Superior Tribunal likewise recommended a higher scale of allowances than the one at present in force.[2] Robertson admitted that he had disobeyed the Government by simply continuing the 1814 scale after it had been rescinded.[3] He thought it 'no more than an adequate remuneration'.[4] Morison had put the accountants whom he had 'employed experimentally' on a lower scale of pay—between 18 and 4 rupees a month—but he declared in 1820 that when he recommended any for permanent appointments he would recommend that they be appointed on a higher scale.[5]

At length, in 1820, the Government laid down some general principles of policy for the Collectors to follow. Accountants were to be paid according to the scale originally prescribed in the 1814 Regulation. They were to be appointed independently of the headmen, but once appointed they were to co-operate with them and help them, attending them while they transacted their business in the village and registering their proceedings. On the other hand, they were to be held liable to show their accounts to the officers of government and to report to the Collector if the headman abused his authority in any way.[6]

Such was the policy. But when Elphinstone visited Broach in 1821 he found that 'the tullatee regulation can scarcely be said to be introduced here. The Tullatees keep their accounts in the old form; and although they are considered as Government officers much more than in the Deccan and are often removed and appointed by the Collector, they seem to be much more closely connected with the Potails than in Ahmedabad and Kaira, and more likely to conceal than to expose any frauds of the village management.' When he used the term 'Patel' of Broach he included in its meaning the sharers in bhagdari villages. What particularly troubled him was the tendency for the sharers, when they were a small minority

---

[1] Shubrick to Government, 12.9.1820, Bom. R.C. 27.9.1820, 5349 ff.
[2] J. Bax (Register, Superior Tribunal), 9.9.1819, B.C. 768/20872, 43 ff.
[3] Robertson to Government, 10.10.1819, para. 45, Bom. R.C. 19.1.1820, 311 ff.
[4] Robertson to Government, 10.6.1820, Bom. R.C. 28.6.1820, 3363 ff.
[5] Morison to Government, 3.2.1820, Bom. R.C. 23.2.1820, 1084 ff.
[6] Minutes of Government for a Circular to the Collectors, 18.11.1820, Bom. R.C. 18.11.1820, 6637 ff.

of the cultivators, to persuade the accountant to throw the weight of the assessment upon the lands of the other cultivators.[1]

In Ahmadabad and Kaira, however, 'the new Tullatee is an officer direct from Government, and looked up to in the village as its agent'. He was even employed to collect the revenue, a duty hitherto generally recognized as belonging exclusively to the headman. Traditionally he had been the servant of the headman. Now he was responsible only to the Collector. It was a revolutionary change. Elphinstone sympathized with the attitude of the Girasia chiefs to these accountants, and he had withdrawn them from their villages. In the government villages he realized that the appointment of these accountants had 'a tendency to extinguish the authority of the Patell, already much weakened by other parts of our management', and he suggested that the Collectors should take care 'to bring the Tullatee's power within its natural bounds, and to withdraw it from all interference with the immediate duties of the Patell'. But he left them in the government villages. Indeed, he declared himself convinced of the 'excellence' of the 1814 Regulation, 'both as promoting the advantage of government and of the ryots'.[2]

Prendergast, on the other hand, thought that the 1814 Regulation was wholly mistaken, and prophesied that 'in as much as it has not been acted upon, for instance, in the Broach collectorship, in so much will there be cause for future rejoicings. Innovations of this nature have seldom or never failed to be followed by the greatest regret'.[3] But he did not make an issue of it.

When an inquiry was made in 1825 there seemed to be general satisfaction among the Collectors that the accountants were keeping their records properly and supplying the Collectors with the information which they required.[4] Broach was the great exception: there the accountants were not yet paid according to the 1814 scale and consequently were not yet resident in their villages; moreover, they were still being used to collect the revenue.[5] The

[1] M.E., Minute, 25.4.1821, S.R.J. iii. 662 f.
[2] M.E., Minute, 6.4.1821, S.R.J. iii. 682 ff.
[3] Prendergast, Minute, 29.6.1821, S.R.J. iii. 704.
[4] Lumsden (Surat) to Government, 28.6.1825, Bom. R.C. 13.7.1825, 18; Crawford (Ahmadabad) to Government, 29.6.1825, Bom. R.C. 20.7.1825, 15; Williamson (Kaira) to Government, 15.7.1825, Bom. R.C. 7.9.1825, 7.
[5] R. Boyd (Collector, Broach) to Sadr Adalat, 13.8.1825, Bom. R.C. 7.9.1825, 13; Ironside (Register, Sadr Adalat) to Government, 4.6.1825, Bom. R.C. 22.6.1825, 4.

Collector was duly instructed to abide by the 1814 Regulation.[1] But the tendency which Elphinstone had noticed with regret in 1821 was still more apparent now: as the Sadr Adalat reported, 'an active intelligent Tulatee too frequently governs the village to which he is attached only as writer and accountant. Care should in consequence always be taken to support the constitutional heads of villages and not permit them to be under the control of the person appointed to assist them in their duties.'[2]

But the accountants were not appointed merely to assist the headmen. Their very existence as officials responsible directly to the Collector implied that the headmen were not trusted. If a headman was obviously not trusted by the Government it may be supposed that he had the less chance of being respected by the people—at least in the nineteenth century.

There was now no lack of recruits. Williamson at Kaira, for example, found that whenever a vacancy occurred a number of 'respectable' men often applied for the post. Lumsden at Surat pointed out that an incidental advantage of the system was that it gave 'a decent and desirable livelihood to the great bulk of the Brahmuns and other educated natives here who would otherwise be reduced to great straits'. The Collectors found several advantages in fostering the growth of a hereditary class of accountants. Directly, so it was hoped, this would develop a sense of loyalty. Williamson at Kaira, for example, usually appointed the son of a deceased accountant, although to a different village, on the ground that 'nothing attaches natives to our government so much as introduction into its service at an early age'. Indirectly, so it was suggested by Lumsden, the Government would gain in influence from the growth of its opportunities of patronage: 'we have or are likely to acquire a greater hold over [the] influential from the extent of our revenue establishments, particularly from the number of Tullatees employed, than any government of these districts ever before possessed'.[3]

The situation was broadly similar in the Konkan. In many villages in the south, particularly in Khoti villages, there were no accountants. Sometimes the same man was the accountant of a

---

[1] Government to Collector of Broach, 31.8.1825, Bom. R.C. 31.8.1825, 79.

[2] Ironside (Register, Sadr Adalat) to Government, 4.6.1825, Bom. R.C. 22.6.1825, 4.

[3] Lumsden to Government, 28.6.1825, Bom. R.C. 13.7.1825, 18; Williamson to Government, 15.7.1825, Bom. R.C. 7.9.1825, 7.

number of villages. In one instance, for example, in Suvarndurg, the local deshpande was also the accountant of 262 villages. Sometimes the number of relatives eligible for office was so large that the allowances could not be divided among them all. The common solution was for each member of the family to do the work and draw the allowances for one year in rotation: it sometimes happened that a member only succeeded to the post once in fifteen or even thirty years.[1]

'Under such a system', wrote Dunlop despairingly, 'it would be in vain to look for regularity or responsibility, men come from Scindia's camp and other parts of India to perform their year's duty as a point of honour or depute someone else to perform it for them.'[2]

He therefore suggested that one member of the family should be appointed to do the duty permanently, that his activities should be confined to such villages as he could manage, and that inadequate allowances should be increased in accordance with the Regulation.[3]

The Governor in Council approved of his proposals, but advised him to proceed gradually when introducing accountants into villages where there was none before.[4] In Khoti villages they need only be appointed where there were tenants with rights to be protected against the Khots—that is, in villages where there were some superior (dharakari) tenants. Since the amount due from the Khot to the Government was fixed, the accountants were of no use save to protect the rights of tenants, and could therefore have no function in Khoti villages where the tenants were all (ardheli) tenants at will.[5]

But whether it was to protect the villagers or to sustain the rights of the Government, the accountant's function necessarily involved restricting the powers of the headman. Indeed, however much Elphinstone wished to maintain the position of the aristocracy of the country, the new system had the general effect of lowering it. The whole revenue and judicial administration of the British was more uniform, more systematic, more closely knit together than that of their predecessors. Of its nature, it was a government of laws rather than of men. The activities of all who

[1] Dunlop to Government, 15.8.1824, Bom. R.C. 12.1.1825, 44.
[2] Ibid.   [3] Ibid.
[4] Government to Collector, 10.1.1825, ibid. 47.
[5] Government to Collector, 12.9.1825, 39.

had authority and influence were thereby restricted, and they themselves reduced in social consequence.[1]

The Deccan was another matter. The Commission lasted until 1826, and Elphinstone devised special measures to preserve some of its essential features thereafter.

[1] In the matter of succession to hereditary district or village offices, the claims of utility and custom were reconciled by an ingenious compromise. Hereditary succession might by the accident of birth produce occasional inefficiency. The annual rotation of offices was bound at the least to reduce efficiency. It was therefore provided that if the sharers in an hereditary district or village office appointed one of their number to officiate, their choice must be subject to the Collector's approval, while if the succession continued to be by rotation among them the Collector might require each person to continue in office for three years (Bom. Reg. XVI, 1827, sec. xvii, cl. 4).

9

THE DECCAN SYSTEM AND THE GOVERNMENT OF BOMBAY

WHEN Elphinstone became Governor of Bombay, William Chaplin succeeded him as Commissioner in the Deccan. At the same time the Deccan was annexed to the Bombay Presidency and the activities of the Commissioner came under the scrutiny of the Bombay Government.

There was a flutter of minutes in the Council at Bombay when it was realized that the Deccan Commission during Chaplin's first year of office was likely to cost no less than Rs.314,390–1–12. This figure included the salaries of Chaplin himself, his two secretaries, and his two accountants, as well as those of a large Indian staff, together with the amounts of Rs.48,000 for 'presents' and Rs.54,000 for Chaplin's personal expenses.[1]

Prendergast at once proposed that the Commissioner's salary should be fixed and made to cover all his expenses. He stated incidentally that he thought Rs.4,500 a month was too much to allow for expenses.[2]

The argument quickly turned to general principles. Elphinstone maintained that a certain amount of display was politically desirable:

The people of Poona are used to the residence of a Prince and of many great Sirdars and the chief authority among them ought to be able to maintain some small portion of the state to which they have been accustomed. Many of the chiefs under Mr. Chaplin's orders have themselves some Lacks of Rupees a year and would be apt to contrast their own rank with that of an officer placed much below what they have been used to see in the Resident.[3]

Bell and Prendergast both hoped nevertheless that the Commission would soon be abolished. They still thought it too expensive.[4]

---

[1] Statement of expenses of Commission, 20.2.1820, Bom. P.C. 29.3.1820, 3188. It was of course only in appearance that the estimate had been brought to the last Rea: the officers' salaries had been so calculated, but the other heads of expenditure had been estimated in round figures.

[2] Prendergast, Minute, 31.1.1820, Bom. P.C. 29.3.1820, 3177 f.

[3] M.E., Minute, n.d., ibid. 3178 ff.

[4] Bell, Minute, n.d., ibid. 3189; Prendergast, Minute, 14.3.1820, ibid. 3190 f.

Prendergast, moreover, disdained the use of pomp and circumstance:

The state, splendour & pageantry of Asiatic sovereignty, to which the inhabitants of Poona have been accustomed whilst that city was the seat of the Paishwa's Government, was so far beyond anything of the kind that can be attempted by any subordinate officer of this Government, I do not think it should be thought of. They have acquired in lieu of it, more substantial advantages, and that pomp and spectacle may perhaps be considered as only removed from Poona to Sattara.[1]

Shortly after this inconclusive discussion the Supreme Government intervened to declare that now that the administration of the Deccan was in the hands of the Governor in Council of Bombay, Rs.5,000 should be enough to cover the Commissioner's salary and expenses.[2]

Elphinstone thought this insufficient and recommended that Chaplin's salary and expenses be continued at Rs.3,000 and Rs.4,000 per month respectively. This was done subject to the Supreme Government's approval.[3]

The home government quickly replied, in December of the same year, that this was 'much too high' and that the Supreme Government's recommendation of Rs.5,000 'went to the utmost bounds of liberality'. Chaplin's salary was to be reduced to that level.[4]

There were personal as well as general reasons for the opposition to the Deccan system. Not one of the senior posts in the Deccan was filled by a Bombay civil servant. Chaplin the Commissioner and Thackeray his successor at Dharwar were both on the Madras establishment; Briggs in Khandesh, Pottinger at Ahmadnagar, H. D. Robertson at Poona, and Grant at Satara were all army officers. Some of their subordinates were also army officers. The idea that these men were all occupying lucrative positions which ought properly to have been occupied by Bombay civil servants must have aroused much bitterness against the Deccan system. Indeed, a memorial of protest against the continued employment of army officers in the administration of the Deccan was drawn up and signed in 1820 by seventy-five civil servants of the Bombay

[1] Prendergast, Minute, 14.3.1820, ibid. 3190 ff.
[2] Supreme Government to Bombay Government, 25.4.1820, Bom. P.C. 7.6.1820, 4929 ff.
[3] Minutes of M.E. and his colleagues, n.d., ibid. 4932 ff.
[4] Political dispatch to Bombay, 29.12.1820, para. 3, Bom. P.D. ii. 243 ff.

establishment.[1] H. D. Robertson was understandably irritated when, as he told Elphinstone, his own Assistant 'Lumsden came to ask *my permission* to sign it'.[2]

In such a situation, the Bombay civil servants on Elphinstone's Council, although they themselves had nothing to gain by the abolition of the Deccan system, nevertheless sympathized with their colleagues who had, and tended all the more to criticize any abuses which came to light and to enlarge upon the extravagance of the Commission itself, just as Prendergast, for example, denounced any suspicion of 'pomp and spectacle' at Poona.[3]

There was little enough of pomp these days at Poona. When Low visited Poona in 1825 he found the new rulers engaging in 'a great variety of out of the way amusements—such as Palankeen Racing— Buffalo fighting—wrestling—Races of men tied up to the necks in sacks—Ram fighting—Tumbling—& Fellows chasing & trying to lift an unhappy pig with his tail greased—all of which sports have their respective rules & regulations'. When describing these excitements to Elphinstone, he told also of a bet recently made there that 'a native could not ride 125 miles a day for four successive days'. The bet was in fact lost.[4] What is significant is that a certain attitude of contempt for the 'native' was already developing.

But there were some who sympathized enough with Indian ways of life to adopt Indian dress. Captain Archibald Robertson, who succeeded Briggs in Khandesh, had several assistants—Dent, Erskine, and Graham—who did this.[5] But he himself strongly disapproved of the practice: 'I do not however at all like gentlemen assuming the native costume. It does not involve any moral turpitude, but does not I think at all add to the respect that natives entertain for the British character—besides which, those who wear that dress, are often tempted after a time to do under its guise what they never would have thought of doing in the costume of their country.'[6] Here the attitude is not so much one of contempt for

[1] Memorial, Bom. G.C. 15.11.1820, 1653 ff.

[2] H. D. Robertson to M.E., 28.6.1820, *Elphinstone*.

[3] Bell and Prendergast in fact supported the memorial (Bom. G.C. 15.11.1820, 1653 ff.).

[4] Capt. John Low (Commissioner with Baji Rao) to M.E., 25.2.1825, *Elphinstone*.

[5] Henry Frederick Dent, writer season 1819; James Erskine, writer season 1822; William John Graham, writer season 1821.

[6] A. Robertson to M.E., 30.6.1824, *Elphinstone*.

some supposed inferiority in manly qualities as, rather, one of suspicion of immorality.

Robertson did his best to eradicate the practice: 'I set my face decidedly against it; so that nothing of the kind has ever, to my knowledge, appeared at office or indeed in any way before me except on one or two casual & very unexpected encounters.'[1]

Robertson claimed that as a result of his efforts, 'Mr. Graham has been made a complete convert of—& given it up altogether.' He thought that Dent was one of the leaders of the fashion, and regarded him as 'a professed votary of pleasure'.[2]

So strongly did Robertson object to this behaviour that although he thought Dent a 'very efficient' Assistant he asked Elphinstone to post him elsewhere, preferably to a larger station where he would be more under the influence of his own countrymen.[3]

James Erskine was a nephew of Elphinstone's. Besides his 'great partiality for the native dress', which Robertson so deplored, 'he mixes a good deal with the natives', with the result that he had improved his knowledge of the vernacular. Robertson thought that it was because of the example set by Dent that he had taken to Indian dress, and determined to take the young man with him on his next tour of the districts so that he would escape his influence.[4]

Elphinstone was less shocked than Robertson by such behaviour, but he did not welcome it. Indeed, at about the same time he himself was writing to caution a young man, perhaps Erskine himself, against becoming too identified with Indian ways of life:

I hear you have turned a great native and great nautcher. It is so very important to get acquainted with the natives and to know their manners and character, that I repress a strong prejudice which I have always had against Europeans adopting the native dress, in the idea that it is worth while even to do that, provided it leads to your taking an interest in the people; but I must caution you against pushing it too far, for I never saw a European who adopted the dress of the natives, and gave much into their pleasures who ever perfectly recovered his place among Europeans. I hope you will like the natives and acquire their language, but do not sink to their level.[5]

It might have been expected that the comparative absence of English society in the Deccan would have encouraged the Englishmen

[1] Ibid.   [2] Ibid.
[3] Ibid. He linked with Dent a Captain Bailie whom I cannot trace.
[4] Ibid.   [5] M.E. to ?, 1.6.1824, Colebrooke, ii. 164.

there to mix more freely with Indians. This was not objected to. Indeed, Chaplin sent a circular to his Collectors in 1823 urging them to cultivate 'an unreserved personal intercourse' with 'the higher classes of natives'.[1] Elphinstone used to go hunting with the great chiefs, and when he visited the Deccan in 1826 his companions on one occasion went to a nautch at Balaji Pant Natu's.[2] What underlay both the objection to Indian dress and also the assumption of cultural superiority may perhaps have been an almost unconscious wish that Europeans, however close their intimacy with Indian friends, should remain Europeans and preserve a distinction between their manners and way of life and those of the Indian population which would mark them out as the ruling class.

At all events, Robertson's admonitions did not prevent either Graham or Dent from becoming so intimate with Mamlatdars as to borrow money from them. After Graham's death it was found, for example, that he was in debt to Mamlatdars to the extent of Rs.1,445.[3]

Chaplin had had considerable experience as a Collector under the Madras Government before he went to Dharwar. Munro thought highly of him: indeed, it was Munro who had recommended him to Elphinstone as his own successor at Dharwar.

At about this time he got married. Macleod, his Assistant Secretary, looked on with covert amusement: 'Mrs. Chaplin hardly knows whether she is standing on her head or her heels, she is so happy & so is he—it is quite delightful to see; tho' so ridiculous that I cannot help laughing in my sleeve to see two such *gulls*.'[4]

Perhaps as a result of this, when Low visited Poona in 1825 he found Chaplin

very greatly improved from what he was formerly as a member of society. He is now really quite gay (tho' all in his own quiet sort of way) & seems to enjoy large company day after day as much as anybody—more so certainly than I do, for I have had so much of it since my arrival here that I have several times been glad to send excuses to parties, and retreat to my solitary book & cup of tea in my own bungalow, while

[1] Chaplin to Collectors, 28.5.1823, Choksey, *Aftermath*, 216–20.
[2] M.E., Journal, 19.8.1826, Colebrooke, ii. 184.
[3] Hodges (Acting Collector, Khandesh) to Government, 4.8.1829, Bom. R.C. 16.9.1829, 22. He had also borrowed Rs.862 from a Saukar upon a Mamlatdar's guarantee and still owed Rs.562 of this when he died.
[4] Macleod to Grant, 29.10.[1820], *Elphinstone*.

Chaplin goes through it all with perfect good will, and generally breaks up each night's feast with 2, 3 & sometimes 4 hours of short whist.[1]

When a couple of months later Chaplin complained to Elphinstone of the headaches he was suffering from, he was met with a warning against 'well dressed dinners & short whist at this season'. Elphinstone added some good advice: 'Depend upon it, if you would have recourse to abstemious habits & regular hours you would soon get rid of your headaches.'[2]

But Chaplin declared, 'I have for some time past followed your plan—eat no tiffin—drink 2 glasses of wine only—no beer for months past—& break up the Bhut Chit at $\frac{1}{2}$ past 11.'[3]

However sociable his habits had become, Chaplin was not popular with all his subordinates. He and H. D. Robertson the Collector of Poona were often at odds, Robertson objecting both to his inquiries into the details of a Collector's work and to the sarcasm with which he was apt to enliven his criticisms. When Robertson complained about this, Elphinstone admitted that 'the satirical way of writing you allude to . . . is a great misfortune in his situation'.[4]

Elphinstone had already warned Chaplin not to arouse ill feeling among his subordinates by sarcasm at their expense. In December 1821, when praising a report of Chaplin's, he added a word of criticism:

It has however a fault that is well worth attending to. It has wit enough for an Edinburgh Review and used with almost as little compunction & it will therefore leave the Collectors pretty much in the humour of reviewed authors. This may possibly produce serious inconvenience in things not now thought of. Great indulgence in all cases where it can be shown and grave censure when necessary would keep them in better temper, but great forbearance is necessary in an irregular government like yours where so much depends on individual zeal.[5]

The individual zeal of each Collector was particularly necessary in the informal hearing of complaints. Like Elphinstone, Chaplin was anxious to foster this practice and urged his Collectors to set aside fixed times for it.[6] This was done. But the Collectors were unable to maintain the practice of hearing oral complaints.

[1] Low to M.E., 25.2.1825, *Elphinstone.*
[2] M.E. to Chaplin, 18.4.1825, *Elphinstone.*
[3] Chaplin to M.E. 20.4.1825, *Elphinstone.* Bhut Chit = batchit = conversation.
[4] M.E. to H. D. Robertson, 6.5.1822, *Elphinstone.*
[5] M.E. to Chaplin, 10.12.1821, *Elphinstone.*
[6] Chaplin to Government, 5.11.1821, para. 99, S.R.J. iv. 335.

Briggs in Khandesh, who had begun by hearing complaints verbal or written between nine and eleven o'clock every morning, confessed a few years later that

in spite of every wish to adopt the system of hearing complaints *viva voce*, I have been compelled to abandon it. Persons in Candeish state at one time before me what they deny to my face another. I have at length adopted the plan of receiving all petitions in writing, which prevents the plaintiff from retracting, and from making frivolous, groundless and malicious complaints, to which I found the *viva voce* plaintiffs too prone. A box with a hole to receive petitions lies in the veranda of the cutcherry, which is opened by me on Mondays, Thursdays and Saturdays, when all those who choose attend. I am always open to complaints against personal violence or outrage, during the whole time I attend the office, from ten till five daily.[1]

H. D. Robertson at Poona used to receive 'respectable natives' on a particular day each week. But, he told Chaplin in 1821, 'as latterly I found those only came to me who could not get what they wanted from you, and that I was liable to be led into interferences with your orders, I gradually abolished the custom of receiving them daily on a stated day, or at all, unless they bring an order from you for a punchayet, or any other business'.[2] He sat two or three times a week, however, to hear complaints from ordinary people: 'complaints are received in writing and explained *viva voce*'. He added with a possible reference to Munro that 'the enviable facility of settling disputes and of giving eight to ten decrees in half an hour, or special order[s] on *ex parte* representations and assertions, enjoyed (I have heard) by gentlemen in some parts of India can never, I am sorry to say, be hoped for here'. Like Briggs, he thought that those who come to him with complaints would only keep to the truth if their words were written down.[3]

Pottinger at Ahmadnagar also seems to have received only written complaints. But he saw members of 'the better classes' whenever they applied for an interview, and any of the lower classes could see him when he sat in his office to deal with petitions. This he did at least twice a week, and at such times, he told Chaplin, 'I make it an undeviating rule to call every person before me who gives in a petition, however trifling the subject of it, and I am led to under-

[1] Briggs, *Replies to queries*, n.d. [1822], S.R.J. iv. 688.
[2] H. D. Robertson, *Replies to queries*, 10.10.1821, ibid. 593.
[3] Ibid. 527.

stand this system is peculiarly gratifying to their feelings'.[1] These complaints were 'all received in writing, and explained verbally'.[2]

Thackeray, an experienced Madras civilian who succeeded Chaplin at Dharwar, used his discretion whether or not to listen to oral complaints. His general principle was that 'querulous persons, who can write and have much to say, are sometimes desired to bring their complaints in writing. This has some effect in checking falsehood and litigation, for the complainant who talks at random is often afraid of committing himself on paper.'[3]

Elphinstone intended panchayats to be the main instrument of civil justice. Even from the beginning, however, it was only in Dharwar and Khandesh that they were in fact the main instrument —judged, that is, by the number of suits which they decided. In Khandesh, moreover, the number of suits decided by all instruments together was remarkably small. In Poona Mamlatdars and subordinate Judges (Amins) were the chief instrument. (It was only in Poona that subordinate Judges had been appointed; by 1821 there were five of them altogether, and no doubt they did much more of this work than the Mamlatdars.)[4] In Ahmadnagar the Collector's Court was the chief instrument. Elphinstone had already had occasion to rebuke Pottinger for not giving enough scope to panchayats. It still seemed that he had not mended his ways, and he was accordingly rebuked by Chaplin on several occasions.[5]

But Chaplin himself admitted that the Collectors did not have enough time for their judicial work. On the other hand, he believed that effective supervision was 'the main-spring of punchayets', indeed, that they needed 'the individual attention of one person'. He therefore recommended in 1821 that a Register should be appointed under each of the Deccan Collectors 'to watch and regulate the proceedings of punchayets'.[6]

In February 1822 Registers were therefore appointed to serve under the Collectors of Poona, Ahmadnagar, and Dharwar— though not Khandesh, where judicial business seemed so small.[7]

---

[1] Pottinger, *Replies to queries*, [1822], para. 38, S.R.J. iv. 725.
[2] Pottinger, *Replies to queries*, 31.7.1822, ibid. 731.
[3] Thackeray, *Replies to queries*, [1822], ibid. 779.
[4] Chaplin to Government, 5.11.1821, para. 86, S.R.J. iv. 333.
[5] Chaplin to Government, 5.11.1821, para. 98, S.R.J. iv. 334 f. See Table, p. 194. [6] Ibid., para. 125, op. cit. 339.
[7] Government to Chaplin, 21.2.1822, Bom. J.C. 27.2.1822, 1472 f. Salary Rs.850 a month.

They were instructed to try to settle all suits by panchayat. Every plaintiff asking them for justice had to be able to prove either that he had been before a panchayat which had been guilty of corruption or partiality or gross injustice, or that he himself was willing for a panchayat and that the defendant had refused one.[1]

TABLE 5

Suits decided in Each Year, 1819–22[2]

Collectorate	Year	By panchayats	By Collector's Court	By Mamlatdars
Dharwar . . .	1819–20	255	2	0
	1820–1	219	34	140
	1821–2	325	54	121
Khandesh . .	1819–20	87	2	0
	1820–1	72	11	5
	1821–2	94	18	13
Poona . .	1819–20	241	41	774
	1820–1	113	13	682
	1821–2	170	5	761
Ahmadnagar . .	1819–20	54	285	111
	1820–1	118	749	104
	1821–2	78	757	29

Note: Suits decided by Amins are included under the heading Mamlatdars.

Chaplin allowed the Registers a wide discretion:

I do not deem it necessary at present to furnish you with specific rules of proceeding on the trial of suits, because any unbending forms of process might prove little congenial to the habits of native gentlemen in the Dekhan, who cannot all at once be reconciled to the equalizing principles of an established judicial code, in which it is hardly possible to draw any line for a distinction of persons. It will be proper however that the proceedings of the Registers should be conducted according to the general rules of our Courts, as far as they can be followed consistently with Mahratta habits and prejudices, in all cases that from particular circumstances cannot be referred to, or settled by Punchayets. But the personal attendance of any sirdar or person of rank, or a Mamlutdar, need not be insisted upon, where the attendance of a Wukeel on their part may be sufficient . . . should it be necessary to possess the evidence of a person of rank in a case of no great moment a Wukeel may be deputed to wait upon him to take down his information. . . .[3]

[1] Chaplin, Circular, 23.2.1822, Bom. J.C. 17.4.1822, 2533 ff.
[2] Chaplin to Government, 20.8.1822, paras. 204 ff., S.R.J. iv. 490 ff.
[3] Chaplin, Circular, 23.2.1822, Bom. J.C. 17.4.1822, 2533 ff.

All the same, however great the care for Maratha custom, this was the first major inroad upon the original simplicity of Elphinstone's judicial plan. Soon, even the utility of the panchayat itself was to be called into question.

However simple the panchayat might seem in principle, in practice its management raised one difficulty after another.

Membership was still one of the main problems. Most people seemed reluctant to serve. There were always some who were only too willing—eager indeed to make a profession of it. But the majority could ill afford the time. Even when members had been found for a panchayat they did not usually attend with any regularity, and this wasted more time.

It was suggested that rosters should be kept of eligible people. But Elphinstone objected that this 'would destroy all the interest which may at present be felt by the members of punchayets in the decision of the cause, and would place each case before persons as little acquainted with the circumstances and character of the parties as an European Judge'.[1]

Payment of members was another remedy suggested—the money to be found by a tax on suits or by a fine payable by the loser. But Elphinstone was also opposed to this idea: payment could not really compensate members for the time which they had lost; it would degrade the character of a panchayat 'by rendering it a business of hire', and it might make panchayats as expensive to suitors as a regular system of Law Courts. The idea was therefore abandoned.[2]

Poor attendance was one reason for the waste of time in reaching a decision. But the waste of time was one reason for poor attendance. One way of reforming the system might have been for the Collectors or their Assistants to maintain a closer supervision over the proceedings of each panchayat. Indeed, Registers had been appointed for that duty, and Elphinstone himself thought that the main reason why panchayats had been so successful in Dharwar was the energetic supervision of Thackeray the Collector.[3] But panchayats were peculiarly difficult for a European to supervise: 'The want of regularity in the proceedings of punchayets makes

[1] M.E., Minute, n.d., S.R.J. iv. 438; Government to Chaplin, 24.1.1822, ibid. 452.
[2] Ibid. Government to Chaplin, 24.1.1822, para. 3, Bom. J.C. 30.1.1822, 538 ff.
[3] St. John Thackeray, Madras writer season 1805 (East-India Register).

them difficult to revise. Their decisions being founded on traditional maxims are not easily understood by a foreigner.'[1]

Panchayats, in short, could not be made efficient save by 'the extraordinary zeal' of an officer like Thackeray. But officers varied. Therefore, panchayats alone were not enough. Subordinate judges (Munsifs) must be appointed to do with speed some of the work now being done with tedious delay by panchayats.[2]

The subordinate judges (Amins) of Poona had been doing useful work, both deciding suits themselves and also supervising the proceedings of panchayats. Chaplin, however, reported in 1822 that they had acquired a bad reputation. In particular, they were disliked by the upper classes—probably, he thought, because of 'their occasionally arrogating to themselves an authority which native gentlemen, unaccustomed to the equality of judicial rules of procedure, can ill brook from persons whom they consider so much their inferiors'.[3]

Elphinstone, however, told the Collectors to appoint their Munsifs 'from amongst the most respectable of the resident inhabitants of the district'. In spite of his forebodings in 1819, he provided them with an incentive to speed by allowing them in addition to a basic salary of Rs.100 a month half an anna in the rupee on the amount of each suit which they tried or referred to a panchayat.[4]

They were empowered to try suits for personal property up to a maximum value of Rs.250 and any suits referred to them by the Collector up to Rs.1,000. They were also to assemble panchayats to decide suits at the request of the parties.[5]

But they were not to supersede panchayats altogether. Harry Borradaile the young Register of Poona had already suggested in an able memorandum that the jurisdiction of panchayats should be limited to certain types of suit.[6] He had approached the question of the usefulness of panchayats by assuming that their great advantage over single judges lay in their superior knowledge of the particular matter at issue: he then asked in what types of suit this

---

[1] M.E., Minute, 14.1.1823, S.R.J. iv. 811.
[2] Ibid.
[3] Chaplin to Government, 20.8.1822, paras. 220, 240. S.R.J. iv. 493, 497.
[4] 'Rules respecting Munsiffs', ibid. 868.
[5] Ibid.
[6] Harry Borradaile, writer 1818, Register of Poona, 1822 (*Personal Records*, xx. 65 ff.).

advantage was most relevant and suggested that they deal with them only.[1]

Elphinstone accepted the general principle. A list was drawn up of matters suitable for panchayats, and it was decided that a Munsif was not to try suits concerning any of these matters unless both parties voluntarily agreed in writing to accept his jurisdiction.[2] The Mamlatdars were empowered to summon panchayats to decide such matters. On the other hand, they could only summon panchayats to try suits for debt or personal property (not above Rs.200) if both parties agreed in writing to accept the decision of a panchayat. In these matters, the onus of asking for a panchayat was upon the parties concerned.[3]

Rules were also laid down to expedite the proceedings of such panchayats as were held. To discourage frivolous suits the Collector was empowered at his discretion to fine the loser up to 10 per cent. of the amount contested. If a panchayat failed to decide within three months it might be dismissed and the case tried by the Collector or referred by him to a Munsif. If a panchayat took longer than two months to decide its members might be made to sit in the office of the Munsif or Mamlatdar.[4]

In order to facilitate the summoning of members, a list of the eligible men in each district (pargana) was to be drawn up, consisting of 'Daismooks, Daispandees, Potails and Koolkurnees (not actually in office), petty Jagheerdars, Enamdars, holders of mokassa, or other umuls of villages, and pensioners of the Government'.[5] It was left to the Mamlatdar's influence to induce members to attend.[6]

---

[1] Borradaile's list of matters for panchayats: (1) 'points of religion', (2) 'customs of the country, of caste, or trade', (3) 'division of property', (4) 'old and intricate accounts', (5) 'cases of wuttuns and hucks', and (6) 'disputes for maintenance'.

Elphinstone's list was longer: (1) 'religion', (2) 'marriage', (3) 'peculiar customs of places', (4) 'wuttuns or hucks', (5) 'division of property', (6) 'maintenance', (7) 'old and intricate accounts', (8) 'disputes between two inhabitants of the same village within the sum of fifty rupees personal property or value', (9) 'suits for damages for alleged personal injuries, and for personal damages of whatever nature', (10) 'boundary disputes'.

(H. Borradaile, 'Note upon Punchayats', n.d., S.R.J. iv. 605; 'Rules respecting punchayats', ibid. 864 ff.)

[2] Or unless the Collector specifically referred such a suit to him. Borradaile's original suggestion had been to limit the jurisdiction of panchayats to these cases; Elphinstone was also concerned to limit the jurisdiction of Munsifs by forbidding them to touch these cases.

[3] Ibid.   [4] Ibid.   [5] Ibid.

[6] M.E., Minute, 14.1.1823, S.R.J. iv. 812. He could impose fines.

Elphinstone considered that these were the least changes necessary to enable the traditional system to work effectively. But after his experience of the Deccan Commission and of the rest of the Bombay territories he had modified his old hostility to the Adalat system. 'The failure of the judicial system, where it has failed', he wrote in 1823, 'is owing to extraneous circumstances.' In the rest of the Bombay territories it was working satisfactorily: 'there is no accumulation of causes like that complained of elsewhere; and if there is some harshness in the manner of proceeding of the courts, it may in part be ascribed to circumstances inseparable from the character of our Government, and partly to the neglect of particular privileges and indulgences, which might be preserved without at all affecting the principles of our jurisprudence'. It might well have to be introduced into the Deccan in time.[1]

The result of these changes was that, judging by the number of suits decided, the Munsifs quickly became the principal instrument of civil justice in the Deccan. Even in Dharwar, where hitherto the largest number of suits to be tried by any one agency had been tried by panchayats, the Munsifs tried more suits than any other single agency in 1823, and more than all the other agencies put together in 1824.[2]

With the aim of making panchayats more popular with suitors and members alike, Elphinstone suggested in 1825 that

appeals be allowed from Punchayets the same as from other tribunals no member being liable to be called on for any explanation of his opinion or to be summoned as evidence to what passes in the Punchayet, more than a Zillah Judge is on an appeal from his decision. I think suitors would more readily take to Punchayets if not thereby deprived of the power of appeal & on the other hand members would be less averse to sit on Punchayets when it ceased to be the interest of either party to accuse them of gross error or corruption.[3]

[1] M.E., Minute, 14.1.1823, S.R.J. iv. 811 f.

[2]

Year	By panchayats	By Munsifs	By Collector, &c.	By Mamlatdars (and Peshkars)
1823	293	471	387	165
1824	413	2614	314	156

(Bom. J.C. 23.3.1825, 44). Munsifs were appointed so late in Dharwar that the number of their decisions for 1823 refers only to the second half of the year. Peshkars had been appointed to help the Mamlatdars in judicial duties.

[3] M.E. to Chaplin, 29.9.1825, *Elphinstone.*

Chaplin disagreed. He thought that this would bring panchayats into disrepute, for their decisions were generally considered as too sacred to be set aside. Yet he admitted that the difficulty of finding members other than those who were trying to make a living out of it was still very real in all large towns. So serious a problem did this seem to him that he concluded that panchayats would never succeed in large towns and that it was best not to encourage them there.[1] Elphinstone thereupon modified his original proposal by suggesting that appeals should be allowed from panchayats held in large towns but not from those held in villages.[2]

It was accordingly provided in 1825 that appeals should be allowed from panchayats held in large towns as freely as from subordinate judges, without the necessity of a complaint of gross error or corruption.[3]

When the Court of Directors came to hear of the changes made in 1823 they condemned the principle that the panchayat should be the only available tribunal in any type of case, and asserted that it should only be used as a means of arbitration when both parties agreed to submit to its jurisdiction. 'Regular courts', they said, should be established as the alternative open to every suitor.[4]

But when the Board of Control saw the draft dispatch containing these orthodox doctrines they struck them out and replaced them with a general expression of approval of the Bombay Government's policy. At the same time they told the Court severely that it would have been 'inexcusable' if the Bombay Government had not tried to make use of the panchayat.[5]

In fact, however, panchayats were never to be the chief instrument of civil justice in the Deccan as Elphinstone had once hoped they would be. But he still thought that they had a useful part to

[1] Chaplin to Government, 7.10.1825, Bom. J.C. 9.11.1825, 31.
[2] M.E., Minute, n.d., ibid. 32.
[3] Government to Anderson (Judge of Poona and Sholhapur), 3.11.1825, ibid. 33.
[4] Quoted in Edmonstone, Minute of Dissent, 10.2.1827, App. C.M. iv. 260 ff.
[5] Board to Court, 9.9.1826, Board to Court, vii. 33 ff. The Court replied with more arguments on 22 December 1826, asking whether 'the dearest rights of the natives' were to be jeopardized in these irregular tribunals, but the Board remained firm, declaring that the Bombay Government were acting in accordance with principles laid down by the home authorities as far back as 1814 (Court to Board, ix. 168 ff., Board to Court, vii. 64 ff.).

play, and the new Code of Regulations published in 1827 made special provision for them.[1]

He even tried to extend their use to criminal trials. When the first drafts for the new Code were being considered in 1822, Elphinstone suggested that an inquiry should be made into the possibility of introducing a jury system in criminal trials. He was thinking of Briggs's experiments with criminal panchayats in Khandesh, and he had heard of the success with which 'native juries' had been used in Ceylon.[2] But there was little support for the idea among the Judges—or even among the Deccan Collectors. Many were particularly afraid of the danger of caste prejudice.[3] Nevertheless, at Elphinstone's suggestion clauses were included in the new Code permitting Judges in criminal trials as well as in civil suits to make use of 'the assistance of respectable natives' by employing them as a panchayat, as assessors, or 'more nearly as a jury'—provided always that the actual decision was for the Judge alone and that their functions were no more than advisory.[4]

The steady undercurrent of disapproval of the Deccan system which disturbed Elphinstone's Council rose to a torrent in 1823 after a series of irregularities had come to light in the administration of justice by the Collectors. Briggs's Assistant Hodges had committed a number of 'enormities' as Elphinstone himself admitted: he considered him to be 'the worst trier of causes that ever sat upon a bench'. Pottinger had treated 'the confessions of prisoners long ago convicted & transported as sufficient proof against a man on his trial'. Thackeray, as Elphinstone complained to Chaplin in September 1823, 'some time ago (indeed I fancy very often) convicted a man on the evidence taken before the Camavisdar or the Assistant without even putting a question to a witness'.[5]

R. T. Goodwin, who had recently succeeded Prendergast as Fourth Member of Council, made the attack.[6] His indignation

[1] Reg. VII, 1827. The Courts were to enforce written panchayat decrees that contained the names of the parties and of the panchayat members, together with mention of the nature of the suit and the decision. This Regulation applied to the whole of the Bombay Presidency.

[2] M.E., Minute, n.d., Bom. J.C. 10.7.1822, 3836 f.; M.E., 'Remark', n.d., S.R.J. iv. 871.   [3] Answers to queries, ibid. 875 ff.

[4] Bom. Reg. IV, 1827, sec. xxiv, cl. 1–4; Bom. Reg. XIII, 1827, sec. xxxviii, cl. 5.

[5] M.E. to Chaplin, 9.9.1823, Elphinstone.

[6] Richard Thomas Goodwin, writer season 1795; 1806, Secretary, Country Correspondence; 1812, Magistrate of Police and Revenue Judge, Bombay Island; 1823, Fourth Member of Council (Personal Records, ix. 127 ff.).

at the absence of regular forms of proceeding led him into an elementary slip: 'the rules of evidence are either unknown or neglected,' he declared, 'and a course of practice is substituted which I shall not describe as irregular and imperfect, but absolutely illegal'.[1]

Elphinstone of course challenged him to say by what law he called these practices illegal, but at the same time he frankly admitted that the administration of justice in the Deccan was 'defective even to a greater degree than in our old provinces'. As remedies he suggested not the drawing up of an ambitious law of evidence but the introduction of the criminal part of the new Code of Regulations, the separation of the office of Judge from that of Collector and Magistrate in charge of Police, and the sending of advice and criticism when the need arose.[2]

Francis Warden, who had also joined the Council in 1823, was as hostile as Goodwin to the union of judicial and revenue powers in the Collector. Apart from that, however, he had little to say against the Deccan system on this occasion. Indeed, he was inclined to welcome simplicity of procedure.[3]

The result of this brief storm was an official letter from the Government to Chaplin which laid down some principles to be followed in the future: for example, hearsay evidence could have no place in a trial; a prisoner should be given the benefit of the doubt if witnesses contradicted each other; the confessions of convicts should not be used as proof against their accomplices; all important criminal cases should be tried by the Collectors themselves.[4] As Elphinstone explained in a private letter to Chaplin, the main advantage of the last provision was that it would exclude Hodges from such trials. He warned Chaplin to avoid such scandals in the future: 'Could you not send back all trials that contain any great irregularity. Their production here & the remarks that are made on them do much harm to the reputation of the Deccan system.'[5]

Chaplin was taken by surprise: 'So few irregularities have of late been pointed out that I fancied matters were going on smoothly and as well as could be expected considering that our Collectors are also Judges, Criminal Judges, Magistrates and Judges of Circuit,

[1] Goodwin, Minute, 6.9.1823, Bom. J.C. 1.10.1823, 4049 f.
[2] M.E., Minute, 27.9.1823, ibid. 4050 ff.
[3] Warden, Minute, n.d., ibid. 4053 ff.
[4] Government to Chaplin, 25.9.1823, ibid. 4057 ff.
[5] M.E. to Chaplin, 9.9.1823, *Elphinstone*.

and cannot therefore be expected to do the duty of all so well as it would be done by separate instruments for each department.' This was dangerous ground, and he went on to admit that 'this is no doubt against the Dekhan system but it has in other respects its advantages'.[1]

The Collectors simply had not the time for all this work: 'Some cases of murder are of such extreme length that the Collectors themselves could hardly get through them without sacrificing their Revenue and other business—and the duty, therefore, necessarily devolves on the Assistants who have not always much experience.' Nor could Chaplin suggest any remedy in the existing situation: 'These are evils which can only be palliated I fear and not entirely corrected under the present system & they of course furnish plaus- ible arguments for the extension of [the] Regular Judicial plan of administration which is so anxiously looked for by the majority of the Bombay C. Service.'[2] The sting in this last remark lay of course in the fact that the appointment of separate Judges in the Deccan would add to the chances of promotion in the Bombay Civil Service.

But it soon became apparent that the Collectors would never have enough time to carry out a revenue survey of the Deccan unless they could be relieved of at least some of their judicial duties. This, and not any argument derived from the theory of the separa- tion of powers, was for Chaplin the decisive factor.[3]

He therefore recommended the appointment of Judges in the Deccan—provided that due precautions were taken to avoid offend- ing 'persons of rank', or 'the native gentry'.[4]

The Governor in Council accepted Chaplin's recommendations and resolved in 1824 to appoint Judges to Poona and Ahmadnagar.[5] But before this resolution could be carried into effect a dispatch was received from the home government conveying their general approval of 'the leading principles' of the Deccan system and directing that 'no important changes' should be made in it without their prior approval.[6]

[1] Chaplin to M.E., 12.9.1823, *Elphinstone*.   [2] Ibid.
[3] Chaplin to Government, 14.4.1824, Bom. J.C. 12.5.1824, 2753 ff.
[4] Ibid. Causes in which Sardars were parties were to go before him as Com- missioner; if Sardars were required to give evidence, 'the forms of civility usual among men of rank must be substituted for all summonses and orders of Court'; they should never be summoned if it could be avoided; in minor cases a Karkun should be sent to them to take down their evidence.
[5] Government to Chaplin, 8.5.1824, ibid. 2763 f.
[6] Political dispatch to Bombay, 5.11.1823, para. 47, Bom. P.D. ii. 397 ff.

The appointment of two Judges seemed at first sight too important a change to be carried out in the face of these orders. Instead,
a single Criminal Judge was appointed to relieve the Collectors of
merely their criminal jurisdiction. Marriott was chosen for this post.[1]

But Elphinstone was soon considering more radical changes that
would afford more adequate relief to the Collectors:

I was thinking [he wrote to Chaplin in July 1825] whether a plan
might not be found more consistent with the present system and with
the important object of bringing forward the natives, than the introduction of regular Courts. The plan that strikes me is to increase greatly
the powers of the natives employed in judicial offices leaving the Europeans nothing to do but hear appeals, by which means they would be
left leisure for their other duties.[2]

Chaplin submitted another plan which provided for an extended
use of panchayats and dispensed with the appointment of another
Judge, but Elphinstone rejected it on the ground, among other
reasons, that these panchayats would be so often composed of
officials and so often liable to be overruled that they would lose
their true character: 'although it might be a good expedient to keep
the Machine going for a while, it would never do for a permanent
system, or supersede the necessity of sooner or later appointing
Judges'.[3]

Elphinstone had in fact decided that the appointment of another
Judge could not be long avoided. Greenhill, the Secretary to
Government, had also submitted a plan, 'suggesting two Judges &
a partial introduction of the Regulations (generally very judicious,
but sometimes rather *judicial*)', as Elphinstone remarked.[4]

Greenhill seems to have admired the Adalat system much more
than Elphinstone or his colleagues in the Deccan could ever do.
He asserted that the introduction of Judges and the Regulation
Code into the Deccan would have the advantage of gradually introducing 'the regularity and despatch of the established Courts of
Adalat in the old provinces'. Elphinstone, on the other hand, inclined rather to think of it as a necessary evil. Although the traditional system had 'many and great faults', it was

capable of preserving the country in peace and tolerable security. If it

[1] Judicial letter from Bombay, 29.11.1824, para. 141, Bom. J.L.R. iv. 303 ff.
[2] M.E. to Chaplin, 14.7.1825, *Elphinstone*.
[3] M.E. to Chaplin, 21.8.1825, *Elphinstone*.
[4] M.E. to Chaplin, 7.8.1825, *Elphinstone*.

could be made to suffice without any change, I would much prefer it for a long period of years, even to a better system that was new; but as it must be altered (partly on account of its own defects, but still more on account of its inconsistency with our notions & institutions which render a continual effort necessary to uphold it) my next wish would be that the alterations should proceed slowly & gradually 1st for the purpose of avoiding every innovation that was not required & 2nd to give the people time to enter a little into the spirit of the new laws imposed on them.[1]

But Chaplin's ill health would soon force him to go home. There was no one competent to succeed him, and the Commission must therefore be abolished on his departure. When the Commission was abolished, there would have to be some judicial authority to whom complaints could be made if a Collector abused his powers. Elphinstone hoped that all important changes could be carried out under Chaplin's supervision. There was therefore no time to waste.[2]

Elphinstone accordingly proposed the appointment of Judges with civil and criminal jurisdiction. But the judicial system of the Deccan was not to be completely assimilated to that of Bombay. He also proposed that the powers of the Indian subordinate judges should be increased.

Dharwar was to be an exception.

Greenhill suggested the appointment of Judges at Poona, Ahmadnagar, and Dharwar. But Elphinstone wanted to avoid such changes where possible: Dharwar was flourishing under the existing Deccan system and might soon be transferred to Madras. It was therefore decided to appoint Judges only to Poona and Ahmadnagar.[3]

Marriott was appointed to Ahmadnagar and Anderson to Poona.[4] In addition, the jurisdiction of the Deccan Munsifs was extended to suits of a maximum value of Rs.5,000. Warden strongly protested against the discrimination which this implied against the

[1] M.E., Minute, n.d., Bom. J.C. 5.10.1825, 44.
[2] Ibid. Chaplin's successor would presumably have been Baber, a Madras civilian who had succeeded Thackeray at Dharwar. But, as Elphinstone told Chaplin, Baber had shown 'an impetuosity and a want of judgement even when his temper is not ruffled that completely satisfies me that the Commission must be abolished whenever you go home' (M.E. to Chaplin, 15.6.1825, *Elphinstone*).
[3] Greenhill, Memorandum, n.d., Bom. J.C. 5.10.1825, 31, and subsequent minutes of M.E. and Council, ibid. 32 ff.
[4] Marriott as Judge of Ahmadnagar and Khandesh, Anderson as Judge of Poona and Sholhapur (Judicial letter from Bombay, 31.5.1826, para. 41, Bom. J.L.R. iv. 435 ff.). George William Anderson, writer season 1806; 1821, Judge of Surat (*Personal Records*, xx. 1 ff.).

Gujarat Munsifs whose jurisdiction was limited in the proposed
Code to suits of a maximum value of Rs.500.[1] As Elphinstone
pointed out, there was a bigger establishment of European Judges
and Registers in Gujarat than was proposed for the Deccan.[2] But
he was also convinced of the need 'to open a door for the employment of the natives. Judicial business under proper superintendence', he asserted, 'is what they seem most fitted for.' He drew
the logical conclusion from this assumption: 'this duty I would
therefore gradually make over to them reserving for Europeans the
business of superintendence and the decision of appeals'. Such
reforms must begin somewhere. Why not now in the Deccan? If
successful they could be extended later on to Gujarat.[3]

In the new Code it was therefore laid down that the jurisdiction
of 'Native Commissioners' should extend at the least to suits worth
Rs.500 and might extend at the most to suits worth Rs.5,000.[4]

The great jagirdars soon settled down without much apparent
difficulty under the new government. Chintaman Rao Patwardhan
was the only serious exception. Elphinstone wrote a little bitterly
in 1823 that Chintaman Rao 'is a professed malcontent, and appears
desirous of being considered as the last representative of Hindoo
independence. His discontent, however, evaporates in long contro-
versial letters, the composition of which appears for some years to
have been almost the only employment of his life.'[5]

Chaplin had already had great difficulty not only in arranging the
final details of Chintaman Rao's settlement with the new government, but also in an even more delicate matter.

Shortly after the beginning of the war the two brothers Vaughan,
one an officer in the Madras Army, the other in the Marine, had
been captured while travelling between Bombay and Poona. They
were then killed, one brother being forced to hang the other.[6]

The officer immediately responsible for this, one Babaji Pant
Gokhale, escaped capture and even detection until Thackeray the
Collector of Dharwar heard that Chintaman Rao had him in con-
finement. He thereupon told Chintaman Rao to deliver him up.[7]

[1] Warden, Minute, 11.5.1826, Bom. P.C. 24.5.1826, 22.
[2] M.E., Minute, n.d., Bom. P.C. 20.9.1826, 23.
[3] M.E., Minute, 5.9.1826, Bom. J.C. 18.10.1826, 30.
[4] Bom. Reg. II, 1827, sec. xxxvii, cl. 3.
[5] M.E., Minute, 14.1.1823, S.R.J. iv. 813.   [6] Grant, *History*, 480.
[7] Thackeray to Chintaman Rao, 16.1.1822, Bom. S.C. 27.2.1822, 8.

But Chintaman Rao refused, in an angry letter in which he said that it would have been derogatory to the honour of his family and caste 'to deliver up for punishment a cow or a Brahmin who may have happened to commit a crime against the Company's Government'. He also claimed that Babaji Pant had only been obeying orders and therefore deserved no punishment.[1]

Chaplin received this news with indignation, declaring that 'the perpetrator of this foul and deliberate murder, involving so gross a breach of the law of civilized nations, even though it should be found that he acted under superior orders, ought not entirely to escape with impunity'. He even wondered whether the impertinent style of Chintaman Rao's letter indicated 'a real or feigned derangement of intellect'.[2]

The Bombay Government decided upon drastic action. According to the terms under which Chintaman Rao held his jagir, they told Chaplin, he was bound to hand over offenders against the British Government—and it rested with them, they added, to decide who were the offenders. Chintaman Rao was to be warned that unless he handed over Babaji Pant at once, he would be treated as a rebel. If he refused yet made no active resistance to a British force, 'it may safely be inferred that he is deranged' and then his jagir should be put in the hands of trustees. If he resisted, his jagir should be seized and 'every means taken to seize or destroy him and his adherents'. The jagir might, however, be continued to his son if his son proved loyal.[3]

In the event, Chintaman Rao surrendered Babaji Pant, who was sentenced to life imprisonment and sent to Singarh Fort near Poona.[4] But when the home government heard of the matter they ordered his release on the ground that his defence that he had acted under orders was a valid one.[5] He was accordingly released.[6]

The episode thus ended without disaster for Chintaman Rao. But, as Elphinstone remarked to Chaplin, 'If the Jageerdars go on in this way, we shall have *simplified* the Carnatic before it is given up to the Madras Government.'[7]

[1] Chintaman Rao to Thackeray, 28.1.1822, ibid. 9 f.
[2] Chaplin to Government, 16.2.1822, ibid. 6 ff.
[3] Bombay Government to Chaplin, 25.2.1822, ibid. 10 ff.
[4] Political letter from Bombay, 31.7.1822, paras. 78 ff., Bom. P.L.R. viii. 683.
[5] Political dispatch to Bombay, 16.2.1825, paras. 54 ff., Bom. P.D. ii. 701 ff.
[6] Political letter from Bombay, 1.9.1826, paras. 9 f., Bom. P.L.R. x. 149 f.
[7] M.E. to Chaplin, 26.2.1822, *Elphinstone*.

Chintaman Rao did not confine his irascibility to his relations with the new government. The dispute between him and the Maraj branch of the Patwardhans continued. Chaplin despaired of an early settlement, 'since neither party is ever at a loss for expedients for protracting the enquiry'. The matter at issue concerned ancestral property, but Chaplin doubted whether this was the real source of difficulty: 'Chintaman Rao's wounded honour is, I fancy, the chief point of litigation; and I really believe he would be sorry to find himself deprived of what he considers to be so substantial a grievance.'[1]

Elphinstone discounted the rumours which he had heard of Chintaman Rao's insanity: such tales seemed to originate among his dependants, and Elphinstone concluded that their real purpose was to protect his lands from confiscation 'in case some fresh extravagance should expose him personally to the resentment of Government'.[2]

Chintaman Rao eventually decided to see Elphinstone about his grievances. He resolved to go to Bombay and see him there. When Elphinstone heard of his project, in 1823, he told Chaplin to try to persuade him not to go, and sketched out a number of different arguments for Chaplin to use. These arguments are of some interest for they point the difference between the old ways of life and the new, as seen by Elphinstone with all his sympathy for the old. Chaplin was to explain to Chintaman Rao the following points:

1st. That His Majesty's Castle and Island of Bombay (or more legally speaking the County of Bombay) is under the exclusive control of H.M.'s Justices and H.M.'s Court of Recorder, and is governed according to the laws of England. 2nd. That in consequence the Governor has no power whatever to protect Chintamun Row or his followers from the ordinary operation of those laws, or from the rules of police which to them will be very irksome. 3rd. That no elephants or camels are allowed on the Island, and no armed men are allowed to enter it. 4th. That there is no ground for encamping and that he must therefore take lodgings, which near the rains are not easy to be had. 5th. That if there were no difficulty in his coming, there is no use in it, as I must refer to you and to Mr. Thackeray on every point, and can never give him an answer till I receive your opinion, which, on the other hand can hardly be made up in Chintamun Row's absence.[3]

---

[1] Chaplin to Government, 20.8.1822, para. 312, S.R.J. iv. 508.
[2] M.E., Minute, 14.1.1823, S.R.J. iv. 813.
[3] M.E. to Chaplin, 9.5.1823, *Elphinstone*.

Chintaman Rao did not go to Bombay.

As the years passed, he continued to complain of the time taken to reach a settlement between him and the Miraj branch. Though often insolent in his letters to the Government, he became reasonably polite to Chaplin in social intercourse: 'To myself personally', Chaplin reported in December 1825, 'he has been rather civil than otherwise for a long time past, a circumstance which I perhaps owe to some exaggerated compliments I paid to him on his taste for statuary, architecture & the fine arts when he showed me his improvements at Sanglee.'[1]

But he was badly shaken by the death of his only son in August 1826 and Elphinstone's refusal to countenance his attempt to adopt an heir without the prior sanction of the Government.[2]

Even after the abolition of the Deccan Commission it was rumoured that Chaplin would use his influence in England to secure justice for Chintaman Rao. When Balaji Pant went to a party given by Gopal Rao of Jamkhandi in February 1827 he heard it related that the home government had sent instructions for Chintaman Rao to be invested with a permanent hereditary title to his jagir. This, it was said, was the result of Chaplin's influence. H. D. Robertson the Collector of Poona, whom Balaji Pant informed of all this, repeated with unkind humour to Elphinstone the story that 'Mrs. Chaplin was related (through Oliver Cromwell I suppose) to the King of England, that Mr. Chaplin had consequently the King's ear, & that in spite of you, who were no favourite of His Majesty, Mr. Chaplin had done justice to Chintamun Row, and would obtain in England a confirmation of his act—or at all events would confirm it himself when he arrived in Bombay to succeed you as Governor.'[3]

The other jagirdars seemed quickly reconciled to their new circumstances. Those most affected by the change of government were those who had been punished for their loyalty to Baji Rao. When Elphinstone went on tour in the Deccan towards the end of 1822 he had visual evidence of this:

I was visited by the chiefs of the families of Poorundera, Rastia, Vinchoorkur, and other Jagheerdars, who have lost the lands assigned

[1] Chaplin to Government, 31.12.1825, Bom. P.C. 18.1.1826, 20.
[2] *Maratha Families* in Forrest, *Selections*, 692; M.E., Minute, 4.1.1827, Bom. P.C. 31.1.1827, 51.
[3] H. D. Robertson to M.E., 7.2.1827, *Elphinstone*.

them for the maintenance of troops and are reduced to those allowed them for their personal support. The retinue of these chiefs was greatly reduced, and they appeared more in the character of private persons than they would have done under the Peishwa. They seem, however, to be treated with consideration both by Europeans and natives, and their situation, on the whole, was less melancholy than I expected.[1]

Those who had not suffered from the war seemed to be flourishing. He thought that they were 'now in greater prosperity than perhaps at any former period'.[2] They had all kept their old jagirs, and many of them had also been rewarded for their conduct during the war by grants of new territories. Now they mostly came in pomp to meet him, 'with considerable bodies of troops, accompanied by elephants and guns'. Chintaman Rao himself brought 1,500 horse and foot with him; Appa Desai brought at least 1,000. Elphinstone commented, however, that 'many of these were raised for the occasion; and some of the other chiefs showed more attention to economy than to display'.[3]

For a while Elphinstone enjoyed their company: 'the Southern Jageerdars are not bad fellows', he wrote to Adam on 30 December 1822. 'Some of them are keen hunters and not bad companions in their way.'[4] But he soon wearied of the Patwardhans' controversies. 'I am plagued to death with Putwurduns', he confided to Grant on 4 January 1823, 'and most heartily envy you the near prospect of deliverance from all such society.'[5]

Appa Desai, the rough and ruthless chief of Nipani, had at first preserved an enigmatic demeanour. Thackeray the Collector of Dharwar reported in 1821 that 'the Nepanee chief remains in grim repose at his capital. His country does not appear to be better managed than usual, but the complaints of his subjects are not so loud.'[6] They were quieter still when Elphinstone visited the Deccan in 1822, for he was then able to report that Appa Desai had 'adapted himself to the new system of government, by entirely abstaining from the acts of tyranny and violence for which he was so remarkable under the Peishwa'.[7]

---

[1] M.E., Minute, 14.1.1823, S.R.J. iv. 812–13.
[2] M.E. to Governor-General, 30.12.1822, *Elphinstone*.
[3] M.E., Minute, 14.1.1823, S.R.J. iv. 813.
[4] M.E. to Adam, 30.12.1822, *Elphinstone*.
[5] M.E. to Grant, 4.1.1823, ibid.
[6] Thackeray, n.d. [1821], ibid. 398.
[7] M.E., Minute, 14.1.1823, S.R.J. iv. 809 ff.

Not that Elphinstone would have interfered with any minor irregularities. In 1825, for example, a newswriter reported that Appa Desai 'has murdered a young girl, it is not known whether one of his mistresses or concubines, she was 15 or 16 years of age'. Chaplin referred the matter to the Governor in Council.[1] But Elphinstone decided that since under the Peshwa the great jagirdars had powers of life and death, there was no justification for the Government to intervene. It had indeed been provided in Appa Desai's agreement that he should govern justly and obey any orders which the British Government might make concerning any complaint which might reach them. But Elphinstone pointed out that this provision was only intended to guard against large-scale disorders which might infect British territories. 'It was never intended', he declared, 'that our Government should interfere unless in very flagrant instances of abuse of power or long continuance of gross misgovernment.'[2]

Elphinstone had long feared that one of the main threats to the independence of the jagirdars would be the desire of Collectors for economy and efficiency and of Judges for justice and equality. When Chaplin returned to England and the Deccan Commission was abolished, he was particularly anxious that the jagirdars should not be left unprotected before the egalitarian Courts.

'Persons of rank' in the Deccan were therefore divided into three classes for civil suits and three classes for criminal trials, and Anderson the Judge of Poona was appointed 'Agent' to decide all civil suits concerning them.[3]

The first class for civil suits consisted of 'individuals of the very first distinction and influence under the Paishwa's Government, on account of their birth, their political importance, or the religious estimation in which they were held', and included the Patwardhans, Appa Desai of Nipani, the Pant Sachiv, and the Pratinidhi. Suits against them were to be decided by the Agent, 'reference being had in the most ample degree to the privileges of the defendant by former usage and custom enjoyed' and no decree against

[1] Intelligence report from Kolhapur, 30.8.1825, Bom. P.C. 21.9.1825, 30.
[2] M.E., Minute, n.d., ibid. 31; Government to Chaplin, 19.9.1825, ibid. 32; Agreement with Appa Desai, 14.6.1820, art. viii., Aitchison, viii. 402.
[3] M.E., Minute, 5.9.1826, Bom. J.C., 18.10.1826, 30. Chaplin wanted the Collectors to deal with all such suits. But Elphinstone preferred to appoint a separate Agent on the ground that the Collectors would not have enough time.

them was to be enforced without reference to the Governor in Council.[1]

The second class for civil suits consisted of 'individuals not equal in consideration to those above adverted to, but of high rank and importance under the Paishwa's Government', and included not only Vithal Narsing the Vinchur jagirdar and Balla Sahib Raste— how fallen, these two, from their former eminence!—but also Balaji Pant Natu, Muhammad Hanif the old Residency Munshi, and others risen from obscurity by the favour of the new government, like 'the Record Keepers of Collectors', and so on.[2] Suits against them were to be decided by the Agent, 'reference being had in a great degree, and in confirmity to former usage and custom, to the rank of the defendant, his situation and privileges, under the Paishwa's Government, as affecting his creditor's means of compelling payment during that period, his present means of discharging the debt, and other points material to the real equity of the plaintiff's claim and the defendant's liability'—the point here being that those who lent money to great men under the Peshwa's Government had had less opportunity for enforcing payment of their debts than under the new and more egalitarian government, and presumably took account of the risk by fixing the rate of interest at a level which it would probably be unfair now to exact in full. The Agent was to decide suits in this class without reference to government, but appeals from his decision were to be allowed to the Governor in Council.[3]

The third class consisted of 'individuals inferior in rank to those of the classes previously described, but still equitably entitled, on account of the privileges hitherto enjoyed by them, to a certain special degree of consideration', and included eminent Brahmans like Nilakantha Shastri, Mulhar Shroti, and Raghu Acharya the Principal of the Poona Hindu College, as well as Ganpat Rao Dengle the son of Trimbakji. Suits against them were to be decided by the Agent 'in like conformity to usage and custom, with some

[1] List No. 1 Civil, Bom. J.C. 18.10.1826, 31; Bom. Reg. XXIX, 1827, sec. v, cl. 1.

[2] Although they implied the contrary, the Government were thus engaged in creating an aristocracy of new men—though they might plausibly have claimed that men with this type of occupation might well have enjoyed special privileges under the former government even though these specific persons might not have done so.

[3] If presented within ninety days (ibid. cl. 2).

relaxation of the rules of the General Regulations, and some portion of attention to the points above specified for regulating his
decisions in suits against individuals of the two Superior Classes'.
Appeals from his decision were to be allowed to the Sadr Adalat.[1]

Exactly how much consideration was to be shown was not defined. The Government's attitude was expressed in general terms,
and much was left to the Agent's discretion. But the aim of these
measures was to protect the jagirdars from ruin as a result of the
strictness of Regulations and Law Courts to which they were unaccustomed. Thus, Elphinstone proposed that 'even in the clearest
case of debt the agent should be empowered to allow the Sirdar to
retain his house and a portion of his income sufficient for his decent
maintenance', and that the Agent's proceedings 'should be conducted rather according to the forms of a Durbar than those of a
Court of Justice'.[2]

Men of rank were also divided into three classes for criminal
matters. Each of these classes was smaller than the corresponding
class for civil matters. In other words, less indulgence was to be
shown in criminal than in civil justice.

Chiefs in the first class were 'exempt from all criminal jurisdiction even by the Governor in Council, except in cases of such
magnitude as to admit of interference under the subsisting engagements; or, in respect to those with whom there are no engagements,
cases of such magnitude as to render their punishment of political
importance'. This class was similar to the first class for civil
matters.[3]

Those in the second class were not exempt from the Courts'
jurisdiction, but it was declared that they 'should be treated with
forbearance, and proceeded with according to the special rules provided for their case'. These rules Elphinstone adopted with some
modifications from the draft which became Regulation XV of 1827.[4]

A third class also was created, to be treated with deference, but
with somewhat less indulgence than the second.[5]

---

[1] Bom. Reg. XXIX, sec. v, cl. 3.
[2] M.E., Minute, 5.9.1826, Bom. J.C. 18.10.1826, 30.
[3] Bom. J.C. 18.10.1826, 32. The Shankaracharya was excluded from this
class and placed in the second, although he was included in the first class for
civil suits.
[4] The modifications were mainly in the direction of greater indulgence (M.E.,
Minute, 5.9.1826, Bom. J.C. 18.10.1826, 30).
[5] For example, the Magistrate was empowered to dispense with the trial of a

The second and third criminal lists were both shorter than the corresponding civil lists. Thus, the second class for criminal trials excluded men who had risen to eminence under the new government and were included in the second class for civil suits—men like Balaji Pant, Muhammad Hanif, the Collectors' Record Keepers, and so on. Some of these, like Balaji Pant and Muhammad Hanif, were included in the third class for criminal trials, but others were not.[1] There was indeed a certain lack of symmetry in these lists, perhaps inseparable from all attempts to define and regulate what is in essence indefinable and intangible. Yet if any of the social privileges of the Deccan were to be preserved from the levelling tendencies of the Law Courts they had first to be set down in writing.

There was general satisfaction with the traditional system of police. There were differences of method in different Collectorates —arising either from local circumstances or from the ideas of the Collectors. One Collector, for example, might hold the local Bhil or Ramusi chiefs responsible for refunding the value of all stolen property (or for producing the thief). Another might hold the village responsible.[2] But in spite of such local difference, law and order was in general maintained. Khandesh was the only exception.

From the beginning, Khandesh had indeed presented Briggs with exceptional difficulties—its geography, its past history of war and misgovernment, and the large numbers and warlike habits of its Bhils. Ahmadnagar, however, had also been ravaged by wars— though not to the same extent—and had also suffered from plundering Bhils—though again not to the same extent. Pottinger's method was, in his own words, that of 'treating the Bheels with kindness', his ultimate aim being 'to give them a place in the society like any

second class Sardar if the accused was prepared to compensate the injured party to his and the Magistrate's satisfaction. But for the third class there was to be 'no particular indulgence in respect to compromise' (M.E., Minute, 5.9.1826, Bom. J.C. 18.10.1826, 30).

[1] List Nos. 2 and 3 (Criminal), Bom. J.C. 18.10.1826, 32.

[2] H. D. Robertson (Poona) began with the idea of making the Ramusi chiefs responsible, but soon decided that to bring home the responsibility to the village itself would be more effective (Robertson to Chaplin, 10.10.1821, para. 197, S.R.J. iv. 594). Pottinger (Ahmadnagar) made the Bhil and Ramusi chiefs responsible. But he was careful to maintain their authority over the Bhil or Ramusi watchmen in the villages (Collector of Ahmadnagar to Government, 7.10.1827, Bom. J.C. 20.2.1828, 8).

other caste'. He made a point of working through the chiefs and supporting them in their authority over their followers.[1]

By his own behaviour towards them he strove to overcome their distrust of government as such. When two of the principal chiefs in his jurisdiction at last came to visit him he allowed them to sit down with him upon chairs and talked to them in a friendly way in the presence of other Indians. This he thought pleased them greatly.[2] He realized also how important it was for his subordinates to follow his example. He found that the Kamavisdars tended to think it 'unbecoming their own individual station and even caste to hold any intercourse' with Bhils and 'equally absurd and unnecessary' to keep faith with them. He went to much trouble to persuade his Kamavisdars and their assistants 'to understand the delicate nature of their interference with the Bheels'.[3]

As a result, no doubt, of his sympathetic policy, he could soon claim that 'very few (if any) Bheels can be said to reside in the Hills now'. Some went there to graze their herds of black cattle and their flocks of sheep and goats; a few might till some ground there; but 'generally speaking the hills are quite deserted'. There were many instances of Bhils working in the fields for Kunbis and even Brahmans. Moreover, in 'large villages where there are weekly bazaars we now find the Bheels bartering their grain, cloth and other necessaries like the Koonbees'. Pottinger declared with satisfaction that he found it 'pleasing to observe the social intercourse that now exists between the Bheels and the other classes of the people'.[4]

On the other hand, Briggs seemed to be having little success in Khandesh. As one chief after another broke his agreement and rose in rebellion, his only remedy was to organize fresh military expeditions. Not even punishments like transportation seemed to deter others from fresh escapades.

Chaplin himself lost all patience: 'Nothing but a war of extermination can put an end to these troubles', he wrote privately to Elphinstone in February 1821, 'for the race of these marauders is evidently not to be reclaimed by any measures of indulgence.'[5]

Briggs himself had little faith in the chiefs. Pottinger always tried to work through them, but Briggs set out to reduce the number of

[1] Pottinger, *Replies to queries*, n.d., Bom. J.C. 30.4.1823, 2056 ff.
[2] Pottinger to Chaplin, 12.6.1823, Bom. J.C. 2.7.1823, 2989 ff.
[3] Pottinger, *Replies to queries*, n.d., Bom. J.C. 30.4.1823, 2056 ff.
[4] Ibid.
[5] Chaplin to M.E., 22.2.1821, *Elphinstone*.

their followers as much as possible by settling them in lowland villages. 'It has been my endeavour', he explained to Chaplin, 'to communicate separately with individuals which, while it prevents me from being imposed on by agents, breaks the links of a community available only for bad purposes.'[1] If the chiefs themselves sensed that this was his aim, they must have been all the more reluctant to co-operate with him. His relations with most of them certainly seemed unhappy.

He was a little more successful in persuading the lowland Bhils who had fled to the hills to return to their posts as watchmen in the villages. By October 1820 he could claim with a perhaps deceptive appearance of accuracy that 'no fewer than 1003 new houses have been constructed by hill Bheels returned to villages within the last twelve months'. He estimated also that 'from 3000 to 4000 Bheels who have always depended upon plunder for their subsistence have returned into the bosom of society, of which it is fair to conclude that 1000 to 1200 were male adults, the whole of whom have been robbers from their birth'.[2]

Yet the daily ration of grain which village headmen had been authorized to allot to each of their Bhil watchmen had never been drawn. Briggs suggested two reasons: that 'the Bheels were unwilling on the one hand to acknowledge themselves as having returned from the hills', and on the other hand that the village headmen were afraid that the cost might fall upon the village expenses. Moreover, he doubted whether even the traditional village allowances to Bhil watchmen were being paid, with the result that 'they must, like other people, depend solely on their own exertions for their livelihood, and a very great proportion of Candeish Bheels do support themselves entirely by labour. They are however constantly called on, in performing their duties as watchmen, in all villages lying on public roads, for which they seldom get paid by the passengers whom they accompany, and never by the villagers where they reside.'[3]

Small wonder, then, that the police system of Khandesh was ineffective. Briggs himself felt 'convinced that no highway robbery is ever committed without its being known in a few days to most of the Bheels in the vicinity'. He suggested that rewards should be offered—one-fourth of any stolen property that was recovered,

---

[1] Briggs to Chaplin, 31.12.1821, Bom. J.C. 30.4.1823, 2042 ff.
[2] Briggs to Chaplin, 31.10.1820, S.R.J. iv. 442.   [3] Ibid.

divided equally between the headman and the informer. But Chaplin thought that this might encourage fraud. Briggs also drew up a plan for reforming the village police system by allotting a definite number of watchmen to each village in proportion to its revenue, their names to be registered by the Mamlatdar and they themselves mustered periodically. But Chaplin thought that this would cost too much, although he had no objection to the mustering and registration of village watchmen.[1]

Meanwhile Briggs had been hearing rumours of corruption among his staff. In September 1819 he was told that there had been some corrupt practice at Malegaon. He soon found evidence against the Mamlatdar, Raghupant Rao, and punished him and others implicated with him by fines and imprisonment. He still had full confidence in his two Daftardars, Appaji Rao of the old Poona Residency and Lakshman Rao of Madras. Appaji Rao had been of great help to him from his first months in Khandesh; Lakshman Rao had only arrived in August 1819. Briggs appointed to succeed Raghupant Rao a Kanarese Brahman whom Lakshman Rao had brought with him. In October Briggs's Assistant Hodges found evidence of corruption at Bhamer: the offender was punished and replaced by another of Lakshman Rao's protégés.[2]

Briggs went to the hills shortly after this to deal with some of the Bhil chiefs. While he was away[3] he heard rumours that Lakshman Rao himself was corrupt. His first impulse was to dismiss them as 'mere calumnies'. Then Chaplin arrived at Dhulia, Briggs's headquarters, for a short visit on tour. Briggs asked him to investigate the matter but he declined the invitation. Briggs himself therefore spent nearly six weeks looking into the various accusations made against Lakshman Rao, and concluded that he had been guilty of corrupt practices to the tune of several thousand rupees. Chaplin, however, did not think that the charges against Lakshman Rao had been substantiated. He was therefore dismissed but not punished in any other way.[4]

Towards the end of 1820 Briggs had to go to Bombay to see his family safely embarked, and Captain Archibald Robertson came from Gujarat to take his place for a few months. Briggs left Khan-

[1] Briggs to Chaplin, 31.10.1820, S.R.J. iv. 442; also Chaplin to Government, 5.11.1821, para. 74, ibid. 330.

[2] Briggs to Chaplin, 16.4.1825, para. 48, B.C. 1022, 376.

[3] Dec. 1819–Jan. 1820.   [4] Ibid., para. 49, 378 ff.

desh with the angry sound of fresh accusations in his ears. Khandu Pant, his Treasurer, had actually accused the redoubtable Appaji Rao, his head Daftardar, together with Narsing Rao, his head assistant Daftardar, of conniving at the corrupt practices of yet another Mamlatdar, Madhav Rao Hari the Mamlatdar of Chandor. Briggs at once demanded proof. It soon appeared, however, that Khandu Pant wanted to withdraw his charges, and Briggs surmised that he had come to an arrangement with the men he had been accusing. Briggs was determined not to let it rest at that: 'I resolved to break asunder the link which I now felt assured had existed between them.' He told Khandu Pant to produce substantial proofs before he left for Bombay, on pain of dismissal. There was an unpleasant scene: 'The day arrived, the whole Cutcherry and others were assembled, and Kundoo Punt was publicly dismissed on the ground either of falsely accusing Appajee Row and others, or of withholding information of malpractices to which he was privy but chose to conceal.'[1]

It transpired that Madhav Rao Hari and Khandu Pant had combined together. Rs.15,800 of the government revenue had been concealed by Khandu Pant and paid to Madhav Rao Hari to liquidate a debt. Khandu Pant himself asserted that he had shared out the money among the Collector's office staff. But he was unable to prove this. It seemed likely that the two of them had been concerned in many frauds practised in the Treasury and that 'they were engaged together in trade' on the basis of their proceeds.[2]

Captain Robertson carried out some investigations while Briggs was away. Soon Briggs received a letter from Appaji Rao complaining of these proceedings which seemed directed against him. Briggs did not reply, but when he returned he asked Hodges to investigate the charges against Appaji Rao since he himself felt under obligation to him for his help in the days when they were establishing British authority in Khandesh.[3]

Fresh revelations were soon made. Janardhan Pant, the Mamlatdar of Sonda and Rawer, confessed that he had gained Rs.2,500 from frauds upon the public revenues. Rajaram Pant, the Sherishtadar of Rawer, confessed that he had gained Rs.500 in the same way.

[1] Ibid., para. 52, 381 ff.
[2] Briggs to Chaplin, 20.8.1821, B.C. 723/19557, 186.
[3] Briggs to Chaplin, 10.8.1825, para. 53, B.C. 1022, 382.

Not even the greatest survived the welter of accusations and confessions. It was soon proved that Appaji Rao, the head Daftardar, and Narsing Rao, the head assistant Daftardar, had accepted bribes and committed various financial malversations. The sums involved were large. In seven divisions alone, with a revenue of about 4 lakhs of rupees, Briggs found that the malversations committed by his office staff over a period of three years amounted to no less than 1 lakh of rupees.[1]

In Appaji Rao's defence Briggs pointed out that he had begun his embezzlements 'at a time when he believed Mr. Wilkins or somebody else was to supersede me and my establishment'. Rs.4,000 of his gains he spent in repairing two temples in Dhulia. But once he had been 'engaged in these dirty practices in conjunction with others of the Cutcherry he never was able to control their conduct and Kondoo Punt, Nursing Row & the rest went on in spite of his threats, remonstrances or entreaties'.[2]

The double Daftar was intended to prevent such happenings by means of the rivalry of parallel officials. What Elphinstone found 'more than ordinarily revolting' was the revelation that the disgrace of Lakshman Rao, the parallel official to Appaji Rao, had been deliberately contrived by Appaji Rao himself. It was Appaji Rao who had worked out the plan; it was Appaji Rao who had supplied the money to be offered to him as a bribe; it was Appaji Rao who had then had him reported to the Collector.[3]

The methods of peculation adopted in Khandesh were various: the Collector's office staff had accepted bribes from jagirdars for real or pretended services, appropriated public money which they set off in the records against the cost of non-existent establishments, appropriated part of the revenue collections by making false statements of the balances due to government, and through the hereditary district officers extorted money from the peasants by levying unauthorized taxes. In the districts also, Mamlatdars and others had extorted up to 5 per cent. from the peasants on all loans made to them by the Government in aid of cultivation (takavi). In the one district of Nasirabad, since the acquisition of Khandesh by the new government, it was calculated that the present Mamlatdar had gained Rs.1,148 by illicit means, former Mamlatdars Rs.2,922, the

[1] Judicial letter from Bombay, 15.1.1822, para. 170 ff., Bom. J.L.R. iii. 597 ff.
[2] Briggs to M.E., 9.12.1823, *Elphinstone.*
[3] M.E., Minute, n.d., B.C. 723/19557, 158 ff.

Collector's office staff Rs.6,385, the hereditary district officers and village headmen Rs.15,720.[1]

Elphinstone's reaction was philosophical:

I believe that every new conquest is in a great degree the scene of extortion and corruption, and, if in some instances no such iniquities have been detected it has frequently been owing to our having long left the country under farmers whose oppressions never came to light, and not having put it under the direct management of our own officers until the knowledge acquired by our Collectors prevented the existence of any great irregularities.

He was no doubt thinking of Gujarat and trying to forestall comparisons between it and the Deccan. He naturally referred to the previously disturbed state of Khandesh before its acquisition by the British, and to the evil effects of that time—'the habits of tyranny acquired by the public officers' and 'the submissive character of the people'.[2]

Chaplin himself had recently visited Khandesh and as early as February 1821 he was writing privately to Elphinstone that 'a great deal too much revenue has been squeezed from the ryots during the last year or two—Had the exactions been confined to the Government settlement all would have been reasonable & well enough—but in many districts it may be estimated that about one third as much more has been eaten up by Jumeendars & public servants.'[3]

After conversation with Colonel Jardine Chaplin came to suspect that the corruption of the administrative staff in Khandesh might explain why the Bhil chiefs kept breaking their engagements: perhaps, as Chil Naik had said, they were not being paid their proper pensions? He found it 'not easy to conceive how they should without some sort of cause renounce engagements so favourable to them'. Moreover, 'an apparent want of due co-operation on the part of the Mamlatdars with the military detachments' made him think that perhaps they were even encouraging disorder so that they themselves might have more scope for their peculations.[4]

Elphinstone and Chaplin therefore began to look about for a possible successor to Briggs in Khandesh. Pottinger was

---

[1] Judicial letter from Bombay, 15.1.1822, paras. 170–6, Bom. J.L.R. iii. 618 ff.

[2] M.E., Minute, 25.8.1821, Bom. J.C. 12.9.1821, 3235 ff.

[3] Chaplin to M.E., 22.2.1821, *Elphinstone*.

[4] Chaplin, 26.6.1821, in Bom. P.D. ii. 521 ff. Also Chaplin to Government, 18.4.25, paras. 9–10, B.C. 1022.

approached, but with profuse thanks he hastily declined the poisoned chalice:

> I feel a degree of gratitude and obligation which I am quite unable to express for this fresh proof of your consideration and friendship for me [he replied to Elphinstone] and had I only myself to think of I should have readily accepted the situation in Kandeish, but as Mrs. Pottinger (whose health is rather delicate) and my sisters would have to accompany me there, I dread the climate on their account, and no pecuniary advantage would of course be a compensation to me were I to see one of them suffering under sickness and *fancy* myself the cause, however remotely, of it.[1]

In the end, Captain Archibald Robertson was permanently appointed to Khandesh, and Briggs succeeded Grant at Satara.

Rumours of the home authorities' reactions to these happenings soon reached the Deccan. On 16 May 1823 Chaplin had a letter from Ravenshaw, one of the Directors, telling him 'that Captain Briggs is called over the coals for having hanged a Bheel without trial—He alludes to Mr. Russell's having been turned out for flogging two thieves who died in consequence—and says that if "Briggs' story be as bad as he hears it is he must expect a similar fate".'[2]

When Strachey had first heard of the small number of civil suits in Khandesh he had written sceptically to Elphinstone in September 1820:

> Your Collector in Candeish I think tells you there is no judicial business there—Is Candeish heaven, are there no injuries there? This looks bad. There are men in Candeish and there is power. 'C'est une expérience éternelle, que tout homme qui a du pouvoir est porté à en abuser; il va jusqu'à ce qu'il trouve de limites' (Montesquieu). I cannot believe that because there is no litigation in Candeish there are no wrongs. I conclude either that there is no redress to be had or that the people from *habit* have not yet got into the way of applying for it.

The moral which he drew was that the Deccan system was inferior to that of Bengal: 'So when in Bengal I see greater numbers of suits I infer that access to justice is more easy there than elsewhere.'[3]

When he had news of the discoveries of corruption in Khandesh,

[1] Pottinger to M.E., 2.8.1821, *Elphinstone.*
[2] Chaplin to M.E., 16.5.1823, *Elphinstone.*
[3] Strachey to M.E., 15.9.1820, *Elphinstone.*

he could not resist reminding Elphinstone in July 1822 of what he had written in 1820: 'I was disposed to chuckle on reading your last Judicial general letter to find that the state of things in Candeish was actually such as I supposed it to be on hearing that there were no complaints there.'[1]

He was shocked not only at the corruption but also at Briggs's dealings with the Bhils. At the beginning of 1823 he told Elphinstone that he had 'looked into some of the proceedings in the Political Department about Candeish & there are some about the Bheels which if noticed in this country cannot I think fail to be most severely censured—whether they are likely to be noticed except in the common course of the official correspondence I am not at all able to judge'.[2]

At length a weighty draft issued from the Political Department of the East-India House condemning both the corruption in Khandesh and Briggs's handling of the Bhil problem, and ordering his dismissal from his post and his return in disgrace to his regiment. The Board of Control, however, expunged some of the more severe passages of the draft and altered others. After an argument with the Court the Board refused to approve of Briggs's dismissal and denied that there was any conclusive evidence that the Bhils' pensions had actually been withheld. They declared, on the other hand, that if it transpired after inquiry that Briggs had had reason to suspect this or had known it, they would consider him unworthy of future employment in a confidential post.[3] And so the dispatch was sent, in July 1824.[4] To the last, however, the Court maintained their right to do as they thought fit with their own servants. This was perhaps because the episode was one more incident in the losing battle which they were fighting with the Board of Control. At all events, after declaring their rights as a matter of principle, they finally agreed to suspend their orders for Briggs to be removed from all political duties and returned to his regiment until they had received the results of Chaplin's inquiries into the affairs of Khandesh.[5]

[1] Strachey to M.E., 2.7.1822, *Elphinstone.*
[2] Strachey to M.E., 2.1.1823, *Elphinstone.*
[3] Board to Court, 18.5.1824, Board to Court, vi. 258; Court to Board, 27.5.1824, Court to Board, viii. 137 ff.; Board to Court, 26.6.1824, Board to Court, vi. 275 ff.
[4] Political dispatch to Bombay, 21.7.1824, Bom. P.D. ii. 457 ff.
[5] Court to Board, 8.7.1824, Court to Board, viii. 169 ff.

Beneath the home government's criticisms of Briggs's dealings with the Bhils lay the assumption that if the hill chiefs had been fairly treated they would have kept their agreements. The chiefs had presumably been alienated either by the terms of their agreements or by the way in which those terms had been carried out. Briggs had been convinced that the great majority of Bhils belonged to the villages as watchmen. He had therefore made it an essential condition of these agreements that all the followers of the chiefs who had come from the plains should be sent home, and he anticipated that only a few would be left in the hills with the chiefs. But did the great majority of Bhils in fact come from the plains? And had the chiefs been left with enough resources to maintain the followers they still had with them?[1] This raised the general question, had the chiefs' pensions been fairly estimated? Did they not only cover all their just claims, including those recently established, but also enable the chiefs to maintain both themselves and the followers they needed to do the duties specified in their agreements? Even if the agreements seemed fair, moreover, had they been fairly carried out?[2]

In accordance with the compromise which they had reached with the Board, the Court declared in their dispatch that they would have ordered Briggs's removal from Khandesh had he not already been posted elsewhere, but that in the circumstances they would defer any further orders about him until they could have answers from the Bombay Government to their three main questions— whether the majority of Bhils belonged to the plains, whether the chiefs' allowances were adequate, and whether they had been paid regularly and in full.[3]

Meanwhile, like Chaplin, they suggested a connexion between the corruption of the administrative staff in Khandesh and the continued rebellions of the chiefs: 'The Treasury Servants appear to have appropriated to themselves all they could so appropriate with a prospect of impunity; and in no case could the prospect of impunity have been more complete than in the case of the Bheel Naiqs, whose complaints, it was evident from experience, would not lead to enquiry and would be answered only by menaces carried into immediate effect.'[4]

---

[1] Political dispatch to Bombay, 21.7.1824, para. 16, Bom. P.D. ii. 472 ff.
[2] Ibid., paras. 13 ff., para. 65.
[3] Ibid.   [4] Ibid., para. 53.

There was no direct evidence that the chiefs had not been paid their full pensions, but they pointed out that Chil Naik had certainly claimed that his proper dues had not been paid. Did he assume that his pension had been given him in return for maintaining law and order and in addition to his traditional dues instead of in lieu of them? He said that he had been promised Rs.600 but had only been paid Rs.175: he had been paid Rs.175 because it was only three months since the conclusion of his agreement, and the figure of Rs.600 was for the year not the month; but no attempt had been made to explain this to him. Instead, he was executed, even though he had voluntarily surrendered himself.[1]

Other instances of military executions were also cited with disapproval in the dispatch. In general the home government disliked Briggs's severity towards the Bhils as much as they disliked his 'unbounded partiality for Appajee Rao'.[2] He should rather have shown 'a liberal indulgence for the jealousies, prejudices and ancient and inveterate habits of a wild and ignorant people, a readiness to receive and investigate complaints, and the power of judging impartially and dispassionately between them and the persons employed under him'.[3]

Meanwhile the policy of punishing the Bhils for rebellion was being continued. Not everyone was able to combine with it a proper spirit of sympathy with them. The climate and the geography of Khandesh made it a hard country for campaigns; again and again different chiefs rebelled; sympathy must have been a difficult emotion to cultivate: even Chaplin had in 1821 forecast 'a war of extermination' against the Bhils.

A certain Lieutenant Livingstone was employed on one of these punitive campaigns in charge of a detachment in 1824. In his instructions Robertson told him that although apprehending the Bhils in their hills was so difficult, 'at all events much good will result from frequently beating up their quarters and keeping them in a state of alarm'.[4] When he found a Bhil camp, with some satisfaction he burned the thirty-five dwellings of which it consisted. He duly reported that he was 'happy to say' that he had 'given them a most confounded drubbing having killed four men and two women besides having taken fourteen prisoners all of whom

[1] Ibid., paras. 21 ff.
[2] Ibid., para. 59.   [3] Ibid., para. 67.
[4] Robertson to Livingstone, 24.1.1824, Bom. P.C. 30.6.1824, 2909 f.

I am sorry to say are females with the exception of one boy'. The episode had excited his ardour: 'On the receipt of pay', he added, 'I shall be after the rascals again and sincerely hope to have the pleasure of spilling more blood.'[1]

Major Archibald Robertson, tactful as he always was, changed the words 'a most confounded drubbing' to 'a very severe chastisement' before he forwarded Livingstone's report through the usual channels.[2] But by some mischance an unaltered copy of the report had already reached Chaplin. He was shocked to see such language in an official document, and forwarded it to the Government with a covering letter in which he solemnly explained how sorry he was that Livingstone 'in reporting upon the execution of so unpleasant a duty should have adopted a tone of exultation instead of expressing his concern that he should have been the instrument of unavoidably inflicting retribution on these misguided people'.[3]

The Governor in Council forthwith ordered Livingstone's replacement on the ground that his choice of language showed 'that he ought not to be entrusted with a service where so much is left to the discretion of the officer in charge'. They also declared that the burning of villages and seizure of cattle were both impolitic since by depriving the inhabitants of the means of subsistence such measures encouraged the peaceful to join the rebellious, and the rebellious to remain in rebellion. Such measures were therefore prohibited. Chaplin was also told to warn his Collectors 'to be careful how they give any general powers to military officers'.[4]

Robertson pointed out that Livingstone had burned, not a village but a temporary encampment, and that there was no indication that he had seized any cattle. But the Governor in Council maintained that in such situations a proclamation should always be issued as a warning to any peaceful inhabitants before any operations were carried out.[5]

Livingstone himself apologized for the language of his report: 'I entirely attribute the style of diction to my having marched all night and been exposed the greater part of the day to the influence

[1] Lieut. A. Livingstone to Brigade Major, Khandesh, 31.3.1824, Bom. P.C. 21.4.1824, 1822 ff.
[2] Robertson to Chaplin, 15.5.1824, Bom. P.C. 30.6.1824, 2896 ff.
[3] Chaplin to Government, 13.4.1824, Bom. P.C. 21.4.1824, 1820 f.
[4] Government to Chaplin, 19.4.1824, Bom. P.C. 21.4.1824, 1824 ff.
[5] Robertson to Chaplin, 15.5.1824, Bom. P.C. 30.6.1824, 2896 ff.; Government to Chaplin, 24.6.1824, ibid. 2912 ff.

of a scorching sun, added to which my overanxiety to communicate quickly the result of the expedition.'[1] But he had already been relieved by another officer before he had even written his apology.[2]

The main result of the episode was the order of government forbidding measures like the burning of homes or the seizure of cattle which might by depriving the Bhils of the possibility of an honest subsistence drive them into rebellion or confirm them in it. But this order, however sensible, was only negative. More than this was needed to bring law and order to Khandesh.

Even Gumani, the chief of the Sindwa area, rebelled in 1824. For several years there had been every sign that he had reconciled himself to the new order of things. He was living in apparent contentment in a village in the Thalner district near his hill post which he called 'Raj Mahal'. He himself he styled with solemn magnificence 'Raja Sri Raja Gumani Naik Mahalkar'. He was not a model citizen, but the Government hoped that 'a very liberal provision and frequent connivance at his irregularities' would enable him to settle down. But some serious deeds of plunder and even killing forced them to send a detachment against him. He was foolish enough to attack it and was put to flight. He was soon captured by some Bhils who supported the new government and was duly tried and transported.[3]

According to Robertson this and similar episodes simply showed how little reliance could be placed in agreements with the chiefs.[4] He had already formed his own opinion of the reason for their frequent rebellions. Hitherto it had been generally assumed that they would be moved by the instincts of economic man: if by their agreements they could secure as much money as by plunder, it was assumed that they would naturally keep their agreements.

But Robertson suggested in April 1824 that the true explanation of their conduct might lie in their attitude to robbery as a sport: he noticed that they 'follow it indeed with a keenness and a relish that is hardly to be accounted for, considering the risk that sometimes attends it, except we view it in the light of a passion the gratification of which affords them as great delight as the pursuit of game does the keenest sportsman'. Pensioning the chiefs was therefore

[1] Livingstone to Robertson, 14.5.1824, ibid. 2896 ff.
[2] Lieut.-Col. Dyson to Chaplin, 28.4.1824, Bom. P.C. 12.5.1824, 2397 f.
[3] Political letter from Bombay, 22.6.1825, B.C. 1022/28050, 1 ff.; Robertson to Chaplin, 10.3.1825, ibid. 205 ff.
[4] Robertson to Chaplin, 10.3.1825, ibid.

unlikely to restrain them. Only 'the most rigid restraint and control' could keep them in order.[1] 'They may be likened to children, who do right more from fear than from a love of good.'[2]

Elphinstone with his respect for the experience of the past was reluctant to abandon the policy of pensioning the chiefs. Such a policy had had 'the most striking success' under the Bengal Government, he remarked, and it had also been followed on occasion by the Peshwa. Moreover, in the western hills of Khandesh the pensioned chiefs had been maintaining law and order: there the chiefs were hereditary rulers of communities of Bhils born to the hills. Elsewhere, on the other hand, the chiefs had been continually rebelling and there was general unrest: but those chiefs were upstarts who had once been village watchmen; they were more like bandit leaders than hereditary rulers, while nearly all their followers were also refugees from the plains. Elphinstone added that he himself had never expected that conciliation alone would pacify the Bhils, but rather a combination of 'rewards on the one hand and punishments on the other'.[3]

He therefore decided that Robertson should be told to continue the chiefs in their pensions so long as they did not encourage robberies but to stop paying them if they were encouraging robberies or failing to restrain their followers.[4]

The arrival of the home government's dispatch of July 1824 prompted a general reconsideration of the policies hitherto adopted towards the Bhils.

Robertson confirmed that the majority of the Bhils in Khandesh were lowlanders and that the pensions fixed by Briggs were fair and in some instances liberal. Moreover, reasoning from the absence of positive evidence to the contrary, he denied that the administrative staff had either provoked or protracted disorders on the part of the Bhils. As for Chil Naik, he thought that his complaints were quite unfounded.[5]

Chaplin duly added his tribute in praise of the wisdom and justice of the policies hitherto pursued towards the Bhils, declaring that 'the claims of the Bheels have been most liberally considered,

[1] Robertson to Chaplin, 10.4.1824, Bom. J.C. 2.6.1824, 3121 ff.
[2] Robertson to Chaplin, 11.3.1825, Bom. J.C. 1.6.1825, 8.
[3] Elphinstone, Minute, n.d., Bom. J.C. 2.6.1824, 3160 ff.
[4] Ibid.; also Government to Chaplin, 1.6.1824, ibid. 3165 ff.
[5] Robertson to Chaplin, 10.3.1825, paras. 31–38, 43, 61, B.C. 1022/28050, 221 ff., 270 ff.

that conciliation and lenity have been exhausted in endeavouring to reclaim those of the plains who have betaken themselves to the fastnesses in the hills, from their inveterate courses, and that the most active measures of coercion, whenever they relapse into those habits, can alone be effectual in checking and alleviating the evils arising from their devastations'. He now recanted his former suspicions that the administrative staff had withheld money due to the Bhils, and even emphasized the fact that Briggs had been 'surrounded with a cloud of difficulties'.[1]

Briggs in his turn composed a lengthy and detailed defence of his tenure of office in Khandesh. When he received a copy of the Bombay Government's official reply to the home government's dispatch he privately wrote a fervent letter of appreciation to Elphinstone:

It is quite delightful to find from the summary you have drawn out that so far from the Candeish proceedings being harsh, they have been proved to be of so different a complexion, and I can with great confidence lay my hand upon my heart & say that towards any individual under my authority am I conscious of never having acted with more rigour than the circumstances of the moment, and the necessity of the case, appeared to demand—upon the whole I think the minute scrutiny & review of all my proceedings are more likely to do me good than harm.[2]

In reply to the three specific queries of the home government, the Bombay Government declared, first 'that all the Bheels against whom military operations were directed were from the plains', secondly that the chiefs' allowances were equitable, and thirdly that they had been regularly paid.[3]

But however much the Bombay Government approved of their own proceedings they had not succeeded in pacifying the Bhils. It was time for new measures.

When Elphinstone was Deccan Commissioner he had suggested the formation of a Bhil Corps, but the idea had been abandoned on advice. Elphinstone now raised the matter again, and in January 1825 an official letter was sent to Chaplin proposing the formation of a Bhil Corps and asking him to suggest other ways of providing employment for the Bhils. This letter also proposed that in view of the prevalent shortage of grain it might be advisable to increase

[1] Chaplin to Government, 18.4.1825, Bom. P.C. 22.6.1825, 48.
[2] Briggs to M.E., 19.5.1825, *Elphinstone*.
[3] Political letter from Bombay, 22.6.1825, B.C. 1022/28050, 1 ff.

the chief's pensions.[1] These matters were duly referred to Robertson.

He already had little faith in pensioning the chiefs, and advised against any increase on the ground that it 'would only add to their importance without improving their morals'. For the future he intended to avoid as far as possible the granting of pensions and instead to persuade the Bhils still in the hills to settle in some of the lowland villages then lying waste, and by loans and favourable rents to encourage them to take to agriculture.[2] One of his assistants, Captain Rigby,[3] had established cordial relations with the Bhils of the north-west, and had succeeded in persuading some to take to agriculture and in settling disputes which might otherwise have led to violence. In order to encourage the Bhils of the south-east to develop habits of industry and peace Robertson suggested the appointment of another officer in the Ajanta hills.[4] Captain Ovans was duly appointed there.

These officers soon acquired a special status and title. The process was accelerated by a quarrel between Rigby and Dent, Robertson's first Assistant. Robertson himself thought that Dent had adopted an overbearing and dictatorial attitude towards Rigby. Such tensions often arose among the Deccan Collectors and Assistants who had such a limited range of acquaintances. He therefore asked that a special title be given to Rigby which should define his status.[5] The Government accordingly conferred upon Rigby the title of 'Agent under the Collector with the Bheels'.[6]

Robertson was not optimistic about the success of a Bhil Corps. But in his choice of a commander for it he showed that he was a good judge of men. He chose Lieutenant Outram, then the Acting Adjutant of one of the Company's Bombay Regiments of Foot.[7] In

[1] Government to Chaplin, 31.1.1825, Bom. P.C. 2.2.1825, 57.
[2] Robertson to Chaplin, 11.3.1825, Bom. J.C. 1.6.1825, 8.
[3] Captain George A. Rigby, 10th Regt., Bombay Native Infantry (East-India Register).
[4] Ibid. In order to influence the Bhils of the north-east he intended that the Bhil Corps, if raised, should have its headquarters at Dharangaon or Erandol.
[5] Robertson to Chaplin, 11.5.1825, Bom. P.C. 8.6.1825, 75.
[6] Government to Chaplin, 7.6.1825, ibid. 76. Captain Ovans was then engaged on survey work in Gujarat. Until his arrival in October 1825 the work was done by Graham, one of Robertson's assistants (Bom. P.C. 22.6.1825, 21; Bom. P.C. 8.2.1826, 38 f.). Captain Charles Ovans, 1st Bombay European Regiment (East-India Register).
[7] 23rd Bombay Native Infantry. Robertson may have been influenced by Outram's conduct in driving out of Mulher Fort a gang of Bhils who had seized

May 1825 Outram was authorized to enlist up to 400 recruits. Robertson asked him to take most of his men from the Chalisgaon, Bhadgaon, and Erandol districts because the Bhils living there had been the most troublesome of all and were probably the most poverty stricken. Later he might go farther afield.[1] When in due course he did so the Government found it necessary to warn him not to enlist any Bhils who seemed likely to lead industrious and peaceable lives as civilians.[2]

Robertson suggested that all the officers and N.C.O.s of the Corps should be taken from 'a few steady commissioned and non-commissioned officers and privates of the line', at least until it could be seen that Bhils themselves could be promoted. He added that a few posts should be left open for Bhils. He also advised Outram to pay the recruits not in cash but in grain, giving only small amounts of cash at intervals, and only substituting cash for grain when he thought a man fit for it—'as all will prefer to have money'.[3]

Outram had some difficulty in finding his first recruits. He stayed for several weeks in the Chalisgaon area. He got into touch with some of the leading Bhil chiefs, 'went alone with them into their jungles, gained their hearts by copious libations of brandy, and their confidence by living unguarded among them'. In this way he finally won their trust. Even so, they were easily alarmed and always inclined to suspicion: this he attributed to 'the treachery and cruelty of former rulers being still fresh in their memory'. They were easily swayed by chance rumours: 'Three or four whom I first enlisted were frightened away by an absurd report that I was enticing them to transportation!'[4]

He left Chalisgaon with five recruits, and travelled on through Bhadgaon and Erandol, collecting more as he went. By the end of June 1825 he had twenty-five.[5]

He still had difficulty in keeping their confidence. Robertson had suggested early in May that it would be politic to defer arming the

it under the leadership of Godaji Dengle, a relative of Trimbakji Dengle (Chaplin to Robertson, 18.4.1825, Bom. P.C. 27.4.1825, 29 ff.; Political letter from Bombay, 16.4.1825, para. 6, Bom. P.L.R. ix. 299; Simcox, *Bhil Corps*, 35 ff.).

[1] Pay between Rs.4 and Rs.4½ per month with Rs.1 batta for serving away from headquarters and with free clothing (Robertson to Outram, 6.5.1825, Bom. P.C. 8.6.1825, 11; Robertson to Chaplin, 11.3.1825, Bom. J.C. 1.6.1825, 8).

[2] Government to Collector, 8.6.1826, Bom. J.C. 14.6.1826, 17.

[3] Robertson to Outram, 6.5.1825, Bom. P.C. 8.6.1825, 11.

[4] Outram to Robertson, n.d. [1.7.1825]; Outram, Memorandum, n.d., Simcox, 41–43, 52–54.   [5] Ibid.

Bhils in the Corps for some time, at least until they showed 'a relish for their new mode of life'.[1] Outram soon found that to encourage the recruits to trust the Government it was necessary for the Government to trust them: at the beginning of August he asked Robertson for authority to buy about twenty swords to give his recruits at once; he also recommended that the Corps should be armed with swords, shields, and matchlocks.[2] All this was approved.

Outram duly bought the swords and distributed them among his Bhils. But he felt that it was only the possession of muskets which would really give them confidence in the Government's intentions towards them. 'The suspicion of our motives gains ground daily', he reported at the beginning of September 1825. What made them particularly nervous was the coincidence that Dharangaon, the town which Outram had chosen as the Corps headquarters, and even the office in which he lived, had been the scene of a massacre of Bhils under the former government. In the hope of lulling their fears and suspicions he talked with them of the cruelty of that massacre 'with marks of detestation and without reserve', and carefully explained 'the advantages we expect from their services (for they could not understand and would suspect any other motive for the liberality of Government)'.[3]

During Muharram he kept his Bhils together and 'endeavoured to make them spend a happy holiday'. But on the final day a rumour spread amongst them to the effect that the crowds of people who had come to the town on that day included agents of the Government who were preparing to slaughter all the Bhils there. The rumour was only believed by 'about 15 of the most timorous and newest' of Outram's recruits, and they fled. When Outram heard of it he had his Bhils assembled and spoke reassuringly to them, emphasizing how he slept every night with only a Bhil guard at his house. His hearers rallied to him and soon eight of the fugitives were returned.[4]

Because of this fundamental lack of confidence he decided not to recruit on too large a scale so long as the Corps were deprived of muskets. By the beginning of July he had 25 recruits, by the beginning of August 62, by the beginning of September 92.[5]

[1] Robertson to Outram, 6.5.1825, para. 12, Bom. P.C. 8.6.1825, 11.
[2] Outram to Robertson, 2.8.1825, Bom. P.C. 31.8.1825, 22.
[3] Outram to Robertson, 1.9.1825, Bom. P.C. 12.10.1825, 75.
[4] Ibid.   [5] Ibid.

Meanwhile he was using various ways of conciliating them. When he had assembled his first recruits he 'separated the old from the young men' and explained that only the young men would have to drill, and that the older men would be exempted so long as the young men did it—'thus causing the older men who had most influence to be interested in persuading the younger to submit'. The younger men he hoped to train as light infantry, the older to employ on police duties.[1]

Again, although Robertson had been most cautious in contemplating the promotion of Bhils, Outram promoted three to the rank of Naik as early as the beginning of July; one he promoted Havildar at the beginning of August. His intention in making these promotions was 'to excite a spirit of emulation, by showing what they have to look up to as the reward of good behaviour and to teach obedience to non-commissioned officers of my own creation in opposition to what they had hitherto been only accustomed to pay to their hereditary Naiks'.[2]

He found that drunkenness was the greatest obstacle to discipline at first. In order to check it he paid them only 2 annas every morning: this was barely sufficient for the necessities of life. The rest of their pay, amounting to between 10 and 12 annas, he paid them at the end of the month, and he soon noticed that they were beginning to spend it on 'articles of finery' or shoes.[3]

The Bhils had fresh suspicions when a detachment from the Line arrived early in November 1825 to help train them. Outram calmed them by sending the detachment's arms away and announcing that the regulars and the Bhils were to be armed together. At length, on the last day of December 1825 the arms arrived. The Bhils, reported Outram, were 'much delighted with and proud of' them.[4]

He was anxious to develop their self-respect. He saw to it that they had a proper uniform. He encouraged social relations between them and the high-caste soldiers of the regular detachment. Once he sent the Corps to Malegaon where his old regiment, the 23rd, was stationed: the Bhils were delighted to be treated as equals, as brother soldiers, by the regulars, who invited them to sit down

[1] Outram to Collector of Khandesh, 8.1.1828, Simcox, 105 ff.
[2] Outram to Robertson, 1.9.1825, Bom. P.C. 12.10.1825, 75.
[3] Ibid.
[4] Outram to Collector of Khandesh, 1.1.1826, Bom. P.C. 1.2.1826, 44.

with them and gave them food. Outram even taught the buglers of the Bhil Corps a special call.[1]

As the months passed he steadily enlarged the Corps. On 1 November 1825 its strength was 109, on 1 January 1826 134, on 1 March 249, on 1 May 280, on 1 July 308.[2]

John Bax,[3] who succeeded Robertson as Collector of Khandesh, realized the need to develop the Bhils' self-respect, and decided to station a small detachment of the Corps with Captain Ovans, the Bhil Agent in the south-east. He himself also took an escort of Bhils with him when he went on tour to settle the revenue. These measures, he wrote, 'besides their utility as Police, will tend to have a good effect on their characters as well as on the Bheel community at large by exhibiting the trust that is reposed in them'.[4] Outram was delighted: these measures would not only show the Collector's confidence in the Bhils, they would also 'raise them in the ideas of other classes'.[5]

And so the Bhil Corps flourished. In November 1827 the Corps was inspected by Lieutenant-Colonel Campbell, the Officer Commanding in Khandesh: he was highly impressed with their discipline and efficiency. In appearance he found them 'generally of small stature averaging about 5 feet 2½ inches in height, spare in their form and very ill-looking in their countenance, but they make up for these imperfections by a sagacity and intelligence probably acquired by the exercise of a previous predatory life'.[6]

In this year, the establishment of the Corps was raised to 600. Already its members were being employed both to man outposts and to suppress insurgents.[7]

The Khandesh Magistrate's Report for 1830 cited the success of Outram's Bhil Corps as proving the truth of the maxim Divide and Rule.[8] This praise may sound faint enough today but it should not

---

[1] Outram to Collector of Khandesh, 1.1.1826, Bom. P.C. 1.2.1826, 44; also Outram to Robertson, 1.9.1825, Bom. P.C. 12.10.1825, 75; Simcox, 70.

[2] Outram to Collector of Khandesh, 1.1.1826, Bom. P.C. 1.2.1826, 44; Outram to Collector of Khandesh, 1.5.1826, Bom. J.C. 14.6.1826, 16; Outram to Collector of Khandesh, 1.7.1826, Bom. J.C. 5.8.1826, 16.

[3] John Bax, Bombay writer, season 1808 (East-India Register).

[4] Bax to Government, 13.11.1826, Bom. J.C. 6.12.1826, 4.

[5] Outram to Bax, 13.12.1826, Bom. P.C. 10.1.1827, 38.

[6] Lieut.-Col. D. Campbell to Assist. Adj.-Gen., Poona Division, 1.12.1827, Bom. M.C. 6.2.1828, 18.

[7] S.B.R., N.S. xxvi. 234.

[8] Cited in W. S. Boyd to Government, 30.4.1833, B.C. 1467, 101.

damn either Outram or his Corps. The main purpose of the Corps was to help to keep law and order. This purpose it fulfilled. The Bhil Agents, on the other hand, had also to promote the welfare of the Bhil population. As instructed by Robertson they had a two-fold duty consisting '1st in preserving the peace of the country and 2nd in ameliorating the condition of the Bheels'. He explained in painstaking detail that this duty could be performed in various ways.

1st by a watchful superintendence of the Bheels in the range committed to their respective charge

2nd by inspiring them with confidence in the Government

3rd by encouraging them to turn their attention to industrious pursuits

4th by being careful that those among them on whom Government has settled pensions are duly paid the same

5th by attending to and redressing their complaints against each other as well as under certain circumstances against other classes, or pointing out to them how redress against such classes is to be obtained as well as in all such cases when mutually agreeable to the parties by acting as arbitrators

6th by apprehending those who may be accused of offences, and committing them for trial if the offence be of a serious nature before the Court of Circuit or in minor cases inflicting such punishment as may be customary among themselves, and if recourse has been usual to such a tribunal or if the Agents think it can be resorted to with advantage, as a Punchayet of their own tribe may award

7th by superintending such military operations as it may be found necessary to carry on to reduce to order any tribes or bands who may be committing depredations.[1]

By entrusting the Agents with 'a watchful superintendence of the Bheels' in their respective areas Robertson explained that he meant them to have power to call on any Bhils to show how they were earning their living, to restrict them from assembling in large numbers, to stop them leaving their homes, even to require security from any who aroused suspicion.[2]

Various methods were used to encourage the Bhils to take to agriculture. Land was granted to them upon special terms. Money was lent to them for the purchase of stock. Graham soon found that

[1] Robertson to Chaplin, 30.7.1825, Bom. P.C. 7.9.1825, 100.
[2] Ibid.

men of substance were unwilling to become security for such loans —'the very idea of the Bheels turning cultivators appearing to everyone chimerical'. He therefore appointed supervisors to instruct the Bhils how best to cultivate their lands and to keep him informed of developments.[1] This expedient was soon adopted more generally. Robertson allowed the Agents to reward Bhils who had distinguished themselves by their industry or by their help in the maintenance of law and order. These rewards were to 'consist of something calculated to promote industry, such as some land free of rent for a given time, a bullock, or even a pair, a plough, a cart, and other implements of husbandry, seed, grain, &c.'[2]

With his experience in Gujarat, where Judges and Law Courts had been established for some time, Robertson thought that serious offences committed by Bhils should be brought under the jurisdiction of the ordinary Courts. Elphinstone was doubtful, but he finally agreed.[3]

At last, a new policy had been introduced into Khandesh. The appointment of Bhil Agents and the formation of a Bhil Corps both signified that the Government now realized the need to find a place for the Bhils in the new order of things.

Reviewing the state of the Deccan, Elphinstone declared in January 1827 that the conduct of the Raja of Satara and 'the success of his administration have exceeded our utmost expectations'.[4]

Much credit was no doubt due to Grant the first Resident at Satara. He had a difficult task—to carry on the administration in the name of the Raja, conforming to the Raja's wishes where possible and giving him 'a taste for business, and a knowledge of the principles of Government'. This meant that he had to reform the machinery of administration by introducing form and regularity and punishing corruption. But Elphinstone had also told him that 'no innovations ought to be attempted unless to remedy great

[1] Graham to Robertson, 28.11.1825, Bom. P.C. 8.2.1826, 38.

[2] Robertson to Chaplin, 30.7.1825, Bom. P.C. 7.9.1825, 100; Graham to Robertson, 27.6.1825, Bom. P.C. 20.7.1825, 22; Graham to Robertson, 28.11.1825, Bom. R.C. 11.1.1826, 34; Bax, Memorandum, 7.1.1828, Bom. R.C. 16.1.1828, 117.

[3] Robertson to Chaplin, 30.7.1825, Bom. P.C. 7.9.1825, 100; M.E., minute, n.d., ibid. 101; Robertson to Chaplin, 30.12.1825, Bom. P.C. 11.1.1826, 77; Newnham to Marriott, 27.6.1826, Bom. J.C. 5.7.1826, 84.

[4] M.E., Minute, 4.1.1827, Bom. P.C. 31.1.1827, 51.

abuses or to meet the wishes of the people'.¹ Satara was not to be governed by Regulations.

He was greatly helped by the Indian officials who came from the Company's old provinces fresh with new ideas and methods which upset the old officials used to traditional ways.

I set Tattya Abeynkur the present Dafturdar and Krishen Row the newcomer together by the ears yesterday [reported Grant in July 1819] in a dispute about the form of Treasury receipts; they were *excessively* polite at first but at last got angry and Tattya Abeynkur told him . . . you may say as much as you will about Genl. Munro and Genl. Gahagan, but if this is their form I see nothing in it but bad writing which no Carcoon in this part of the country could read and broken Persian which *no real Hindoo* will pretend to understand.²

Grant soon lost one of his most helpful and able officials. Fearing that Balaji Pant might have taken advantage of the confidence which he had placed in him, Grant began to investigate all his activities. But Balaji Pant came to hear of it: 'these enquiries having got to his ears', Grant explained to Elphinstone, 'he is if guilty, alarmed, & if innocent, offended. I really think him a very respectable fellow & perhaps it was something not altogether fair in me to indulge, that induced me to watch him very closely of late—it is perhaps something mean, but I could not help suspecting him.'³

One morning towards the end of October 1819⁴ Balaji Pant came to Grant 'in extreme agitation real or pretended' and announced that 'he could stay no longer in Satara or ever look on the Raja's face, that he had told several respectable persons that Grant Sahib had mentioned to him that Ballajee Pant was taking bribes, that he was taking everything into his hands like Bhow Maunkaiser, but that he was now Raja & should take care to prevent him.'⁵

Grant 'endeavoured to appease him' by denying that he had said anything of the sort to the Raja. But Balaji insisted on leaving Satara.⁶

Grant could 'not clearly see what he is after unless it be . . . to re-establish the power which he has of course lost'.⁷

¹ M.E. to Grant, 8.4.1818, Choksey, *Aftermath*, 259.
² Grant to M.E., 11.7.1819, *Elphinstone*.
³ Grant to M.E., 26.7.1819, ibid.
⁴ The morning of 22 October.
⁵ Grant to M.E., 22.10.1819, ibid.
⁶ Ibid.   ⁷ Ibid.

Grant refused to be coerced: 'He is a sensible, clever & I think faithful servant but although he will be a great loss to me I cannot allow him to take the power into his hands which I am bound to deliver over to the Raja.'[1]

When he offered to stay as Grant's servant not the Raja's, Grant told him that this was what he wanted—'for him to remain here & superintend, but to have no power of appointing the servants of the Raja's Govt.' Grant explained that his duty would be 'to tell me when any improper person was appointed by the Raja and to keep me informed of anything that seemed improper'.[2]

Unfortunately, in Grant's phrase, 'this was the *touchstone*, he could not submit to descending at once from a Raja to a Carcoon. He trembled with passion and said he could have a Carcoon to give me intelligence, that he was desirous of going to Benares'.[3]

And so Balaji Pant left Satara. At his departure, on 4 November 1819, Grant 'showered all possible & proper honour upon him'.[4] On the other hand, the Raja, so Grant reported, seemed 'half mad with joy at his departure, & Mai Sahib with the others have had a rejoicing though she sent for Ballajee Punt and had a crying match at parting'.[5] Grant assured Elphinstone that he had treated him 'with all possible honour', lest, as he wrote, 'you shd. think I had not *done the handsome* by Ballajee'.[6]

Upon Chaplin's recommendation Balaji Pant was awarded Rs.12,000 a year, partly on account of his pension as former Agent to the Resident at Poona and partly in 'compensation for the loss of his situation at Satara which circumstances in which he was [in] no way to blame obliged him to leave'—according to Chaplin's official memorandum.[7]

One reason for Balaji Pant's unpopularity with the Raja and his mother was no doubt the way in which Grant had used him in his negotiations to limit the Raja's personal expenses. Grant had further trouble over this soon after Balaji's departure. He was now authorized to allow the Raja Rs.5 lakhs. But he only allowed him

[1] Grant to M.E., 22.10.1819, *Elphinstone.*
[2] Grant to M.E., 23.10.1819 (postscript to Grant to M.E., 22.10.1819), ibid.
[3] Ibid.
[4] Grant to M.E., 3.11.1819, ibid.
[5] Grant to M.E., 4.11.1819, ibid.
[6] Grant to M.E., 12.11.1819, ibid.
[7] Enclosure No. 2 with Chaplin to Government, 21.11.1821, Bg. P.C. 10.2.1821, 4.

Rs.4 lakhs for the time being on the ground that if he had allowed him the full amount, 'he would immediately have settled it in monthly expenditure & been equally importunate for money *to buy things*'. The result was 'a violent quarrel about the division of the 4 lacks' between the Raja and his mother and brothers. Grant did not want to be involved; he felt ill, and hoped that his 'illness was a good excuse', but, so he told Elphinstone, 'Maharaj came to my bedside almost crying if not really so & made me promise that if I would not interfere on the part of the Sirkar, I would at least do so as his dost.'[1]

Grant accordingly saw the Raja's mother and brothers. He found that they really wanted 'to have *the lands divided*'. He 'told the old Lady that I would not hear of it'. He added that he thought that the Raja was generous in proposing Rs.60,000 a year for each of his brothers and Rs.40,000 a year for his mother. There was an un-comfortable scene: the Raja's mother 'began to cry and sob as if her heart would break'. But the younger brother later told Grant privately that he would for his part be content with the Raja's decision. Grant saw the Raja's mother again and reported to Elphinstone that the episode had ended amicably enough: 'After a long talk we parted, oh never were there two such friends *not to be lovers* in this world, & she now tells the Raja that Nana Farnavese was not fit to hold a candle to me.'[2]

In general, Grant was satisfied. 'We are getting on very well', he reported towards the end of 1819, 'the Raja attends daily to *administer justice* to his people, and can give instructions in any common case without looking into Burnett's face to see if he be right or wrong'.[3] Burnett was one of Grant's Assistants. By May 1820 Grant himself had ceased altogether to attend the Raja's court of justice. His assistants still attended, but only to give advice if the Raja asked for it. If they thought that injustice was being done, they told Grant and he took it up afterwards in private with the Raja.[4]

Grant praised this system in glowing terms: 'The lower orders of the people are literally delighted at being able to state their complaints to the Raja seated on his gadee, and, all are pleased at the ready access and the prompt means of redress which this plan

---

[1] Grant to M.E., 28.12.1819, *Elphinstone*. Dost = friend.
[2] Grant to M.E., 28.12.1819, ibid.
[3] Grant to M.E., 28.12.1819, ibid.
[4] Grant to Chaplin, 25.5.1820, B.C. 703/19071, 41 ff.

seems to afford, but', he added with a peroration which no doubt
seemed convincing enough to the Englishmen of his day, 'it is the
presence of the English gentlemen that completes their assurance
of finding justice.'[1]

Nevertheless, he intended within another month to remove all
appearance of superintendence in judicial matters, with a view to
handing over control of the administration by stages to the Raja.
The judicial administration he proposed to transfer first, the revenue
later.

In revenue work also he was well pleased with the Raja's grasp of
affairs. The Raja went into the office and treasury two or three
times a week to examine the accounts, and Grant told Chaplin that
he had noticed the Raja 'requiring explanations which show that he
observes essentials, and understands something of what is transacting'.[2]

Chaplin, however, objected to the idea of handing over power by
stages. Indeed, he hardly liked the idea of handing it over at all:
'the longer the evil day can be postponed the better, provided it
can be done in consistency with the Treaty which has been by ourselves dictated to him'. In opposition to Grant, with all the latter's
personal knowledge of the Raja, Chaplin declared that as 'a Maratha
youth, unaccustomed to business, who has been all his life a
prisoner', he was unlikely to cope properly with judicial work. He
even objected in principle to the idea of a king doing justice:
'history', he wrote, 'is full of examples of rapine and oppression
which have resulted from princes personally sitting as judges'.[3]

In general he declared that 'though admirable in theory', Grant's
plan was probably 'too speculative for execution . The treaty's
provisions were broad enough, he thought, to permit of deferring
the transfer of power for another year or so, and 'while we do retain
our control we should keep it unimpaired, in order to avoid that
jarring and conflict of interests and the consequent endless in-
trigues which must result from a division of authority'.[4]

The Governor in Council accepted Chaplin's argument that the
transfer of power should be effected in one operation rather than in
stages, but declared that it should be done as soon as possible.[5]

---

[1] Grant to Chaplin, 25.5.1820, B.C. 703/19071, 41 ff.   [2] Ibid.
[3] Chaplin to Government, 20.7.1820, B.C. 703/19071, 17 ff.
[4] Ibid.
[5] Government to Chaplin, 18.8.1820, ibid. 242 ff.

But Grant wrote privately to Elphinstone two months later that 'Chaplin's plan of retaining all to the last is *wrong*', on the ground that 'if all be given over now it is certain *wreck*, if nothing be relaxed it will create disgust'. In fact he had already transferred the judicial administration to the Raja. He explained to Elphinstone that in spite of Chaplin's opinion 'the nature of things, however, obliges me to relax and although I have retained the full power in my hands, I have made nearly the arrangements which the Raja would have introduced this Dussera, and this I have done because I am confident it will meet your wishes. I have taken care to preserve the letter though I have deviated from the spirit of Chaplin's orders'.[1]

In January 1821 he confessed to Chaplin that 'the judicial administration was already in a measure transferred to the Raja' and that various administrative measures and appointments which the Raja wanted had been promulgated at the Dasahra festival.[2]

Grant eventually proposed to transfer the whole internal administration to the Raja on 5 April 1822, the anniversary of his accession.[3] 'I think in my own mind', he remarked to Elphinstone, 'that I have done *wonderfully* proper in coming to the *magnanimous* resolution of *abdicating* after all the public labour has been brought to a close'.[4]

He was optimistic about the future: 'I do think that although what has been effected does not come up to the castles I built, that things at this moment are farther advanced than you expected. I have very good hopes of the Raja, I think him a very good little fellow'.[5]

But the Raja was in a difficult position, under the shadow of British strength. In 1819, before any power had been handed over, Grant reported an unpleasant incident which indicated how the Raja was regarded by some of his staff. Grant remonstrated with him for having 'interfered improperly' with a panchayat. Dajiba Upadhyaya, one of the Raja's entourage, thereupon asked Grant 'what was the use of being a Raja if he could not act according to his inclination. To this the Raja turned round suddenly and replied laughing "Dajeeba you're a blockhead—don't you see I may do whatever I like provided I do what is right"—"that is as you may

[1] Grant to M.E., 12.10.1820, *Elphinstone*.   [2] Grant to Chaplin, 23.1.1821.
[3] Political letter from Bombay, 29.8.1821, para. 83, B.C. 703/19071, 14–15.
[4] Grant to M.E., 21.2.1822, *Elphinstone*.   [5] Grant to M.E., n.d., ibid.

be ordered" was said in a loud whisper by some of the attendants outside, and was succeeded by a tittering.'[1]

In August 1822, several months after the transfer of power, a cat tied neck and heels was sent to the Raja with a message addressed to him as Maharaja Chhatrapati—'an order from one of the Sahib log to try this prisoner in his Udalut for having killed one of his fowls'. Grant suspected that it was Chintaman Rao who sent both cat and message.[2]

In such a situation, the way in which the Resident used his influence was of considerable importance. Grant always behaved with tact towards the Raja, but he was succeeded in 1823 by Briggs, and soon Chaplin was complaining that 'Briggs instead of holding the confidential sort of intercourse with him which Grant did is getting rather *diplomatic*—addressing notes "to the Durbar" and receiving written answers—a system which by relaxing too suddenly the control formerly exercised promises I think to be attended with a bad effect, the little Raja being I fear at bottom but a very degenerate scion of the House of Seewajee.'[3]

Elphinstone was 'sorry to hear of Briggs' alteration in the manners of Sattara'. He suggested that 'a word of advice now and then both from you and me may do something', but commented also that Briggs's 'fault is his self-confidence which prevents his ever improving'.[4]

The course of events ran smoothly enough, however, during Briggs's period of office at Satara. Briggs himself was greatly impressed by the Raja's administrative ability. Looking back over the years which he had spent at Satara he wrote in 1827 that

the aptness with which the Raja took to business under Captain Grant-Duff is truly surprising, and the steadiness with which he pursues the system laid down by him, is highly creditable to His Highness. He usually attends his office daily at about eleven or twelve o'clock, where he sits and hears all complaints 'viva voce', with secretaries around him making notes of such circumstances as require further investigation, or reference. After the complaints are exhausted, he retires to his private office, where he has the letters read received from the districts, and dictates replies; after which, having heard the answers to the letters of

[1]   Grant to M.E., 23.3.1819, Choksey, *Aftermath*, 265.
[2]   Grant to M.E., 29.8.[1822], *Elphinstone*.
[3]   Chaplin to M.E., 10.7.1823, *Elphinstone*.
[4]   Elphinstone to Chaplin, 2.8.1823, *Elphinstone*.

the preceding day, they are sealed in his presence before being des-patched.[1]

The Raja's brother, Appa Sahib, was entrusted with 'the super-intendence of the criminal court of justice and the business of the Jageerdars'.[2] This criminal court consisted of five members in-cluding himself as President.

All civil suits were decided by panchayats nominated by the parties, or by the Government if they could not agree upon nominees.

The traditional village police system was as effective as that in the British territories, in Briggs's opinion.[3]

It was almost the Deccan system to perfection. But not all its details accorded with Briggs's notions of propriety. Instead of pay-ing his domestic officials their full wages the Raja allowed them to accept gifts (Briggs called them bribes) in return for conveying petitions to him.[4]

Briggs regarded it as a serious fault that the Raja allowed his private feelings of antipathy towards Brahmans to lead him 'to make low and ignorant persons his associates',[5] and to appoint incom-petent non-Brahmans to important offices. As his agent to com-municate with the Resident he employed one Balwant Rao Bhonsle, although according to Briggs Balwant Rao 'writes & reads indiffer-ently', and was therefore 'not very equal to transact business of himself'.[6]

Moreover, the Raja was impatient of restraints upon his authority. 'He endeavours to forget the Treaty', Briggs complained, 'and to persuade himself and his people that he is quite his own master. He frequently regrets rather *too publicly* that there is a Resident here at all, whenever his wishes are checked.'[7]

On the other hand, he tried to make use of the Resident's authority to support unpopular policies of his own devising. When he anticipated a fall in the revenue for 1823/4 he decided to reduce

---

[1] Briggs to Government, 1.1.1827, para. 3, Bom. P.C. 17.1.1827, 24–27.
[2] Ibid. The Raja's elder brother, Raja Ram (Bhau Sahib), died in January 1821 (Political letter from Bombay, 29.8.1821, para. 89, B.C. 703/19071, 15).
[3] Briggs to Government, 1.1.1827, para. 5, Bom. P.C. 17.1.1827, 24–27.
[4] Ibid., para. 28.   [5] Ibid., para. 27.
[6] Ibid., para. 26. In a private letter to Elphinstone Briggs described him as 'not being able to read or write (tolerably even)' Briggs to M.E., 8.10.1826, *Elphinstone*.
[7] Ibid.

official salaries. He consulted Briggs. But Briggs advised against it.
Then he got his officials to agree to a temporary reduction of 25 per
cent., and he told Briggs that they had suggested the idea in the
first place. But Briggs was later informed by several officials that the
Raja had told them that it was the Resident's idea.[1]

The Raja had much difficulty with his great jagirdars. They had
chosen to come under his authority instead of under the British
Government's. But he saw no need to thank them for it. As Briggs
remarked, 'whatever the world may think, His Highness conceives
that he is only raised to that station which is due to his birth, and
which common justice would have assigned to him'. He therefore
looked upon them as proper subjects of his. But they themselves
had been used to virtual independence, and resented any attempt
on his part to enforce his authority over them.[2]

Grant had had trouble with the Pant Sachiv and suspected him
of conniving at the lawlessness of the Ramusis. 'I am somewhat
afraid', he told Elphinstone in 1820, 'that the police in the Punt
Suchew's territory may be neglected, or rather that he will be a
Muqadam of Ramoossee Naiks, but I shall endeavour to show him
the danger of such a trade.'[3]

When the Pant came to see the Raja several months later, Grant
remonstrated with him. He of course denied the truth of all
rumours of his complicity with the Ramusis and claimed that they
must have originated in reports of engagements which he had made
with them to protect his territory. Grant had to be satisfied with
that. 'I am inclined to hope', he concluded, 'that he is sincere, at all
events I am convinced he is intimidated, and that he at least intends
to act more circumspectly for the future.'[4]

But Briggs found no improvement. 'The police of his district is
scandalous', he reported in 1827. 'He seizes robbers only to extort
part of their booty.' For the past fifteen months there had been
complaints from inhabitants of the Pant's territories. Both the Raja
and Briggs had warned him but 'although he promises fairly, the
plaintiffs continue as clamorous as ever'. Briggs suspected that
the Pant encouraged robbers in his own districts to prey upon the
Company's territories—a policy with which Briggs of all people

[1] Briggs to Government, 1.1.1827, Bom. P.C. 17.1.1827, 24 ff.
[2] Ibid.
[3] Grant to M.E., 28.4.1820, *Elphinstone*.
[4] Grant to Chaplin, 23.1.1821, B.C. 703/19072, 300.

should have been familiar enough. The Pant was also said to be in the habit of exacting heavy fines from his subjects, 'levied principally on the plea of punishing the infidelity of married persons of both sexes'.[1]

The Pant himself Briggs described as 'a young man of acute & active mind, extremely prone to intrigue'. Like Chintaman Rao, he was 'fond of horticulture', and had 'a large garden laid out in the Europe style full of English fruits and plants' and 'several different kinds of Europe poultry which he keeps as curiosities'.[2] But in spite of these peaceful avocations indicative of Western influence the Pant was the most turbulent of the Raja's great jagirdars.

The Raja was also vexed by what Briggs's acting successor Simson called the 'imbecility and profligacy' of Ram Rao Daphle, who was in financial difficulties.[3]

The Raja of Akalkot, too, treated the Raja of Satara 'with great indifference' according to Simson.[4]

Small wonder that the Raja 'hinted' to Simson 'pretty plainly and on more than one occasion that it was not without design that all allusion to the continuing of their jageers to the descendants of the present holders was omitted in the articles of guarantee'.[5]

When Elphinstone saw him in 1826 he did in fact argue from the terms of these agreements that the jagirs were personal to their present holders and could therefore lapse on their death. Elphinstone denied this. When the agreements were made, he recalled, it was intended 'to provide for those old families by rendering their jaghires perpetual, a point which was decided on before they were given their choice of holding the lands either of the Raja or of the Company'.[6]

Elphinstone admitted that if a family became extinct its jagir would lapse to the Raja, but he added that 'it is by no means desirable that such extinction should take place'.[7]

The Raja also drew up in painstaking detail a graduated system of procedure to be adopted for the coercion of refractory jagirdars,

[1] Briggs to Government, 1.1.1827, paras. 21–22, Bom. P.C. 17.1.1827, 24–27.
[2] Ibid.
[3] Simson to M.E., 5.11.1826, *Elphinstone*. William Simson, Bombay writer, 1818 season (*East-India Register*).
[4] Ibid.
[5] Ibid.
[6] M.E., Minute, 13.12.1826, Bom. P.C. 10.1.1827, 70.
[7] M.E. to Raja, 25.1.1827, Bom. P.C. 14.2.1827, 22.

beginning with the simple requirement that the jagirdar should remain at Court until he had given satisfaction and culminating in the permanent resumption of some of his villages.[1]

To this Elphinstone replied that 'the scale of graduated compulsion recommended by your Highness is very judicious as long as it is applied with moderation, but would be ruinous if pressed on with too much eagerness', and he pointed out that since the jagirdars' agreements provided that all transactions affecting them should be carried out in consultation with the Resident, 'it will therefore be necessary to consult with him on each case of complaint and in every stage of the proceedings'.[2]

Ram Rao Daphle, however, had become so involved in debt that at his request and with the Resident's approval the Raja took over the administration, and when Briggs took his leave of Satara he reported that Ram Rao was living at the capital 'in a most distressed and disreputable condition'.[3]

The Raja was particularly anxious to make the Pant Sachiv and the Pratinidhi, as descendants of the Ashta Pradhans or Ministers of Shivaji, more dependent upon his own authority and to have them render some service to the state. He called them Karkuns in contrast to the Sardars who furnished troops for his service.[4]

In 1827 the Pant Sachiv was brought low by sickness. He wanted a son and asked the Raja for permission to adopt one. This was the Raja's opportunity, and he took it eagerly. He declared that he would allow the Pant Sachiv to adopt an heir only on condition that henceforth the heir would perform certain obligations like furnishing a contingent of troops.[5] He also made a pointed reference to the Company's policy towards their own jagirdars. To this Elphinstone returned that 'our own jagirdars are not ancient nobles', and therefore could provide no precedent, but he thought it reasonable for the Raja to demand a gift in token of allegiance (*nazar*), just as the Peshwa had done.[6] Privately he remarked to Colonel Archibald Robertson, the new Resident, 'the best thing for the Raja would be to have the Suchew die before the question was settled, the successor would then stand on his own merits alone', the Pant him-

---

[1] Raja's Memorandum, Bom. P.C. 10.1.1827, 68.
[2] M.E. to Raja, 25.1.1827, Bom. P.C. 14.2.1827, 22.
[3] Briggs to Government, 1.1.1827, para. 25, Bom. P.C. 17.1.1827, 24–27.
[4] Simson to M.E., 25.6.1827, B.C. 1161/30460, 5 ff.
[5] Ibid., and Robertson to Government, 13.8.1827, ibid. 25 ff.
[6] M.E. to Simson, 10.7.1827, ibid. 20 ff.

self having deserved special consideration for his conduct during the war.[1]

In the end, it was agreed that the Raja should allow the Pant to adopt on condition of paying a gift of allegiance and furnishing a contingent of horse. The Raja accordingly allowed him to adopt a son. He did so, and died a day or so later.[2]

Apart, however, from the Raja's severity towards his jagirdars, Satara retained more of the characteristics of the Deccan system than did any of the Collectorates.

Chaplin left Bombay for England on 21 June 1826, and the Deccan Commission was abolished with effect from that date.[3]

The immediate effects of the change were small. To take the place of the Commissioner in his relations with the jagirdars, an Agent for Sardars was appointed. To take over his judicial duties the Judges of the Sadr Adalat were appointed Commissioners of Criminal and Civil Justice in the Deccan.[4] To harmonize the system of government of the rest of the Bombay territories with that of the Deccan, the new Code of Regulations had already been modified and added to. The Deccan system was least changed in the Southern Maratha country: first because it had worked best there, and secondly because it seemed unwise to assimilate the Southern Maratha country to the rest of the Bombay territories until the Court of Directors had decided whether it should be permanently joined to Bombay or Madras.

And so the Deccan Commission was abolished. Elphinstone had been considering the possibility for several years. As early as 1822 he was asking Chaplin to examine how far the Deccan could be brought under the same Regulation Code as the rest of the Bombay territories: 'bear in mind', he told him, 'that although the blind application of a code to one country which was made for another, is absurd, yet that when the same Regulations do suit, there are many advantages in a simple and uniform system throughout'.[5]

As early as 1822 he was also emphasizing to Chaplin that if any

---

[1] M.E. to Robertson, 20.8.1827, *Elphinstone*.

[2] Political letter from Bombay, 24.5.1828, para. 58, B.C. 1161/30460, 1 ff.

[3] Government to Judges and Magistrates in Deccan, 22.6.1826, Bom. J.C. 28.6.1826, 5.

[4] Government to Sadr Diwani and Sadr Faujdari Adalat, 8.6.1826, Bom. J.C. 14.6.1826, 6.

[5] M.E. to Chaplin, 10.2.1822, *Elphinstone*.

parts of the Deccan system were to survive, they must be incorporated into Regulations. 'If we mean to make any modifications or to keep up anything of the present system, it must be established in a printed book before the present actors quit the scene, when possibly the respect commanded by print may get our improvements to be ranked with the wisdom of our ancestors & spared in consequence.'[1]

He soon realized, too, that a system that relied on men rather than measures was incompatible with the spirit of the age. As he told Lord Hastings in 1824, 'the plan of proceeding on native customs without precise Regulations cannot I am persuaded be kept up after the first set of public officers shall have passed away, & it will then be necessary to introduce as in other places a system depending less on personal character & requiring less experience & knowledge of the people'.[2]

Regulations were essential to preserve a system of which the essence was the relative absence of Regulations. 'The most extensive exercise of discretion', he wrote in 1827, 'passes unquestioned if authorized by a statute and exerted in a specified form; but the smallest act of authority becomes suspected if there is anything informal in the proceedings.'[3]

On the one hand, Regulations could preserve to the individual officer a scope for the use of his discretion. On the other hand, Regulations could set bounds to his enthusiasms. Such bounds would become all the more necessary in the years to come. Each new civil servant, fresh from England, who had never seen the Maratha administrative system at work under a Maratha government, was likely to be hostile to whatever of that system he found remaining in the Deccan.

Elphinstone feared that social intercourse between 'the higher orders' and English officials would steadily decrease as the new men arrived. Hence the necessity for preserving the hitherto informal privileges of the jagirdars in a Regulation to protect them from the zeal of egalitarian Judges.

The mere separation of powers, he wrote in 1827, had already had the result that 'intercourse between those of the higher orders and Europeans' was 'already much less than it used to be': when

[1] M.E. to Chaplin, 21.2.1822, *Elphinstone*.
[2] M.E. to Hastings, 13.2.1824, *Elphinstone*.
[3] M.E., Minute, 4.1.1827, Bom. P.C. 31.1.1827, 51.

each officer had charge only of one branch of administration—
revenue or justice—he tended to come into contact with Indians
only in so far as related to the duties of his particular branch.[1]

Such tendencies had not yet taken full effect in the Deccan.
Indeed, Elphinstone intended, as he said, 'to prevent, or at least
delay that result'. And he could claim in 1827 that 'the whole
system there is still much more conformable to the native habits,
and less repugnant to their feelings than in most other parts of
India'. But he was not optimistic for the future: 'there is nevertheless a tendency to an opposite state of things which it will probably
be impossible altogether to withstand'.[2]

[1] Ibid.   [2] Ibid.

10

EDUCATION AND RELIGION

RELIGIOUS neutrality was the Company's aim, but it became all the more difficult of achievement as the Company's social policies increasingly pressed upon areas of men's lives hitherto guarded by their religion. Not that those of the Company's servants who advocated such policies necessarily ignored their religious implications. C. E. Trevelyan, for example, would support the cause of English education by Utilitarian arguments in public, but when writing in private to the Governor-General he had no hesitation in presenting it as the means for the eventual conversion of India to Christianity.[1]

In his private correspondence Elphinstone similarly welcomed the spread of Western knowledge in India as weakening the Hindu religion. Anxious lest the supporters of Western education should raise up enemies by associating it with Christian teachings he wrote to Captain Irvine[2] in 1819:

I confess myself firmly convinced that the most effective, perhaps the only, means now remaining for checking the improvement & even *the conversion* of the Natives is to attempt to convert them by forcing our Doctrines upon them before they are prepared to receive them. I consider the Hindoo religion to be one great cause of the people of this country being so far behind Europeans in laws & morals & I should be very glad to see that obstacle to their improvement removed. I am fully persuaded that so absurd a superstition could not keep its ground among an enlightened people & I am likewise persuaded that the Natives must gradually become enlightened & that their religion must fall unless an injudicious spirit of opposition to it should inspire it with new life & give its professors that energy in which they are now so deficient. I have often considered the state of our Empire in India & it has always appeared to me that notwithstanding the small numbers of those who uphold it & its want of a root in the feelings of the people, it would probably stand for a long time unless chance should raise up some false prophet who

[1] See my 'The home government and Bentinck's educational policy', *Cambridge Historical Journal*, x. 2 (1951), 224 ff.

[2] Probably Captain Francis Irvine, 11th Regt. Bengal Native Infantry, Secretary to Calcutta Madrasa Committee (*East-India Register*).

should unite a plan for the reformation of the existing religion with one for the deliverance of the country from foreigners. Against such a storm as an able & enthusiastic man might raise by these means, I do not think our power could stand one moment & this is exactly what attempts at conversion are likely to produce. It is worth comparing the stake with the object for which it is risked. I do not suppose the advocates for conversions think it signifies much that the great work should be accomplished by *their* hands in particular & if they do not, there stands on one side the chance of converting the natives 50 or 100 years (or 200 years, what is a century in the history of mankind?) sooner than they would otherwise be converted, & on the other the chance of confirming them in their errors, producing the destruction of our Eastern Empire, & shutting out for ages that light the first rays of which would be overwhelmed in the common ruin.[1]

Elphinstone fully realized the possible political implications of fostering Western education in India. When Briggs saw a pile of printed Marathi books in his tent one day he 'asked him what they were meant for. "To educate the natives.", said he, "but it is our highroad back to Europe".' Briggs commented, 'I wonder you, as Governor of Bombay, have set it on foot', but Elphinstone 'answered coolly, "we are bound under all circumstances to do our duty to them" '.[2] The date of this incident is uncertain, but it seems from a letter which he wrote to Malcolm that in 1819 at least he had considerable doubt even of the political danger of such a policy.

The acquisition of knowledge by their subjects [he wrote on that occasion] may have lost the French Hayti & the Spaniards South America, but it preserved half the world to the Romans, gave them a hold on the manners & opinions of their subjects & left them a kind of moral Empire long after their physical power was destroyed. Knowledge seems to overturn tyrannical and to maintain moderate Governments & it is therefore to be hoped it may strengthen ours but at any rate the danger from it is distant & uncertain & we have no more right to stifle the growing knowledge of our subjects than Herod had to massacre the innocents because he believed some one of them was to dethrone him.[3]

When he wrote to James Loch on the subject several years later, he had become more certain about the eventual political result of promoting education in India. Loch was a friend with whom

[1] M.E. to Capt. Irvine, 10.1.1819, *Elphinstone*.
[2] T. E. Colebrooke, *Memoir*, 72, quoting from Briggs.
[3] M.E. to Malcolm, 27.1.1819, *Elphinstone*.

Elphinstone was conducting a desultory correspondence. He had been describing educational activities at home, and Elphinstone replied in September 1823:

> We are educating the Natives from the same feeling but not with the same enthusiasm as you describe at home. Here it is even a more important & more hazardous experiment than in Europe, but it is I think our very first duty & it will be better for us to lose the country by the effects of our liberality than to keep it like Dutchmen or Spaniards, not that I think the immediate danger of our losing the country increased by education, on the contrary the immediate danger is much diminished; but there can be no doubt that when the natives get more extended notions they will expect first a share of their own Government & then the whole.[1]

Elphinstone thus came to think that the spread of education would not only destroy Hinduism as a religion but also foster a spirit of political independence among the people. But he also thought it the duty of the British Government to foster education even though it might be their own 'high road back to Europe'.

Fundamentally he regarded education as a duty of government because it was a moral influence. In the report which he wrote on leaving the Deccan in 1819 he declared that there was no way 'to improve the morals of the people, except by improving their education'.[2] He elaborated upon this theme in Benthamite terms in the course of a lengthy minute upon educational policy which he wrote in 1823:

> It is now well understood that, in all countries, the happiness of the poor depends in a great measure on their education: it is by means of it alone that they can acquire those habits of prudence & self-respect from which all other good qualities spring, & if ever there was a country where such habits are required, it is this. We have all often heard of the ills of early marriages and overflowing population; of the savings of a life squandered on some one occasion of festivity; of the helplessness of the Ryots, which renders them a prey to moneylenders; of their indifference to good clothes or houses, which has been urged on some occasions as an argument against lowering the public demands on them; &, finally, of the vanity of all laws to protect them when no individual can be found who has spirit enough to take advantage of those enacted in their favour. There is but one remedy for all this, which is education.[3]

[1] M.E. to James Loch, 4.9.1823, *Elphinstone*.

[2] M.E., *Report*, 56.

[3] M.E., Minute, n.d. [13.12.1823], para. 41, Bom. G.C. 10.3.1824, 702.

He thought that education, besides inculcating these virtues of prudence and self-reliance, would also lead to the disappearance of sati, infanticide, and 'superstition'—and that nothing else would.[1]

The sort of 'superstition' which the Bombay Government were most anxious to eradicate was the belief that epidemics like cholera were the result of witchcraft. Outbreaks of cholera in the Northern Konkan were followed by the murder of many unfortunate individuals popularly believed to have magical powers. When they reported these events to the Court of Directors the Government took care to emphasize the need to promote education as the remedy.[2]

Conscious as Elphinstone was of 'the slippery foundation of our Government, owing to the total separation between us and our subjects', he also hoped that education would remove popular prejudices against the British and spread a knowledge of their principles and opinions.[3]

On the other hand, if the Government took no interest at all in education, not only might 'the fountain of native talent' dry up, but also 'the actual learning of the nation' would be 'likely to be lost & the productions of former genius to be forgotten'.[4]

He was thus concerned with the education both of the learned classes and also of the peasantry. '

The peasants, it might be thought, would have little opportunity to read even if they had once learned how to do so. He was, however, anxious not only to eradicate 'superstition' by the spread of Western knowledge but also to teach the peasants to read so that they might understand the declarations of the Government, decipher their own revenue certificates (pattas), and work out their own accounts.[5] Under a ryotwari system each peasant would have at least this much of immediate personal concern to read.

His aim, he declared in 1823, was not 'to provide clerks for offices but to diffuse knowledge among all orders of the people of this country'.[6]

---

[1] Ibid., para. 42.
[2] Judicial letter from Bombay, 29.11.1824, para. 9, B.C. 925/25944, 1 ff.
[3] M.E., Minute, n.d. [13.12.1823], para. 43, Bom. G.C. 10.3.1824, 703.
[4] Ibid., para. 44.
[5] Cf. Elphinstone to Chaplin, 3.11.1823: 'My views are very humble, the principal object being to have reading enough among the ryots to enable them to understand the intentions of Government regarding them and to take their own accounts' (*Elphinstone*).
[6] M.E., Minute, n.d., para. 4, Bom. G.C. 10.3.1824, 825.

He thought that the promotion of education was one of the most important duties of a government. Not the most important of all, however, and on one occasion in 1825 he laid down the duties of a government in what he considered to be the proper order of precedence: first, the repression of violence; secondly, the fixing of 'moderate and equal assessments' of the land revenue; thirdly, the administration of justice; fourthly, the establishment of freedom of trade; and fifthly, the promotion of education. On the other hand, he added, education was the best means of promoting all these other objects as well.[1]

When he was Commissioner in the Deccan Elphinstone had at first contemplated the establishment of colleges at Nasik and Wai. But he had subsequently abandoned this notion in favour of a more limited but more systematic distribution of Dakshina gifts to learned Brahmans than had taken place under the former government. In the report which he drew up on leaving the Deccan he had suggested that these gifts might be awarded for proficiency in 'more useful branches of learning' than 'Hindoo Divinity' and that some professors might be appointed to teach such subjects.[2]

Towards the end of 1820 Chaplin accordingly submitted to the Government a plan for a college at Poona. In order to make it popular with Hindus he 'proposed the appointment of teachers in almost all their branches of learning, although,' he added, 'many of them are perhaps worse than useless'. For the same reason he avoided all provision for 'European science'. But in his plan he tried, as he said,

to direct the attention of the College principally to such parts of their own Shasters as are not only most useful in themselves but will best prepare their minds for the gradual reception of more valuable instruction at a future time. When we have once secured their confidence, but not till then, will be the time to attempt the cautious and judicious introduction of those improvements in the education of our Hindoo subjects by which alone, joined with good Government, we can hope to ameliorate their moral condition.[3]

He therefore proposed that it should be declared that the study of the Vedas would be 'held secondary' to the study of the Shastras, that no student would be allowed to study the Vedas alone, and

[1] M.E., Minute, n.d., Bom. E.C. 31.12.1825, 20.
[2] See Chap. 5, above.
[3] Chaplin to Government, 24.11.1820, B.C. 667/18622, 193 ff.

that whoever chose 'to study any of the Veds must also study some one of the Shasters, which latter will be held his primary qualification'.[1]

Chaplin also proposed that an annual examination should be held at the time of the Dakshina and that the preference in awarding Dakshina prizes should be given to students of the college. Besides the encouragement already given to the Shastras over the Vedas, he proposed that the study of law, mathematics, and medicine should be particularly encouraged by larger prizes. In addition, the Government should grant 5 rupees a month each to 100 students, 'children of poor, respectable and learned men'. The staff was to consist of a Principal and eighteen teachers.[2]

At the command of the Court of Directors the Governor in Council was at this time already considering how best to train junior civil servants in the vernacular languages.[3] It was assumed that this should be done in a college. A Committee had been set up, and was examining the possibility of combining three colleges in one institution, namely, 'a College for instructing gentlemen on the civil and military establishments in the eastern languages', 'a College for instructing the Hindoos in their own sciences', and 'a College for teaching languages and laws to the natives'.[4] The Committee submitted a detailed plan to this effect. Elphinstone preferred it to Chaplin's more limited proposals, which at his suggestion were referred to the Committee in case they might suggest any modifications of the Bombay College plan.[5]

But both Bell and Prendergast, the two civil members of Elphinstone's Council at this time, objected to the Bombay College plan, and it was therefore suspended pending a reference to the Court of Directors.[6]

The Committee in due course submitted their verdict upon Chaplin's plan. They conceded that it was 'admirably well calculated to preserve and promote the study of Brahminical learning,

[1] 'Sketch of the general plan proposed to be published in the native language', enclosed with Chaplin to Government, 20.11.1820, ibid.
[2] Ibid.
[3] Revenue dispatch to Bombay, 14.7.1819, para. 57, Bom. D. xlvi. 589 f.
[4] The Committee consisted of Warden, Goodwin, Vans Kennedy, Erskine, and Dr. Taylor (M.E., Minute, 2.6.1820, B.C. 667/18622, 27 ff.).
[5] J. B. Simson (Secretary to M.E.) to Government, 23.12.1820, ibid. 185 ff.
[6] Prendergast and Bell, Minutes, n.d., ibid. 176 ff.; M.E. to Malcolm, 31.1.1821, *Elphinstone.* Also Public letter from Bombay, 29.8.1821, para. 72, Bom. G.L.R. ix. 273.

and to provide a moderate provision for a certain number of learned men and students, at a period when, from the fall of the Hindoo Dynasty they are not likely to receive their accustomed patronage and support'. But they declared that the college was less likely to succeed in the eventual aim of· spreading Western knowledge if it was situated at Poona than it would be if it were situated at Bombay.

A Mahratta, especially if young [they wrote enthusiastically] can hardly visit Bombay without feeling his mind enlarged. He sees customs different from his own; he sees the wonders produced by wealth and trade, our busy harbours, our warehouses, our docks, our carriages and public roads, the appearance of ease, industry and comfort diffused over a large population; he can hardly help comparing the scene in which he is placed with that which he has left, and his education is begun before he has opened a book: curiosity is the best foundation for knowledge. ...

They thought optimistically that he would be filled with admiration.[1]

But as Elphinstone pointed out, the most eminent Shastris would never come to Bombay. Yet since the college would be 'a sort of compensation' for the lakhs of rupees which the former government used to distribute among Brahmans, it ought at least to provide for some of them. The college must therefore be at Poona.[2]

Prendergast objected that the expense would be 'very heavy as a Seminary for Brahmins exclusively, and if these will not readily consent to leave Poona, the advantage to be derived by the Departments of Government from their learning will . . . be very limited'.[3]

But the most important advantage which the Government could expect to derive from the college was the training of Shastris for the Law Courts. The Sadr Adalat were feeling the lack of qualified Shastris and Maulvis, and Elphinstone used this as an argument for pressing forward with the establishment of the Poona College.[4]

Prendergast, however, did not fail to point out that there was

---

[1] Committee to Government, 18.5.1821, B.C. 667/18622, 207 ff.
[2] M.E., Minute, n.d. (Colville and Bell subscribing), ibid. 219 ff.
[3] Prendergast, Minute, n.d., ibid. 221 ff.
[4] e.g. Sutherland (3rd Judge of Circuit) to Bax (Register, Superior Tribunal), 1.8.1820, paras. 25 ff., Bom. J.C. 11.10.1820, 4252 ff.; Vibart (Register, Sadr Adalat) to Government, 27.6.1821, Bom. J.C. 15.8.1821, 2482 ff.; Sutherland to Register, Sadr Adalat, 1.8.21, Bom. J.C. 5.9.1821, 2736 ff.

a much greater need for learned Muslims than for learned Brahmans, and that the Poona College could only supply the Courts with the latter.[1]

Chaplin's plan was eventually approved. At Elphinstone's suggestion, he was told to reduce the distribution of Dakshina gifts to as low a level as possible in all cases where it did not help to promote learning. He was also warned that the encouragement to be given to the study of the Shastras in preference to that of the Vedas, 'might be inferred indirectly rather than in express terms; the enunciation of the preference might lead to questions among the natives, as to the cause of such preference, which it is unnecessary to excite'.[2]

Chaplin opened the new Poona Hindu College on 6 October 1821. 'All the principal inhabitants', he reported, attended the ceremony. He made a speech explaining the aims of the Government in founding the college, and presented honorary dresses to the Professors.[3] He had revised his original scheme, and it was now announced that only Brahmans between 10 and 18 years of age would be scholars, that the annual examinations to be held in the presence of government officers would not include any parts of the Vedas or Shastras which Hindus might consider particularly sacred, and that 70 of the scholarships awarded would be for students of the Shastras, the remaining 30 for students of the Vedas.[4]

When Chaplin visited the college in 1822 he reported that he 'invited a few of the principal Sirdars and Shastrees in Poona to witness the exhibition of the scholars', and that they 'appeared to be much gratified' with what they saw. Clearly, in his opinion the college was fulfilling its task of conciliating the upper classes.[5]

He recommended in 1822 that the Dakshina should not fall below Rs.35,000 on the ground that 'it certainly conduces much to our popularity, and promotes in a considerable degree the preservation of national learning'. The distribution of the prizes was now regulated by a Committee of Shastris who examined each candidate upon his learning.[6] The Governor in Council

[1] Prendergast, Minute, n.d., B.C. 667/18622, 221 ff.
[2] Government to Chaplin, 10.8.1821, ibid. 223 ff.
[3] Raghu Acharya, a learned Brahman, was appointed Principal of the College.
[4] Chaplin to Government, 7.10.1821, B.C. 667/18622, 225 ff.
[5] Chaplin to Government, 20.8.1822, para. 397, S.R.J. iv. 522.
[6] Ibid., para. 396.

agreed that 'it would be illiberal and impolitic to direct any further reduction' of the Dakshina, and the amount was therefore fixed at Rs.35,000 as Chaplin suggested.[1]

The authorities at home had not yet pronounced upon these developments. While the Bombay Government had suspended the Bombay College plan pending a reference home, they had gone forward with the establishment of the Poona Hindu College on the ground that the Supreme Government had sanctioned the expenditure of 2 lakhs of rupees a year 'for the support of native literature in the Deccan' and on the assumption that 'the faith of the Government' seemed 'to have been pledged to the learned classes of our own subjects in the Deccan'.[2]

In 1823, however, the Court of Directors replied with a cold rebuke to the Bombay Government for having set up the Poona College. They questioned the Bombay Government's assumption that the establishment of the Poona College would have 'a very favourable effect' on 'the minds of the Natives', and they quoted at length from one of their own dispatches to the Supreme Government in which they criticized both the Benares Hindu College and the Calcutta Madrasa. In this dispatch they cast scorn upon the traditional Oriental learning:

With respect to the sciences, it is worse than a waste of time to employ persons either to teach or learn them, in the state in which they are found in the Oriental books. As far as any historical documents may be found in the Oriental languages, what is desirable is that they should be translated, and this, it is evident, will be best accomplished by Europeans who have acquired the requisite knowledge. Beyond these branches, what remains in Oriental literature is poetry, but it has never been thought necessary to establish Colleges for the cultivation of poetry....[3]

The harsh overtone of Utilitarianism became ever more distinct as the Court proceeded to explain that the plan of the Benares Hindu College and the Calcutta Madrasa had been 'originally and fundamentally erroneous'. Their aim should not have been 'to teach Hindoo learning or Mahomedan learning but useful learning'. It was a question not of the language of instruction but of its

[1] Government to Chaplin, 19.3.1823, para. 24, Bom. J.C. 30.4.1823, 2178 ff.
[2] Public letter from Bombay, 29.8.1821, paras. 68–69; B.C. 1172/30648, 1 ff.
[3] Public dispatch to Bombay, 11.6.1823, paras. 21 ff., Bom. D. xlviii. 290 ff.

content. The Court applied the same criticisms to the new Poona College. Since, however, the Bombay Government had not only founded the college but also laid down its syllabus—'wherein we see nothing to which we can attach almost any expectation of utility'—the Court contented themselves with a recommendation to the Bombay Government to attend to the principle of utility in future. They added a further criticism which seems to equate education with training: 'an institution in which study is not cheered by the hopes of preferment in the Church, of emolument at the Bar, or of literary distinction will be in danger of considering the provisions it affords as an eleemosynary supply for pauperism or an easy retreat for lazy indifference'.[1]

In short, the Court of Directors objected both to the content of the education provided at the Poona College and also to its purpose or lack of purpose. The Utilitarian influence upon their dispatch was clearly strong, and it has since been suggested that James Mill was its author.[2] Elphinstone himself suspected as much, and drew up a lengthy minute in defence of his educational policy. Then he wrote to Strachey:

My minute is about as big as the Beej Gunnit: among other things it contains a defence of the Poona College against the Court of Directors (your friend Mill I fancy) who decry or deny all Hindoo learning & think 14,000 Rupees a year (saved out of the Dukhshna, a stupid piece of almsgiving) too much to give for paying 15 or 20 professors & 100 exhibitions to students; so as to keep up the little learning there is & to afford a vehicle for introducing more, besides keeping the people in good humour & doing something to distinguish our occupation of the country from that of the wild beasts to whom Burke has likened us. Tell me if it was Mill that wrote it.[3]

Strachey confirmed this. 'In one of your letters about education', he replied, 'you ask me whether the attack on the Poona College was written by Mill—It was—but this I say only generally —no particular passage can be fixed on as his—Drafts of letters are you know altered at the Board of Control & indeed at the India House.'[4]

[1] Ibid. Quoting from the College Committee's report.
[2] See Spear, 'Bentinck and Education', *Cambridge Historical Journal*, vi. 1 (1938), 78 ff.
[3] M.E. to Strachey, 19.1.1824, *Elphinstone*. Beej Gunnit, *Vija Ganita*, a Sanskrit treatise on Algebra which Strachey had translated from a Persian text.
[4] Strachey to M.E., 20.1.1825, *Elphinstone*.

While the Court allowed the Poona College to continue, they firmly rejected the Bombay College plan. This merely spurred Elphinstone forward. In the minute on education which he drew up after receiving the Court's dispatch he explained his other plans which, as he told Chaplin, he had 'put off until the grand question about the College should be decided'.[1] In these plans he assumed that the Government should promote the education of 'the lower orders'. Not the lowest, however:

> it is observed [he wrote in 1823] that the missionaries find the lowest castes the best pupils; but we must be careful how we offer any special encouragement to men of that description; they are not only the most despised, but among the least numerous of the great divisions of society; and it is to be feared that if our system of education first took root among them, it would never spread further, and that we might find ourselves at the head of a new class, superior to the rest in useful knowledge, but hated and despised by the castes to whom these new attainments would always induce us to prefer them. Such a state would be desirable if we were contented to rest our favour on the attachment of a part of the population; but inconsistent with every attempt to found it on a more extended basis.[2]

The idea that the Government should take an active part in the promotion of education was not accepted by all of Elphinstone's colleagues. Hitherto the initiative had been taken by a private organization, the Bombay Education Society. Founded in 1815 to superintend the education of poor European children upon a Christian basis, this society turned its attention to the education of Indian children in 1818, when it established three 'native schools'. Their plan was to teach 'both the English and native languages', as the Rev. George Barnes, the Archdeacon of Bombay, explained to Elphinstone, but their main difficulties were 'the want of good English masters, & the almost total deficiency of good native schoolbooks'.[3]

In 1820, however, it was decided at a general meeting of the Education Society held in St. Thomas's Church to form a special committee for 'native education', called 'the Native School and

[1] M.E. to Chaplin, 3.11.1823, *Elphinstone*.
[2] M.E., Minute, 13.12.1825, para. 55, Bom. G.C. 10.5.1824, 708.
[3] Barnes to Government, 13.5.1818, Bom. G.C. 20.5.1818, 1126 ff.; Barnes to M.E., 6.1.1819, *Elphinstone*.

School Book Committee', and to raise a separate fund for the purpose. Elphinstone himself gave a large sum of money: this he did in his private capacity as President of the Society.[1]

But when Marriott, the Collector of the Northern Konkan, asked for the help of the Government in 1821 there was immediate opposition in Elphinstone's Council. Marriott wanted to establish a schoolmaster at Panwell, upon the application of a number of the inhabitants, at a salary of 35 rupees a month, a_ _l another at a cost of 50 rupees a month, for educating the children of the Indian officials on his establishment.[2]

Prendergast strongly opposed these suggestions. Panwell, he argued, was so near Bombay that schools were unnecessary there: 'for on this Island', he wrote, 'there is already abundant facility for young natives acquiring the English language as almost every English writer, Purvoo, Parsee, and Portuguese have pupils who when they have made a little progress, are allowed to practice and make themselves useful without pay in almost every public office, in which they afterwards succeed to vacancies, and it is the same at almost every subordinate [station]'.[3]

He also objected to Marriott's proposals on general principles: if they were sanctioned, he thought that they would be followed by many similar proposals, resulting in 'an intolerable burthen on the Hon'ble Company's finances'.[4]

In order to reinforce his objections to the promotion of education by the Government he declared in addition, 'I need hardly mention what every member of the Board knows as well as I do, that there is hardly a village [however] small throughout our territories, in which there is not at least one school, in larger villages more, many in every town and in larger cities in every division.' Reading, writing, and arithmetic were taught in these schools to such effect, he thought, that 'there is hardly a cultivator or Pattydar who is not competent to keep his own accounts with a degree of accuracy in my opinion beyond what we meet with amongst the lower orders in our country'.[5]

Elphinstone, however, welcomed Marriott's proposals, and he

[1] *Bombay Courier*, 19.8.[1820], 26.8.[1820], quoted in *Asiatic Journal*, Feb. 1821, 192–4.
[2] Marriott to Government, 23.5.1821, Bom. G.C. 27.6.1821, 1020 ff.
[3] Prendergast, Minute, n.d., ibid. 1023 ff.
[4] Ibid.
[5] Ibid.

was supported by the rest of his Council.[1] The plan was therefore sanctioned.[2]

Meanwhile the Native School and School Book Committee had been collecting money. By 1822 they had over Rs.6,000.[3] But Elphinstone was vexed that the archdeacon could 'neither find a Native to assist him nor a European acquainted with the languages who will take any interest in the cause'.[4] The Government had had a collection of fables, the Panchatantra, printed in Marathi, and it was typical of Elphinstone that he quickly sent a copy to Chaplin, explaining that 'some improper passages' and 'repetitions' had been left out, and asking him to show it to 'some intelligent & unsophisticated natives' for their opinion.[5]

Both Elphinstone and Archdeacon Barnes were anxious to press forward with the establishment of schools and the training of teachers to conduct them according to the monitorial system developed by Lancaster and Bell.

But the archdeacon in a private letter to Elphinstone expressed his doubts about the advisability of continuing the Committee as a part of the Education Society: 'I am not sure that anything is gained by making the Native School & School Book Committee so connected with the Education Society for though the object is different & kept distinct, yet the natives may confound these schools for them with ours for Christian education. If this be the case, it may be better . . . to separate them & make two societies.'[6]

Elphinstone thought this 'a very judicious arrangement', and the Committee accordingly became a separate society—the Native School Book and School Society—with the task of promoting the 'general diffusion of useful knowledge among the Native Inhabitants of India subject to the Presidency of Bombay'.[7] Lieutenant George Jervis became its Secretary.[8]

---

[1] M.E., Minute, n.d., Colville (Commander in Chief) and Bell subscribing, ibid. 1026.

[2] Minutes of Council, 21.6.1821, ibid.

[3] Barnes to M.E., n.d. [June/July 1822], Elphinstone.

[4] M.E. to Erskine, 22.7.1822, Elphinstone.

[5] M.E. to Chaplin, 25.7.1822, Elphinstone.

[6] Barnes to M.E., 26.[7.]1822, Elphinstone.

[7] M.E. to Barnes, [27].7.1822, Elphinstone. See also B. K. Boman-Behram, Educational Controversies in India, 501.

[8] Brother of T. B. Jervis who founded a 'Native School Society' in the South Konkan which opened several schools which subsequently received help from the Government (W. P. Jervis, T. B. Jervis, 19; also cf. 32–33).

A Committee of this Society then made an analysis of the problem of reforming the existing system. Its main defects they considered to be 'the deplorable deficiency of books for education and mental improvement'; the lack of 'an easy and efficacious method of imparting instruction', the lack of trained teachers and of people to superintend schools, and finally the lack of money for educational purposes. They concluded that books must be translated into the vernaculars and published, the monitorial system introduced, teachers trained to use it, and the Secretary empowered to superintend the schools where they taught. It was suggested, finally, that the Government might contribute some money to help pay for these activities.[1]

This report was the occasion for a lengthy minute by Elphinstone on educational policy. Indeed, it was mainly at his suggestion that the Society had turned to the Government for money.[2]

Typically enough, he suggested a compromise between the promotion of education indirectly through the Society and its promotion directly by the Government. He assumed that some measures must depend upon 'the spontaneous zeal of individuals' and should therefore be left to the Society. The Government, on the other hand, should undertake measures requiring 'an organized system, and a greater degree of regularity and permanence than can be expected from any plan, the success of which is to depend upon personal character'.[3] The Education Society should train teachers; the Government should establish new village schools where needed.[4] The Government should pay for the printing of books in the vernacular; the Society should supervise the actual printing and organize the distribution of the books.[5]

Such an arrangement, he emphasized, presupposed that the Society would take great care that 'neither religion nor any topic likely to excite discontent among the natives should ever be touched on in its schools or publications'.[6] But this principle was more difficult to apply than to formulate. 'It is of comparatively little use that people are taught to read', he declared, 'if their studies are to be confined to legends of Hindu Gods.' Hence there

---

[1] Jervis to Government, 4.10.1823, and enclosed Report, 13.9.1823, Bom. G.C. 10.3.1824, 725 ff.
[2] M.E., Minute [13.12.1823], para. 2, Bom. G.C. 10.3.1824, 670.
[3] M.E., Minute [13.12.1823], para. 5.   [4] Ibid., para. 10.
[5] Ibid., para. 18.
[6] Ibid., para. 6.

was a need for vernacular books on secular subjects and in particular for a 'tract containing those prudential maxims which are
most important to the poor and which are least known in India'.
He wanted, in fact, an education to change men's lives. But a
religion like Hinduism might be involved in the smallest details
of daily life and could not therefore remain untouched by the
implications of such an educational system as he had in mind. He
therefore added a warning that criticisms of customs like infant
marriage and expensive caste ceremonials should be introduced
as delicately as possible.[1]

While he regarded such elementary vernacular education as of
fundamental importance, he also suggested the foundation of a
school at Bombay for the teaching of the English language and of
history, geography, and 'the popular branches of science' through
the medium of English. This he envisaged as a school for the
children of the upper classes: 'to prevent such a mixture of ranks
as might prevent the higher order of natives from using the school,
no boy should be admitted until he was approved by the Committee, and a preference should be given to the sons of wealthy
natives and to boys that show particular promise of talent'. This
was only to apply in the early years, however: 'when the School
became more extended', he added, 'a separate class should be
instituted for the lower castes'.[2]

Such extensive governmental activity to promote education was
unprecedented either in the Company's territories or in Britain.
Elphinstone defended it on the ground that without it learning and
even literacy would decline because British rule gave Indians no
opportunity to accumulate wealth. But Warden opposed the idea
of extensive governmental activity, and argued that even though
there were less highly paid posts under the British than under the
Maratha Government, there were more that afforded 'a comfortable maintenance'. Moreover he pointed to the great jagirdars and
to the district and village officers, who, he thought, still had the
same salaries and allowances as before.[3] Elphinstone replied, 'it is
large fortunes alone that can encourage letters. Almost the whole
of our great expenditure is distributed among the very lowest
orders & even our largest salaries (200 or 250 Rupees a month)

---

[1] M.E., Minute [13.12.1823], para. 25.
[2] Ibid., para. 27.
[3] But their perquisites were practically gone.

will not enable a man to maintain a few scholars, much less a college.'[1]

Almost the only part of Elphinstone's plans of which Warden approved was the proposal to establish a central school at Bombay. Such a school he thought would supply teachers who could be appointed to each zilla. He opposed all distinction of persons: the teachers he thought could be of any social origin—Christians, Parsis, Muslims, or Hindus.[2] Elphinstone of course objected to this 'lack of consideration for the native prejudices' and doubted the existence of a sufficient demand for English teaching in the country at large.[3]

Warden even suggested that the Government should, 'not ostensibly but indirectly, give every encouragement to the missionaries'. He so disliked the traditional Indian system of education that he wanted the village schools to be left 'untouched and unnoticed'. Not only did he object to the idea of sending trained teachers to the villages, but he also objected to Elphinstone's suggestion that the village schools might be encouraged by the holding of occasional examinations and the distribution of prizes to the most proficient pupils and teachers.[4]

All Warden's enthusiasm was for a centralized system of education. 'All our efforts and resources' should be concentrated upon the proposed school at Bombay.[5] He himself had never served in the districts: he had spent the whole of his official career at Bombay. Elphinstone was quick to point out the weakness of an educational policy concentrated upon a Bombay school:

The people of the nearest parts of the Concan hardly ever visit Bombay & with the remotest places there is no intercourse at all, except the occasional visit of a Vakeel to the Presidency & the journeys of some servants & settlers to the interior. When they do meet the people of the Presidency and of the country do not readily mix: the former have the blunt bustling manners of a commercial town which are of all things the most disagreeable to a native. This character extends to the upper classes, by whose example of course the diffusion of knowledge must be effected, and as these are generally men of humble origin who have

[1] Warden, Minute, 29.12.1823, para. 4, Bom. G.C. 10.3.1824, 798 ff.; M.E., Minute, n.d., para. 3, ibid. 823.
[2] Warden, Minute, 29.12.1823, para. 14, ibid.
[3] M.E., Minute, n.d., para. 12, ibid. 831.
[4] Warden, Minute, 29.12.1823, para. 10, ibid. 803.
[5] Para. 13, ibid. 805.

raised themselves by commerce, the upper classes in the interior regard them as vulgar purse-proud traders whose manners and habits it would be better to shun than to imitate.[1]

The main defect of Warden's plan, Elphinstone concluded, was that 'every improvement among all classes of the natives is to be postponed until they shall have learned English'.[2] To this Warden retorted that he had never intended that English should be the only language taught but that it should have an equal place with the vernaculars.[3] Even so, it was unlikely to be wanted at all in the districts. Moreover, at the proposed central school at Bombay, upon which he thought the Government should concentrate its resources, he accepted Elphinstone's intention that English should be the language taught. His proposals would therefore have had the effect of neglecting the vernaculars in favour of English.

After much further argument, it was decided to suspend taking action upon Elphinstone's main suggestions except that of an English school at Bombay until a full inquiry had been made into the existing state of education in the country and until a decision upon the major issues had been made by the Court of Directors.[4]

Some officers no doubt took a personal interest in the village schools and tried to encourage them. Williamson, the Collector of Kaira, for example, reported in 1824 that when he went on tour he 'sent for the best scholars from the village school' and got them to read and write in his presence before 'dismissing them with a present of sweetmeats'. He himself considered that 'the distinction seemed to please them', and he understood, he added, that it 'was thought and talked of a good deal by the boys'.[5]

But such men were exceptional. Elphinstone himself thought in November 1823 that in general 'the want of superintendence' was the greatest difficulty which he had to face—greater even than the want of money.[6]

While some village schools were no doubt flourishing under the

[1] M.E., Minute, n.d., para. 11, ibid. 829.
[2] Para. 26, ibid. 843.
[3] Warden, Minute, 8.1.1824, para. 5, ibid. 849.
[4] The English School at Bombay was established under the superintendence of the Native School Book and School Society in July 1824. By June 1826 it had fifty Maratha and five Gujarati pupils (Jervis to Government, 6.6.1826, Bom. E.C. 14.6.1826, 4).
[5] T. Williamson to Government, 27.2.1824, Bom. G.C. 26.1.1825, 30.
[6] M.E., Journal, 3.11.[1823], Elphinstone.

encouragement of individual officers, in general little was known about them. If the existing system was to be improved, it had first to be understood. Hence the general inquiry which was begun in 1824: it was a logical accompaniment of Elphinstone's plans.

As statistics, the numbers of schools and pupils which were reported to exist in each Collectorate now seem of little value. But Elphinstone himself had never expected anything more than a very rough picture of the situation.[1] In general, the reports of the Collectors and Judges, so the Bombay Government informed the Court of Directors, only confirmed their

former impressions of the low state of education throughout the country: that the instruction imparted in schools extends, with very limited exception, only to such an elementary acquaintance with writing and arithmetic as is absolutely necessary for the business of a shop-keeper or tullatee, that but a small proportion of the people acquire even this knowledge and that the aid of Government in providing or assisting in the remuneration of Schoolmasters is essential to any advancement of learning, if not to the preservation of the very inefficient and defective means of instruction now existing.[2]

Administrative necessity had already forced the Government to undertake a certain amount of vernacular education. They had to have trained men to carry out revenue surveys of their enlarged territories, and the first aim of the Engineer Institution founded in 1823 was to train boys from the Education Society's Charity School as surveyors. It was soon decided

to graft on the survey establishment a plan for instructing natives in some of the mechanical arts and the lower branches of sciences which might render them useful in superintending public works under European Engineers and further the grand design of the institutions already in full operation in other parts of India for introducing generally among the natives of the country a more perfect knowledge of science in its most useful branches founded on European practice.[3]

In the latter department of the Engineer Institution the students were taught in Marathi and Gujarati as appropriate, and George Jervis the Superintendent translated several textbooks for them.

[1] e.g. in his minute of 13.12.1823, para. 17, when proposing an inquiry, he writes that the Collectors 'might, for instance, give a guess at the number of boys taught at each' school. See the comments of Shri R. V. Parulekar, xvi ff.
[2] General letter from Bombay, 15.3.1826, para. 4, Bom. L.R. xlvii.
[3] This decision was in fact made before the College was actually founded.

If Indians were to be trained for subordinate posts in the engineer department there was surely no logical reason why they should not also be trained for the revenue work which they were already undertaking. In 1825 Captain Sutherland accordingly suggested the formation of an institution for this purpose: this he thought would make it possible to create 'a well-organised body of native revenue servants', formed into 'a native civil service' of some 250 officers.[1]

Elphinstone of course heartily supported the idea but found wider implications in it. Such an institution, he declared, would not only provide the Government with 'a better description of revenue officers', but also make possible 'the safe admission of the natives into a larger share than they now possess of the administration of the Government'. Without it, he forecast that Indian revenue officers would be supplanted by Eurasians, and even by Europeans when the free immigration of Europeans came to be allowed. As a result 'the Natives would by degrees be removed from every station of power or profit even of the most subordinate rank'. This process would either create 'a dangerous spirit of disaffection' or 'if it were completed without producing a destructive explosion the result would be such as is perhaps still more to be deprecated, for the whole of the people of India would sink to a debased and servile condition far below that of the Greeks in Turkey and nearly resembling that of the Indians in Spanish America'.[2]

On the other hand, 'if care were taken to qualify the natives for the public service and afterwards to encourage their employment the picture would soon be reversed'. Soon there might well be Indian Sub-Collectors, or even Collectors and Judges. 'It may not be too visionary to suppose a period at which they might bear to the English nearly the relation which the Chinese do to the Tartars, the Europeans retaining the Government and the military power, while the Natives filled a large portion of the civil stations, and many of the subordinate employments in the army.'[3]

They might not be content with only a part. They might eventually demand the whole. Even so, Elphinstone thought it 'better for our honour and interest as well as for the welfare of mankind that we should resign our power into the hands of the

---

[1] Sutherland to Government, 14.3.1825, Bom. E.C. 31.12.1825, 9.
[2] M.E., Minute, n.d., ibid. 10.
[3] Ibid.

people for whose benefit it is entrusted, than that it should be wrested from us by a rival nation or claimed as a birthright by a handful of creoles'.[1]

He therefore proposed that the plan should be referred to the Court of Directors and that meanwhile Chaplin should be asked to send a few young men to the Engineer Institution for instruction so that if the plan were approved they would be ready to instruct others, while if it were not they could be appointed to the government service.[2]

But Warden objected that there was no need for such a scheme. Further, he opposed the idea of training Indians specifically for revenue work on the ground that it would narrow their minds.[3] In his view there was only one thing needful: 'whatever expense the British Government may incur in the promotion of education should have but one object in view, the formation of an efficient Institution for the diffusion of the English language'.[4]

Elphinstone wrote privately to Chaplin explaining the plan in detail. The course of instruction he thought should include 'Arithmetic, Mensuration, the Regulations of Government and the most approved principles of assessment: to this such studies should be added as might form the young men to habits of order, regularity & industry & might gradually inspire them with some principles of integrity.'[5]

But not even Chaplin welcomed the plan. He explained privately to Elphinstone that he could 'get no aid from natives in throwing any light on the subject of revenue education. The position that experienced revenue servants are wanting', he reported, 'is denied, & consequently our want of management in not being able to find & turn their services to account called into question.' He himself thought that experience would be the best training.[6]

In accordance with Elphinstone's proposals the plan was officially referred to Chaplin for his opinion. He remained 'not very sanguine' about its success in producing more efficient revenue officials, but he conceded that it might be of 'some benefit in removing native prejudice and advancing European science'.[7]

[1] Ibid. [2] Ibid.
[3] Warden, Minute, 25.3.1825, ibid. 11.
[4] Warden, Minute, 6.4.1824, ibid. 15.
[5] M.E. to Chaplin, 9.4.1825, *Elphinstone.*
[6] Chaplin to M.E., 28.5.1825, *Elphinstone.*
[7] Chaplin to Government, 9.7.1825, Bom. E.C. 31.12.1825, 19.

But he could never share Elphinstone's broader visions: 'as conquerors differing toto coelo from the conquered, we can never allow the natives to compete with us for the superior offices of administration though we may somewhat enlarge the share they now possess. The best educated must limit their prospects to the middling or subordinate stations, for if they ever ascend higher. they must push us from our seats to make room for themselves.'[1]

Like Elphinstone he thought that orthodox Brahmans would be reluctant to go to Bombay: 'I think it likely', he reported, 'that few Brahmin boys of respectability will be found willing to proceed as students to Bombay [where][2] there is such a mixture of classes and inhabitants of various nations that all distinctions of caste are in a great degree confounded.'[3]

Nevertheless he published a proclamation inviting 'candidates, whether students or others, of the Brahmin and other respectable Hindoo castes, or Mussalmans' for instruction at Bombay in 'land surveying, accounts and the arts of fiscal administration, as well as the duties required of public servants in the judicial department'. The Government, he added, would provide the students with servants of their own caste. The course would last two or three years, after which each student would receive a certificate of his qualifications entitling him to immediate employment in a subordinate post under a Collector or Judge.[4]

In spite of his scepticism about the success of the plan, his proclamation went further than Elphinstone wished. Elphinstone therefore suggested that he should be told that not more than twenty-five pupils should be sent to Bombay and that they could only be trained for revenue and not for judicial work.[5]

But Chaplin's lukewarm report seemed only to arouse fresh misgivings among Elphinstone's colleagues. Warden repeated his opinion that experience was the best training and demanded a reference to the Court of Directors before any money was spent on the plan.[6] Goodwin supported his demand for a reference to the Court.[7]

[1] Chaplin to Government, 9.7.1825, Bom. E.C. 31.12.1825, 19.
[2] 'whether' in text.   [3] Ibid.
[4] Public notice by Chaplin, encl. with Chaplin to Government, 9.7.1825, ibid.
[5] M.E., Minute, n.d., 20.
[6] Warden, Minute, 26.7.1825, Bom. E.C. 31.12.1825, 21.
[7] Goodwin, Minute, 27.7.1825, ibid. 22.

In view of this opposition, Elphinstone decided to cancel the arrangements already made.[1]

But contrary to expectation Brahmans were already flocking to volunteer. Early in August 1825 young John Warden reported to Jervis from Poona that 'two hundred persons have entered their names as candidates for instruction in your school; and 20 or 30 are still daily coming in to the Principal of the College for the same purpose.[2] Of the whole there are I think 6 Mahrattas & two boys of the Prabhoo caste, the remainder are Brahmins: not a single Mussalman has made his appearance, & the Prabhus are much older than the generality of the other candidates—none however are I believe more than 25 years of age'.[3]

Chaplin decided to select by examination twenty-five candidates aged between fourteen and eighteen.[4]

Before he heard this news, Elphinstone wrote privately to Chaplin,

The plan of inviting a certain number of boys to Captain Jervis's institution having been reconsidered, it is thought desirable to stop the whole proceeding. I do not think many will have come in on your proclamation, if any have they will reap the benefit held out in it, but it is desirable that you should announce the invitation to have ceased as soon as you can do so without occasioning disappointment to people who may have taken steps in consequence of your proclamation. In such cases if you could make them quite satisfied by means of a gratuity it would be better than to send them down, as no part of the plan is cordially received here, and under all circumstances it is impossible it can thrive.[5]

As soon as Jervis had shown him John Warden's letter, however, he wrote an urgent note to Chaplin, stating that in view of the large number of volunteers, 'the plan of gratuities would never do, as it would create everlasting distrust', and telling him, 'you must therefore send down your 25 and specify what they expect that it may be scrupulously fulfilled'.[6]

All the volunteers, according to Chaplin, belonged to the neighbourhood of Poona, mostly within fifteen miles of the city. He selected twenty-five and decided that 'to the others who have

[1] M.E., Minute, n.d., ibid. 26.
[2] He means that they were giving in their names to the Principal of the Poona Hindu College as volunteers to go to the Bombay Engineer Institution.
[3] John Warden to [Jervis], 4.8.1825, *Elphinstone*.
[4] Ibid.   [5] M.E. to Chaplin, 5.8.1825, *Elphinstone*.
[6] M.E. to Chaplin, 7.8.1825, *Elphinstone*.

passed a tolerable examination something must be given to re-
munerate them for their trouble & attendance'.[1]

When the young men finally arrived in Bombay Jervis was
disappointed at their appearance: 'The greater part are very *ill-
looking*', he complained.[2] Elphinstone himself no longer had any
enthusiasm for the plan, wrote in unusual irritation of 'these
miserable paupers who have so unexpectedly exposed themselves
to the contamination of Bombay', and declared that he would 'have
been much better pleased if they had stayed away'.[3]

He proposed that Jervis should be told to procure a house and
Brahman servants for them, and be authorized to spend a maximum
of 8 rupees a month on the subsistence of each student. He also
proposed that Rs.200 a month should be allowed as the salary of
a superintendent for them.[4]

This seemed extravagant to both Warden and Goodwin. 'Rupees
392 a month for 24 Natives must prove a very costly system',
remarked Warden. It only went to show, he added, how injudicious
it was for the Government to interfere like this in the promotion
of education.[5] Goodwin for his part declared that the idea of
paying Rs.200 a month to the Superintendent was 'preposterous',
and added that American missionaries had educated 2,000 children
during the past year at a cost of only Rs.3,419.[6]

It was eventually decided, however, to authorize the costs of
subsistence and of the Superintendent's salary as originally proposed.[7]

Fresh evidence was soon forthcoming that the Brahmans of
Poona were not precluded by caste prejudice from coming to
Bombay for Western knowledge.

Warden had meanwhile been finding fresh arguments from the
history of education in Bengal to support his thesis that the resources of the government should be devoted to the teaching of
the English language. His strongest argument was always that
Western knowledge was obtainable only in English books, and that

---

[1] Chaplin to M.E., 9.8.1825, *Elphinstone*; Chaplin to M.E., 10.8.1825, ibid.
He finally decided to give them 'a few days batta'.
[2] Jervis to [M.E.], 7.9.1825, ibid.
[3] M.E., Minute, n.d., Bom. E.C., 31.12.1825, 30.
[4] Ibid. Twenty-four young men had actually arrived.
[5] Warden, Minute, 5.9.1825, ibid. 31.
[6] Goodwin, Minute, 5.9.1825, ibid. 32.
[7] Government to Jervis, 10.9.1825, ibid. 35.

to make translations would waste both time and money. He now learnt from a recently published book by Lushington that students in the highest classes of the Calcutta Sanskrit College had to learn English. He even quoted from Lushington that 'the Raja of Burdwan and two other individuals of consideration each established a school, the former of whom subsequently transferred his school to English superintendence. From the earliest stage one third of the children in attendance at the schools were Brahmins. At first a Brahmin boy would not sit down on the same mat with one of another caste. The teachers also made the same objection, which has of late been voluntarily relinquished.'[1]

From this he argued that the Poona College should be enlarged and rendered 'more extensively beneficial by dissolving the Brahminical prejudices by which it is controlled'. He also suggested that the study of English should be introduced at the Poona College and at the Bohras' College at Surat of which the Collector had spoken highly. With this end in view he formally proposed that the Government should offer to instruct in the English language at Bombay and at the public expense one or more of the most intelligent students at each of these colleges.

The offer was accordingly made.[2] The Bohras' College refused it; but the Poona College accepted, and four of their students quickly volunteered to come to Bombay to learn English. It was accordingly decided to make similar arrangements for their subsistence and accommodation as had been made for the young men from Poona now studying at the Engineer Institution.[3] In short, the Poona College, which Warden so detested as a citadel of Brahmanical orthodoxy and exclusiveness, was soon to be invaded.

The last encounter between Elphinstone and Warden in the field of education was joined in 1826. Early in June the Native

[1] Warden, Minute, 2.10.1825, Bom. E.C. 12.10.1825, 14.
[2] Ibid. 16.
[3] W. A. Jones (Judge of Surat) to Government, 25.9.1826, Bom. E.C. 11.10.1826, 1; Jervis to Government, 15.2.1826, Bom. E.C. 1.3.1826, 1. Of the four who came from Poona three were not satisfied with the terms and conditions laid down for them and returned to Poona. Jervis waited a month in the expectation that three more would be sent from Poona, but none came. He therefore accepted three young Brahmans who had been asking him to admit them. He learnt only after this that three more were coming from Poona. He therefore suggested that all seven should stay, and this was approved (Jervis to Government, 17.5.1826, Bom. E.C. 31.5.1826, 1; Government to Jervis, 25.5.1826, ibid. 2).

School Book and School Society reported that they had succeeded
in training fourteen Brahmans as Marathi schoolteachers. They
suggested that these teachers should be established in 'second
order' schools—schools to be founded between the existing village
schools on the one hand and schools for higher branches of education on the other. The pupils of such second order schools would
become efficient village schoolmasters, teaching according to the
monitorial system which the Society was promoting.[1]

The Society asked the Government to pay each of the fourteen
20 rupees a month and establish them at strategic places under the
Collectors' supervision: four in the Poona district and two each at
Admadnagar, Dharwar, Dhulia, Nasik, and Satara.[2]

This was done.[3] Briggs, however, soon reported from Satara
that the Raja did not want the Society's teachers, and that besides
a palace school there were no less than 43 schools with 505 pupils
'in other parts of this small town'.[4] The two teachers concerned
were therefore sent to Ratnagiri instead.[5]

In spite of this incidental mishap, the provision for the fourteen
teachers had been arranged smoothly enough, perhaps because
Warden was away in the Deccan at about this time.[6] But he was
stung to complain of the Society's report on the progress of the
Bombay English school.

This school, as Elphinstone remarked, had 'evidently made little
progress'.[7] In their report, the Society emphasized their difficulties, but they also declared that 'the moral and intellectual
culture of the native mind is most successfully effected by employing the native language as the medium of communication'. For
them to learn a language wasted time which might otherwise 'be
much more beneficially employed in enlarging and improving
their minds'. Moreover, they added, 'the acquisition also of
English has hitherto invariably tended to render a native negligent
of his own vernacular dialect' and hence less able to spread his

[1] Jervis to Government, 6.6.1826, Bom. E.C. 21.6.1826, 1.
[2] Ibid.
[3] Government to Jervis, 15.6.1826, ibid. 5.
[4] Briggs to Newnham (Secretary to M.E.), 12.7.1826, Bom. E.C. 5.8.1826, 5.
[5] Government to Native School Book and School Society, 29.7.1826, ibid. 8.
[6] Warden signed the Proceedings of 21.6.1826 in which the letter to Jervis
of 15.6.1826 had been recorded. But in the previous Proceedings, viz. of
14.6.1826, it was stated that he was away at Poona. No doubt the matter was
decided before his return.
[7] M.E., Minute, 8.6.1826, Bom. E.C. 14.6.1826, 5.

knowledge among his countrymen. They therefore concluded that 'the teaching of the English language is of secondary importance in effecting the mental and moral improvement of the natives'.[1]

Elphinstone drew the moral that 'the English language and the higher branches of science can only be taught by well-educated Englishmen', and proposed to ask the Court to send out one or more from England. He added that he thought the Society's arguments conclusive against an exclusive reliance upon English schools.[2]

Warden thereupon elaborated at length upon the desirability of pressing forward with the teaching of English, and declared that 'whatever sum of money the Honourable Court may appropriate towards the promotion of education should in my opinion be chiefly applied to the diffusion of the English language'.[3]

The Society had suggested the appointment of Superintendents of schools in Gujarat and the Deccan. Warden objected to this, and repeated his former objection to the distribution of prizes—except at the Bombay English school.[4]

'If the failure of my plans . . . were necessary to the success of Mr. Warden's', Elphinstone at last declared in exasperation, 'I could understand the resistance which he offers to them in every step, but, as I have again and again expressed my perfect readiness to concur in all his proposals, I must be excused if I cannot comprehend the reasons of his unwearied opposition.' And he pointed out with justice that he himself had in fact been the first to propose that English should be taught as the language of science—the only way, he added, in which it could be useful.[5]

The Native School Book and School Society had now completed the training of 10 Gujarati Brahmans—3 for Surat, 3 for Ahmadabad, 2 for Broach, and 2 for Kaira—and they asked the Government to make similar provision for them as for the 14 Marathi teachers.[6] But Warden objected that the Government had no right 'to distribute schoolmasters at the public expense throughout the provinces'. On the contrary, 'their maintenance should depend

---

[1] Jervis to Government, 6.6.1826, ibid. 4.
[2] M.E., Minute, 8.6.1826, ibid. 5.
[3] Warden, Minute, 26.6.1826, Bom. E.C. 5.7.1826, 1.
[4] Warden, Minute, 27.6.1826, ibid. 4.
[5] M.E., Minute, 22.8.1826, Bom. E.C. 6.9.1826, 1.
[6] Jervis to Government, 22.8.1826, Bom. E.C. 6.9.1826, 5.

on their own exertions which', he added, 'will not be very great if Government support them'.[1]

Goodwin, however, maintained that the Government should carry out its original policy, pending the decision of the Court, and he referred to Munro's experience at Madras as indicating the need for some system of government allowances to teachers.[2]

Thus fortified, Elphinstone declared that since the policy had already been decided upon, 'it can be of no use to have a new debate every time it becomes applicable'.[3] It was therefore decided to send the teachers to Gujarat at the public expense and to pay them each Rs.20 a month, 'agreeably to the sense of the majority consisting of the Honourable the Governor and Mr. Goodwin'.[4]

By now Elphinstone had come to the conclusion that it was unlikely that 'any extensive progress' could be made in education while he was Governor. But he wrote a minute to define his aims for the benefit of the Court of Directors who would have to decide between him and Warden.[5]

He explained that his only objection to Warden's plan had been 'its limited nature': he had always been willing to 'graft' it on to his own. There was no objection to Warden's plan. The only question for the Court to decide was, how much of his own could be adopted?[6]

He suggested that besides encouraging the translation and printing of books in the vernaculars, 'the same means of instruction to the lower orders be afforded as at Madras, and the same encouragement held out to the higher branches of learning as in Bengal'. He looked forward to the establishment of 'a superior sort of school, teaching English as well as the languages of the country, at each Collector's station; and a smaller school, for the native languages, in each pergunnah'. In addition he proposed a college for 'the higher branches of the native literature, combined with European sciences'.[7]

As he himself claimed, his plans gave a considerable place to

[1] Warden, Minute, n.d., Bom. E.C. 6.9.1826, 8.
[2] Goodwin, Minute, n.d., ibid. 9. A minute of Munro's on the subject had recently been received (Bom. E.C. 16.8.1826, 5) in which Munro had argued that the Government should pay them a basic minimum, to which they could add whatever they could earn (by fees, &c.).
[3] M.E., Minute, n.d., Bom. E.C. 13.9.1826, 4.
[4] Minutes of Council, ibid.
[5] M.E., Minute, n.d., Bom. E.C. 13.9.1826, 1–2.
[6] Ibid.   [7] Ibid.

English education, even though he always thought that the vernaculars were of more far-reaching importance as means of instruction for 'the lower orders'. He was not content to leave the middle classes to spread Western knowledge of their own accord: he knew that there were schools in some at least of the villages, and he wanted to reach the peasantry through them. In this way he hoped not only to spread a knowledge of reading, writing, and elementary accounting, but also to change their ways of thought and thus their way of life.

This view of education as a panacea for social evils was widely held in all three Presidencies. Looking forward to the abolition of sati 'at some future period', the Governor-General in Council declared in 1824 that 'the more general dissemination of knowledge and the discussion of the question amongst the better informed Hindoos themselves may be expected to have some effect in gradually preparing the minds of the natives for such a measure'.[1]

The prohibition of sati by a direct order of the Government was generally thought to be inexpedient on the ground that it would be an interference with the Hindu religion. It was known, however, that the Shastras contained a number of restrictions upon the practice of sati. The Government of Bengal, where the vast majority of sati ceremonies took place, accordingly instructed their officers to see that these restrictions were observed. This meant that the Magistrate or one of his subordinates had to attend every ceremony and ensure, for example, that no force was used, that the widow was not drugged, or below the age of puberty, or pregnant, and that if she had any infant children some relative would guarantee to provide a suitable maintenance for them.[2]

However, the increase in the number of satis which accompanied a cholera epidemic led the Governor-General in Council to express the fear in 1819 that the official sanction implied in this supervision might be encouraging the practice.[3] They changed their opinion two years later when they noticed that a decrease in the number of satis had accompanied a decline in the cholera epidemic.[4]

---

[1] Resolutions of Governor-General in Council, 3.12.1824, P.P. 1825, xxiv. 150 ff.

[2] Instructions to Magistrates, P.P. 1821, xviii. 32 f., 41 f.

[3] Resolution, 30.7.1819, ibid. 252 f. (sent to the Bombay Government for information).

[4] Resolution [1821], P.P. 1823, xvii. 64–65.

But the home government objected in 1823 to the enactment of a Regulation on the subject for the same reason, that 'a law, which shall explain . . . the cases in which it ought not to be followed may be taken as a direction for adopting it in all others', and that 'in a district where the practice, if ever known', had 'fallen into disuse, any public mention of it whatever would appear impolitic'.[1]

The home government added, as a general principle, that 'neither this plan of discriminating and qualified permission, nor any plan of repression, should be positively and generally prescribed to the magistrates'. On the other hand, they declared that they would approve of all measures for protecting widows against the use of violence or drugs to make them become satis.[2] In short, the home government had no positive and definite policy.

There were comparatively few satis in the territories under the Bombay Government. The practice was almost non-existent in Gujarat. In reply to an inquiry in 1819 the Judge of Kaira reported that there had only been three satis there within living memory; the Magistrate of Surat reported that the last sati there had been in 1814; according to both the Magistrate and the Judge of Broach satis were of very rare occurrence there; in the Ahmadabad zilla a widow had indeed become sati in 1819, but this was a solitary instance.[3] In the Konkan, on the other hand, the practice still prevailed.

When Vicesimus Hale was Resident at Malwan, several applications for his permission were made to him. The general impression among the people seemed to him to be that the Company's Government would not allow it. He therefore took care not to deny this, and merely declared that he could neither give nor withhold his permission as he had had no instructions. He himself thought that this devious policy had had excellent results: 'The state of doubt in which these evasive answers left the minds of the applicants', he wrote in 1819, 'I found had all the effect I could have hoped for, and in a very short time I heard no more of them, the result being that within the boundaries of the late Malwan Residency not a single case of Suttee has occurred, at least not in my time, and I

[1] Judicial dispatch to Bengal, 17.6.1823, P.P. 1824, xxiii. 44 f.
[2] Ibid.
[3] Anderson (Kaira) to Government, 27.9.1819, Bom. J.C. 1.11.1819, 2897–8; Morison (Surat) to Government, 21.9.1819, ibid. 2881–2; Shubrick (Broach) to Government, 25.9.1819, ibid. 2885–6; Barnard (Broach), 29.9.1819, ibid. 2899 f.; Norris (Ahmadabad) to Government, 25.9.1819, ibid. 2895 ff.

believe I am correct when I add neither within the 4 years my predecessor was stationed there.'[1]

More direct measures were taken in the Northern Konkan. When a widow applied to Hockley, a junior civilian, for permission to become sati, he refused to give it. As Babington the Judge described the incident, 'the woman was brought into Bassein in a perfectly frantic state, and was placed under restraint, until her mind should become in some measure tranquillized'. This treatment seems to have been successful, for Babington concluded, with satisfaction, that 'she has at length been restored to coolness and reason, and has quitted Bassein with a strong feeling of gratitude towards Mr. Hockley, whom she regards as her preserver'.[2]

Nepean's first reaction was to approve of Hockley's action.[3] But Prendergast objected that 'the local authorities should be restrained from noticing or at all interfering with the natives in the exercise of any of their religious ceremonies'.[4] After a brisk argument it was decided to ask the Bengal and Madras governments to explain what policies they had adopted towards the practice of sati.[5]

Meanwhile, a widow had actually been burnt at Bassein, and the Judge was asking for instructions.[6] It was decided to tell him not to prohibit the practice until the policy of the Supreme Government was known.[7]

In due course the Supreme Government forwarded copies of their orders to their Magistrates, and the Bombay Government circulated them to the Magistrates under their own authority.[8]

In the same year, 1818, the office of Magistrate was transferred from the Judge to the Collector, and in the Northern Konkan it was henceforth the ponderous but conscientious and determined Marriott who had to deal with the problem. He thought like Hale that there was a general idea among the people that the Company's

[1] Hale to Government, 4.10.1819, ibid. 2900 ff.
[2] Babington to Government, 17.10.1817, P.P. 1821, xviii. 245 f.
[3] Proposed order by Nepean, ibid. 246.
[4] Prendergast, Minute, n.d., ibid. 246.
[5] Bombay Government to Supreme Government, 5.11.1817, ibid. 247 (also to Madras).
[6] Babington to Government, 19.11.1817, ibid. 247.
[7] Minutes, 24.11.1817, ibid. 248.
[8] Minutes, 1.10.1818, ibid. 252. The Madras Government merely stated, in effect, that a direct prohibition of the practice was inexpedient, although they allowed Magistrates to try to persuade widows not to become satis (ibid. 248).

Government would not allow widows to burn themselves. He therefore refrained from publishing the Bengal orders. Nor did he delegate the responsibility of seeing that the restrictions imposed by the Shastras were observed, on the ground 'that if the prohibitory points to the sacrifice were to be determined by Native Police Officers, the practice of that awful rite would shortly multiply manifold', since the knowledge of the Bengal orders would spread and these officers might themselves be bribed. He therefore examined into the circumstances himself.[1]

He claimed success for his policy: 'I now have the happiness of believing that the course which I have adopted has been the means of saving many poor, infatuated, or intoxicated, females from destruction.'[2]

From October 1818, when he received the Bengal orders, until September 1819, he had only two applications for permission to perform the ceremony, but, he added, 'as they were not made' in the prescribed form 'they did not take place'. One sati had indeed been consummated without any application for permission. But he punished the parties most concerned 'for this breach of Police Law'.[3]

Prendergast was quick to object. Marriott, he declared, should be told that the Government did not intend to check or forbid any act done under the authority of the religion of the people. Nor was there any justification for requiring that the Magistrate's permission must first be sought. Therefore, 'the police law' which Marriott had 'taken upon himself to enact' was unwarrantable. For her act to be of merit, the widow must sacrifice herself within a short time of her husband's death; but if Marriott was away it might take too long to apply for his permission.[4]

But Warden was now in the Council, and with his enthusiasm for things Western he strongly supported Marriott's policy. He declared that he was 'convinced of the practicability of abolishing not only this but also every other sanguinary practice of the Hindoos, and without endangering either the popularity or the security of our supremacy'. This was one instance in which he held that the custom of the country should be followed: it had been the

[1] Marriott to Government, 25.9.1819, Bom. J.C. 1.11.1819, 2887 ff.
[2] Ibid.
[3] Ibid.
[4] Prendergast, Minute, 30.9.1819, ibid. 2917 ff.

custom under the former government to apply to it for permission; this procedure should be continued.[1]

Prendergast, however, retorted that to require people to ask for a permission which could not in fact be refused amounted to 'nothing more than a show of impotent opposition, just sufficient to increase the propensity it is so desirable to suppress'.[2]

The recent opinion of the Governor-General in Council, which had been communicated to the Bombay Government, was also to the effect that attempted restrictions might only encourage the practice, and Marriott was accordingly warned of this danger and told that he had acted properly in refraining from publishing the Bengal orders. But against Prendergast's advice he was also told that the custom of asking for official permission should be continued, although the Government would have preferred him to have refrained from punishing those concerned in the sati ceremony which had been performed without his permission. As a general principle he was told to ignore all such cases where there had been no time to obtain his permission.[3]

With the acquisition of the territories newly conquered from the Peshwa in the Southern Konkan the problem became more serious for the Bombay Government. Fifty widows resolved to become satis there in 1819. Of this number, three ceremonies were subsequently 'prevented by the police as contrary to the Shasters', one was similarly prevented by 'a military officer', five widows were 'dissuaded' by relatives and others, and one ceremony was 'delayed and finally abandoned owing to questions being discussed between the parties and the Magistrate personally'.[4] Forty widows perished.

The practice also prevailed to a certain extent in the Deccan. When Elphinstone was Commissioner he therefore had to consider what was the best policy to adopt towards it.

When Marriott wrote privately to him to argue that 'policy does not require the British Government to abstain from preventing this cruel practice', he replied that the risk was too great:[5] 'If we succeed we save 100 or 1000 victims from voluntary immolation.

---

[1] Warden, Minute, 4.10.1819, ibid. 2924 f.
[2] Prendergast, Minute, 8.10.1819, ibid. 2928 ff.
[3] Government to Marriott, 1.11.1819, ibid. 2934 ff.
[4] Judicial letter from Bombay, 16.5.1821, para. 163, Bom. J.L.R. iii. 415.
[5] Marriott to M.E., 31.8.1819, *Elphinstone*. As Marriott was then Collector in the Northern Konkan he was not, of course, under Elphinstone's authority.

If we fail we involve sixty millions in all the horrors of war &
revolution; and by occasioning the down fall of our own Empire,
we shut out every hope of that slow but certain improvement that
is now going on among the natives.' Such calculations, he emphasized, must always be carefully made: 'as perfection is confessedly
unattainable, every Govt. must submit to many evils & it is in
weighing each of them against the greater evils that would result
from its removal that it chiefly shows its wisdom'.[1]

Marriott had also argued that the practice of sati was 'not enjoined by the Hindoo Religion'. To this Elphinstone replied 'that
it is not with the precepts of the written law that we have to do as
politicians, but with the opinions & prejudices of the vulgar; that
those prejudices are not always strongest where the interest of the
individual is affected; & that the operations of fanaticism are as
irregular & uncertain as its effects are tremendous'.[2]

Marriott had also argued that when a widow in the Konkan had
actually been forbidden to become a sati, the incident had passed
off quietly. But Elphinstone replied that 'that interference created
a general & strong sensation throughout all the parts of the Deccan
which I was then visiting. So easy is it for general effects to be
produced without exciting much observation at the spot where
they originate.'[3]

Only a few months after the end of the war Elphinstone had had
to decide how far the policy of the former government could be
followed. In August 1818 Pottinger reported from Admadnagar
that the widow of a Brahman 'of considerable sanctity' had asked
him to allow her to become a sati. 'As she had gone through all the
preliminary ceremonies,' he explained, 'it would have been a
heavy breach of Braminical law, as well as of an acknowledged
custom, to have prevented the woman following the bent of her
inclinations.' He therefore 'tacitly consented', but he 'positively
refused' to help pay for any special clothes for her to wear or for
any wood for the pyre, or to give any official sanction to the ceremony by attending either in person or by proxy.[4] Elphinstone fully
approved: 'I cannot sanction the slightest interposition of authority
in a case so closely connected with the religious prejudices of the
Hindoos.'[5]

---

[1] M.E. to Marriott, 9.9.1819, *Elphinstone*.   [2] Ibid.   [3] Ibid.
[4] Pottinger to M.E., 10.8.1818, Bg. P.C. 3.10.1818, 12.
[5] M.E. to Pottinger, 18.8.1818, ibid. 13.

From what he had heard from 'several very respectable Brahmins', Pottinger was 'almost satisfied' that the practice could easily be stopped altogether. He understood that Baji Rao had often dissuaded widows from becoming satis and paid for their support thereafter. Pottinger therefore asked Elphinstone to allow him to do likewise.[1] Elphinstone consented: Pottinger could use Brahmans to dissuade widows from becoming satis, and grant subsistence allowances to all widows who were in fact dissuaded.[2] The Supreme Government also approved of this policy.[3]

Several widows in the Deccan were dissuaded in this way. Briggs gave 7 rupees a month to the widow of one of his officials (Karkuns) and a reward of Rs.50 to the Brahman who persuaded her not to become a sati.[4] H. D. Robertson the Collector of Poona even granted to one widow her travelling expenses to Benares on condition that she renounced her intention of becoming a sati.[5]

But satis were few in the Deccan, and the policy of pensions and rewards was clearly open to abuse. Soon after the Deccan had come under the authority of the Bombay Government it was decided to abandon the policy on the ground that it might 'lead persons to pretend a resolution to sacrifice in the hope of being thus paid for desisting'. It was also decided to tell Chaplin that satis were in general so rare in the territories under the authority of the Bombay Government that 'we are of opinion that the less we interfere in the practice the better'.[6] The Southern Konkan was in fact the one exception.

In the Southern Konkan, moreover, widows might become satis in circumstances which in Bengal would have precluded them from doing so. In Bengal a widow could only be burnt in company with her husband's corpse. If she had any infant children it was necessary for someone to guarantee them a suitable maintenance before she could be allowed to burn. But in 1822 the widow of a Brahman who had died at Poona was burnt at Ratnagiri in company with his bones but not his corpse, while the only guarantee to provide for her two children had been given by an old lady of

[1] Pottinger to M.E., 10.8.1818, ibid. 12.
[2] M.E. to Pottinger, 18.8.1818, ibid. 13.
[3] Supreme Government to M.E., 3.10.1818, ibid. 14.
[4] Briggs to Chaplin, 20.11.1819, Bom. J.C. 15.12.1819, 3631 ff.
[5] H. D. Robertson to M.E., 28.5.1819, Bg. P.C. 10.7.1819, 23.
[6] Minute, 18.11.1819, Bom. J.C. 24.11.1819, 3268 f.

eighty. The Sarkamavisdar had forbidden the ceremony and referred the matter to Sparrow the Collector. Sparrow himself
thought that in the circumstances it was contrary to the Bengal
circular orders that the widow should have been burnt, but he
refrained from punishing any of those concerned and asked for the
Government's instructions, on the ground that 'in order to reduce
the frequency of this horrid rite it should be neglected and treated
with as little notice as possible'.[1]

The Governor in Council decided that Sparrow had shown
'great prudence and judgement'. The Sarkamavisdar had done his
duty in prohibiting the ceremony. But punishing those who had
disobeyed his order 'might excite a spirit of discontent, if not of
opposition'. It was therefore decided that 'no further notice be
taken of this transaction'.[2]

This 'defeat' led the Governor in Council to 'doubt the policy of
the circular orders'. The subjection of the Hindus of Bengal to a
Muslim government might have made them more 'submissive' in
such matters than the Marathas. It was generally known to be a
custom of Maharashtra that a widow might be burnt in company
with the bones, or even merely the turban or the dagger of her dead
husband. As Elphinstone had written to Marriott in 1819 it was to
custom rather than to the Shastras that the Government should
turn. Such practices might well be 'contrary to the Shaster, but
the Shaster is entitled to no attention except as it is the object of
popular veneration, and if the attachment of the people is in this
instance transferred from the written law to their own customs',
the Government must take account of the latter.[3]

Education would no doubt solve these problems. 'At no very
distant period the worst of these delusions will vanish . . . before
the general diffusion of knowledge . . . attempting to lop off one
branch of their superstition we run the risk of interrupting . . .
those causes which are already consuming it at the root.'[4]

The authorities in the Konkan were therefore told to consider the
orders as having been suspended, except that care must still be
taken to see that no widow was drugged or forced to burn and that
suitable provision had been made as hitherto for all infant children.[5]

[1] Sparrow to Government, 24.2.1822, B.C. 920/25883, 11 ff.
[2] Resolution, ibid. 23 ff.   [3] Ibid.   [4] Ibid.
[5] Government to Magistrate, Southern Konkan, 14.3.1822, repeated to Judge,
Southern Konkan, and to Magistrate and Judge, Northern Konkan, ibid. 27 ff.

But even if it was possible for the Magistrate to ensure that no force was used to compel a widow to mount the funeral pyre, there remained the fact that she would probably be prevented from leaving it once it had begun to burn. In September 1823 the *Bombay Courier* published a letter signed by 'a decided enemy to suttees' which described a recent ceremony at Poona when the widow escaped from the pyre once and returned of her own accord, escaped again and was forced back into the flames by bystanders, escaped a third time and was rescued by some Englishmen and sent to hospital. She died there in agony on the following day from the burns which she had received.[1]

Goodwin brought the matter up in Council, and suggested that under the principles laid down by the Supreme Government those concerned should be punished.[2] Elphinstone therefore proposed that the Bengal orders should be sent to Chaplin for him to publish or refer to the pandits of Poona at his discretion.[3]

But Robertson's report of the ceremony then arrived. It appeared that by some mistake the Indian official who should have attended the ceremony had not in fact gone to it. Robertson nevertheless thought that those who had taken the leading part should be brought to trial, and Chaplin agreed. A petition for their release without trial had indeed been presented to Robertson. It was signed by 'the greatest shastrees'. But the Government decided that the trial should go forward and directed that 'the petitioners be informed that as the prisoners are to be tried by the laws and customs of their own country and religion, there seems to be no occasion for suspending the proceedings'. Chaplin had already been told 'in trying the prisoners to give due weight to the universal opinion and admitted practice of the Hindoos as well as to their written laws'.[4]

Two of the three accused were therefore released after conviction and the third was acquitted, but it was at the same time

The Home Government agreed that Sparrow had shown 'great prudence and judgement' (Judicial dispatch to Bombay, 12.12.1827, para. 3, Bom. J.D. i. 544 f.).

[1] *Bombay Courier*, 29.9.1823, reproduced with Goodwin, Minute, 6.10.1823, Bom. J.C. 5.11.1823, 4559 f.

[2] Goodwin, Minute, 6.10.1823, Bom. J.C. 5.11.1823, 4559 f.

[3] M.E., Minute, n.d., ibid. 4564.

[4] Robertson to Chaplin, 9.10.1823, ibid., 4566 ff.; Chaplin to Government, 11.10.1823, ibid. 4565 f.; Robertson to Chaplin, 25.10.1823, ibid. 4771 ff.; Chaplin to Government, 25.10.1823, ibid. 4769 f.; Government to Chaplin, 5.11.1823, ibid. 4775 f.; Government to Chaplin, 30.10.1823, ibid. 4653 ff.

solemnly proclaimed that henceforth persons found guilty of similar acts would be liable to punishment as murderers.[1]

Meanwhile, Robertson with his accustomed fondness for Brahmanical disputation had taken the opportunity to begin discussions with the leading shastris of Poona about the proper conduct of sati ceremonies. They were unable to justify the use of force. Arguing from the generally accepted premiss that to have any spiritual merit a widow's self-sacrifice must be voluntary, he wanted to persuade them to stipulate that the pyre must be so constructed as to allow the widow to escape even after it had been set alight. On the last occasion the widow had indeed been able to do so, but it was usually impossible.[2]

He assumed that few if any women would have confidence in their own courage either to endure the disgrace of having escaped from the pyre or to withstand the pain of being burnt to death if they could in fact escape at any time after they had felt the flames. He therefore concluded that if it became generally known that pyres would henceforth be constructed so as to allow a widow to escape whenever the pain became too great, few or none would decide to become satis. In such circumstances the practice would in effect be abolished.[3]

He felt that such an opportunity might not occur again in half a century, and arranged for a final conference on the subject to be held at the time of the Dakshina, in December, when Brahmans from every quarter of Maharashtra would have come to Poona.[4]

The Government's reaction was shrewd. They told Chaplin that they had no doubt that Robertson would realize how important it would be 'to attend more to the feelings of the people than to the degree of solidity belonging to the arguments by which their erroneous notions may be supported and that much care' was 'necessary to avoid any discussion likely to give to the question the character of a doctrinal dispute, which could not fail to excite a strong spirit of opposition in the breast of the weaker party.'[5]

Those present at the conference in December included a number of eminent Brahmans—Mulhar Shroti, whom Robertson

[1] Proceedings of trial, Bom. J.C. 17.12.1823, 4972 ff.
[2] Robertson to Chaplin, 9.10.1823, Bom. J.C. 5.11.1823, 4566 ff.
[3] Ibid.
[4] Ibid.
[5] Government to Chaplin, 11.12.1823, Bom. J.C. 17.12.1823, 4993 f.

called 'the most highly respected Brahmin in the country'; Nila-kantha Shastri and Vithal Upadhyaya of Pandharpur, 'esteemed the most able men, and the most deeply versed in the learning of the shasters in the whole of the Deccan'; Raghu Acharya, 'an eminent scholar', then Principal of the Poona Hindu College, and many more. Robertson estimated the total number present to be 'at least' five hundred.[1]

He himself took an active part in the discussions. Mulhar Shroti defended the existing custom not by reference to the Shastras but on the ground of expediency. Robertson's main argument in reply was to emphasize the principle that the sacrifice must be voluntary. He was strongly supported by Vithal Upadhyaya, who gave a de-tailed description of the way in which a pyre ought to be built in order to conform to the Shastras and enable the widow to escape if at any time she wished to do so.[2]

Vithal Upadhyaya's description was 'unanimously pronounced to be excellent', and Robertson thereupon 'declared that piles upon that model would for the future be the only ones allowed in this district'.[3]

It was also agreed at the conference that when a widow declared that she wished to become a sati, the pile should be 'minutely described to her, and her relations ordered to give her no com-bustible materials'. If she remained determined she was to be told that if she failed to endure it to the last she would be 'consigned to the outskirts of the town and to the society of Chandals (Derhs)'.[4]

Chaplin himself thought that the rules would prove a powerful deterrent, and he reported to the Government that he had 'taken some pains' to find out if the Brahmans' agreement had been 'en-tirely sincere, free and unconstrained'. He was satisfied that it had been, and he hoped that the rules would be extended elsewhere.[5]

The Government agreed that the rules were likely to have a deterrent effect and told him to send particulars of Robertson's

[1] Robertson to Chaplin [10] December 1823, Bom. J.C. 4.2.1824, 750 ff.
[2] Ibid. As reported by Robertson: 'The foundation of the pile on which the corpse rests to be as high or as low as the friends or widows chuse to make it. Resting upon this foundation four sticks to be firmly erected at the four corners; and on these cross pieces of wood placed so as to support a roof of sticks; the sides to be composed of grass, and the height of this room to be such as the widow can easily walk in; at one end a door or entrance which is not to be shut up; and the four supports not to be removed by the bystanders.'
[3] Ibid.   [4] Ibid.
[5] Chaplin to Government, 15.12.1823, Bom. J.C. 4.2.1824, 750 ff.

proceedings to the other Collectors, 'that they may adopt a similar rule or not according to the receipt which the opinions of the Poona Shastrees may meet with among those of their districts.' He was to emphasize to them that the rules were only to be introduced if 'voluntarily and cordially agreed to by the Shastrees of most authority among the people under their jurisdiction'.[1]

But the Government also suggested that the penalty prescribed for widows who escaped the pyre was too severe: it seemed more likely to encourage than to deter them once they had begun the ceremony.[2]

Robertson, however, replied that although the penances prescribed by the Shastras were comparatively light, the Brahmans at the conference, 'well knowing that very few women' would 'venture to burn in the new pile without immediately coming out of it again', wanted to prescribe the more serious penalty of outcasting, 'thereby diminishing the chances of families losing their character by the escape of victims'.[3]

Robertson took this opportunity to claim that in the couple of months since the rules had been promulgated, six widows who had decided to become satis had abandoned the idea when they realized the implications of these rules.[4]

In view of these considerations, the Government sent particulars of Robertson's proceedings to the Collectors of the Northern and Southern Konkan and authorized them to adopt similar rules if the local Shastris freely accepted them.[5]

Some months later, however, the *Bombay Courier* published a letter from Suvarndurg describing a sati ceremony in a nearby village which showed on the one hand that the new rules were not being obeyed in the Southern Konkan, and on the other hand that the Government's permission might popularly be interpreted as approval.[6]

The writer declared that when he argued against the ceremony with bystanders they replied by referring to the Government's

[1] Government to Chaplin, 30.1.1824, Bom. J.C. 4.2.1824, 770 ff.

[2] Ibid.

[3] Robertson to Chaplin, 1.3.1824, Bom. J.C. 12.5.1824, 2287 ff.

[4] Ibid. In view of the paucity of satis in the Poona Collectorate hitherto it is possible that Robertson's informants were telling him what they thought he would like to hear.

[5] Government to Collectors, Northern and Southern Konkan, 8.5.1824, ibid. 2318 f.

[6] *Bombay Courier*, 16.10.1824, P.P. 1825, xxiv, 211 ff.

permission. '"Sircar Ka Hookum"[1] seemed to form a triumphant answer to all my arguments'. Moreover the pile had been so constructed that the widow could never have escaped: there was a wooden roof about 2 feet thick above her, one end resting on the pile itself, the other end raised about 2 feet by being 'slightly tied' to two posts; large quantities of dried grass were heaped around the posts; when a light was applied, the dried grass 'instantly' led the fire to the rope supporting the roof, which thereupon fell on to the widow and effectively prevented her escape.[2]

The rules had been formally established in the Southern Konkan, and the Government therefore told Dunlop the Collector that 'as far as the rule in question can be rendered effectual to the prevention of suttees that natives should strictly adhere to it'.[3]

The rules were not promulgated in the Northern Konkan in view of the absence of satis there. It was thought expedient not to recall men's minds to the practice in areas where it did not exist.[4]

The grant of pensions to widows who retracted their original intention to become satis had been abandoned in 1819. But Robertson was a man of ingenuity. On one occasion a Mamlatdar persuaded a widow not to become a sati. The widow had no means of subsistence, but a relative promised to maintain her. Robertson thereupon told the Mamlatdar to tell the widow's relative that 'I shall have much pleasure in giving him an office suitable to his abilities from the enjoyment of which he will not be liable to repent of this humanity to his female relative.'[5] The Government approved of this attempt to show that humanitarianism was the best policy.[6]

At this time, in January 1825, Robertson was full of confidence in the success of the new rules: 'the Brahmins of the city seem reconciled to the belief that the custom will no longer be preserved unless some outrageous zealot of affection and religion ventures and actually endures the torture before the memory fades away.

[1] Sircar ka Hookum = Government's order.
[2] Ibid.
[3] Government to Dunlop, 20.10.1824, ibid. 210 f. There had been no opposition to the adoption of the rules, according to Dunlop, as reported in Farish to M.E., 16.10.1824, *Elphinstone*.
[4] Government to Mills (Acting Collector and Magistrate, Northern Konkan), 28.2.1825, Bom. J.C. 23.3.1825, 62. The same presumably applied to the Gujarat Collectorates.
[5] Robertson to Chaplin, 5.1.1825, Bom. J.C. 9.2.1825, 52.
[6] Government to Chaplin, 8.2.1825, ibid. 53.

I am inclined to think with the Brahmins that there will never be another suttee in the town of Poona.'[1]

In the Southern Konkan, however, it was soon apparent that the rules had not always prevented a widow from burning even when they were strictly observed—as at one ceremony at Ratnagiri which was witnessed by the Europeans, so the Assistant Magistrate reported in February 1825.[2]

In June 1825 two widows were burnt in Poona within a week or so of each other. This made Chaplin doubt the efficiency of the new rules as a deterrent.[3]

He too fell back upon education as the sovereign remedy—'a long and gradual process of improvement in knowledge, which can alone subvert such superstitious ceremonies'.[4]

He now deprecated all interference beyond ascertaining that the sacrifice was voluntary—'that point decided, the pile cannot in my opinion be too combustible'. Apart from that he objected to official interference on grounds both of humanity and expediency. On the one hand, he questioned 'our right to harrass the afflicted widow by long, frequent and pernicious visitations' in an attempt to dissuade her from her intention. On the other hand, he suggested that the rules might even encourage the practice: 'the natural instinct of self-preservation will be a sufficient tie to prevent suttees ever becoming very fashionable, unless we make them so by interfering and by adding to the merit of the sacrifice by increasing and multiplying the torments of it'.[5]

Besides these two unlooked for satis at Poona in June 1825, another was reported from Surat in the same month—the first there since 1814. These events led to fresh discussions in Council.[6]

Warden suggested that the Magistrate of Surat should be asked about the expediency of prohibiting satis there as such a long time had elapsed without any until this solitary one in June 1825.[7] Elphinstone objected on the ground that while a prohibition would have hardly any practical effect at Surat where satis were so

[1] Robertson to Chaplin, 5.1.1825, ibid. 52.
[2] D. A. Blane (Assistant Magistrate) to Government, 10.2.1825, Bom. J.C. 2.3.1825, 3.
[3] Chaplin to Government, 15.6.1825, Bom. J.C. 3.8.1825, 37.
[4] Chaplin to Government, 17.6.1825, Bom. J.C. 6.7.1825, 28.
[5] Ibid.
[6] G. W. Anderson (Judge of Surat) to Government, 18.6.1825, Bom. J.C. 6.7.1825, 7.
[7] Warden, Minute, n.d., ibid. 9.

rare, the news of it might attract undesirable attention else-where.[1]

Elphinstone also thought that the new rules had not had 'a fair trial'. Robertson's zeal had been too apparent. 'When our principal authority in the district appears himself and shows a strong per-sonal interest in obstructing an act so contrary to his religious notions the intended sufferer derives a fresh excitement and an additional influence from the circumstance and obtains the honour not only of fidelity to her husband but of martyrdom for her religion.' He therefore turned to what he called 'the established maxim that fanaticism can only be successfully combated by neglect and indifference'. He accordingly proposed that 'Captain Robertson should be told that although the Governor in Council highly appreciates his anxiety to suppress the practice of self-immolation he is of opinion that his measures would be attended with more success if they were less apparent, that the Governor in Council has still great confidence in the effects of enforcing an adherence to the legal pile, provided it be left to its undisturbed operation'.[2]

Warden, on the other hand, again suggested that the practice of sati should be prohibited. 'Any intermediate measure between a positive prohibition and perfect neglect and indifference appear to me to be most impolitic.' In his view, 'all the sanguinary practices of the Hindoos might be prohibited without affecting either the security or popularity of our supremacy'. Alternatively, as effective deterrents he mentioned possible measures like the resumption of jagirs and pensions on the occurrence of a sati in the holder's family, or the imposition of a heavy tax upon sati pyres, graded according to the family's wealth, the proceeds being devoted to some charitable purpose such as the maintenance of a fund for the support of widows who had been dissuaded from becoming satis.[3]

Elphinstone of course objected to all such drastic measures:

I think we should see that the sacrifice is voluntary and that the woman is of full age and in possession of her faculties. I think also that we should take advantage of the Hindoo law which forbids the sacrifice in cases of pregnancy or of infants dependent on the mother. Whether we should have interfered with the construction of the pile is a question, but we have done it, and to retract would now create more sensation than to go

[1] M.E., Minute, n.d., ibid. 10.   [2] M.E., Minute, n.d., ibid. 29.
[3] Warden, Minute, 24.6.1825, ibid. 30.

on while it would lose the chance of success which I think we still have
by persevering—further I would not go.[1]

Elphinstone, however, suggested that the grant of pensions to
widows who retracted might again be authorized.[2] But Warden
now objected on the ground that the Government might be defrauded—the reason why it had been decided in 1819 that such
pensions should no longer be granted.[3] At Elphinstone's suggestion
the matter was referred to the Governor-General in Council, who
advised against it. The idea was therefore abandoned.[4]

The only positive result of these discussions seems to have been
a warning to Chaplin that Robertson should be more cautious.
This was based upon Elphinstone's minute on the subject.[5]

Doubtful cases had always to be referred to the Shastris. In
accordance with Elphinstone's reluctance to interfere in any
matter affecting the Hindu religion, the Government refrained
from deciding upon such matters. Dunlop, as Magistrate of Ahmadnagar, reported in 1826 that a Brahman lady of Nasik had applied
to him for permission to become a sati on the ground that she had
not seen her husband for twenty-five years and he must therefore
be presumed to be dead. Dunlop asked for advice, but he was told
that 'you must regulate your proceedings by the opinion of the
Shasterees with respect to the legality of the proposed act'. Rational
consideration would be out of place. 'These sacrifices being entirely contrary to natural reason, the rules regarding them must be
sought for in the superstition that renders it necessary to tolerate
them.'[6]

The Regulation Code of 1827 enshrined the indefinite attitude of
the Government towards the practice of sati in contrast to their
strict prohibition of the murder of supposed witches: 'The belief
that sorcery was practised by the deceased shall not be admitted as
a justifiable cause for putting him or her to death, nor shall the
deceased's own request be so admitted; but assisting at any rites of

---

[1] M.E., Minute, n.d., Goodwin subscribing, ibid. 31.
[2] M.E., Minute, n.d., Bom. J.C. 3.8.1825, 37A.
[3] Warden, Minute, n.d., ibid. 40.
[4] M.E., Minute, n.d., and Bombay Government to Supreme Government,
2.8.1825, ibid. 41–41A; Supreme Government to Bombay Government,
1.9.1825, and Minutes of Council, 2.10.1825, Bom. J.C. 5.10.1825, 14 f.
[5] Government to Chaplin, 4.7.1825, Bom. J.C. 6.7.1825, 32.
[6] Dunlop to Newnham (Secretary to M.E.), 29.6.1826; Newnham to Dunlop,
7.7.1826; Bom. J.C. 19.7.1826, 38.

self-immolation, as directed by the religious law of the person performing such immolation, shall not subject any one to the penalty of murder.'[1]

Expediency was the reason for this difference in policy. The Government were prepared to prohibit the killing of witches but not the burning of widows for the reason that all governments appreciate—the fear of revolt in the latter case but not in the former. Both practices were regarded as 'superstitions'. Both offended against Western notions of right and wrong. But only a few citizens indulged in the killing of witches, while it was thought that the majority accepted the suicide of widows as a religious duty of high spiritual merit and might well rise in revolt against a government that tried to prohibit it. It was therefore thought that although the killing of witches might be prohibited by a Regulation, the burning of widows could be ended only by the spread of education—the great solvent, it was hoped, of all 'superstition'.

TABLE 6

Satis[2]

Collectorate	1821	1822	1823	1824	1825	1826	1827	Total
Northern Konkan	..	..	..	1	1	1	..	3
Southern Konkan	50	47	38	27	32	28	27	249
Surat .	..	..	..	..	1	..	..	1
Broach	..	..	..	..	..	..	..	0
Kaira .	..	..	..	..	1	..	..	1
Ahmadabad	..	..	..	..	..	..	..	0
Khandesh .	..	..	..	1	1	2	6	10
Poona	..	..	1	..	6	3	2	12
Ahmadnagar	..	..	..	..	..	..	1	1
Dharwar .	..	..	..	8	4	1	4	17

[1] Bom. Reg. XIV, 1827, sec. xxvi, cl. 2.
[2] *Elphinstone.* Also P.P. 1830, xxviii (178), 264, 269.

PART THREE

11

EPILOGUE: THE FATE OF ELPHIN-STONE'S POLICIES UNDER MALCOLM

(1827–30)

In 1827 Sir John Malcolm succeeded Elphinstone as Governor of Bombay. In their personalities the two men were very different. Elphinstone was of an intellectual disposition, shy and reserved in manner, and aristocratic in breeding; Malcolm was more extroverted, bluff and hearty in manner and of humbler origins. But their Indian experience had been similar: they were both essentially of the 'political line'; they knew more of Indian ways of life and sympathized with them more than did the average civil servant of the Company's settled provinces. Malcolm himself heartily approved of Elphinstone's policies: 'the only difference between Mountstuart and me is that I have mulligatawny at tiffin, which comes of my experiences at Madras'.[1] But he realized that there were strong tides moving in the opposite direction. 'I fear', he wrote in 1828, 'my views of governing this country are too opposed to the pride of conquerors & the general plans of cold calculators to be much approved.'[2] He did not think of himself as a great reformer: 'I am not a new era man', he wrote towards the end of his Governorship, 'though the fact may be I am getting old and too much alarmed at what others deem trifles.'[3] He was concerned rather to preserve Elphinstone's major policies.

He was soon at odds with Elphinstone's chief opponent, Francis Warden. However, Warden and also Goodwin left Council in 1828. But Malcolm was little pleased with their successors, James Sparrow and John Romer. Romer had been a Judge, and Malcolm thought that he had the typical Judge's excessive respect

---

[1] Quoted in Kaye, *Malcolm*, ii. 498.
[2] Malcolm to H. Wood, 21.9.1828, *H.M.* 734, 517 f.
[3] Malcolm to Sir S. Beckwith, 21.1.1830, ibid., 794 f.

for rules and regulations and forms of procedure. Sparrow was too often ill, but even when he was fit he generally followed Romer's lead.

When Elphinstone left Bombay some of the leading Indian citizens like Jamshetji Jijibhai and Framji Kawasji formed themselves into a committee with the aim of raising funds to endow in his memory Professorships under the Native Education Society. They explained to the Society in December 1827 that they hoped to secure at least three Professors from England to teach the English language and also 'the arts, sciences and literature of Europe'. At the same time they were careful to emphasize that they had no intention of superseding the vernaculars by English in the education of the people but only of teaching English as a classical language to the few who would in turn diffuse European arts and sciences by translations.[1]

Nevertheless, Warden was soon asserting that the scheme only confirmed him in his opinion of 'the policy of directing our chief effort to one object, to a diffusion of a knowledge of the English language as best calculated to facilitate the intellectual and moral improvement of India'.[2]

Defiantly trailing his coat before Malcolm he added, 'I subscribe entirely to the opinion expressed by the author of the Political History of India, that it is better and safer to commence by giving a good deal of knowledge to a few than a little to many, to be satisfied with laying the foundation stone of a good edifice, and not desire to accomplish in a day what must be the work of a century.'[3]

This was an obvious reference to Malcolm's recently published *Political History of India* in which he had quoted from a letter of his own to Marshman, the celebrated Baptist missionary, expressing the hope that future missionaries would follow the example of Serampore and proceed slowly and cautiously in their educational work, considering it 'safer to commence by giving a good deal of knowledge to a few than a little to many'.[4]

Warden concluded his provocative minute with an attack upon the Engineer Institution, which taught in the vernaculars, as an unnecessary extravagance.

[1] Mahoodas Runchodas, Jamsetjee Jeejeebhoy, and others to Secretary, Native Education Society, 1.12.1827, Bom. G.C. 27.2.1828, 18.
[2] Warden, Minute, 24.3.1828, Bom. G.C. 28.4.1828, 49.
[3] Ibid.
[4] Malcolm, *Political History of India*, ii (1826), 291.

Malcolm replied by emphasizing the need to train Indians to take a larger part in the work of government. It was 'essential' to do this 'on grounds of economy, of improvement and of security'. In particular, the Engineer Institution had already trained some competent Indian survey officials, and was thereby providing a path for Indians 'to rise to respectable employment'. The majority of its students, Malcolm was pleased to see, were Brahmans—the class who had suffered most from the establishment of British rule. This alone was a reason for fostering the Engineer Institution. 'I prize every opportunity, however slight, that presents itself of conciliating this class.' The study of mathematics and science, moreover, seemed to Malcolm particularly likely to wean the Brahmans from their 'habits of intrigue' and 'superstitious prejudices' and 'to instill insensibly the love of truth into their minds'.[1]

Meanwhile, the fund for the Elphinstone Professorships continued to grow, and with the help of a grant from the Bombay Government the Elphinstone College was eventually founded and Professors were sent from England.[2] This was the only education which Warden could fully support—English teachers teaching 'Western knowledge' in the English language. His antipathy to Indian learning was revealed even more clearly in a brisk clash which he had with Malcolm over the Poona Hindu College.

In February 1828 the Principal asked if he could give honorary dresses and from six to twelve months' pay to students who were leaving. He cited the example of the Engineer Institution as a precedent: there those who passed their examinations were given certificates and the top three or four were also given prizes of between Rs.30 and Rs.100.[3] Malcolm accordingly proposed that the Principal should be told to give certificates to students who passed their examinations and 'rewards of a small amount to a few of the most deserving'.[4]

Warden strongly objected: 'I cannot consent to entrust the distribution of rewards to a Native.' Moreover the 'final orders' of the Court of Directors would soon arrive and decide the issue between

[1] Malcolm, Minute, n.d., Bom. G.C. 28.4.1828,50.
[2] It was decided to appoint two Professors. Their subjects of instruction were to embrace mathematics and natural science—including mechanics, &c. (Malcolm, Minute, n.d., Bom. G.C. 3.11.1830, 43).
[3] Deputy Agent for Sardars to Government, 29.2.1828; Native Education Society to Government, B.C. 1173/30649, 223 ff.
[4] Malcolm, Minute, n.d., ibid. 228–9.

Elphinstone and himself. Until then, they should 'abstain from entangling ourselves with pledges and plans, which may be soon superseded'.[1]

But Malcolm replied by appealing to political expediency: The Poona Hindu College had been 'established to conciliate the Natives by liberality and by conferring distinction on learned Hindus. It may perhaps be deemed more a charitable than a useful institution, but if it tends to the popularity and good name of Government, it is politic to support it.'[2] His other colleagues agreed with him, and it was therefore decided to tell the Principal to grant certificates and small prizes as Malcolm had originally proposed.[3]

Warden seems in fact to have been confidently expecting that the home government's decision upon his controversy with Elphinstone would be in his own favour. He was mistaken. The Court of Directors eventually declared in 1829 that 'we on the whole concur in the more comprehensive, and we think, sounder views of your late Governor', and pointed out that 'his plans . . . as he has himself observed, are not inconsistent with those of Mr. Warden, but go beyond them'.[4] This indeed was what Elphinstone had claimed. But the difference between their plans was not merely that Elphinstone's were more 'comprehensive' than Warden's: the plans of each were based upon different attitudes to Indian life and thought which were reflected in their other controversies. In Malcolm's language, Warden was a 'new era man', eager for root and branch reforms. Wherever Indian customs offended against his Western view of life he was determined to change them as quickly and effectively as possible. Unlike Elphinstone, who had spent so many years in Indian states, Warden had spent his whole career at Bombay, thus seeing Indian ways reflected always against a distorting mirror of Western prejudice.

On the other hand, viewing their respective proposals simply as possible measures that a government could undertake, and without searching into the assumptions behind them, it was possible for the Court of Directors to accept Elphinstone's diplomatic attempt to soften the sharpness of the controversy as an accurate statement of fact.

[1] Warden, Minute, n.d., ibid. 229.   [2] Malcolm, Minute, n.d., ibid. 230.
[3] Government to Agent for Sardars, 30.4.1828, ibid. 231–2.
[4] Public dispatch to Bombay, 18.2.1829, para. 10, B.C. 1172/30648, 157 ff.

The Court blandly continued, 'Because an attempt is made to communicate to the natives the elements of useful knowledge in their own languages, it by no means follows that to those who desire them facilities may not be afforded for learning English. But such knowledge as suffices for the common purposes of life may, without doubt, be more easily taught to the natives in their own than in a foreign language.'[1]

On the other hand, the Court objected to Sutherland's suggestion that Indian revenue officials needed a special course of training. As Chaplin had pointed out, they could pick up the technical details of their work in the field. Moreover, in strong Benthamite accents the Court declared that they had 'less confidence in the efficiency of any moral tuition which can be imparted to the natives in a public school, than in the skilful employment of those means of rewarding good and encouraging bad conduct which every government has at its disposal'.[2]

The Court had, however, sanctioned Elphinstone's main proposals, and Malcolm could now proceed to carry them into effect.

The existing village schools were to be regarded as the basis— 'since', so the Collectors were told, 'it is only by exciting locally a thirst for knowledge that the objects of government can be fully accomplished'. Moreover, the Government's policy was 'to be introduced upon principles of strict economy'.[3] These village schools were to be improved. The village schoolmaster was to be paid 5 rupees a month if he had more than thirty pupils, 3 rupees a month if he had less. This was to be charged to village expenses, 'with the view of identifying the school with the village constitution, and thus raising it in the estimation of the community'.[4]

The Native Education Society were producing good teachers, but only a limited number of these would be needed. They should be stationed at the 'Provincial capitals' from which they could make tours twice a year to the smaller towns and villages, advising, reporting on the qualifications of village schoolmasters and the progress of their pupils, and distributing books. Malcolm was particularly anxious to have trained teachers installed in 'the principal towns' because he wanted the new education to be 'brought

---

[1] Public dispatch to Bombay, 18.2.1829, para. 10, B.C. 1172/30648, 157 ff.
[2] Ibid.
[3] Circular, 21.12.1829, Bom. G.C. 31.12.1829, 52, based upon Malcolm, Minute, n.d., ibid. 48.   [4] Ibid.

nearer to natives of rank and consideration in our provinces' and felt sure that 'none of any rank could be tempted' to go to Bombay for his education.

However well educated the pupils of the Engineer Institution might be, he thought gloomily that they were unlikely to be suitable for revenue appointments on the ground that they would 'probably not be found such as from birth, influence or local reputation it may be expedient to select for employment'. He recommended the abolition of the present Engineer Institution and its replacement by a Government Institution with the same establishment but a different purpose. Henceforth students would have neither stipends nor any guarantee of government service. The Institution would be thrown open to all, not merely those in government service. Finally, its course of instruction would still be given without charge. The only amendment proposed by the Court of Directors was to limit the privilege of free tuition to those who distinguished themselves by their attainments or by their conduct.[1]

Malcolm was convinced of 'the inexpediency as well as the impracticability of conveying general instruction to our native subjects in India through the medium of the English language'. On the other hand, there was a place for English schools: indeed, he thought that there should be more of them. The pay of English language clerks seemed to him 'immoderately high', and 'the real mode to decrease price' was in his view 'to multiply the article'. So he looked forward to the foundation of more English schools.[2]

He hoped that the village schools, too, would provide recruits for government service. In large towns the best pupils could be appointed to the Collector's Office when they left school, to act as copyists on 'a few rupees per mensem', with the prospect of attaining the post of Karkun. In villages and small towns the best pupils could be appointed to the local district Cutcherry. Specially gifted pupils might even be sent to Bombay to study at the Government Institution or in one of the Native Education Society's schools.[3] In his mind, it was only right and proper that government service should be the goal of every intelligent and ambitious boy.

Elphinstone, on the other hand, had disclaimed any intention of training clerks for government offices. His view had been that

[1] General dispatch to Bombay, 29.12.1830, Bom. G.D. ix.
[2] Malcolm, Minute, n.d., Bom. G.C. 31.12.1829, 48.
[3] Ibid.

the education of the peasant should make him better able to deal with the problems of his life as a peasant. But Malcolm's vision was narrower: people's education, he declared, 'should be suited to those occupations which the government have the power of enabling them to pursue and to the character and construction of the community among whom they are expected thro' their better education to obtain a respectable livelihood.[1]

Nor was this a time for ambitious experiments: the home government were anxious for retrenchments, and Malcolm himself was distracted by interminable legal disputes with the Supreme Court. Moreover, in a matter which involved no fresh expenditure—the policy to be pursued towards satis—Malcolm proved more cautious even than the Supreme Government.

The Deccan Collectors had become accustomed to exercising a wide discretion under the Deccan Commission. They might well have been expected to take vigorous advantage of it to put down customs which offended most against Western ideas of right and wrong. Hitherto the widest use of such discretion against the custom of sati had been by H. D. Robertson, the Collector of Poona, who had held discussions with learned Brahmans and secured their agreement to new rules for the ceremony which were designed to make it all the more difficult for a widow to endure.

Giberne, however, the new Collector of Khandesh, went even further in October 1827. Hearing that a certain widow was determined to become a sati he 'intimated to all the cutchery servants, and to those in any way dependent on Government, that the Sircar never wishing to interfere in the customs and usages of the natives of the country forbears to issue orders to prevent the suttee, but that all classes must be aware that it is neither required by their religion nor grateful to Government'. And he added grimly that 'those who choose to attend and assist at the ceremony must never expect favour, that of course I should issue no order to prevent their attending, but that I should take care to have a person to write down the names of those who did assist, and their conduct should not be forgotten; they had their choice either to hold the favour of the Sircar or to lose it by assisting at a ceremony which all must confess was not obligatory or necessary'.[2]

In the end, the widow abandoned her resolution. Giberne had a

---

[1] Malcolm, Minute, n.d., Bom. G.C. 31.12.1829, 48.
[2] Giberne to Government, 23.10.1827, Bom. J.C. 16.1.1828, 32.

cynical explanation: 'fortunately the principal number of Brahmins are employed here under government; self interest prevailed; and whether they used more persuasive arguments, or threatened to be absent at the sacrifice, and which latter is very probable, considering that courage before a multitude will sink to cowardice in solitude, the effect was the widow gave up all idea of it before morning'. He awarded her a monthly pension of 7 rupees.[1]

Malcolm strongly objected to Giberne's use of threats as contrary to existing policy. 'Collectors and magistrates cannot be allowed a latitude as to the expedients their feelings or their judgement may prompt. If they were, the consequence would be confusion and alarm on points where we desire to inform and tranquillize.' He also doubted the policy of granting pensions in such circumstances, but agreed to the pension awarded by Giberne because it had already been promised.[2]

Warden objected to the granting of such pensions on the ground that it might tempt other widows to feign a desire to become sati in order to gain the pension as a reward for retracting. But he heartily approved of the rest of Giberne's proceedings: 'there can be no doubt', he declared, 'that suttees are encouraged by the presence of spectators, and especially of natives in the employ of government'. Moreover, he added, 'if the native functionaries, among whom there are many Brahmins, obtain information that the Magistrate's conduct has been disapproved of, we incur the risk of disseminating an impression that the present government has no disposition to discourage, but every disposition to sanction suttees'.[3]

Malcolm was unconvinced: even if the Collector's Indian subordinates absented themselves from the ceremony for fear of punishment, this must have 'degraded them with their own sect' and therefore 'diminished the benefit that might hereafter be derived from their influence and example'. Rather than play upon men's weaknesses he preferred, he said, to rely upon their good feelings: as Indians came to appreciate the 'painful emotions' which satis aroused in the British, they would try to stop the practice.[4]

---

[1] Ibid.
[2] Malcolm, Minute, n.d., ibid. 34, Commander in Chief and Goodwin subscribing.
[3] Warden, Minute, n.d., ibid. 35.
[4] Malcolm, Minute, n.d., ibid. 36, Commander in Chief and Goodwin subscribing.

Malcolm was supported by the rest of his Council, and the Collector of Khandesh was accordingly told that the Governor in Council disapproved of the threats which he had made to his Indian subordinates. 'Whatever further measures are adopted to discourage this shocking usage should be the proclaimed acts of Government, and as such fully understood by its subjects. The Governor in Council cannot allow the Collectors and Magistrates a latitude as to the expedients their feelings or their judgement may prompt, otherwise the consequence would be confusion and alarm on points on which the Government is desirous to inform and tranquillize.'[1]

The Court of Directors had meanwhile given a guarded approval to Robertson's rules, with the exception that no sort of official declaration was to be made that any widow had lost caste.[2] It now appeared that Marriott in the Northern Konkan had also used his initiative with some success. J. B. Simson, the new Collector of the Northern Konkan, attributed the absence of satis there to Marriott's policies.[3] Marriott had avoided all discussion of the legality of sati ceremonies, but 'at the same time he rigorously enforced all the forms enacted by the former government when they operated as restraints; thus leading the people to a general opinion', wrote Simson, 'that these barbarities were barely tolerated by the British Government, and that they would not be permitted where any circumstance presented itself by which such an act might be forbidden or avoided. Indeed I may say that he endeavoured to impress a belief upon the natives that the ceremony was not allowed by us'.[4]

Marriott had never revealed either the policy of the Supreme Government or the rules evolved by H. D. Robertson. As Simson explained, 'so careful indeed was Mr. Marriott to prevent any impression going abroad that the Government had legislated upon the subject of suttees and legalized the ceremony, that the correspondence which passed was not even placed on record; and the original documents have been to this day retained in the immediate charge of the collector'.[5]

[1] Government to Collector of Khandesh, 15.1.1828, Bom. J.C. 16.1.1828, 37.
[2] Judicial dispatch to Bombay, 12.12.1827, Bom. J.D. i. 543 ff.
[3] Simson to Government, 31.1.1828, Bom. J.C. 20.2.1828, 26.
[4] Simson to Government, 19.3.1828, Bom. J.C. 2.4.1828, 26.
[5] Ibid.

The success of these policies now won the Government's approval.[1] Otherwise Malcolm was extremely cautious.

It was still in the Southern Konkan that the practice seemed most popular. In 1829 Malcolm suggested asking the Collector whether he could exert 'an influence among the powerful inhabitants of the Concan that would tend to decrease this barbarous custom'. He himself, he claimed, had secured promises from some of 'the principal Brahmins in the Deccan' that they would do their best to abolish sati—'a practice which they are quite sensible produces the most unfavourable impression of their character not only in those to whom they are immediately subject, but in the minds of the British community at large'.[2]

In accordance with his aim of enlisting 'the influence of the leading natives of the country', Malcolm wrote to Balaji Pant to ask his help: 'Pray repeat to your friends and all men of rank and influence what I have so often stated, that the continuance of the custom weakens the power of persons like me, who am their friend and advocate, to be useful to them in England, where the practice of suttee is held in such abhorrence.'[3] Balaji Pant suggested that the Collectors might be told that when their permission was sought for a sati ceremony they should appoint a panchayat of 'the most respectable natives' to advise on the matter. This he claimed would give a clear indication of the Government's view and thereby a lead to public opinion.[4] Instructions to this effect were accordingly issued to the Judges and Magistrates.[5]

H. D. Robertson, now Collector and Magistrate of Ahmadnagar, was quick to see that these instructions needed clarification. Of what caste should be the members of this panchayat? Who was to choose them? Still more important—was the Magistrate supposed to carry out their decision?[6] Malcolm proposed that such a panchayat should be composed mainly of influential Brahmans, although some members of the widow's family might be included. The Brahman members might well include government officials,

---

[1] Government to Simson, 29.3.1828, ibid. 27.
[2] Malcolm, Minute, 9.5.1829, Bom. J.C. 10.6.1829, 21; Government to Collector, Southern Konkan, 5.6.1829, ibid. 22.
[3] Malcolm to Balaji Pant, 26.11.1829, Bom. J.C. 31.12.1829, 32.
[4] Malcolm, Minute, n.d., Bom. J.C. 31.12.1829, 31.
[5] Government to Criminal and Sessions Judges and Magistrates, 21.12.1829, ibid. 33.
[6] H. D. Robertson to Government, 28.12,1829, Bom. J.C. 17.2.1830, 25.

and 'they should be carefully selected by the Collector with the object of discontinuing the practice'. Moreover, 'under all circumstances natives in public employ and those who desire to see or maintain an intercourse by visits with European officers should be prohibited from attending suttees'. It was to be expected under these conditions that the panchayat would decide that the widow should not become a sati: if it so decided, then the ceremony should not be allowed.[1]

Malcolm told Balaji Pant Natu and other Brahmans that the Supreme Government had prohibited satis, but they assured him that this new policy of using panchayats would 'in a very short period put an end to suttees ... and that in a safe manner, for it will appear the act of the natives themselves and not be liable to that misrepresentation which may attend another course.'[2]

The legal-minded Romer, however, wanted to abolish satis by passing a Regulation just as the Supreme Government had done.[3] Malcolm had recently appointed Newnham, formerly Secretary to Government, in place of Sparrow. But Newnham supported Romer in this matter, just as Sparrow would probably have done. What was there to prevent the Bombay Government from following the example of Bengal?[4] Malcolm called up the spectre of Brahman discontent. The Deccan and Konkan had only been under British rule for a short time; 'a great proportion of the inhabitants of these countries are Brahmins, many of whom have lost influence and power and must be ready to seize any pretext for exciting [a] spirit of discontent and sedition'.[5]

Romer and Newnham were unconvinced.[6] But Malcolm had the support of the Commander in Chief, and the question was therefore decided by majority vote.[7] The Judges and Magistrates were accordingly told to use panchayats as Malcolm had proposed and to see that Indian officials and those who wanted friendly intercourse with Europeans did not attend sati ceremonies. They

[1] Malcolm, Minute, 11.1.1830, Bom. J.C. 17.2.1830, 27.
[2] Ibid.
[3] Romer, Minute, n.d., ibid. 28.
[4] Newnham, Minute, n.d., ibid. 29, and 20.1.1830, ibid. 32.
[5] Malcolm, Minute, n.d., ibid. 33.
[6] Romer and Newnham, 'Remarks', n.d., ibid. 34.
[7] Malcolm and the Commander in Chief being the majority (Malcolm, Minute, n.d., ibid. 35).

were also to inform the inhabitants of the Supreme Government's abolition of satis and to explain that

this Government affords, by its forbearance in not immediately introducing a similar enactment, an opportunity to the principal natives which the Government trusts they will not neglect, of recommending themselves to increased favour & protection by accomplishing through their influence & example the abolition of a usage which is not enjoined by any positive dogma of their religion, which is revolting to human nature, & abhorrent to the feelings of those under whose rule they are placed.[1]

In reply to a query from the Collector of Broach about the proper composition of such panchayats the new policy was explained further. In accordance with Malcolm's recommendation it was declared that 'Government has no desire to ascertain the wishes of the people as to suttees' but to abolish them in such a way as to avoid any suspicion by the people that the Government wished to interfere with their religious customs. To succeed in this seemingly impossible task, the Government was thought to have 'a right on the present occasion to demand the aid of Hindus employed in its service. Their decisions will not be so conclusive with the people as that of persons not employed, but it is better that any unpopularity that this measure may arouse should fall on them than the European authorities.'[2]

Difficulties soon arose when the new policy was tried in practice. Late in January 1830 the widow of a Brahman Karkun in the Southern Konkan Collector's office announced her determination to become a sati. The Senior Assistant Judge attempted to deal with the situation by summoning a panchayat. According to the Government's instructions he chose as members 'respectable' Indians chiefly in government service and explained to them the Government's wish that they should try to make the widow change her mind; he also emphasized how they would gain credit if they succeeded in this, or if they·discovered any legal impediments to the ceremony. Moreover, he told one of the Indian officials of his Court to go to the spot and take down the names of every one engaged in building the funeral pyre.[3]

---

[1] Government to Judges and Magistrates, 15.2.1830, Bom. J.C. 17.2.1830, 39.

[2] Government to R. Mills, Collector of Broach, 19.2.1830, Bom. J.C. 24.2.1830, 23, based on Malcolm, Minute, n.d. (Commander in Chief concurring), ibid. 21.

[3] J. Brown (Acting Senior Assistant Judge, Southern Konkan) to Government, 3.2.1830, Bom. J.C. 10.3.1830, 19.

But all his efforts were unsuccessful. The majority of names taken down were of 'persons in no way connected with her and who appeared to have a pleasure in hastening the immolation of the unfortunate young woman'. But for the intervention of these people who were unconnected with the widow he thought that with the help of the panchayat he might have persuaded her to change her mind. He therefore wanted to fine them, or at least summon them to his Court and admonish them.[1]

Malcolm shared in his feelings, and proposed that he should be allowed in addition to announce that no relatives of a sati would be eligible for government service and that any near relative already in government service would be dismissed. Moreover, in future the panchayat might be asked if they thought that prohibiting a particular ceremony would cause any outrage to public feeling. 'Their opinion that there would not, or even their silence, might be a just ground for its prevention.' Malcolm explained that he wanted to abolish satis in such a way that their abolition would be associated 'with the most respectable natives whom we have a right to insist upon taking their share in any unpopularity that may attend this act of power, and whose names being associated I consider calculated to prevent future evil consequences'.[2]

Romer and Newnham, however, still advocated an uncompromising prohibition of satis by Regulation.[3]

In the result, the Judge was allowed to express the Government's official approbation to any persons unconnected with the widow who had tried to make her change her mind. He was also instructed to announce publicly that no relatives of a sati would be eligible for government service and that any near relations of a sati who were already in government service would be dismissed. In accordance with Malcolm's other proposal he was told, finally, that panchayats should henceforth be asked whether prohibiting the ceremony in question would be likely to outrage Hindu feeling at large and that he might consider a negative reply or even silence as a just ground for prohibition.[4]

Satis had in fact been prohibited by Regulation in Bengal in

[1] J. Brown (Acting Senior Assistant Judge, Southern Konkan) to Government, 3.2.1830, Bom. J.C. 10.3.1830, 19.
[2] Malcolm, Minute, n.d., Commander in Chief concurring, Bom. J.C. 10.3.1830, 20.
[3] Romer, Minute, n.d., and Newnham, Minute, n.d., ibid. 21 and 22.
[4] Government to Brown, 5.3.1830, ibid. 23.

December 1829, and in Madras in February 1830. In March 1830 the Supreme Government wrote officially to the Bombay Government, explaining that they deferred to Malcolm's intimate knowledge of Western India, agreed to a further trial of his policy, but trusted that the experiment would be short.[1] In the following month Malcolm grasped the nettle. But instead of a Regulation specifically prohibiting sati he proposed merely to repeal that part of the 1827 Regulation which declared that 'assisting at any rites of self-immolation, as directed by the religious law of the person performing such immolation, shall not subject anyone to the penalty of murder'. He thought that this would attract less notice than a direct prohibition. On reflection, he did not think that 'popular tumults' would result, but he did fear that Hindus might derive 'dangerous impressions' of what the Government might do in the future. It was certainly an interference with Hindu religious customs, and it was therefore necessary to make it quite clear to the public that it was an exception.[2]

Romer, that great lover of forms, now revealed that at least in this matter he was so anxious to prohibit the practice that he cared little about the form in which it was done.[3]

In accordance with Malcolm's proposal a Regulation was therefore enacted which rescinded the relevant passage in the 1827 Regulation and declared that henceforth anyone assisting at a sati ceremony would be held guilty of culpable homicide and that anyone who had used force would be held guilty of murder.[4] But he was still uneasy, and in his farewell minute he solemnly declared that the abolition of satis 'must be quoted to our native subjects as an exception to that rigid rule we had prescribed to ourselves, and meant scrupulously to maintain, as a general principle, of not interfering on any point connected with their religious usages'.[5]

Malcolm was no more anxious to make changes in Bhil policy than in sati policy. The measures of conciliation begun during the later years of Elphinstone's Government were continued with success.

[1] Supreme Government to Bombay Government, 23.3.1830, Bom. J.C. 23.6.1830, 25.
[2] Malcolm, 16.4.1830, Bom. J.C. 23.6.1830, 27; Bom. Reg. XIV, 1827, sec. xxvi.
[3] Romer, Minute, n.d., ibid. 28.   [4] Bom. Reg. XVI, 1830.
[5] Malcolm, Minute, 30.11.1830, para. 249, Malcolm, *Government of India*, app. A, 84–85.

The Bhil Corps was being used for diverse kinds of police duty
—chasing plunderers, escorting prisoners and treasure, even
manning outposts in unhealthy places.[1] The Bhils who had been
encouraged to settle down in village colonies and take to agriculture seemed to be flourishing—Giberne the Collector noted in
1828 that 'a kind of village pride seems to have arisen in the minds
of those longer established'. He was encouraged by the activity
which he saw in some colonies: 'the trees of the jungle were falling
under the axe of one Bheel cultivator, another would be burning
the wood, a third endeavouring to manage a plough under the
tutorage of the Patell or Koonbee'. Not that they were entirely
transformed: 'they still require a constant surveillance and appear
naturally enough to prefer idleness to labour'.[2]

All told, Ovans could claim in 1831 that since 1825 when his
Agency was first established, 641 families had been settled in agriculture and 533 families as watchmen and labourers. Allowing five
to a family—'a small average for Bheels'—he estimated that 'about
6000 souls' had been thus 'rescued from crime and misery'.[3]

As the colonies developed, those village watchmen who were not
needed in the villages could be settled there. This left those remaining in the villages with enough work and pay to keep them out of
mischief. By 1831 Ovans, as Bhil Agent in the Ajanta hills, could
report that the village watchmen had become 'our best and most
effective police'.[4]

The introduction of the Regulations into Khandesh, consequent
upon the abolition of the Deccan Commission, at first threatened
difficulty. To control a wild people like the Bhils it seemed desirable to give the man on the spot more power and more discretion
than was customary in a government of laws rather than of
men.

Outram, for example, wanted to use panchayats for trying
offences in his Bhil Corps which in an ordinary regiment would be

---

[1] S.B.R., N.S. xxvi. 234.

[2] Giberne (Collector) to Government, 1.8.1828, para. 43, Bom. R.C. 8.10.1828,
4.

[3] Ovans to Boyd (Collector), 17.10.1831, Bom. J.C. 14.12.1831, 29. Less had
been done elsewhere, and in 1827 the North Western Agency was abolished.
In 1845 an Agency was established in the west. The Agent soon began to found
colonies as Ovans had done. Ovans calculated that 6,908½ bighas were sown in
the Ajanta colonies in 1829–30 (Ovans to Collector, 19.7.1830, Bom. R.C.
13.10.1830, 69; S.B.R. xxvi, N.S., 238).

[4] Ovans to Boyd (Collector, Khandesh), 17.10.1831, Bom. J.C. 14.12.1831, 29.

tried by courts martial.[1] The Collector approved, and recommended
that the Government should authorize Outram to do so, merely
suggesting the reservation that punishments awarded by such
panchayats 'should be limited to two dozen stripes or running the
gauntlet the latter to be carried into effect with the ends of turbans
or slippers, and 30 days imprisonment on conjee diet'.[2]

Warden and Goodwin were both reluctant to sanction such
picturesque deviations from a regular system of government.[3]

Eventually, it was decided to appoint Outram an Assistant Magistrate for the purpose. But his powers were limited: he was not
allowed to sentence a flogging, and 'any other punishment not mentioned in the regulations', it was declared, 'must first be generally
sanctioned by the Sudder Faujdaree Adawlut before it can in any
case be executed'.[4]

Ovans, the Bhil Agent in the Ajanta area, also felt hampered by
the new Regulations, particularly when he had to deal with offences
like the breach of tenancy agreements and 'the abduction of each
other's women'. He was accustomed to refer such matters to panchayats of Bhils, who usually awarded sentences like 'public disgrace, and a few stripes'. He wanted these panchayats to have the
power to award sentences of up to three months' imprisonment.
But none of the present Regulations seemed to him to authorize
such procedure, and he suggested that the Government should pass
a new one.[5]

But they decided, in accordance with the advice of Boyd, the
Collector of Khandesh, that it would be 'inexpedient' to pass a new
Regulation formally investing Bhil panchayats with such powers.
Instead, Ovans was to draw up some rules based upon Robertson's
original instructions to him in 1825; these rules might then be
formally issued to him by the Governor in Council and remain in
force until the Bhils became sufficiently reformed to be put under
the ordinary Regulations.[6]

In civil disputes also Ovans had been acting at his own discretion. Civil suits between Bhils were 'all of the most trifling

[1] Outram to Giberne (Collector of Khandesh), 23.3.1828, Bom. J.C. 21.5.1828,
71.
[2] Giberne to Government, 30.3.1828, ibid.   [3] Minutes, ibid. 73–81.
[4] Government to Giberne, 20.5.1828, ibid. 82.
[5] Ovans to Collector, 19.7.1830, Bom. R.C. 13.10.1830, 69.
[6] Boyd to Revenue Commissioner, 17.8.1830, ibid.; Government to Revenue
Commissioner, 8.10.1830, ibid. 72.

description', and he could usually settle them at once by confronting the parties and getting them to come to some agreement. Such prompt action, he claimed, had the advantage of preventing the Bhils from 'taking the law into their own hands, as they are but too apt to do'.[1]

The rules which he drew up empowered the Bhil Agent to punish Bhils who broke their agreements or abducted each other's women. When trying such cases he could use Bhil panchayats or Bhil assessors and award up to a year's imprisonment with hard labour, thirty stripes and public disgrace, all sentences above six months' imprisonment being subject to the Collector's confirmation. The Agent was also formally authorized to hear all civil suits between Bhils, subject to an appeal to the Collector, and to decide either by himself or with a panchayat or as an arbitrator, cases of importance being submitted for the Collector's confirmation.[2] Ovans's proposed rules also declared that the Bhil Agent should in general continue to be guided by Robertson's instructions of September 1825.[3]

These rules were sanctioned by the Government.[4]

The revenue policies of Malcolm's Government were as careful of established rights as those of Elphinstone's had been. The Government even ventured a sly rebuke at the dogmatism of the home authorities who had strongly criticized Marriott's plan for fostering an hereditary class of zamindars. The Bombay Government replied that they thought it 'prudent' not to circulate the Court's remarks to the Collectors as those remarks were 'decidedly in favour of the ryotwar system so much so as to express strong disapprobation of all others', while 'in the present state of our knowledge we deemed it better to attend to the particular circumstances of each district than to act on general rules'.[5]

The home government had even declared that they would have liked to see the ryotwari system established throughout Broach. Malcolm, however, approved of the bhagdari system as much as Elphinstone had done. When he visited Gujarat in 1830 he was particularly impressed with the prosperity of Broach: 'the appearance of the people was favourable and their large well-built tiled

---

[1] Ovans to Boyd, 10.11.1830, Bom. R.C. 29.12.1830, 127.
[2] Proposed rules, 10.11.1830, ibid.
[3] Ibid.
[4] Government to Collector of Khandesh, 22.12.1830, ibid. 128.
[5] Revenue letter from Bombay, 23.7.1828, Bom. R.L.R. vii. 497 ff.

houses denoted a degree of comfort and subsistence which is rarely witnessed among an Indian peasantry even when they enjoy prosperity and good government'. He concluded that 'it ought to be a chief aim of our revenue officers to uphold this tenure'.[1] At his suggestion the Collectors were told to preserve it wherever they found it and to assess at specially low rates if they found the sharers of any village in difficulties.[2]

The policy pursued in Gujarat under Elphinstone's Government of giving village leases to headmen also came under the criticism of the Court of Directors. The Court were particularly concerned with 'the powers of extortion' which they thought that such a plan would give to the headmen and with 'the inattention to the wrongs of the ryots' which they thought that it would be 'apt to generate on the part of the revenue officers'.[3]

Malcolm's Government, however, suggested that the Court had an exaggerated idea of the power of these headmen. 'The former indiscriminate authority of the Patells', they claimed, had been 'abolished'. In particular, the rents payable by the ryots were recorded in the village accountants' books.[4]

But the Court remained sceptical. In their suspicion of the village officers they even turned to panchayats. They warned the Bombay Government that little trust could be placed in the accountants, and commended the use of panchayats to decide disputes between village farmers and their cultivators.[5] When a panchayat appointed by both parties decided what was the proper rent, its decision should be recorded upon the cultivators' revenue certificates (pattas).[6]

Elphinstone's Government had protected the privileges of the Pandharpeshas of the Northern Konkan against the levelling tendencies of Marriott, their Collector. Marriott's successor Simson was equally hostile to such privileges, and Malcolm therefore had an independent inquiry made by Williamson, then the Collector of Kaira.

---

[1] Malcolm, Minute, n.d., para. 13, Bom. R.C. 17.11.1830, 79.
[2] Government to Principal Collector, Ahmadabad, 6.11.1830, ibid. 80.
[3] Revenue dispatch to Bombay, 6.8.1828, Bom. R.D. iii. 275 ff.
[4] Revenue letter from Bombay, 2.9.1829, paras. 65 ff., Bom. R.L.R. viii. 128 ff.
[5] As in the leasing rules of 1826.
[6] Revenue dispatch to Bombay, 11.8.1830, paras. 17 ff., Bom. R.D. iii. 377 ff.

Williamson reported that they paid 'by no means a trifling rent', although it was admittedly less than that paid by ordinary cultivators. In the Kalian district, for example, the Pandharpeshas had to pay Rs.4 As.1 a bigha while the ordinary cultivators had to pay Rs.5 As.2. Altogether Williamson estimated that these privileged rates did not cost the Government more than Rs.25,000 a year, and he recommended that they should be continued.[1]

Malcolm agreed. Although the Pandharpeshas did no manual labour, they possessed 'means from character and credit of extending cultivation and improvement beyond what is enjoyed by the common coonbee or labouring ryot'.[2]

Like many of the Company's civil servants, however, Warden was opposed to such social privilege. Referring to Williamson's translation of the term Pandharpesha as meaning a well-dressed person, he declared: 'If the Pandra Peyshas of Callian are to be assessed at Rs.4–1 per beegah or at the rate of one fourth of the value of the crop raised, I would prefer favouring the undressed rather than the well-dressed classes of the community' by assessing the ordinary cultivators at favourable terms—Simson himself had made some such suggestion.[3]

But Malcolm got the support of Goodwin and the Commander-in-Chief, and Simson was accordingly told to respect the Pandharpeshas' privileges as they stood at the acquisition of the North Konkan by the Company.[4]

This was almost more than Simson could bear. He proceeded to question the details of the Government's order: he could hardly question the principles behind it once the formal declaration of policy had been made. For example, in the ponderous official language of the time, the Government's order had spoken of 'persons styling themselves Pandrapeshas'. Simson now asked whether the Government meant him to protect the rights of Pandharpeshas alone or also those of any other persons who might claim to be Pandharpeshas even if they were not so in reality.[5]

Malcolm was too experienced to be deceived by such delaying tactics. The Collector, he said, must carry out the Government's

[1] Williamson to Government, 18.1.1828, Bom. R.C. 26.3.1828, 69.

[2] Malcolm, Minute, 5.2.1828, ibid. 71.

[3] Warden, Minute, 18.2.1828, ibid. 72.

[4] Goodwin, Minute, 25.2.1828, ibid. 73; Malcolm, Minute, Bradford concurring, ibid. 74; Government to Collector, 25.3.1828, ibid. 76.

[5] Simson to Government, 30.4.1828, Bom. R.C. 28.5.1829, 29.

policy 'instantly' and ask questions afterwards about any doubtful points that might arise in practice.[1]

Under Ellenborough's vigorous prodding the Court of Directors had ordered drastic retrenchments. 'The days of liberality are gone', remarked Malcolm on one occasion, 'and we live in those of clippers and calculators and our long *coats* are every hour in danger of being made *coatees*.'[2] He was, however, quick to see in this an opportunity for extending the employment of Indians who cost less than Europeans. The 'doctrines of reductions of officers & the extension of native agency' were, he told Melvill, 'equally required by the principles of economy & policy'.[3]

He found opposition in Bombay and claimed that in some ways even the Court of Directors were not trying to help him. Romer in particular was anxious to protect the Judges. 'You may as well slay Mr. Romer as hint at any reduction in the judicial line.' On the other hand, Malcolm complained to Melvill, 'you gentlemen in Leadenhall Street send out writers we do not want & give us at least two European Regts of His Majesty's beyond what we can under any circumstances require'.[4]

He was met in Bombay with the warning 'that change is undesirable, & that the Natives must prove themselves worthy of the encouragement they have received before they can be further trusted'. But he was determined. As early as December 1828 he was declaring, 'I will here or elsewhere break down illiberal bars, that deny from pride & love of power, a nation that fair scope & generous confidence which can alone advance their improvement.'[5]

In private correspondence Bentinck and he were soon discussing the policy of giving Indians original jurisdiction over all civil suits. In April 1829 Malcolm wrote that this would 'work excellently well & be a political benefit as well as a great saving'.[6] He proposed it

[1] Malcolm, Minute, 9.5.1829, ibid. 30.
[2] Malcolm to Lieut.-Col. Goodfellow, 10.1.1830, *H.M.* 734, 784 ff. The allusion was no doubt to Burke (*Reflections on the French Revolution*): 'But the age of chivalry is gone. That of sophists, economists and calculators has succeeded.'
[3] Malcolm to J. Melvill, 1.2.1829, ibid., 257 ff. James Cosmo Melvill, Auditor of Indian Accounts.
[4] Malcolm to Melvill, 1.2.1829, ibid., 257 ff. Cf. Malcolm to Loch, 3.2.1829, 'I must entreat you, send us no more writers, and recall some of His Majesty's Regiments' (ibid. 259 f.).
[5] Malcolm to Barnewell, 5.12.1828, ibid., 225 ff.
[6] Malcolm to Bentinck, 28.4.1829, *Bentinck*.

officially in December 1829. Romer accepted it only as 'a measure forced upon us by the necessities of our situation' and doubted whether any good would come of it 'until the natives of this country come to regard each other, in stations of trust, with more confidence than it is notorious they now do'.[1]

The measure was duly carried into effect by Regulation in 1830. But a petition was soon presented to the Senior Assistant Judge at Poona protesting against the change on the ground that the existing system was satisfactory and that the Native Commissioners who were to have all original jurisdiction could not be trusted. The petition purported to express the views of 'the sirdars, privileged classes, ryots and others of the Zillah of Poona'. It was signed by 'about 650 persons'. The Judge himself believed that the privileged classes had been 'the principal movers' in this matter, for, he said, 'they seem to regard it in some way degrading that their cases should be heard by those they consider their inferiors'.[2] Romer did not miss the opportunity of observing that this bore out his own views.[3]

However, in his farewell minute Malcolm declared that 'there cannot be the slightest doubt of the complete success of this measure'. Justice had been brought nearer to the homes of 'the lower orders', and he also thought that 'the higher classes' were pleased to see the confidence which the Government was showing in these Indian Judges.[4]

He was also well satisfied with the quality of the Indians serving in the revenue department. Indeed, he said that he had 'seldom met more intelligent and able natives'. But he was sorry that 'natives of high rank' did not in general seem eager for employment as revenue officials.[5] This was a problem which had greatly worried Elphinstone—how to encourage 'the higher classes' to join the service of the new government. They lacked the incentives of high responsibility or ample reward: Elphinstone and Malcolm had both done as much as they could to improve the prospects of Indian officials in these matters, but it was little enough that could be done in the

---

[1] Malcolm, Minute, 1.12.1829, para. 28, *Government of India*, app. B, 110; Romer, Minute, 15.12.1829, Bom. J.C. 31.12.1829, 2.
[2] Petition, 25.2.1830, Bom. J.C. 17.3.1830, 2; B. Hutt (Acting Senior Assistant Judge, Poona) to Government, 4.3.1830, ibid. 1.
[3] Romer, Minute, n.d., ibid. 3.
[4] Malcolm, Minute, 30.11.1830, para. 117, *Government of India*, app. A, 42.
[5] Ibid., para. 216 f.

existing structure of the Company's administration. All that remained was exhortation. In 1829 the Collectors were told to employ young men of good family whenever possible both because their 'respectability' was 'good security for their conduct' and also 'because it is more agreeable to the ryots to transact business with those they have been in the habit of looking up to with deference and respect, than with those who, like most of our revenue servants, are taken from the inferior classes of society'.[1]

On the other hand, like a true Scot Malcolm would have no man excluded because of humble origins from the opportunities of government service, such as they were. In 1829, for example, the Collector of the Southern Konkan recommended increasing the size of the local force of irregular police (Sibandis) but suggested that henceforth Mahars and other low castes should be excluded. This, he argued, was a force 'in which it can never be expected that the strict notions of military discipline will be so completely entertained as to supersede the prejudices of caste, and from which small parties are constantly detached throughout the country and have daily communication with the police department from the Mamlatdar of the district down to the subordinate villagers': therefore, he concluded, 'the exclusion of men whose conduct conveys pollution' would promote the success of the force.[2]

But Malcolm disagreed; 'It is my opinion', he said, 'that orders or regulations making such distinctions among our subjects should be avoided. It is right to respect the prejudices of all, and give, where expedient, preference to the castes, but we should not proclaim any exceptions that might evince contempt for the lowest.'[3] The Collector was accordingly told not to make any such exclusions.[4]

In general, however, Malcolm was as anxious as Elphinstone to preserve the social hierarchy. When in December 1827 he received the great jagirdars at Poona, he found them alarmed 'at the tendency of our system of rule to destroy all those distinctions they cherish'. He realized that this was a common result of British rule, but he thought that in view of the system evolved by Elphinstone

---

[1] Government to Collectors, 20.8.1829, Bom. R.C. 26.8.1829, 5.
[2] Reid to Government, 24.2.1829, Bom. J.C. 10.6.1829, 17.
[3] Malcolm, Minute, 9.5.1829, ibid. 21.
[4] Government to Collector, 5.6.1829, ibid. 22. He was authorized to increase the size of the corps from 200 to 300 men; henceforth the corps was to be called the 'Conkan Rangers'.

there was 'a better prospect of preserving a native aristocracy in this part of India than in any other quarter of our territories'.[1]

The jagirdars seemed to value their exemption from regular judicial procedure. 'In politic attention to their prejudices', the Agent for Sardars had found it advisable to receive their visits in a room distinct from that in which he acted as Judge of Poona. Even so, Malcolm thought that the Agent lacked sufficient time to attend thoroughly to their problems, and at his suggestion a Deputy Agent for Sardars was appointed. The creation of such a post was regarded as a needless extravagance at Calcutta. The Bombay Government referred the matter to London, but the Court of Directors ordered them to abolish the post at once.[2]

The Court of Directors, in fact, had no liking for the system of privileged classes. When they delivered their considered verdict upon it in 1829 they declared that 'the obvious objection' to these arrangements was the fact that 'they render the operation of the law unequal'. They regarded the system as 'an evil', although necessary because it was 'at present impossible to enforce the peremptory and undistinguishing process of our Courts on all occasions without danger to the public peace'. But they hoped that the size of the privileged classes would be reduced as far as was possible without political danger.[3] Malcolm, however, took little account of such hopes. In 1830, for example, some ambitious men made application to be included in the lowest of the privileged classes. The Acting Deputy Agent for Sardars suggested that such claims should be considered by a panchayat of five of the most distinguished and respectable members of the first and second classes in Poona.[4] Upon Malcolm's advice this was approved, it being understood that the panchayat would only make recommendations and that the Government would have the deciding power.[5] Romer protested that the Government should be considering not how to increase the size of the third class but how to reduce it, in view of the instructions of the home government, but he was alone in this view.[6]

[1] Malcolm, Minute, 16.1.1828, Bom. J.C. 30.1.1828, 31.
[2] Judicial dispatch to Bombay, 12.6.1833, Bom. J.D. ii. 329.
[3] Judicial dispatch to Bombay, 27.5.1829, Bom. J.D. ii. 9 ff. Also dispatch to Bombay, 15.2.1832, P.P. 1831–2, xii. 232.
[4] P. W. Le Geyt (Acting Deputy Agent for Sardars) to Government, 2.2.1830, Bom. J.C. 24.3.1830, 24.
[5] Malcolm, Minute, n.d., subscribed by Commander in Chief and Newnham (appointed in place of Sparrow), ibid. 25; Government to Acting Deputy Agent for Sardars, 19.3.1830, ibid. 27.   [6] Romer, Minute, n.d., ibid. 26.

Far from being weakened in any way under Malcolm, the structure of the privileged classes was in fact confirmed and strengthened by a Regulation of 1830 which provided for the administration of civil justice by them under the authority of specific charters (sanads) to be issued by the Government. What had hitherto been in many cases informal, and therefore vulnerable in an age of Law Courts and Regulations, was now given legal recognition and support. The Regulations of 1827 had already conferred powers of criminal justice and exemption from the criminal and civil procedures of the Company's Courts. The Regulation of 1830 merely filled an obvious gap. Appeals from the decisions of jagirdars in the first two classes were to be heard by the Agent, appeals from those in the third class by the Judge. It was specifically laid down, moreover, that 'decrees by a jagheerdar shall not be liable to be set aside for want of form in the proceedings; but only for matters affecting the justice of the decision'.[1]

More important to the great jagirdars, however, than any judicial privileges must have been the fear that their name might be extinguished if they died without heirs. What they must have found particularly unsettling was that no one knew whether in any given instance the Government would allow an adoption. The great Chintaman Rao himself was anxiously waiting for the Government to sanction the adoption which he had made in 1826. Nisbet, the Political Agent at Dharwar, wrote a moving description of his plight in 1829:

He is a man of nearly sixty years of age, and can therefore at present anticipate nothing, but the certainty of his estates being seized, and of his adopted child, whom he no doubt regards nearly in the light of a blood relation, becoming a pensioner on the bounty of Government, added to which, he is doomed to listen to the melancholy forebodings of at least three hundred dependants, all men of some consequence, who derive their entire support from him.[2]

With some astuteness Chintaman Rao claimed that it was in order to dissuade his daughter-in-law from becoming a sati that he had consented to adopt a son.[3]

---

[1] Bom. Reg. XIII, 1830. These provisions were not of course needed by the greatest jagirdars who had final powers of civil and criminal jurisdiction according to charters granted in 1818–19.

[2] Nisbet to Government, 21.3.1829, Bom. R.C. 22.4.1829, 43.

[3] Chintaman Rao, Memorandum, n.d., Bom. P.C. 8.12.1830, 2.

Malcolm thought that there ought to be some fixed rule: it seemed cruel to leave such decisions to the discretion of the Government at the time. Like Elphinstone and all opponents of the Bengal system, he disliked inflexibility, but he was forced in this matter to admit that there might be advantages in inflexible rules. His solution was that a Nazarana or succession duty should be levied in every instance of hereditary succession to office or property, and that the natural or adopted heir should always be allowed to succeed if he paid it. But the Bengal Government objected that this would tend 'to confirm in perpetuity the alienation of the public revenue', and the Court of Directors refrained from laying down any fixed rules.[1]

One of the main reasons why Malcolm wanted to impose succession duties on the jagirdars was the idea that their usefulness to the state would thereby be emphasized. It was for the same reason that he tried to make effective the military service which some of the great jagirdars were liable to render. He had their contingents assembled for police duties under a Muslim Jamadar of the Poona Auxiliary Horse, an 'old friend' of his and the son of a Subadar in the Madras cavalry. But the jagirdars were deeply offended, and the experiment evoked a severe rebuke from the Court of Directors for such neglect of the jagirdars' feelings.[2]

In general, however, he tried hard to maintain friendly personal relations with the upper classes just as Elphinstone had done.

When he went on tour he always took care to receive them with proper courtesies. During a fortnight that he spent at Ahmadnagar in 1828, for example, he held a reception 'almost every day'. In his own words 'more than two hundred persons were introduced to me, who from birth, property or law had a right to be received as gentlemen. They seemed much gratified by personal communication with the Governor and in conferences I had with many of them on subjects of petty grievances or complaints I found them reasonable and in general contented and grateful for the favour and protection they enjoyed.'[3]

In this way he hoped to compensate for the abolition of the post of Deccan Commissioner: if the Governor of Bombay visited the

[1] Supreme Government to Bombay Government, 13.11.1828, Bom. R.C. 22.4.1829, 41.
[2] Political dispatch to Bombay, 11.6.1834.
[3] Malcolm, Minute, 20.8.1828, Bom. G.C. 27.8.1828, 47.

Deccan at regular intervals he could receive the great jagirdars and
discuss their problems with them.[1] At the end of his term of office
he elaborated with enthusiasm upon the good effects of these visits
to the Deccan upon the people in general: 'They give life and
animation to all classes; they are a check upon bad conduct, and
an encouragement to good. The natives of India refer everything
to persons. They are slow to understand the abstract excellence of
our system of government. They see in the governor when he visits
the provinces the head of the government. The timid acquire confidence, and the turbulent are checked by his presence.'[2]

Bluff, good-humoured, full of self-confidence, Malcolm certainly seems to have mixed well with all classes. We may suspect,
nevertheless, that however gratifying his condescension may have
been to the humble, the great must at times have found it galling.

When he visited the Southern Maratha country in 1829 he was
deeply impressed by the prosperity and good administration of the
Patwardhans' estates. There the village system was preserved unimpaired. The officials of 'many of the finest districts' had succeeded to their duties 'like an inheritance'. They were local men.
In consequence, 'all the money made in the districts is spent in
them, and the local officers are so connected with those over whom
they are placed and so associated with them in interests that they
cannot be instruments of misrule and oppression without the for-
feit of that influence and reputation which afford them the means
of collecting more revenue than any stranger could realize'.
Malcolm thought highly of a system under which self-love and
social were the same. Moreover, he thought that since the administration of justice was in the same hands as the collection of the
revenue it was generally well managed. 'Notwithstanding the impressions of some of the contrary, I must from all I saw and
heard be of opinion that justice is in most cases administered in a
way fully as satisfactory to the inhabitants as under our improved
system.' In general, he considered that 'the towns and villages
under these Jagheerdars' were 'in a better condition than any of
our provinces in the Deccan'.[3]

Chintaman Rao, the greatest and of old the most turbulent of
the Patwardhans, Malcolm found to be a changed man. 'The spirit

[1] Malcolm, Minute, 16.1.1828, Bom. J.C. 30.1.1828, 31.
[2] Malcolm, Minute, 30.11.1830, para. 275, *Government of India*, app. A, 94.
[3] Malcolm, Minute, 23.2.1829, paras. 63–66, Bom. P.C. 18.3.1829, 40.

of Chintamun Row has been broken by the loss of his only son, a
fine youth on whom he doted, and who was worthy of all his
affection.'[1]

He was paying much attention to horticulture. Malcolm was
both 'surprized and gratified' to see the acres of gardens and plan-
tations at Sangli and to learn how Chintaman Rao was trying to
extend the cultivation of different plants and vegetables, and he
encouraged him in these peaceful pursuits.[2]

The other great jagirdars also seemed to be settling down under
the new government. Even the ferocious Appa Desai of Nipani was
said to be 'personally improved', but Malcolm noted that 'he is
surrounded by old companions in arms to whom he is much
attached and whose wants and habits are unfavourable to economy
and to the good rule of his country.'[3]

But the spacious days which such chieftains had once enjoyed
were over. Appa Desai lacked the patience to wait for the new
government's permission to adopt a son. He tried to pass off another's child as his own, and even, it appeared, had the mother
killed so as to reduce the chance of discovery. The new government
proved inexorable: they told Appa Desai that they would recognize
neither this nor any future child of his, real or supposititious, and
moreover that they would resume his estates at his death.[4]

Vithal Narsing, the jagirdar of Vinchur, who had suffered so
severely for his loyalty to the Peshwa, was in such financial difficulties that he had to ask the help of the Government in 1830 towards the marriage of his daughter to one of Sindhia's ministers.
At Malcolm's suggestion it was decided to give him Rs.15,000.[5]
The Court of Directors put little trust in the Bombay Government's assurance that this grant would not be taken as a precedent:
'we do not place much reliance on the efficacy of such declarations'.
But they admitted that few claims as strong as his were likely to
arise and they approved of the grant.[6]

Balaji Pant Natu was still consolidating his gains. In 1830 he
submitted a memorandum to the effect that Elphinstone had in
1826 granted him the honour of a palanquin but that by some over-

---

[1] Malcolm, Minute, 23.2.1829, para. 53.   [2] Ibid., paras. 54 ff.
[3] Ibid., para. 35.
[4] Political dispatch to Bombay, 11.6.1834, paras. 8–9, Bom. P.D. iv.
[5] Malcolm, Minute, 11.5.1830, Bom. P.C. 23.6.1830, 344A.
[6] Political dispatch to Bombay, 11.6.1834, para. 13, Bom. P.D. iv.

sight the customary grant of an allowance for maintaining bearers
for it had not in fact been made. He wanted a piece of land near
Poona worth Rs.600 a year instead of a cash allowance of the same
amount.[1] Malcolm supported his request: 'He is always at the call
of the authorities in the Deccan and it is well known how much his
advice and assistance are valued by them.'[2] The grant of land was
sanctioned.[3]

But he seems to have felt insecure. Only two years later, for
example, R. C. Money, a perceptive Bombay civilian, was writing
home to Elphinstone that Balaji was not the only one to feel like
this:

I think he is afraid of being or of having been too great a friend once
of our Government—that evil of the present system, *change*, affects him
as it must every respectable native who has risked much for us & been
well rewarded. His face is new to most now & almost all are new faces
to him—new collectors and assistants—& I fear they do not pay him
the respect which he used to receive—This he has himself remarked to
me. This is what all the natives of rank feel very painfully—They are
sick of such changes. . . . [4]

[1] Balaji Pant, Memorandum, n.d., Bom. P.C. 15.12.1830, 76.
[2] Malcolm, Minute, ibid. 77.
[3] Government to Collector of Poona, 13.12.1830, ibid. 77A.
[4] R. C. Money to M.E., 6.11.1832, Elphinstone; R. C. Money, Persian Secretary to Government, Secretary to Native Education Society. Compare Sardesai, *Selections from the Peshwa Daftar*, xlii. 59.

APPENDIX I

Abbreviations used in Footnotes

P.P.   Parliamentary Papers.
P.R.C. Poona Residency Correspondence.
S.B.R. Selections from the Records of the Bombay Government.
S.R.J. Selection . . . from the Records at the East-India House Relating to . . . Revenue . . . and . . . Justice.

The rest of the abbreviations refer to India Office Records:

Eur.MS.	European Manuscript.	G.	General/Public.
H.M.	Home Miscellaneous Series	J.	Judicial.
Bg.	Bengal.	L.R.	Letters Received.
Bom.	Bombay.	M.	Military.
C.	Consultations.	P.	Political.
D.	Dispatches.	R.	Revenue.
E.	Educational.	S.	Secret.

For example, Bg. S.C. stands for Bengal Secret Consultations.

APPENDIX II

Bibliography

I. MANUSCRIPT SOURCES

A. *The Mountstuart Elphinstone Papers* (denoted *Elphinstone* in the footnotes).

B. *At the India Office Library and Record Department (Commonwealth Relations Office).*
Consultations/Proceedings of the Bengal Government in the Secret and Political Departments.
Consultations/Proceedings of the Bombay Government in the Secret, Political, Revenue, Judicial, Military, Education and General/Public Departments.
Dispatches to and letters from Bengal and Bombay, in the relevant departments, as above.
Board's Collections.
Court Minutes, and Appendixes.
European Manuscripts Series, Item 295 (Eur.MS. B.7): 'Macleod's Dekhan Journal MS. 1816–1821'.
Home Miscellaneous Series, Item 734 (Sir John Malcolm's Private Correspondence).
Personal Records.

C. *Church Missionary Society Records.*
Western India Mission Letters Received.

D. *The Bentinck Papers* (denoted *Bentinck* in the footnotes).

E. *The W. H. Mill Papers.*

II. PRINTED SOURCES

A. *Selections from the Records of the Bombay Government* (denoted S.B.R. in the footnotes).
No. iii (Survey Report on Broach—Monier Williams), 1852.
Nos. x–xi (Survey Reports on Parganas in the Ahmadabad and Kaira Collectorates), 1853.
No. xxvi, new series, pp. 201–52 (Historical sketch of the Khandesh Bhils, with an outline of the Bombay Government's 'conciliatory line of policy', 1825–43, by Captain D. C. Graham, Commanding, Bhil Corps; continued to 1855 by Captain J. Rose, Second in Command and Acting Commandant, Bhil Corps), 1856.
No. xxix, new series (Concealment of the revenue records of the former government by hereditary district officers and others), 1856.
No. xli, new series (Satara), 1857.
No. cvi, new series (Talukdars of Ahmadabad), 1867.
No. cxxxiv, new series (Khots), 1873.

No. clxxiv, new series (Hereditary district officers' watans), 1895.

No. cclxxviii, new series (Land tenures), 1894.

No. ccccxlvi, new series (Khots), 1907.

B. *Other Works.*

AITCHISON, C. U., *A Collection of Treaties, Engagements and Sanads Relating to India and Neighbouring Countries* (5th ed., Calcutta and Delhi, 1929–).

BADEN-POWELL, B. B., *The Land Systems of British India* (3 vols., Oxford, 1892).

BALLHATCHET, K. A., 'The Home Government and Bentinck's Educational Policy', *Cambridge Historical Journal*, vol. x, no. 2 (1951).

BELL, E., *Memoir of General John Briggs, of the Madras Army: with Comments on Some of his Words and Work* (London, 1885).

BOMAN-BEHRAM, B. K., *Educational Controversies in India: the Cultural Conquest of India under British Imperialism* (Bombay, n.d.).

Brief Notice of the Services of Mr. Cumming, Late Head of the Revenue and Judicial Departments in the Office of the Right Honourable the Board of Commissioners for the Affairs of India (London, 1824).

BRIGGS, J., *Letters Addressed to a Young Person in India: Calculated to Afford Instruction for his Conduct in General, and More Especially in his Intercourse with the Natives* (London, 1828).

CHAPLIN, W., *A Report Exhibiting a View of the Fiscal and Judicial System of Administration, Introduced into the Conquered Territories above the Ghauts, under the Authority of the Commissioner in the Dekhan* (Bombay, 1824).

CHOKSEY, R. D., *The Aftermath (Based on Original Records), 1818–1826. With Select Documents from the Deccan Commissioner's Files, Peshwa Dafter, on the Administrative and Judicial Organisation of Maharashtra by the British* (Bombay, 1950).

—— *Economic History of the Bombay Deccan and Karnatak (1818–1868)* (Poona, 1945).

—— *A History of British Diplomacy at the Court of the Peshwas (1786–1818)* (Poona, 1951).

—— *The Last Phase: Selections from the Deccan Commissioner's Files (Peshwa Daftar), 1815–1818. With an Introductory Note on the British Diplomacy at the Court of the Peshwa* (Bombay, 1948).

—— *Selections from the Deccan Commissioner's Files (Peshwa Daftar): Period of Transition (1818–1826)* (Poona, 1945).

COLEBROOKE, Sir T. E., *Life of the Honourable Mountstuart Elphinstone* (2 vols., London, 1884).

—— *Memoir of the Honourable Mountstuart Elphinstone* (London, 1861).

CUMPSTON, I. M., *Indians Overseas in British Territories, 1834–1854* (Oxford, 1953).

DRACUP, A. H., and SORLEY, H. T., *Census of India, 1931. Volume VIII. Part I. Bombay Presidency: General Report* (Bombay, 1933).

DREWITT, F. D., *Bombay in the Days of George IV: Memoirs of Sir Edward West* (London, 1907).

Dublin University Magazine, vol. xxviii, no. clxvi (October 1846), pp. 426–42, 'The Right Hon. Sir Henry Pottinger, Bart., G.C.B.'

East-India Register.

ELPHINSTONE, M., *Report on the Territories Conquered from the Paishwa* (2nd ed., Calcutta, 1821, reprinted Bombay, 1838). Where the version printed in S.R.J. iv is the fuller, I have used that.

ENTHOVEN, R. E., *The Tribes and Castes of Bombay* (3 vols., Bombay, 1921–3).

FORREST, Sir G. W., *Selections from the Letters, Despatches, and Other State Papers Preserved in the Bombay Secretariat: Maratha Series*, vol. i, part iii (Bombay, 1885).

—— *Selections from the Minutes and Other Official Writings of the Honourable Mountstuart Elphinstone, Governor of Bombay. With an Introductory Memoir* (London, 1884).

FRASER, Sir W., *The Elphinstone Family Book of the Lords Elphinstone, Balmerino and Coupar* (2 vols., Edinburgh, 1897).

FROUDE, J. A., *Thomas Carlyle: a History of the First Forty Years of His Life, 1795–1835* (2 vols., London, 1882).

GLEIG, G. R., *The Life of Major-General Sir Thomas Munro, Bart. and K.C.B., Late Governor of Madras, with Extracts from his Correspondence and Private Papers* (3 vols., London, 1830).

GOLDSMID, Sir F. J., *James Outram: a Biography* (2 vols., London, 1880).

GORDON, R. G., *The Bombay Survey and Settlement Manual* (2 vols., Bombay, 1917).

GRANT DUFF, J. C., *A History of the Mahrattas.* Revised with Introduction by S. M. Edwardes (2 vols., Oxford, 1921).

GRANT DUFF, Sir M. E., *A Victorian Vintage: Being a Selection of the Best Stories from the Diaries of the Right Hon. Sir Mountstuart E. Grant Duff, G.C.S.I., F.R.S.* Edited by A. Tilney Bassett. With a Biographical Introduction by Mrs. Ruth Jackson (London, 1930).

GUPTA, P. C., *Baji Rao II and the East India Company, 1796–1818* (Oxford, 1939).

—— *The Last Peshwa and the English Commissioners, 1818–1851* (Calcutta, 1944).

HARTOG, Sir P., *Some Aspects of Indian Education Past and Present* (Oxford, 1939).

HEBER, R., *Narrative of a Journey through the Upper Provinces of India from Calcutta to Bombay, 1824–1825 (with Notes upon Ceylon), an Account of a Journey to Madras and the Southern Provinces, 1826, and Letters Written in India* (2 vols., London, 1828).

HOWELL, A., *Education in British India, prior to 1854, and in 1871* (Calcutta, 1872).

Imperial Gazetteer of India.

JERVIS, T. B., *Geographical and Statistical Memoir of the Konkun. The Revenue and Land Tenures of the Western Part of India, Considered with Reference to their First Institution and Present Working* (Calcutta, 1840).

JERVIS, W. P., *Thomas Best Jervis, Lt.-Colonel, H.E.I.C.'s Bombay*

Engineers; F.R.S., F.R.G.S., F.R.A.S., F.G.S.; Director of the Geographical and Statistical Depot, War Department (now Intelligence Division): as Christian Soldier, Geographer, and Friend of India, 1796–1857 (London, 1898).

KAYE, J. W., *The Life and Correspondence of Major-General Sir John Malcolm* (2 vols., London, 1856).

LAMBRICK, H. T., *Sir Charles Napier and Sind* (Oxford, 1952).

LUSHINGTON, C., *The History, Design and Present State of the Religious, Benevolent and Charitable Institutions Founded by the British in Calcutta and its Vicinity* (Calcutta, 1824).

MALCOLM, Sir J., *The Government of India* (London, 1833).

—— *The Political History of India from 1784 to 1823* (2 vols., London, 1826).

MARKHAM, C. R. (ed.), *Narrative of the Mission of George Bogle* (2nd ed., London, 1879).

MEAD, P. J., and LAIRD MACGREGOR, G., *Census of India, 1911. Volume VII. Bombay. Part I. Report* (Bombay, 1912).

Papers Respecting the Pindarry and Mahratta Wars. Printed in Conformity to the Resolution of the Court of Proprietors of East-India Stock, of the 3rd March 1824 (cited as Maratha War Papers).

Parliamentary Papers.

PARULEKAR, R. V., *Survey of Indigenous Education in the Province of Bombay (1820–1830)* (Bombay, 1951).

PATEL, G. D., *Agrarian Reforms in Bombay (The Legal and Economic Consequences of the Abolition of Land Tenures)* (Bombay, 1950).

PHILIPS, C. H., *The East India Company, 1784–1834* (Manchester, 1940).

ROGERS, A., *The Land Revenue of Bombay* (2 vols., London, 1892).

SARDESAI, Rao Bahadur G. S., *New History of the Marathas* (3 vols., Bombay, 1946–8).

—— (ed.), *Poona Residency Correspondence: Volume 12: Poona Affairs (Elphinstone's Embassy) (Part I, 1811–1815)* (Bombay, 1950) (cited as P.R.C. xii).

—— (ed.), *Poona Residency Correspondence: Volume 13: Poona Affairs (Elphinstone's Embassy) (Part II, 1816–1818)* (Bombay, 1953) (cited as P.R.C. xiii).

—— (ed.), *Selections from the Peshwa Daftar: Volume 42: Papers Referring to Pratapsinh, Raja of Satara* (Bombay, 1934).

Selection of Papers from the Records at the East-India House, Relating to the Revenue, Police, and Civil and Criminal Justice under the Company's Governments in India (4 vols., London, 1820–6) (cited as S.R.J.).

SEN, S., *Administrative System of the Marathas* (Calcutta, 1923).

—— *Military System of the Marathas: with a Brief Account of their Maritime Activities* (Calcutta, 1928).

SHARP, H., *Selections from Educational Records, Part I, 1789–1839* (Government of India, Bureau of Education) (Calcutta, 1920).

SIMCOX, A. H. A., *A Memoir of the Khandesh Bhil Corps 1825–1891* (Bombay, n.d.).

SPEAR, T. G. P., 'Bentinck and Education', *Cambridge Historical Journal*, vol. vi, no. 1 (1938).

STOCK, E., *History of the Church Missionary Society* (4 vols., London, 1899–1916).

STOKES, E. T., *Utilitarian Influence and the Formation of Indian Policy, 1820–1840* (Ph.D. Thesis, Cambridge University, 1952).

STRACHEY, E., *Bija Ganita, or the Algebra of the Hindus* (London, 1813).

TREVELYAN, C. E., *On the Education of the People of India* (London, 1838).

TROTTER, L. J., *The Bayard of India: a Life of General Sir James Outram, Bart., G.C.B., etc.* (London, 1903).

GLOSSARY

Adawlut, adalat, Law Court.
Batta, bhata, Additional pay or allowances.
Beega, bigha, A measure of land.
Carcoon, karkun, Clerk.
Coolcurnee, kulkarni, Village accountant.
Coonbee, Kunbi, An agricultural caste.
Cos, kos, A measure of distance.
Cowl, kaul, Revenue contract.
Crore, kror, Ten million.
Cutcherry, kachahri, Government office.
Dufter, daftar, Record, the office in which records are kept.
Dufterdar, daftardar, Record-keeper.
Durbar, darbar, Levee, audience.
Fatwa, Judicial opinion.
Ghat, Mountains, mountain pass.
Guddee, gadi, The seat of royalty.
Hoozoor, huzur, The presence, superior authority.
Huck, hak, Emoluments of office.
Inam, Rent-free land.
Jageer, jagir, (The assignment of the revenues of) an estate.
Jageerdar, jagirdar, Holder of a jagir.
Lack, lakh, One hundred thousand.

Maamool, mamul, Custom.
Mocaddum, mukaddam, Village headman.
Mootasuddy, mutasaddi, Clerk.
Naick, naik, Tribal chief, official.
Nuzzer, nazr, Gift.
Oomedwur, umedwar, A candidate for office, one who is hopeful.
Potail, patel, Village headman.
Potta, patta, Revenue certificate.
Puggee, pagi, Watchman, tracker.
Ryot, raiyat, Peasant.
Ryotwari (raiyatwari) settlement, Revenue settlement between Government and peasant without intermediaries.
Sebundy, sibandi, Irregular soldier.
Seer, ser, A measure of weight.
Sheristadar, sarishtadar, Record-keeper.
Sirdar, sardar, A man of consequence.
Tuckavee, takavi, Advance of money to agriculturist for purposes of cultivation.
Tulatee, talati, Village accountant.
Wukeel, vakil, Agent.
Zamindar, Landholder; district official.
Zamindari settlement, Revenue settlement between Government and (substantial) landholder.

INDEX

Aba Purandhare, 57 and n., 61 n., 208.
Abdul Ghaffar, 144.
Adalats, 36, 153; Elphinstone's attitude changing, 198, 203.
Adam, John, 35, 39, 105, 136, 209.
Ahmadabad: statistics, 140; revenue system, 155-7, 160, 164; village headmen, 175; village accountants, 180-2; teachers, 273; satis rare, 276.
Ahmadnagar, 24, 96, 105, 106, 110, 117 n., 120 n., 122, 124, 187, 202, 204, 213 n., 272, 301; occupation, 22; statistics, 23; panchayats, 110, 112, 193; Bhils, 213-14; sati, 290; Malcolm's visit, 316.
Aitchison, C. U., 73 n.
Akalkot, Raja of, settlement, 76; and Raja of Satara, 243.
Amins, see Munsifs.
Amrit Rao, 43.
Anderson, George William, 204 and n., 210.
Appa Desai, of Nipani: surrender, 47; character, 53; helped Wellesley, 54; loyal to Baji Rao, 56; settlement, 61-62; Munro's opinion of, 62, 74; adapts himself to new system, 209; murder of concubine, 210; first class sardar, 210; attempted adoption, 318.
Appa Sahib, brother of Raja of Satara, 241.
Appaji Krishna Rao, Briggs's Daftardar, 95, 216-18, 223.
Arabs, 27, 28, 81, 82.
Ashti, 6 n., 18, 59.
Assaye, 3.

Babaji Pant Gokhale, 205-6.
Baber, 204 n.
Babington, 277.
Bagalkot, 71.
Baglana, 124, 125.
Baji Rao, last Peshwa, 1, 2, 5, 6, 11, 17, 18, 46, 49, 82; and jagirdars, 5, 51-61, 71, 74; surrender, 6, 43, 44, 57; exile, 45, 48; settlement, 43-44, 74; charities, 11, 85-86; revenue

under, 97, 118, 119; attitude to sati, 281; Elphinstone's opinion of, 5, 55, 74; Malcolm's opinion of, 74.
Balaji Pant Natu: early career, 93-94; rewards, 94; at Satara, 21-22, 235-6; investigates Varanasi Bai, 46; Grant on, 94-95, 235-6; nautch, 190; and sati, 301-2; palanquin allowance, 318-19; fears for the future, 319.
Balla Sahib Raste, 211.
Balwant Rao Bhonsle, 241 and n.
Bankot, 141 n., 143, 144.
Barnes, Rev. George, 258, 260.
Baroda, 5.
Bassein, 1, 48; Treaty, 1, 2, 149.
Bax, John, 232 and n.
Bell, Alexander, 139 and n., 186, 188 n., 253.
Bellari, 15, 92.
Benares, 2, 31, 32, 44, 48, 51, 68, 104, 256.
Bengal: manners, 101; sati, 275, 278, 281, 301; system of government established by Cornwallis in, 31-33, 35-36, 145, 147, 220.
Bentham, Jeremy, and Benthamism, 34-36, 42, 90, 109, 114; see also Utilitarianism.
Bentinck, Lord William, 27, 311.
Bhadgaon, 229.
Bhagalpur, 125, 130.
Bhagdari system, 159-65, 308-9.
Bhamer, corruption, 216.
Bhau Sahib (Raja Ram), brother of Raja of Satara, 241 n.
Bhils, 26, 124; statistics, 125; Maratha policy, 125, 226, 230; under Briggs, 124-34, 213-23, 226, 227; under Pottinger, 213; under A. Robertson, 224-34; under Malcolm, 306-8; Bhil Agents, 228, 233-4, 306-7; Bhil Corps, 130-1, 227-33, 306-7.
Bithur, 45-46.
Board of Control, 31, 33, 257; support Munro system, 34; favour use of panchayats, 199; protect Briggs, 221.
Bohras' College, 271.

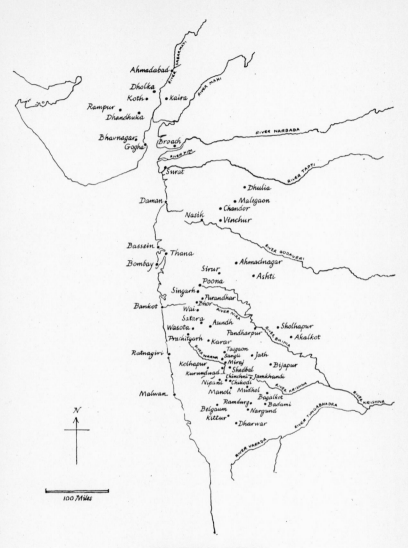

Ahmadabad
Dholka
Koth • Kaira
Rampur
Dhandhuka
Bhavnagar
Gogha Broach
Surat
Daman
Dhulia
Malegaon
Chandor
Nasik Vinchur
Bassein
Bombay Thana
Ahmadnagar
Sirur Ashti
Poona
Singarh Purandhar
Bankot Bhor
Wai
Satara Aundh
Wasota Sholhapur
Prachitgarh Pandharpur Akalkot
Karar
Ratnagiri Taigaon
Sangli Jath
Kolhapur Miraj Bijapur
Kurundwad Shedbal
Nipani Chinchni Jamkhandi
Chikodi
Malwan Manoli Mudhol
Ramdurg Bagalkot
Belgaum Nargund Badami
Kittur
Dharwar

RIVER SABARMATI
RIVER MAHI
RIVER NARBADA
RIVER KIM
RIVER TAPTI
RIVER GODAVERI
RIVER NIRA
RIVER BHIMA
RIVER WARNA
RIVER KRISHNA
RIVER KRISHNA
RIVER TUNGABHADRA
RIVER VARADA

N

100 Miles

WESTERN INDIA

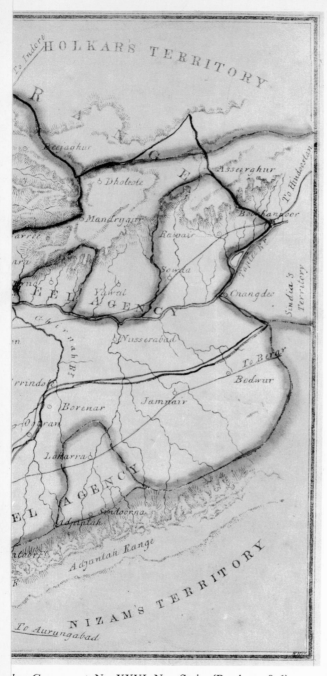